P SMOKING...

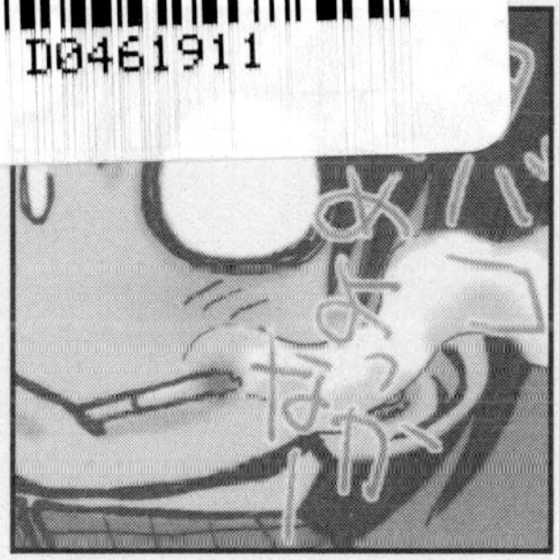

叶 恭弘

The setting of this manga is basically Hokkaido. I lived in Hokkaido throughout my high school years, so I thought it would be easy. But the timing of school events is different than in Tokyo, there's snow on the roofs in winter…it could become a hassle…

When this second book comes out, the snow will be on the ground in Hokkaido. I love the winter in Hokkaido. There is something special about the beauty of a snowy landscape in the bitter cold that you can't get in warmer climates.

—Yasuhiro Kano, 2002

Yasuhiro Kano made his manga debut in 1992 with *Black City*, which won *Weekly Shonen Jump*'s Hop★Step Award for new artists. From 1993 to 2001, he illustrated Mugen's serialized novels *Midnight Magic* in *Jump Novel* magazine, and also produced a manga adaptation. *Pretty Face* appeared in *Weekly Shonen Jump* from 2002 to 2003. Kano's newest series, *M x O*, began running in *Weekly Shonen Jump* in 2006.

PRETTY FACE
VOL. 2

The SHONEN JUMP ADVANCED Manga Edition

STORY AND ART BY
YASUHIRO KANO

Translation & English Adaptation/Anita Sengupta
Touch-up Art & Lettering/Eric Erbes
Design/Hidemi Dunn
Editor/Jason Thompson

Editor in Chief, Books/Alvin Lu
Editor in Chief, Magazines/Marc Weidenbaum
VP of Publishing Licensing/Rika Inouye
VP of Sales/Gonzalo Ferreyra
Sr. VP of Marketing/Liza Coppola
Publisher/Hyoe Narita

PRETTY FACE © 2002 by Yasuhiro Kano. All rights reserved. First published in Japan in 2002 by SHUEISHA Inc., Tokyo. English translation rights in the United States of America and Canada arranged by SHUEISHA Inc. The stories, characters and incidents mentioned in this publication are entirely fictional.

Printed in the U.S.A.

Published by VIZ Media, LLC
P.O. Box 77010
San Francisco, CA 94107

SHONEN JUMP ADVANCED Manga Edition
10 9 8 7 6 5 4 3 2
First printing, October 2007
Second printing, November 2007

www.viz.com

www.shonenjump.com

Pretty Face

Vol. 2

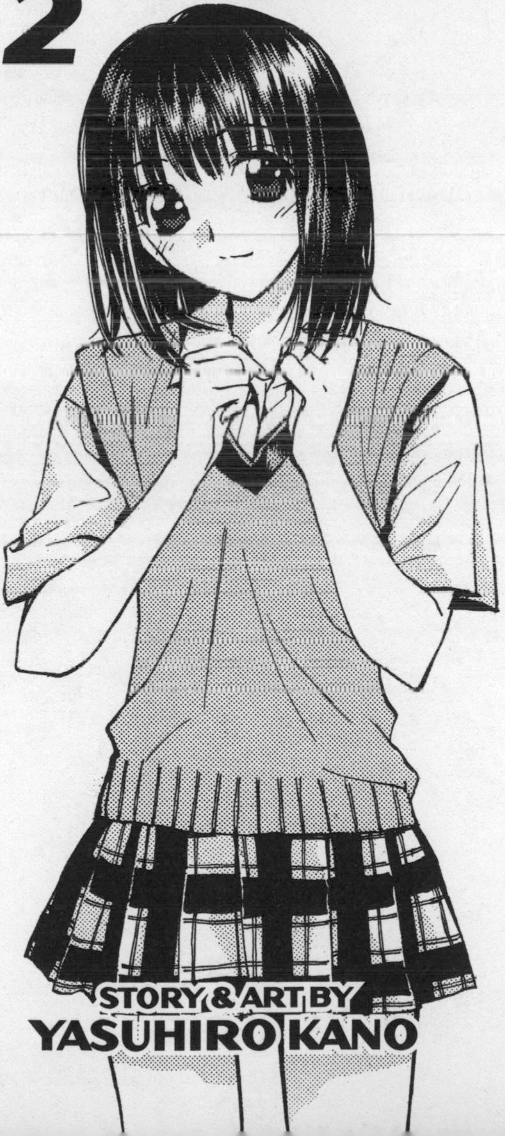

STORY & ART BY
YASUHIRO KANO

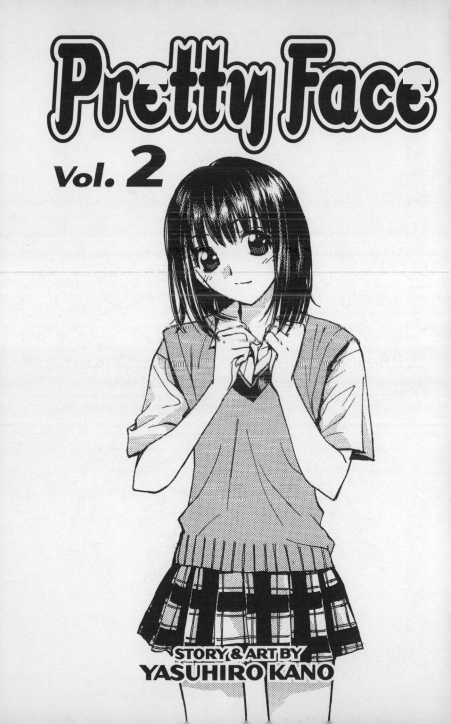

CHARACTERS

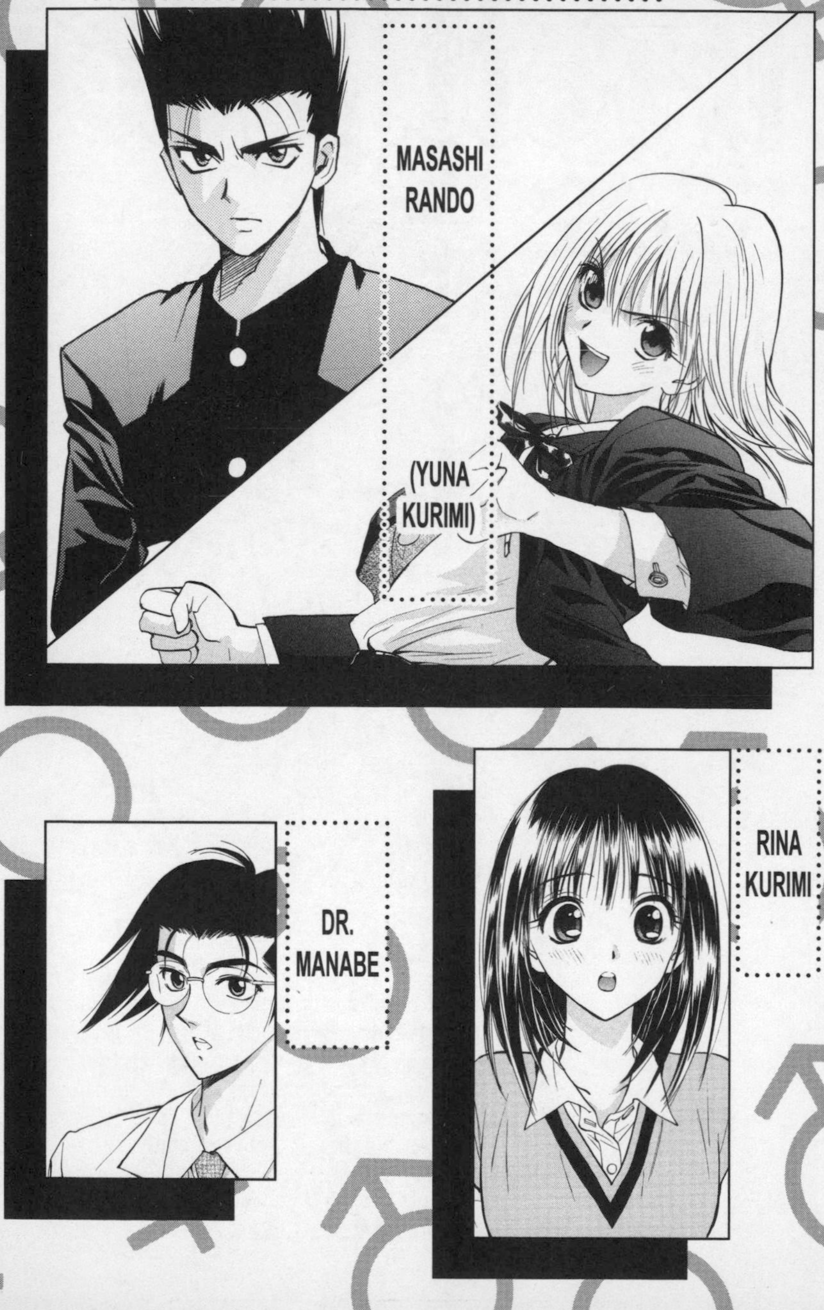
MASASHI RANDO
(YUNA KURIMI)
RINA KURIMI
DR. MANABE

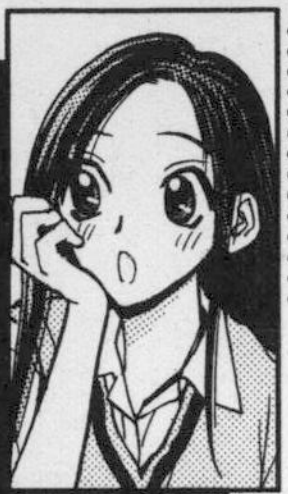

YUKIE SANO

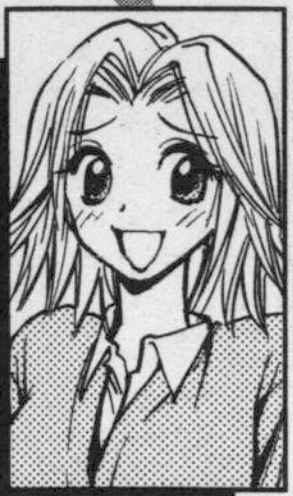

MIDORI AKAI

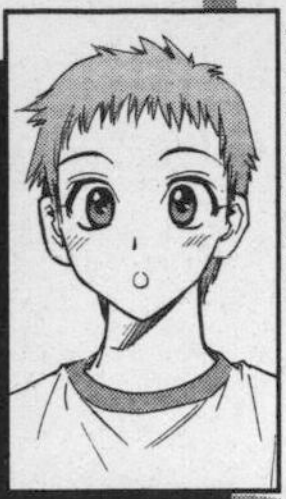

KEIKO TSUKAMOTO

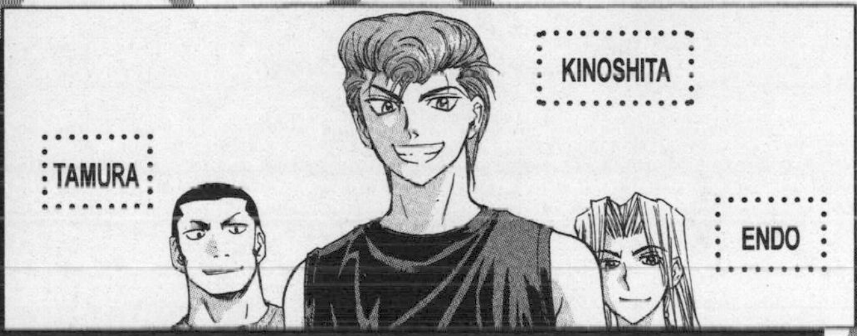

KINOSHITA
ENDO
TAMURA

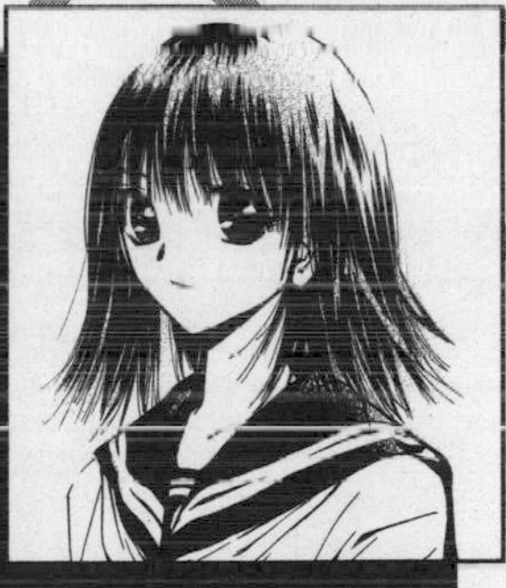

YUNA KURIMI (THE REAL ONE)

STORY

On the way home from a karate tournament, teenage badass Masashi Rando is caught in a horrible bus accident. When he wakes up from his coma a year later, his disfigured face has been reconstructed into the image of Rina Kurimi, the girl he has a crush on! Not knowing what Rando originally looked like, the mad plastic surgeon Dr. Manabe used a photo of Rina in Rando's wallet as the model for his reconstruction. Abandoned by his friends and parents, Rando is mistaken for Rina's long-lost half-sister and adopted into her family. Can he put aside his impure feelings and be a good "big sister" to Rina...while he's still a teenage boy from the waist down?

PRETTY FACE
Vol. 2
CONTENTS

Chapter 9: The All-Girl (?) Okinawa Trip

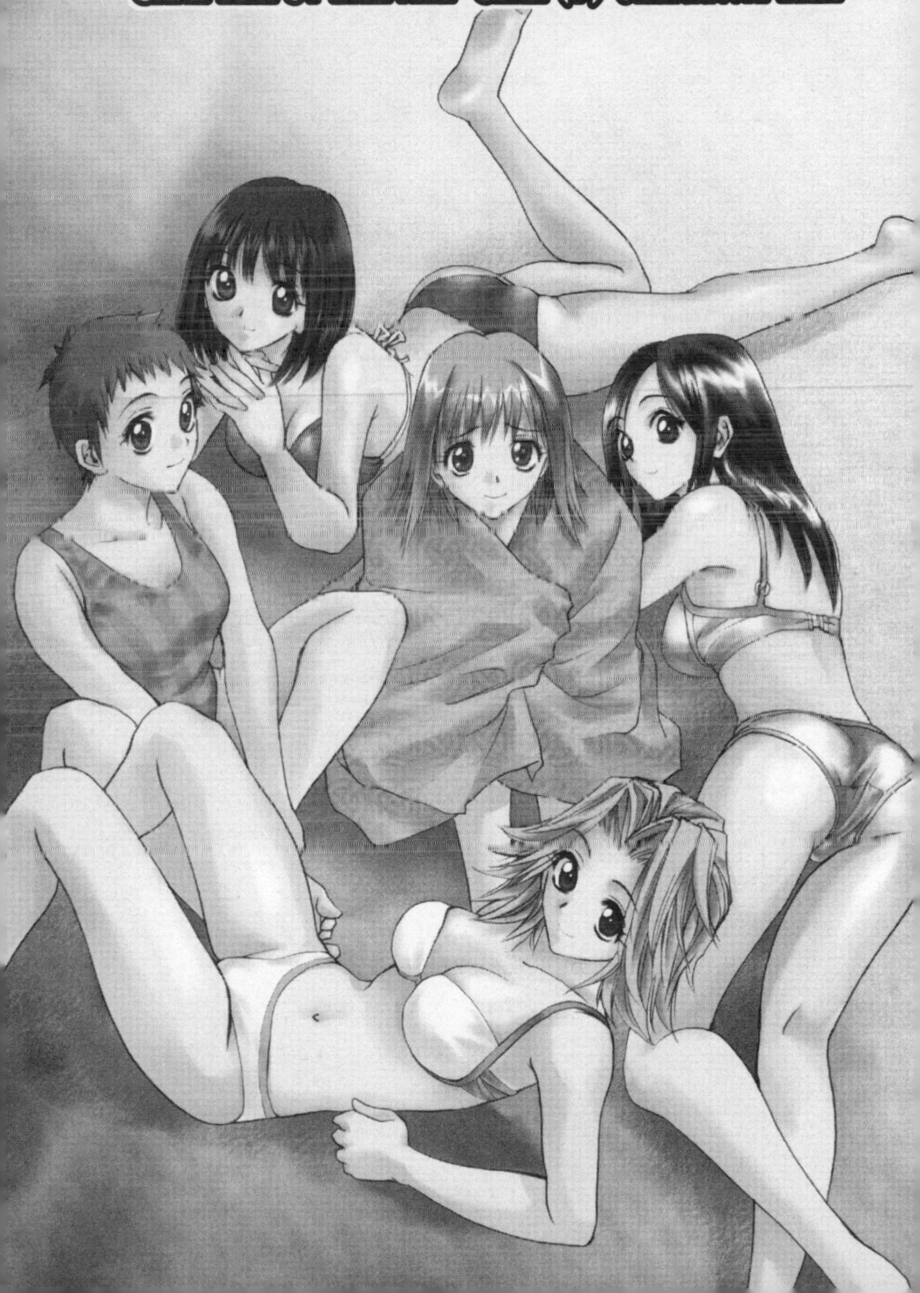

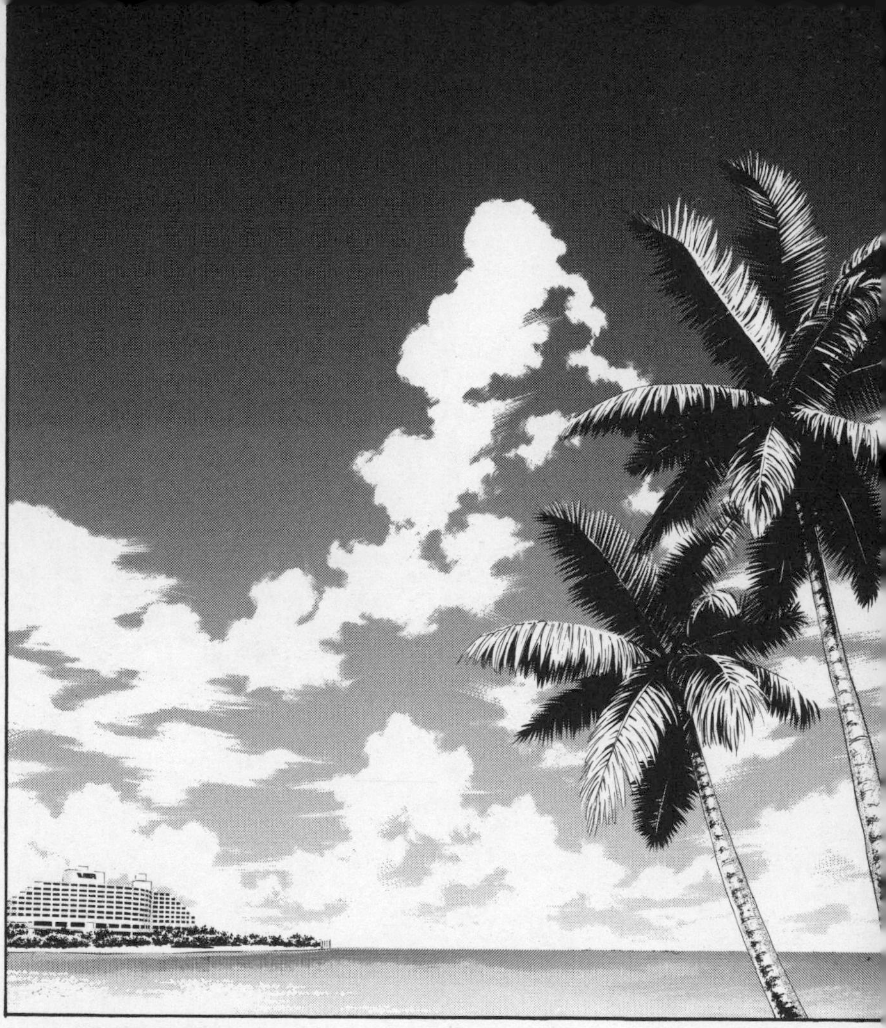

NO GOOD REASON

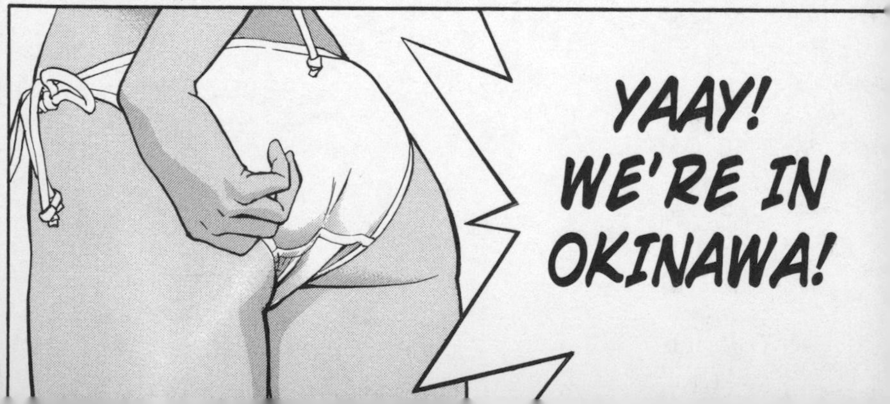
YAAY! WE'RE IN OKINAWA!

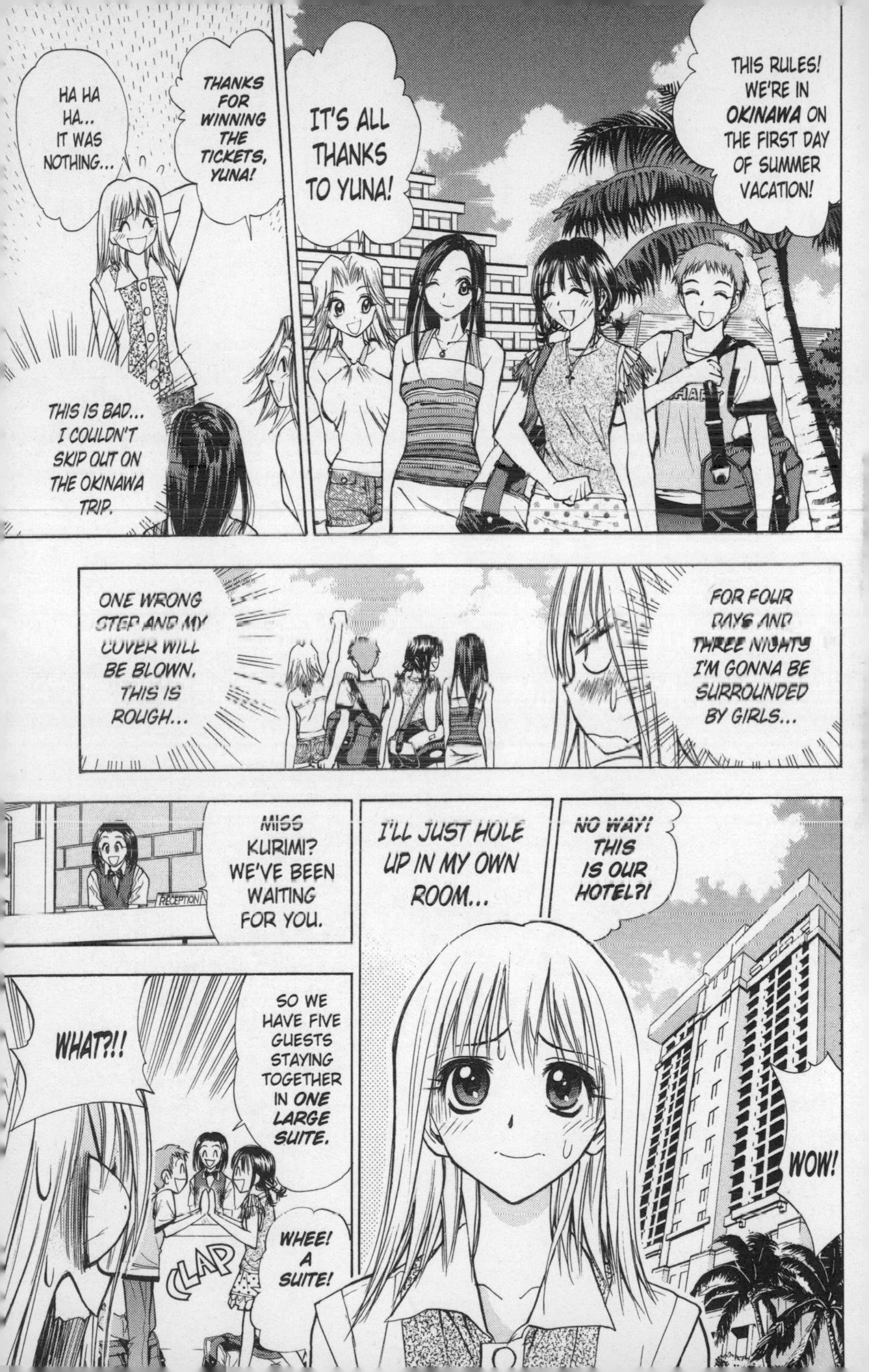
THIS RULES! WE'RE IN OKINAWA ON THE FIRST DAY OF SUMMER VACATION!
IT'S ALL THANKS TO YUNA!
THANKS FOR WINNING THE TICKETS, YUNA!
HA HA HA... IT WAS NOTHING...
THIS IS BAD... I COULDN'T SKIP OUT ON THE OKINAWA TRIP.
FOR FOUR DAYS AND THREE NIGHTS I'M GONNA BE SURROUNDED BY GIRLS...
ONE WRONG STEP AND MY COVER WILL BE BLOWN. THIS IS ROUGH...
NO WAY! THIS IS OUR HOTEL?!
WOW!
I'LL JUST HOLE UP IN MY OWN ROOM...
MISS KURIMI? WE'VE BEEN WAITING FOR YOU.
RECEPTION
SO WE HAVE FIVE GUESTS STAYING TOGETHER IN ONE LARGE SUITE.
WHAT?!!
WHEE! A SUITE!
CLAP

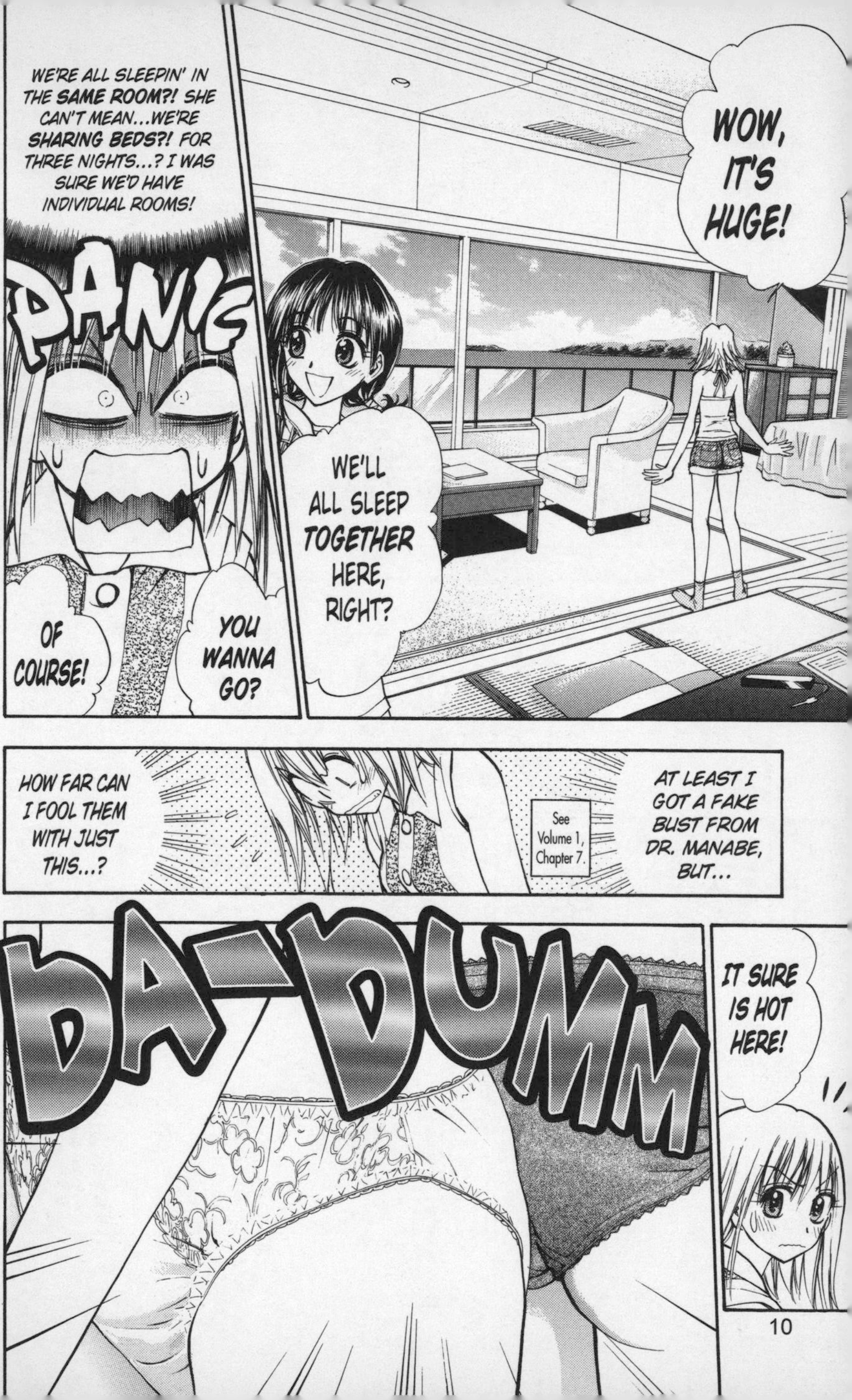
WOW, IT'S HUGE!
WE'LL ALL SLEEP TOGETHER HERE, RIGHT?
WE'RE ALL SLEEPIN' IN THE SAME ROOM?! SHE CAN'T MEAN...WE'RE SHARING BEDS?! FOR THREE NIGHTS...? I WAS SURE WE'D HAVE INDIVIDUAL ROOMS!
PANIC
YOU WANNA GO?
OF COURSE!
AT LEAST I GOT A FAKE BUST FROM DR. MANABE, BUT...
See Volume 1, Chapter 7.
HOW FAR CAN I FOOL THEM WITH JUST THIS...?
IT SURE IS HOT HERE!
DA-DUMM

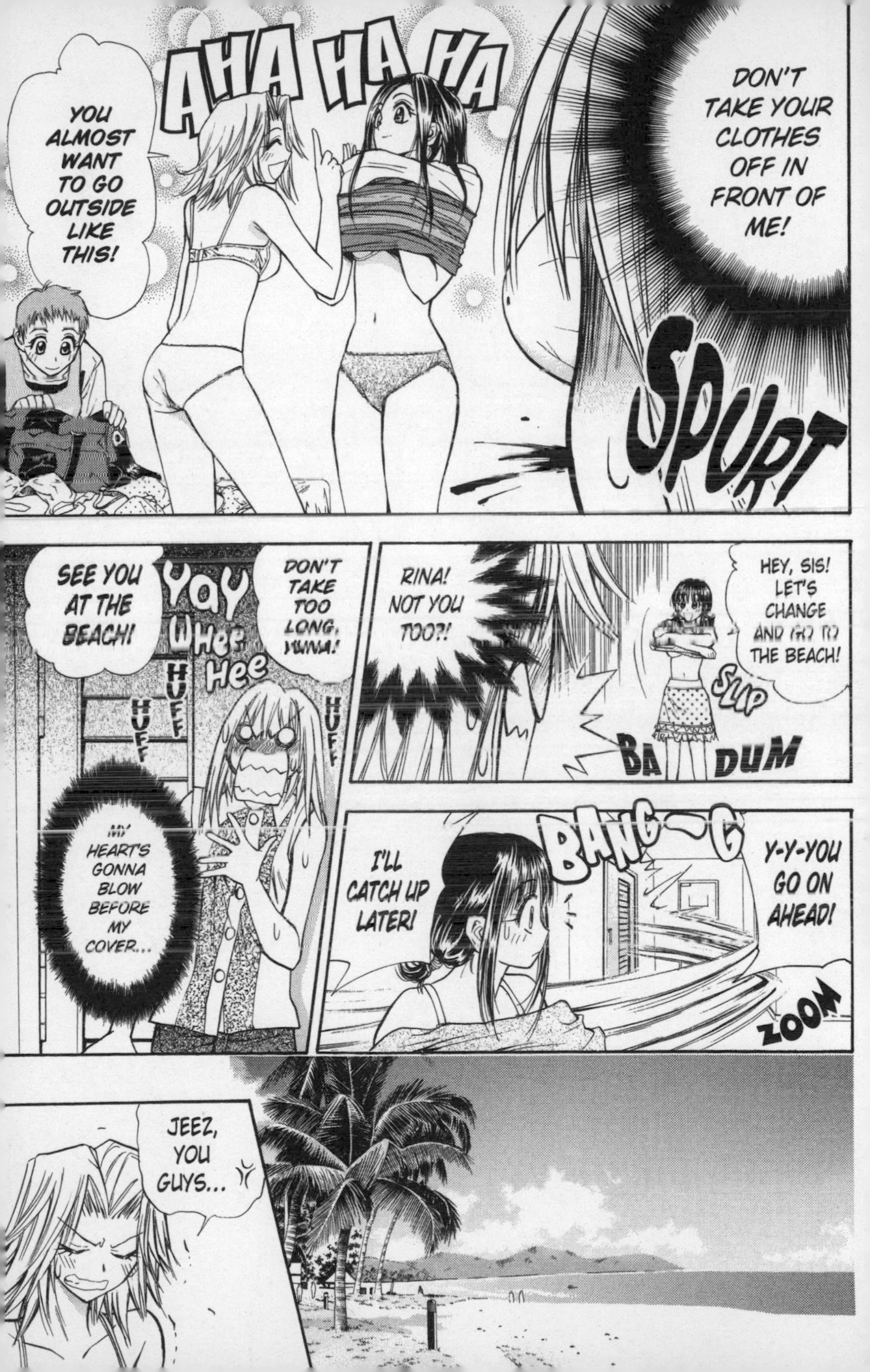
DON'T TAKE YOUR CLOTHES OFF IN FRONT OF ME!
SPURT
AHA HA HA
YOU ALMOST WANT TO GO OUTSIDE LIKE THIS!
HEY, SIS! LET'S CHANGE AND GO TO THE BEACH!
SLIP
BA DUM
RINA! NOT YOU TOO?!
Y-Y-YOU GO ON AHEAD!
BANG-G
I'LL CATCH UP LATER!
ZOOM
DON'T TAKE TOO LONG, RINA!
YaY
WHee Hee
SEE YOU AT THE BEACH!
HUFF
HUFF
HUFF
MY HEART'S GONNA BLOW BEFORE MY COVER...
JEEZ, YOU GUYS...

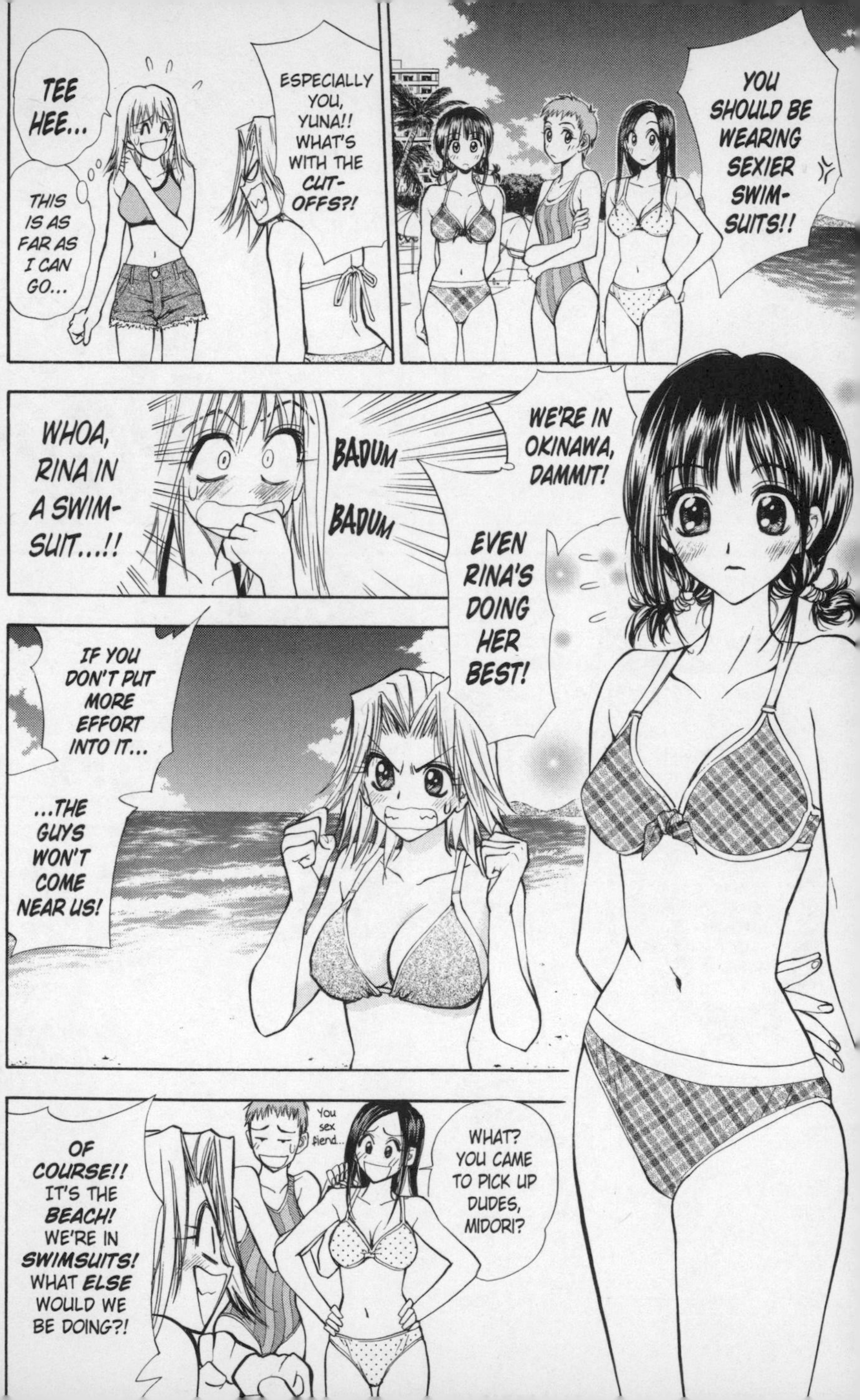
YOU SHOULD BE WEARING SEXIER SWIM-SUITS!!
ESPECIALLY YOU, YUNA!! WHAT'S WITH THE CUT-OFFS?!
TEE HEE...
THIS IS AS FAR AS I CAN GO...
WE'RE IN OKINAWA, DAMMIT!
EVEN RINA'S DOING HER BEST!
BADUM
BADUM
WHOA, RINA IN A SWIM-SUIT...!!
IF YOU DON'T PUT MORE EFFORT INTO IT...
...THE GUYS WON'T COME NEAR US!
WHAT? YOU CAME TO PICK UP DUDES, MIDORI?
You sex fiend...
OF COURSE!! IT'S THE BEACH! WE'RE IN SWIMSUITS! WHAT ELSE WOULD WE BE DOING?!

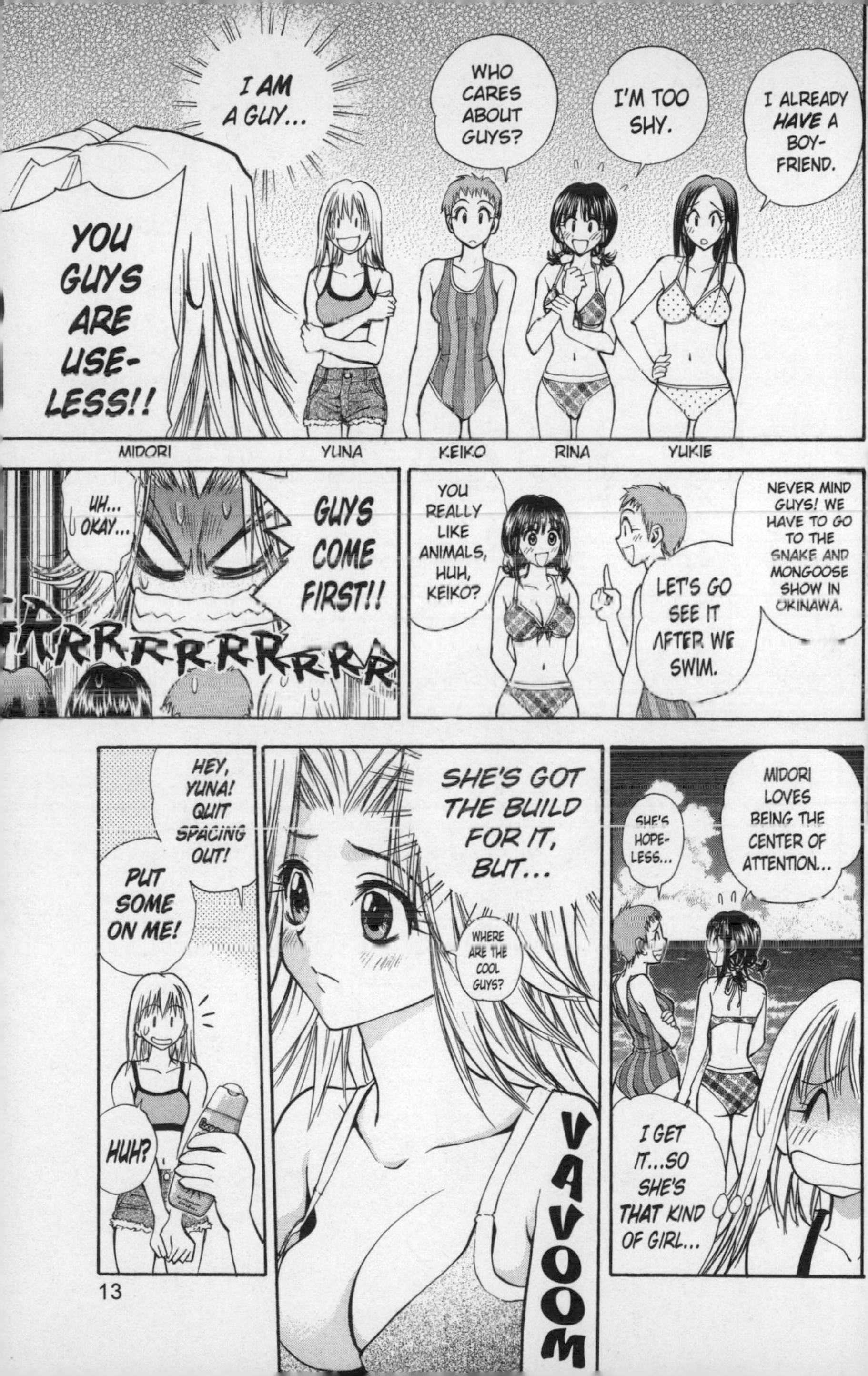
I ALREADY HAVE A BOY-FRIEND.
I'M TOO SHY.
WHO CARES ABOUT GUYS?
I AM A GUY...
YOU GUYS ARE USE-LESS!!
MIDORI YUNA KEIKO RINA YUKIE
NEVER MIND GUYS! WE HAVE TO GO TO THE SNAKE AND MONGOOSE SHOW IN OKINAWA.
YOU REALLY LIKE ANIMALS, HUH, KEIKO?
LET'S GO SEE IT AFTER WE SWIM.
GUYS COME FIRST!!
UH... OKAY...
RRRRRRRRRRRR
MIDORI LOVES BEING THE CENTER OF ATTENTION...
SHE'S HOPE-LESS...
I GET IT...SO SHE'S THAT KIND OF GIRL...
SHE'S GOT THE BUILD FOR IT, BUT...
WHERE ARE THE COOL GUYS?
VAVOOM
HEY, YUNA! QUIT SPACING OUT!
PUT SOME ON ME!
HUH?

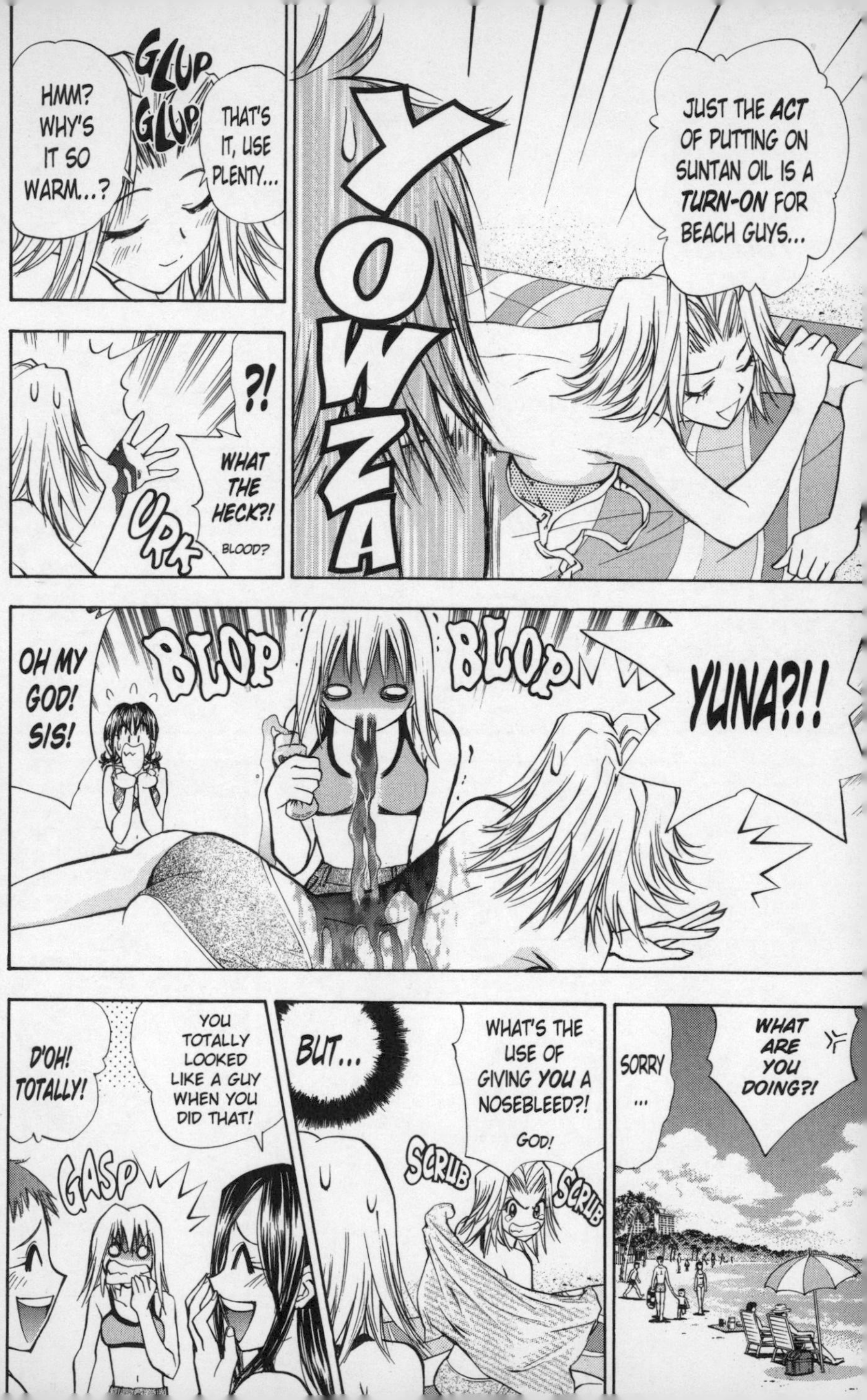
JUST THE ACT OF PUTTING ON SUNTAN OIL IS A TURN-ON FOR BEACH GUYS...
YOWZA
THAT'S IT, USE PLENTY...
GLUP GLUP
HMM? WHY'S IT SO WARM...?
?!
WHAT THE HECK?!
BLOOD?
URK
YUNA?!!
BLOP
BLOP
OH MY GOD! SIS!
WHAT ARE YOU DOING?!
SORRY...
WHAT'S THE USE OF GIVING YOU A NOSEBLEED?!
GOD!
SCRUB
SCRUB
BUT...
YOU TOTALLY LOOKED LIKE A GUY WHEN YOU DID THAT!
D'OH! TOTALLY!
GASP

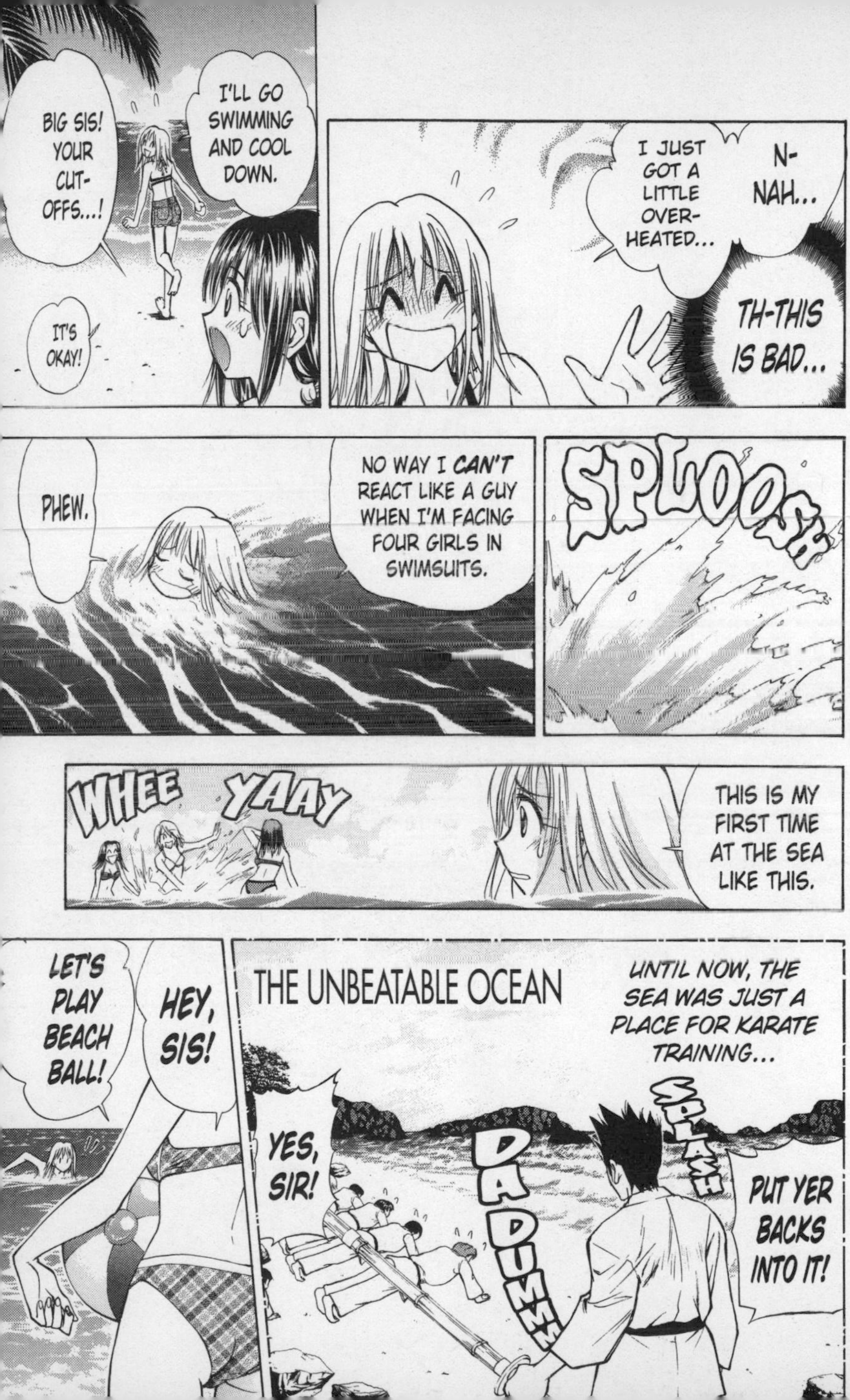
N-NAH...
I JUST GOT A LITTLE OVER-HEATED...
TH-THIS IS BAD...
I'LL GO SWIMMING AND COOL DOWN.
BIG SIS! YOUR CUT-OFFS...!
IT'S OKAY!
SPLOOSH
NO WAY I CAN'T REACT LIKE A GUY WHEN I'M FACING FOUR GIRLS IN SWIMSUITS.
PHEW.
THIS IS MY FIRST TIME AT THE SEA LIKE THIS.
YAAY
WHEE
UNTIL NOW, THE SEA WAS JUST A PLACE FOR KARATE TRAINING...
THE UNBEATABLE OCEAN
PUT YER BACKS INTO IT!
SPLASH
DADUMM
YES, SIR!
HEY, SIS!
LET'S PLAY BEACH BALL!

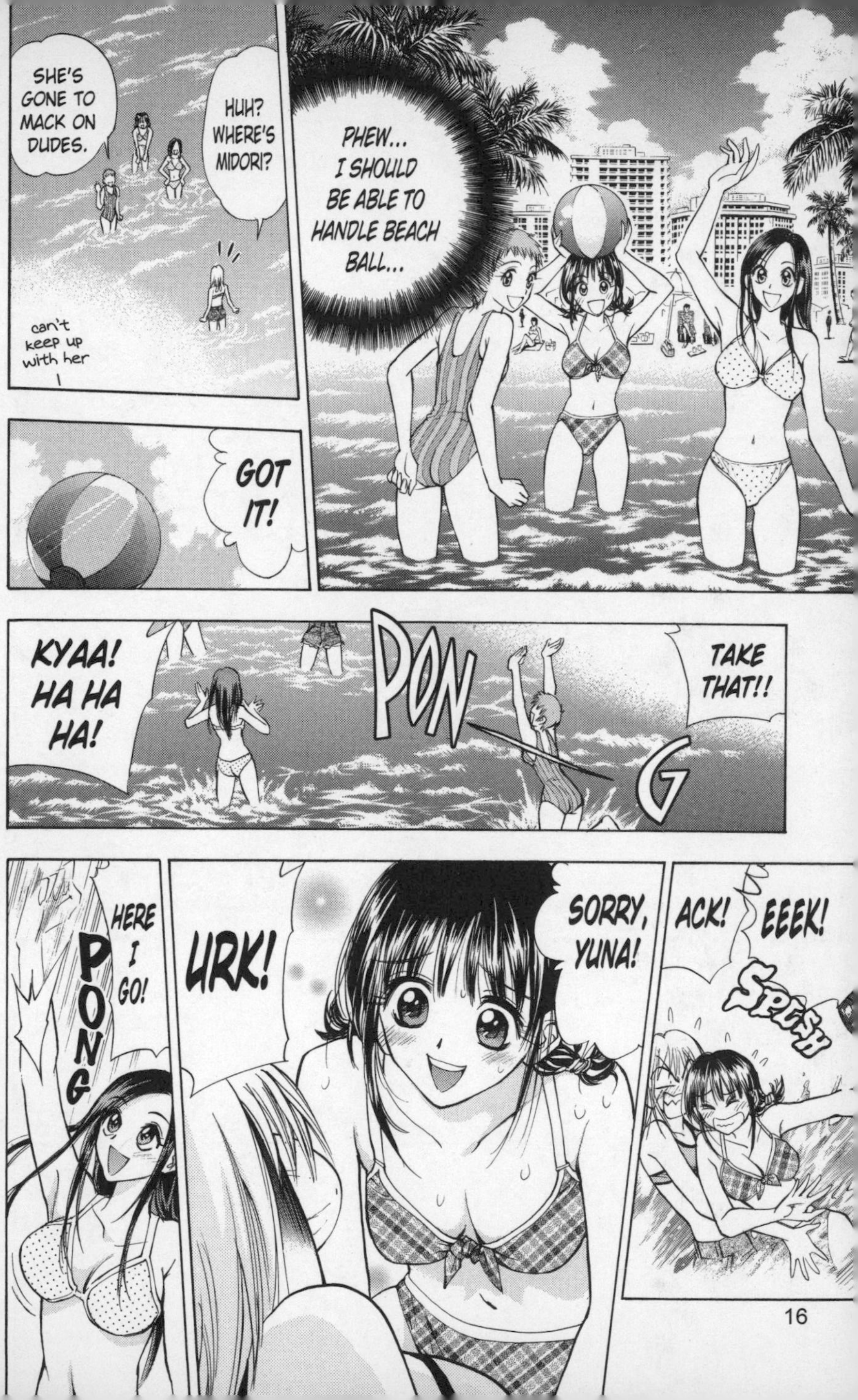
PHEW... I SHOULD BE ABLE TO HANDLE BEACH BALL...
HUH? WHERE'S MIDORI?
SHE'S GONE TO MACK ON DUDES.
can't keep up with her
GOT IT!
TAKE THAT!!
PONG
KYAA! HA HA HA!
ACK!
EEEK!
SPLISH
SORRY, YUNA!
URK!
HERE I GO!
PONG

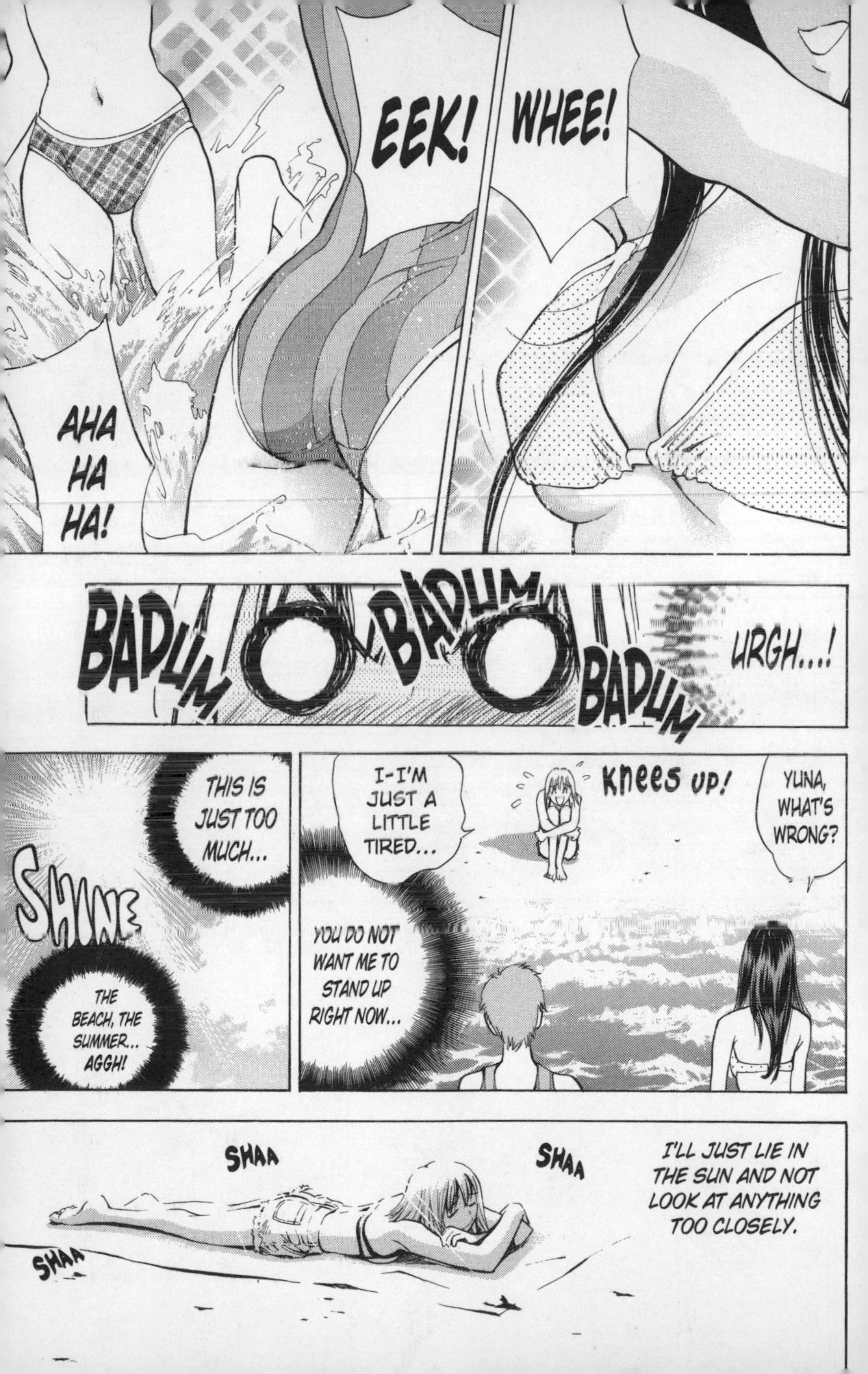
WHEE!
EEK!
AHA HA HA!
URGH...!
BADUM
BADUM
BADUM
YUNA, WHAT'S WRONG?
Knees up!
I-I'M JUST A LITTLE TIRED...
YOU DO NOT WANT ME TO STAND UP RIGHT NOW...
THIS IS JUST TOO MUCH...
SHINE
THE BEACH, THE SUMMER... AGGH!
I'LL JUST LIE IN THE SUN AND NOT LOOK AT ANYTHING TOO CLOSELY.
SHAA
SHAA
SHAA

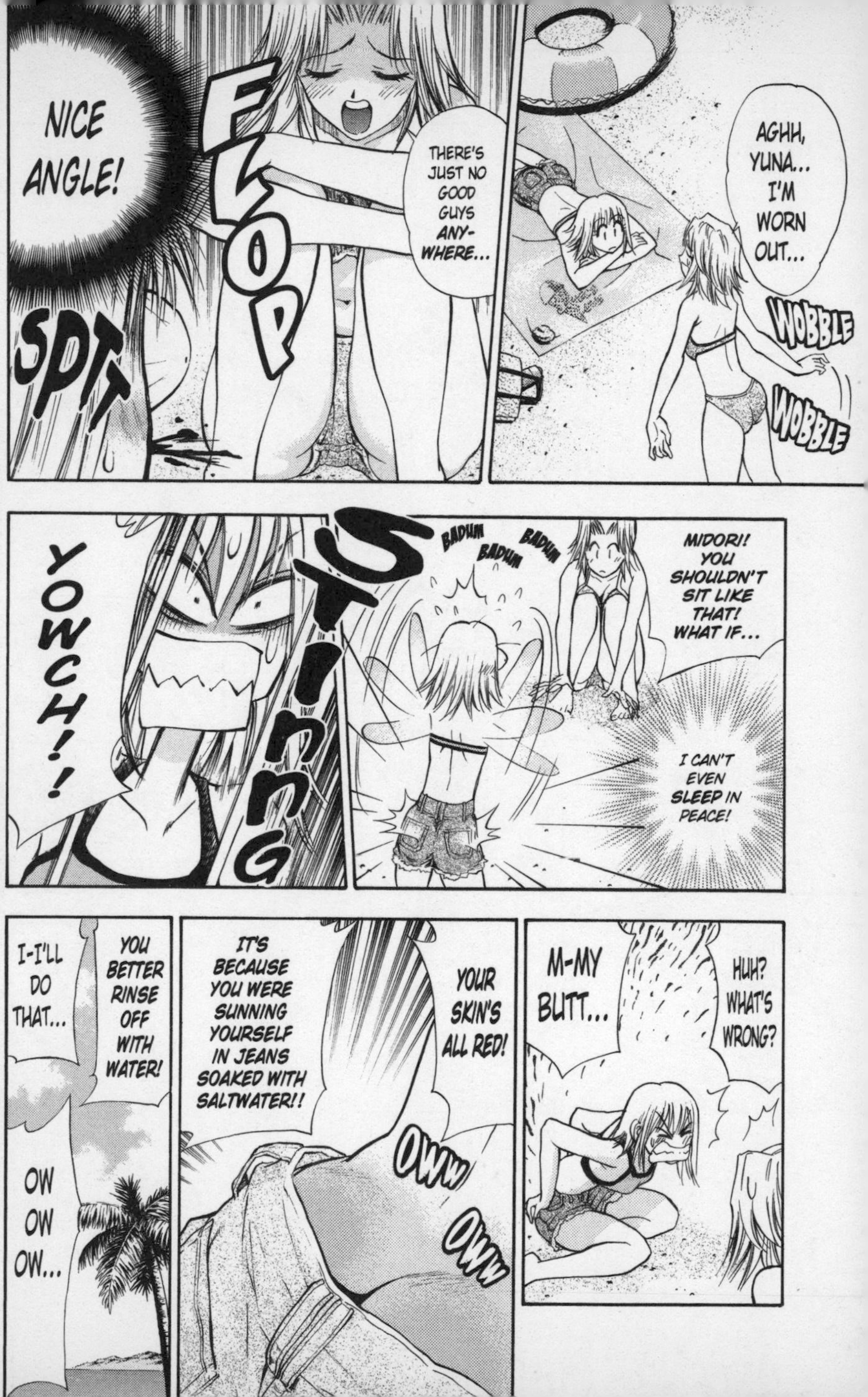
AGHH, YUNA... I'M WORN OUT...
WOBBLE
WOBBLE
THERE'S JUST NO GOOD GUYS ANYWHERE...
FLOP
NICE ANGLE!
SPIT
BADUM
BADUM
BADUM
MIDORI! YOU SHOULDN'T SIT LIKE THAT! WHAT IF...
I CAN'T EVEN SLEEP IN PEACE!
STInnG
YOWCH!!
HUH? WHAT'S WRONG?
M-MY BUTT...
YOUR SKIN'S ALL RED!
IT'S BECAUSE YOU WERE SUNNING YOURSELF IN JEANS SOAKED WITH SALTWATER!!
OWW
OWW
YOU BETTER RINSE OFF WITH WATER!
I-I'LL DO THAT...
OW OW OW...

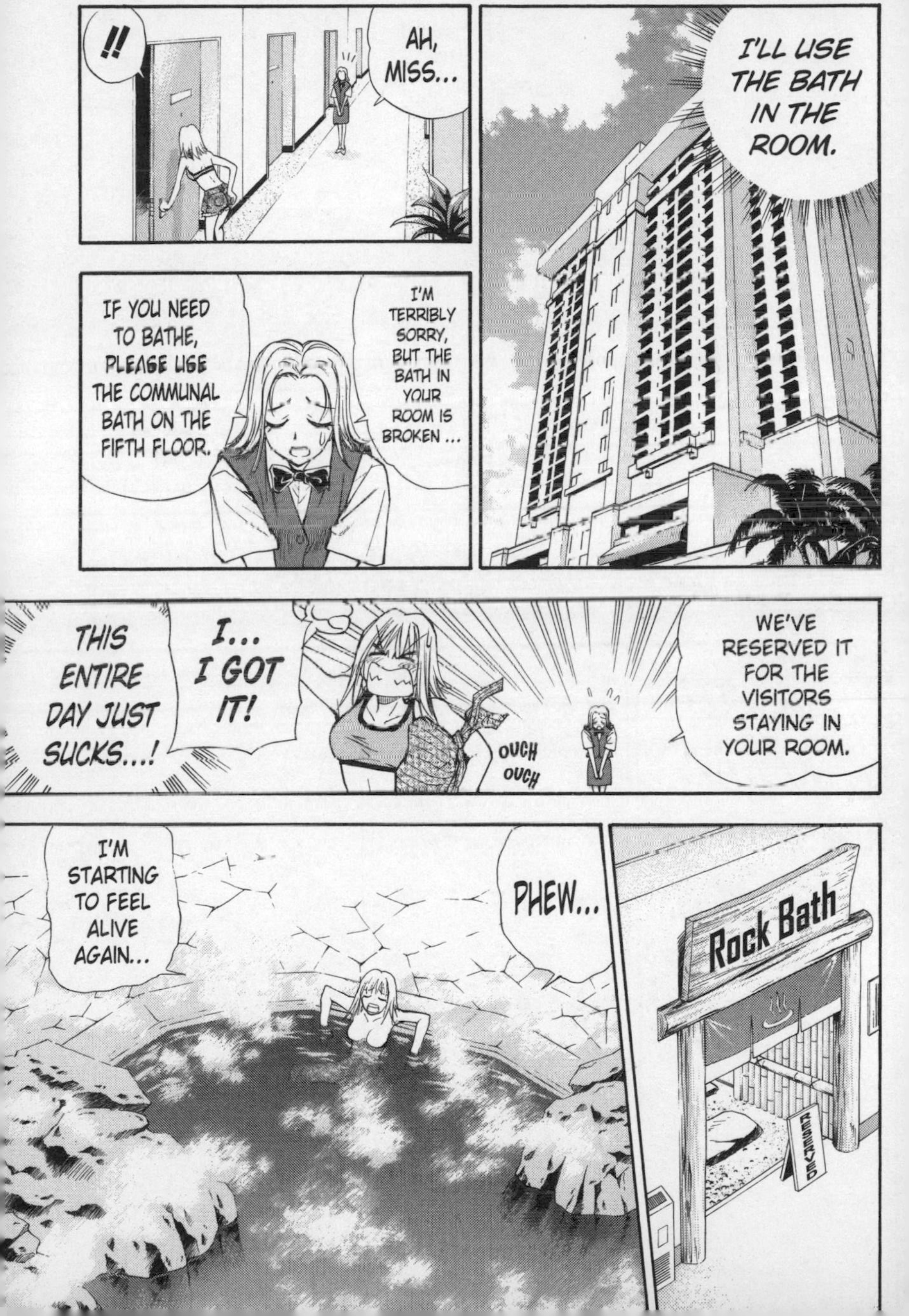
I'LL USE THE BATH IN THE ROOM.
AH, MISS...
!!
I'M TERRIBLY SORRY, BUT THE BATH IN YOUR ROOM IS BROKEN ...
IF YOU NEED TO BATHE, PLEASE USE THE COMMUNAL BATH ON THE FIFTH FLOOR.
WE'VE RESERVED IT FOR THE VISITORS STAYING IN YOUR ROOM.
OUCH OUCH
I... I GOT IT!
THIS ENTIRE DAY JUST SUCKS...!
Rock Bath
RESERVED
PHEW...
I'M STARTING TO FEEL ALIVE AGAIN...

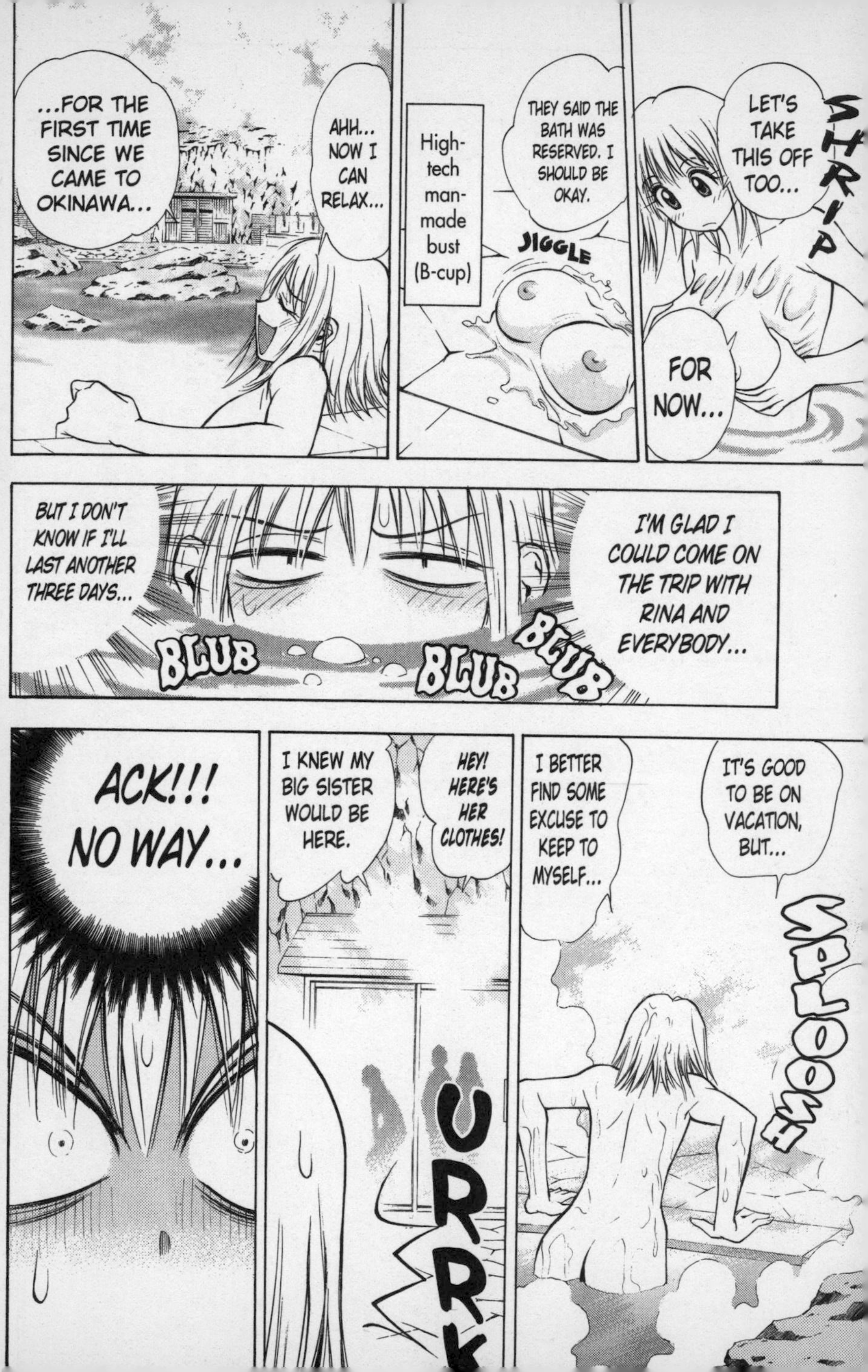
LET'S TAKE THIS OFF TOO...
SHRIP
FOR NOW...
THEY SAID THE BATH WAS RESERVED. I SHOULD BE OKAY.
High-tech man-made bust (B-cup)
JIGGLE
AHH... NOW I CAN RELAX...
...FOR THE FIRST TIME SINCE WE CAME TO OKINAWA...
I'M GLAD I COULD COME ON THE TRIP WITH RINA AND EVERYBODY...
BLUB
BLUB
BLUB
BUT I DON'T KNOW IF I'LL LAST ANOTHER THREE DAYS...
IT'S GOOD TO BE ON VACATION, BUT...
SPLOOSH
I BETTER FIND SOME EXCUSE TO KEEP TO MYSELF...
HEY! HERE'S HER CLOTHES!
I KNEW MY BIG SISTER WOULD BE HERE.
URRK
ACK!!! NO WAY...

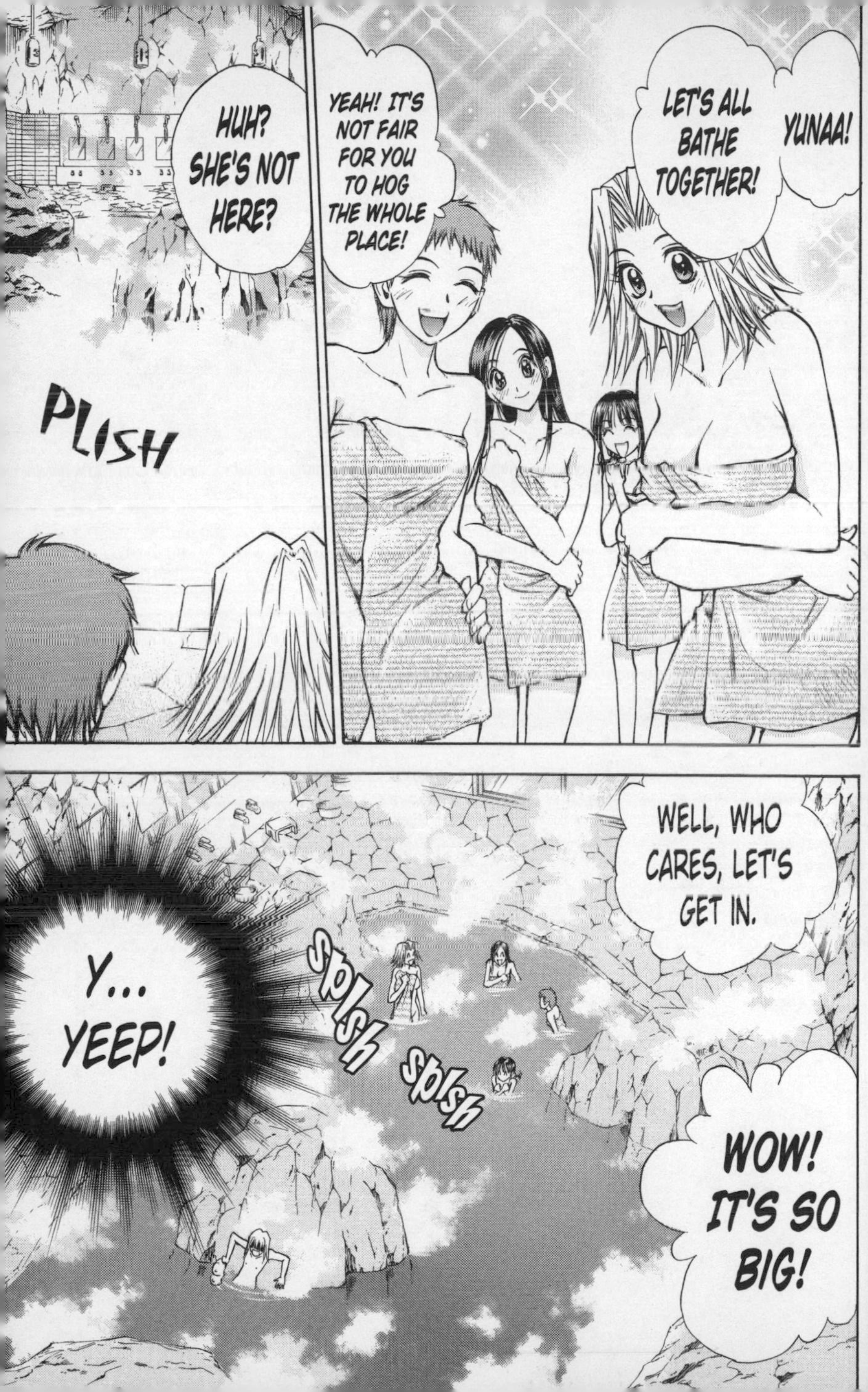
YUNAA!
LET'S ALL BATHE TOGETHER!
YEAH! IT'S NOT FAIR FOR YOU TO HOG THE WHOLE PLACE!
HUH? SHE'S NOT HERE?
PLISH
WELL, WHO CARES, LET'S GET IN.
WOW! IT'S SO BIG!
splsh
splsh
Y... YEEP!

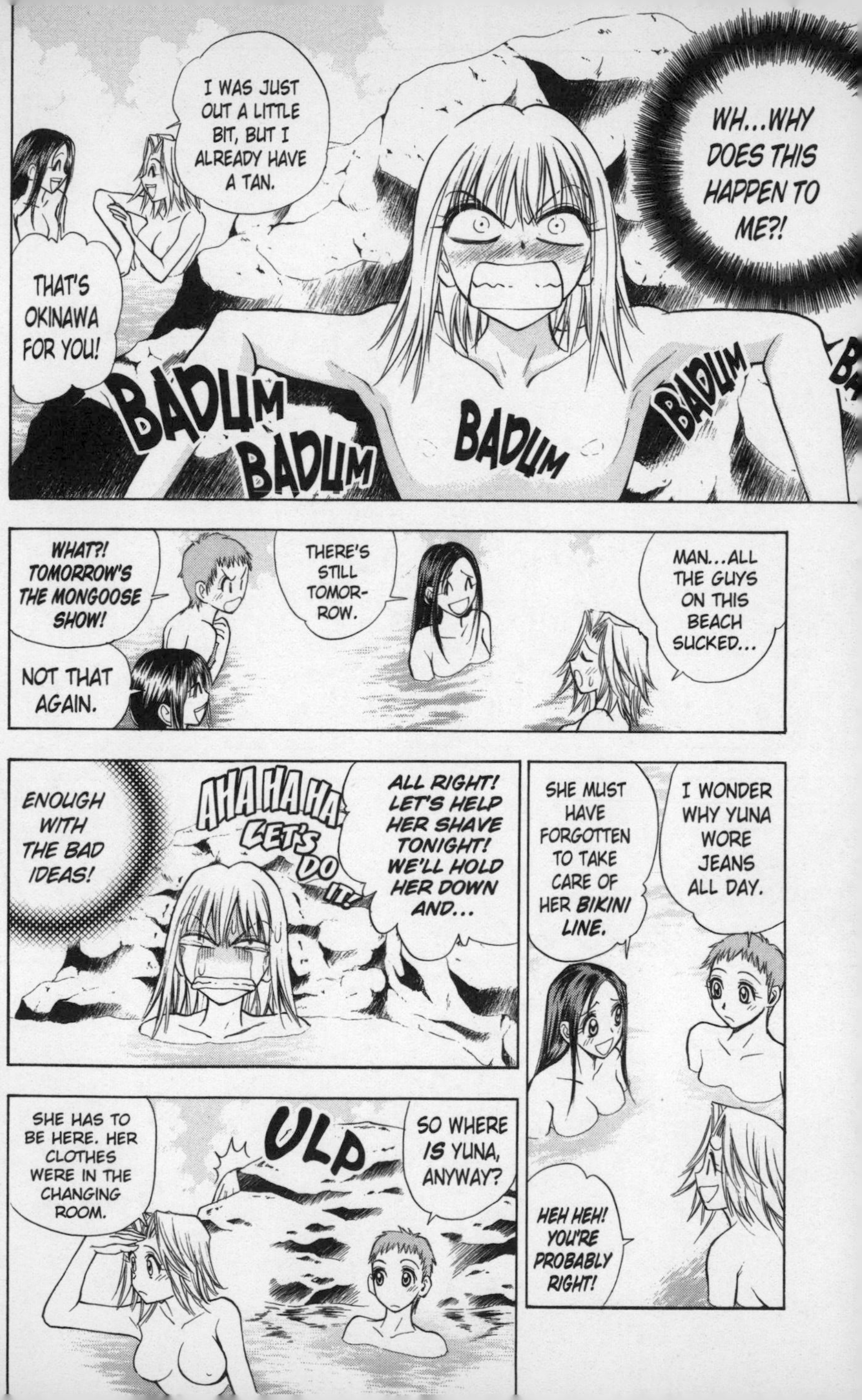
WH...WHY DOES THIS HAPPEN TO ME?!
I WAS JUST OUT A LITTLE BIT, BUT I ALREADY HAVE A TAN.
BADUM
BADUM
THAT'S OKINAWA FOR YOU!
BADUM
BADUM
MAN...ALL THE GUYS ON THIS BEACH SUCKED...
THERE'S STILL TOMORROW.
WHAT?! TOMORROW'S THE MONGOOSE SHOW!
NOT THAT AGAIN.
I WONDER WHY YUNA WORE JEANS ALL DAY.
SHE MUST HAVE FORGOTTEN TO TAKE CARE OF HER BIKINI LINE.
HEH HEH! YOU'RE PROBABLY RIGHT!
ALL RIGHT! LET'S HELP HER SHAVE TONIGHT! WE'LL HOLD HER DOWN AND...
AHA HA HA
LET'S DO IT!
ENOUGH WITH THE BAD IDEAS!
SO WHERE IS YUNA, ANYWAY?
ULP
SHE HAS TO BE HERE. HER CLOTHES WERE IN THE CHANGING ROOM.

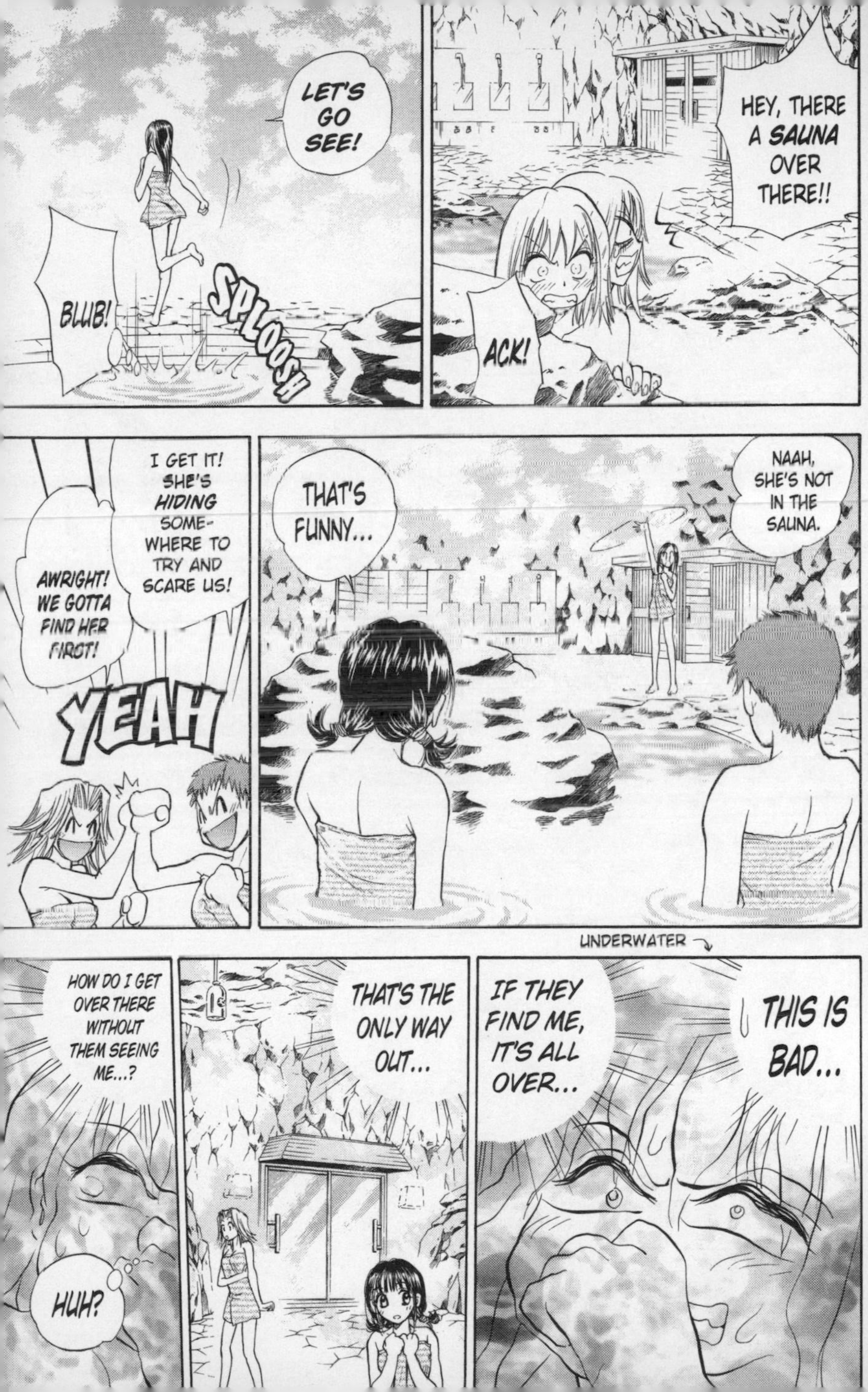
HEY, THERE A SAUNA OVER THERE!!
ACK!
LET'S GO SEE!
BLUB!
SPLOOSH
NAAH, SHE'S NOT IN THE SAUNA.
THAT'S FUNNY...
I GET IT! SHE'S HIDING SOME-WHERE TO TRY AND SCARE US!
AWRIGHT! WE GOTTA FIND HER FIRST!
YEAH
UNDERWATER
THIS IS BAD...
IF THEY FIND ME, IT'S ALL OVER...
THAT'S THE ONLY WAY OUT...
HOW DO I GET OVER THERE WITHOUT THEM SEEING ME...?
HUH?

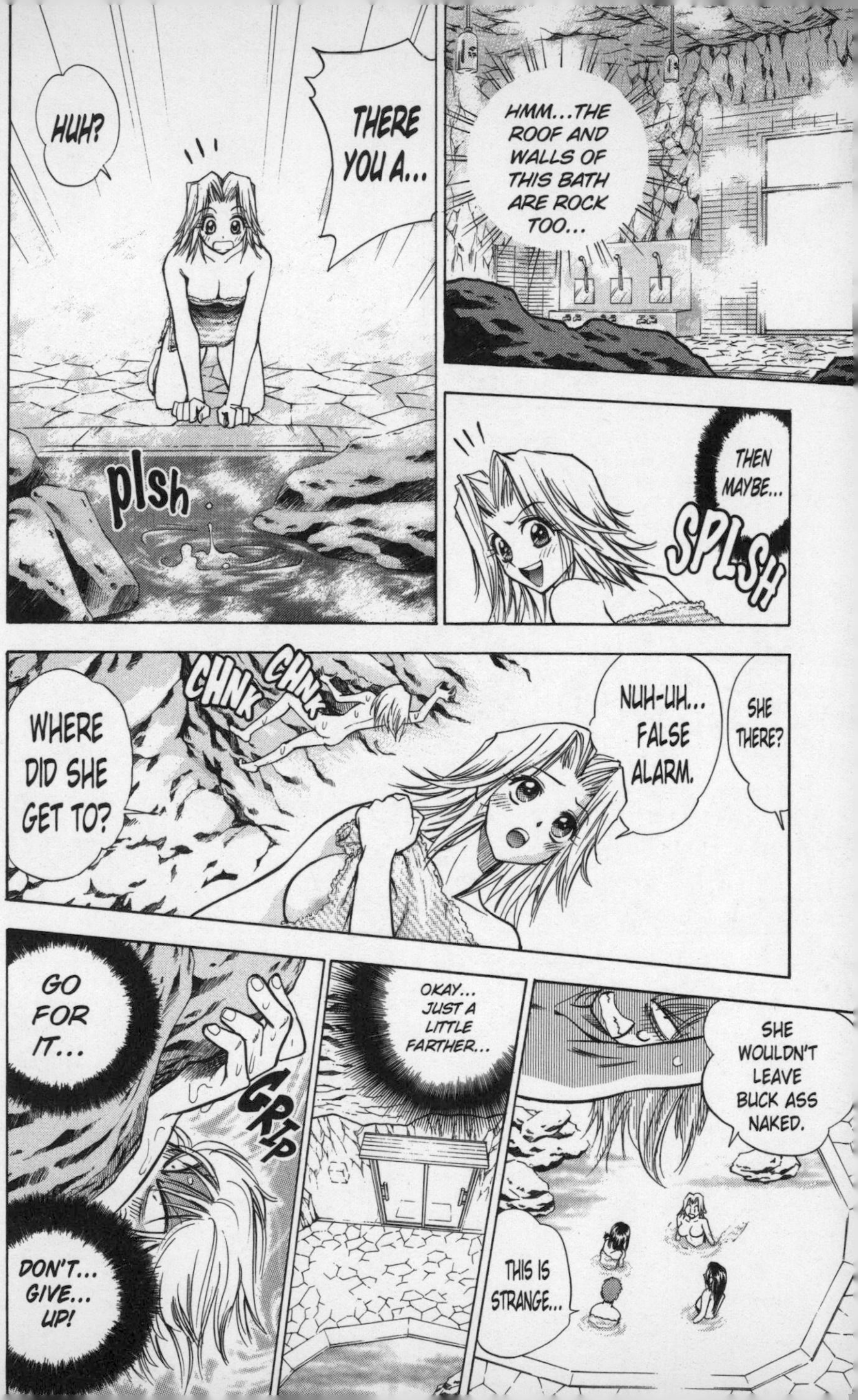
HMM...THE ROOF AND WALLS OF THIS BATH ARE ROCK TOO...
THEN MAYBE...
SPLSH
THERE YOU A...
HUH?
plsh
SHE THERE?
NUH-UH... FALSE ALARM.
CHNK
CHNK
WHERE DID SHE GET TO?
SHE WOULDN'T LEAVE BUCK ASS NAKED.
THIS IS STRANGE...
OKAY... JUST A LITTLE FARTHER...
GO FOR IT...
GRIP
DON'T... GIVE... UP!

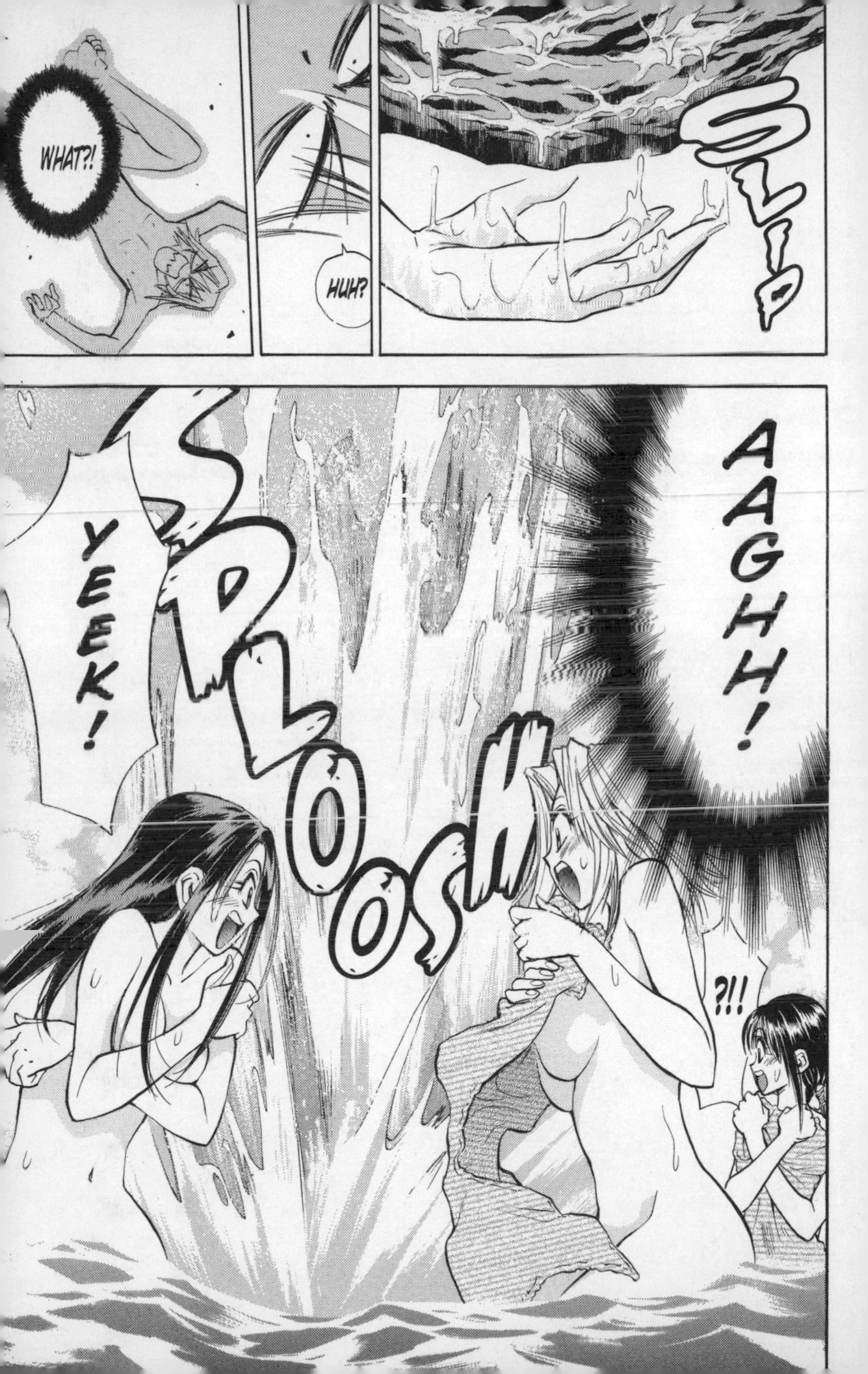
SLLIP
HUH?
WHAT?!
AAGHH!
SPLOOSH
YEEK!
?!!

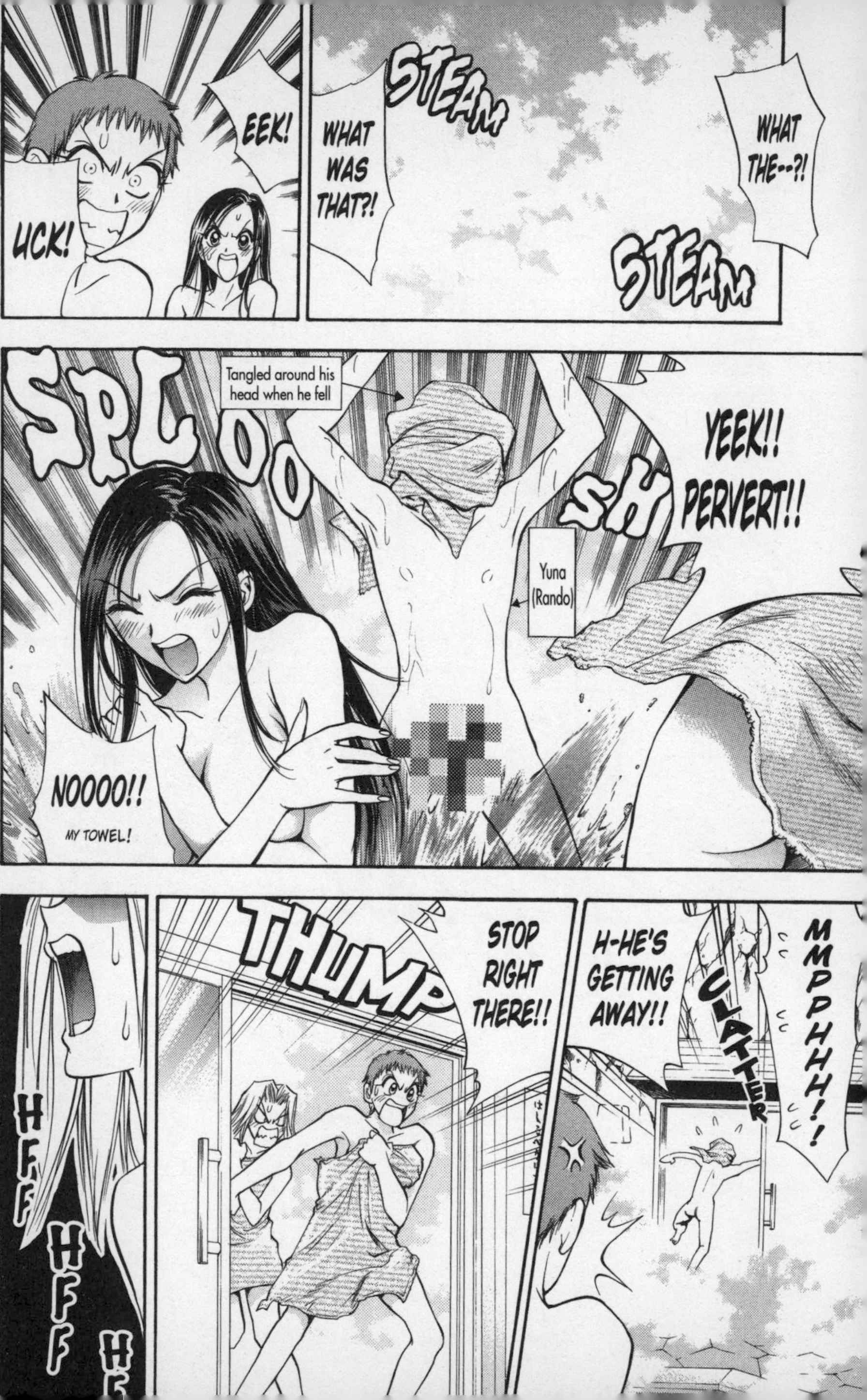
WHAT THE--?!
STEAM
WHAT WAS THAT?!
STEAM
EEK!
UCK!
YEEK!! PERVERT!!
SPLOOSH
Tangled around his head when he fell
Yuna (Rando)
NOOOO!!
MY TOWEL!
MMPHHH!!
CLATTER
H-HE'S GETTING AWAY!!
STOP RIGHT THERE!!
THUMP
HFF
HFF

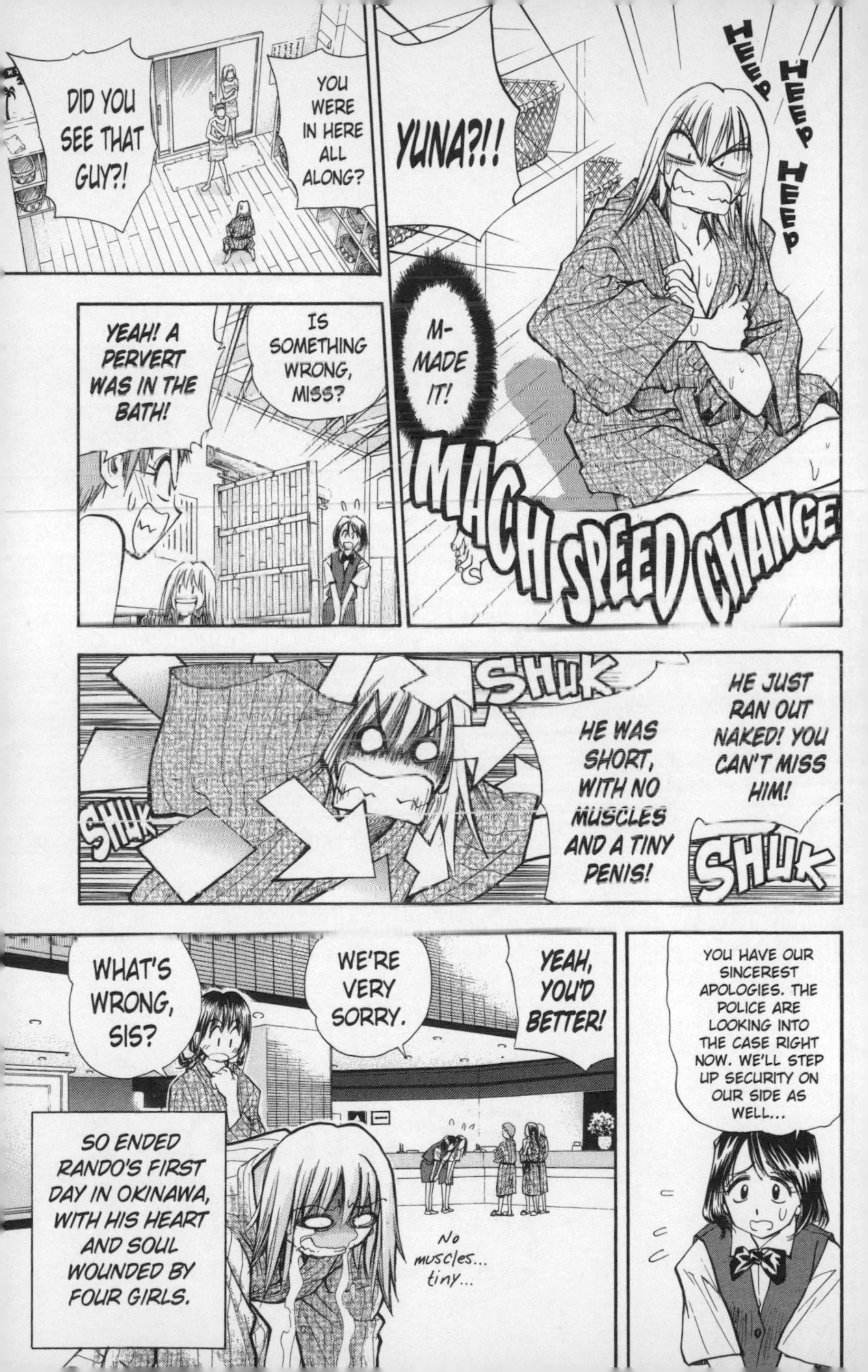
YUNA?!!
HEEP HEEP HEEP HEEP
M-MADE IT!
MACH SPEED CHANGE
YOU WERE IN HERE ALL ALONG?
DID YOU SEE THAT GUY?!
IS SOMETHING WRONG, MISS?
YEAH! A PERVERT WAS IN THE BATH!
SHUK
HE JUST RAN OUT NAKED! YOU CAN'T MISS HIM!
HE WAS SHORT, WITH NO MUSCLES AND A TINY PENIS!
SHUK
SHUK
YOU HAVE OUR SINCEREST APOLOGIES. THE POLICE ARE LOOKING INTO THE CASE RIGHT NOW. WE'LL STEP UP SECURITY ON OUR SIDE AS WELL...
YEAH, YOU'D BETTER!
WE'RE VERY SORRY.
WHAT'S WRONG, SIS?
SO ENDED RANDO'S FIRST DAY IN OKINAWA, WITH HIS HEART AND SOUL WOUNDED BY FOUR GIRLS.
No muscles... tiny...

Pretty Face

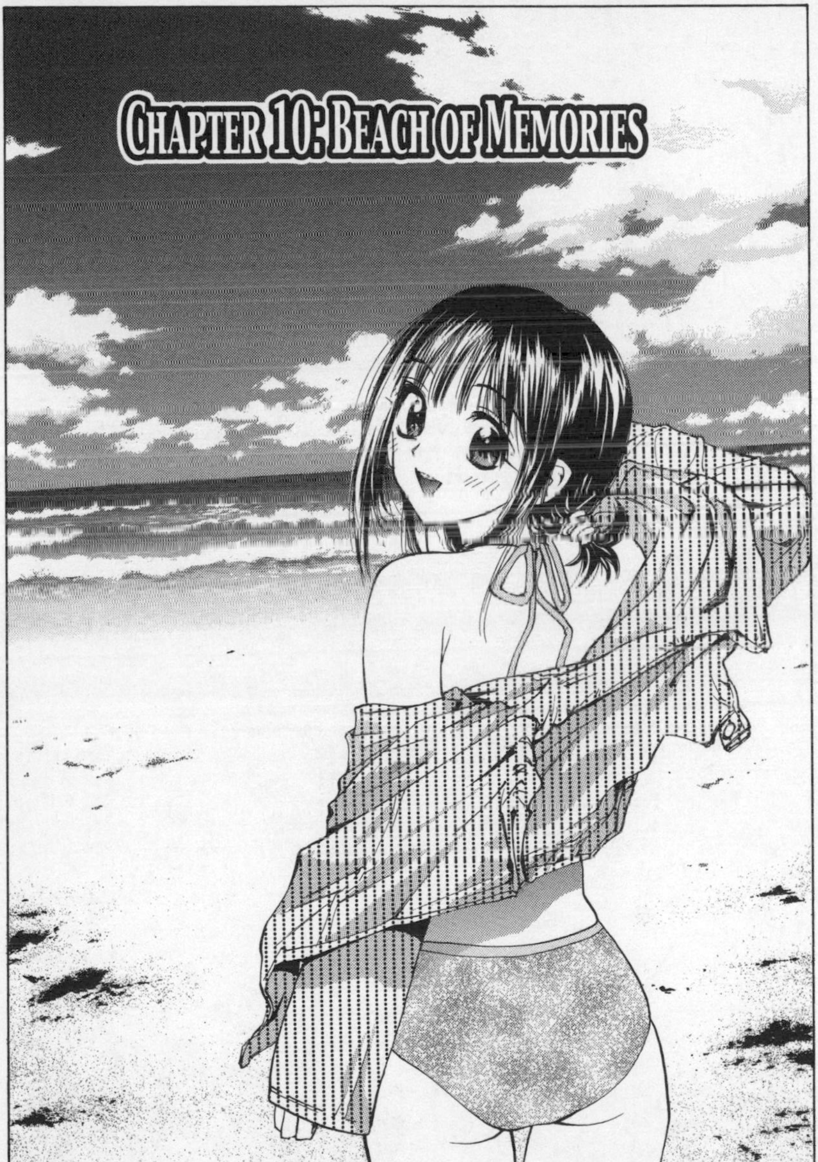
CHAPTER 10: BEACH OF MEMORIES

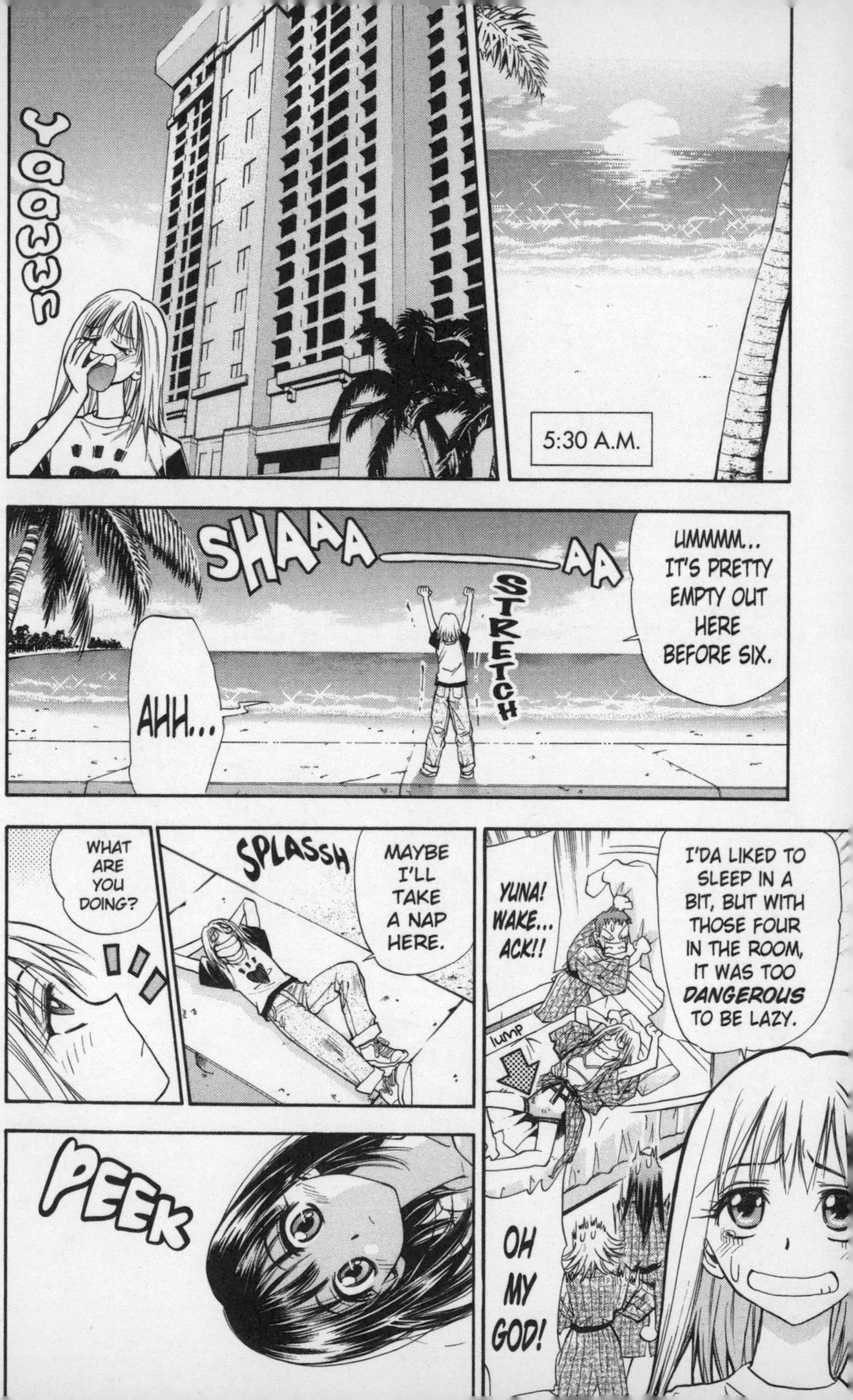
5:30 A.M.
Yaawwn
UMMMM... IT'S PRETTY EMPTY OUT HERE BEFORE SIX.
SHAAA——AA
STRETCH
AHH...
I'DA LIKED TO SLEEP IN A BIT, BUT WITH THOSE FOUR IN THE ROOM, IT WAS TOO DANGEROUS TO BE LAZY.
YUNA! WAKE... ACK!!
lump
OH MY GOD!
MAYBE I'LL TAKE A NAP HERE.
SPLASSH
WHAT ARE YOU DOING?
PEEK

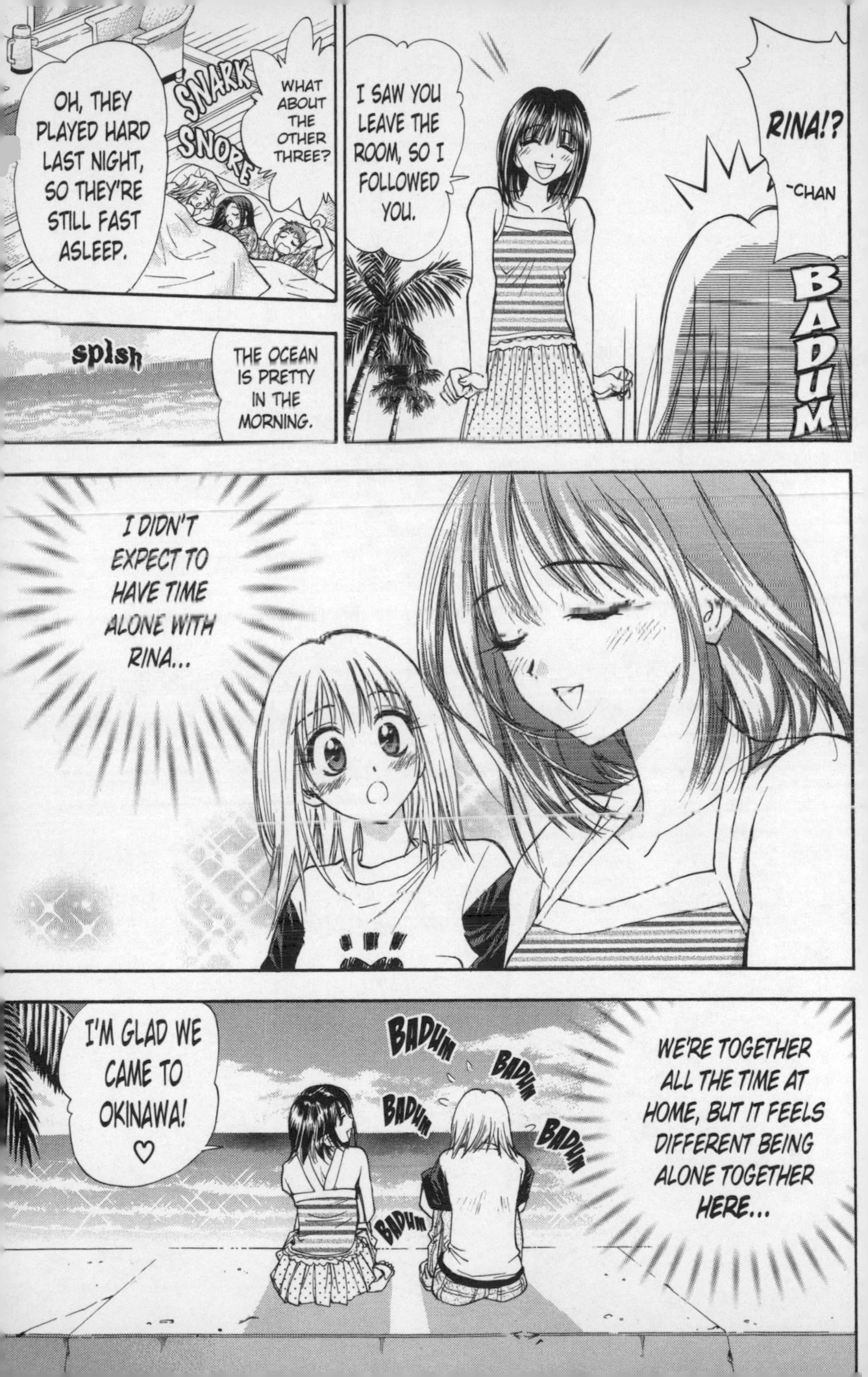
RINA!?
-CHAN
BADUM
I SAW YOU LEAVE THE ROOM, SO I FOLLOWED YOU.
WHAT ABOUT THE OTHER THREE?
SNARK
SNORE
OH, THEY PLAYED HARD LAST NIGHT, SO THEY'RE STILL FAST ASLEEP.
THE OCEAN IS PRETTY IN THE MORNING.
splsh
I DIDN'T EXPECT TO HAVE TIME ALONE WITH RINA...
WE'RE TOGETHER ALL THE TIME AT HOME, BUT IT FEELS DIFFERENT BEING ALONE TOGETHER HERE...
BADUM
BADUM
BADUM
BADUM
BADUM
I'M GLAD WE CAME TO OKINAWA! ♡

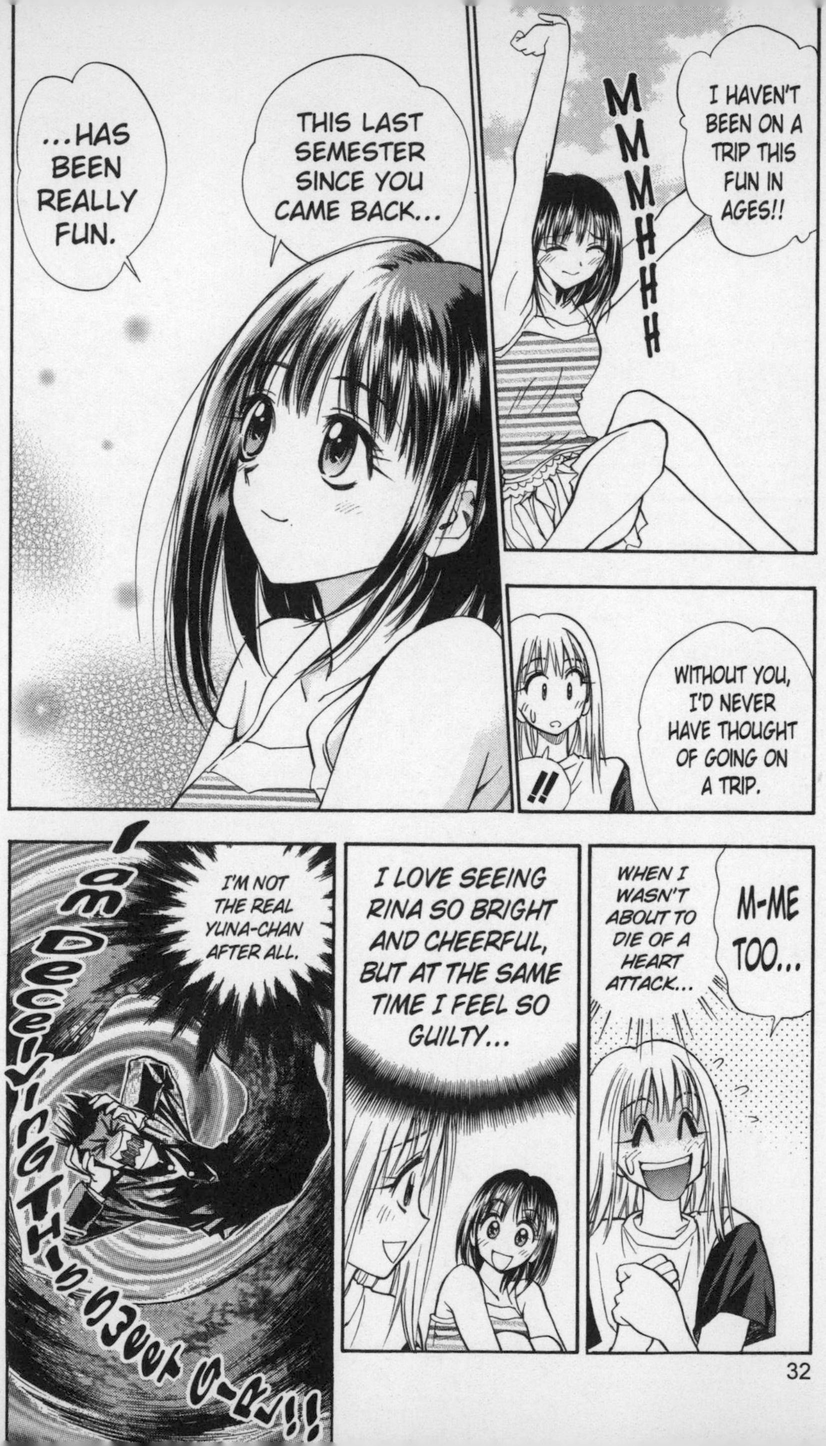
MMMHHH
I HAVEN'T BEEN ON A TRIP THIS FUN IN AGES!!
!!
WITHOUT YOU, I'D NEVER HAVE THOUGHT OF GOING ON A TRIP.
THIS LAST SEMESTER SINCE YOU CAME BACK...
...HAS BEEN REALLY FUN.
M-ME TOO...
WHEN I WASN'T ABOUT TO DIE OF A HEART ATTACK...
I LOVE SEEING RINA SO BRIGHT AND CHEERFUL, BUT AT THE SAME TIME I FEEL SO GUILTY...
I'M NOT THE REAL YUNA-CHAN AFTER ALL.
I'M DECEIVING THIS SWEET GIRL!!

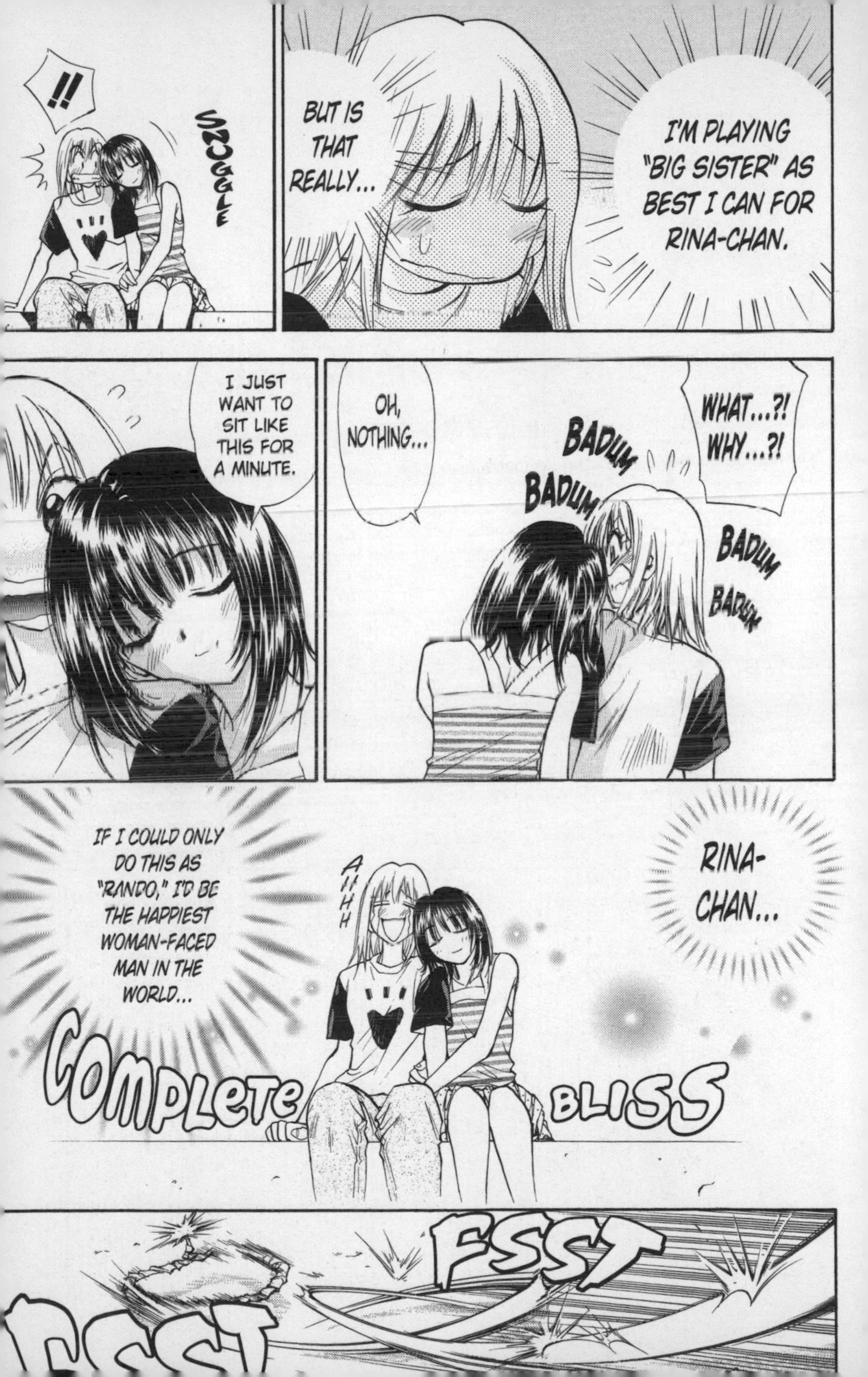
I'M PLAYING "BIG SISTER" AS BEST I CAN FOR RINA-CHAN.
BUT IS THAT REALLY...
!!
SNUGGLE
WHAT...?! WHY...?!
BADUM
BADUM
BADUM
BADUM
OH, NOTHING...
I JUST WANT TO SIT LIKE THIS FOR A MINUTE.
RINA-CHAN...
AHHH
IF I COULD ONLY DO THIS AS "RANDO," I'D BE THE HAPPIEST WOMAN-FACED MAN IN THE WORLD...
COMPLETE BLISS
FSST

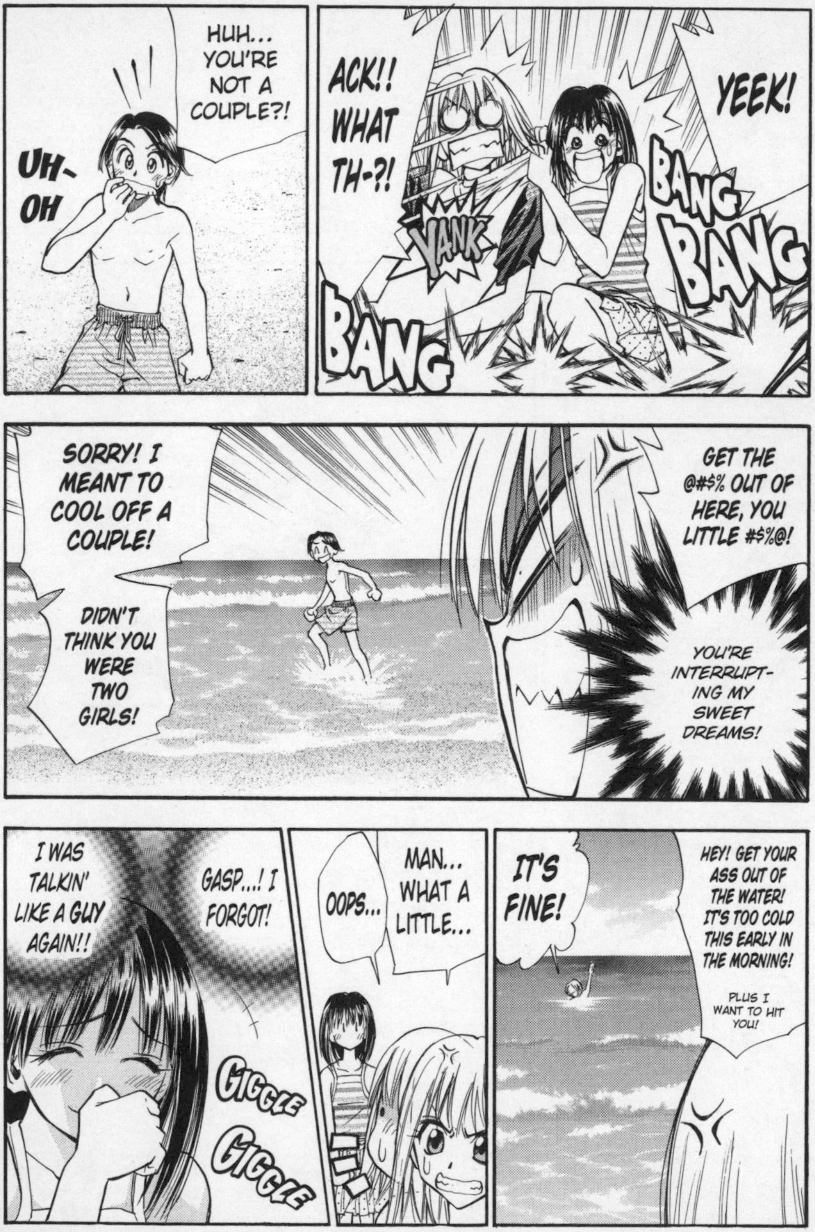
YEEK!
BANG BANG
ACK!! WHAT TH-?!
YANK
BANG
HUH... YOU'RE NOT A COUPLE?!
UH-OH
GET THE @#$% OUT OF HERE, YOU LITTLE #$%@!
YOU'RE INTERRUPT-ING MY SWEET DREAMS!
SORRY! I MEANT TO COOL OFF A COUPLE!
DIDN'T THINK YOU WERE TWO GIRLS!
HEY! GET YOUR ASS OUT OF THE WATER! IT'S TOO COLD THIS EARLY IN THE MORNING!
PLUS I WANT TO HIT YOU!
IT'S FINE!
MAN... WHAT A LITTLE...
OOPS...
GASP...! I FORGOT!
I WAS TALKIN' LIKE A GUY AGAIN!!
GIGGLE
GIGGLE

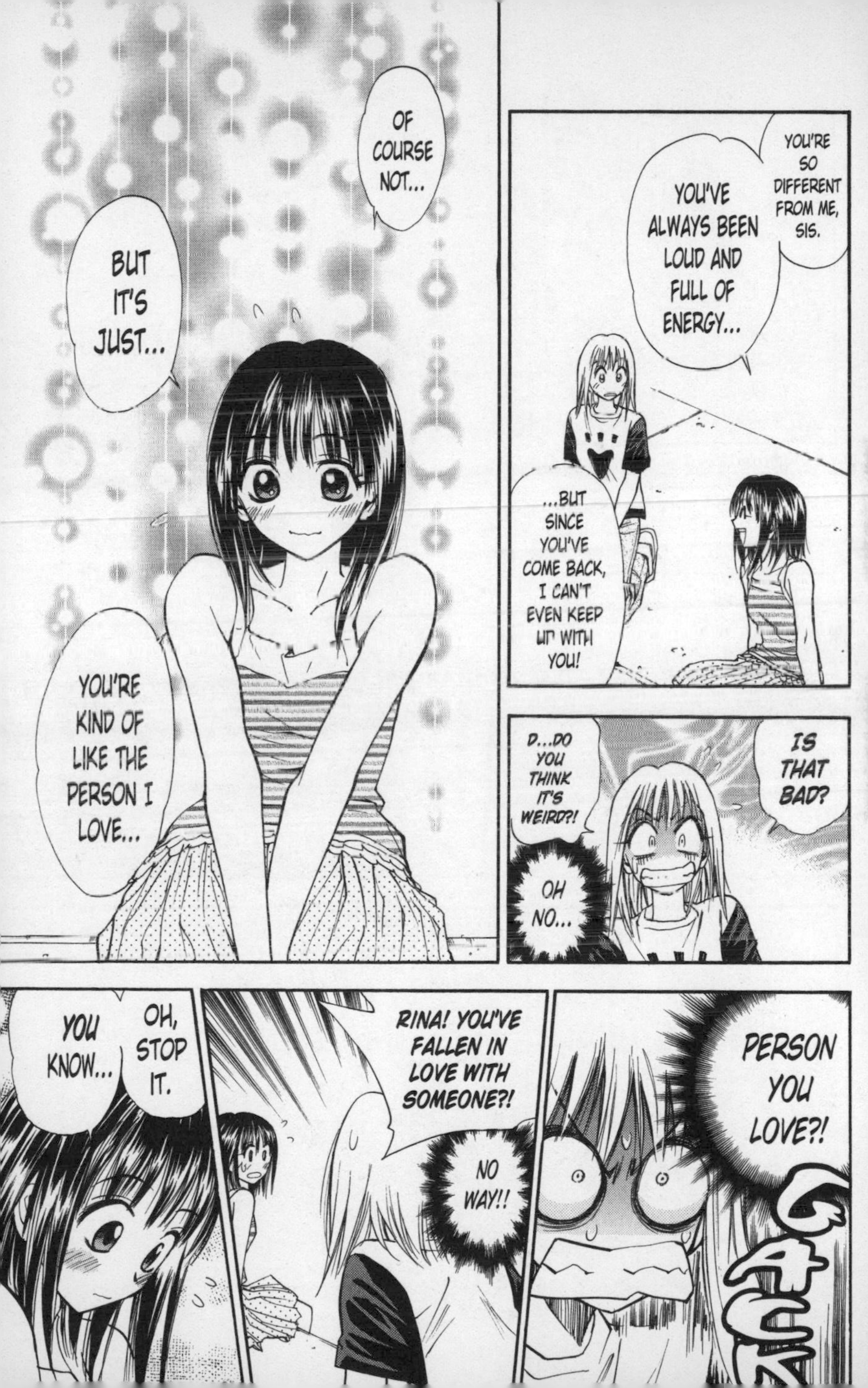
YOU'RE SO DIFFERENT FROM ME, SIS.
YOU'VE ALWAYS BEEN LOUD AND FULL OF ENERGY...
...BUT SINCE YOU'VE COME BACK, I CAN'T EVEN KEEP UP WITH YOU!
IS THAT BAD?
D...DO YOU THINK IT'S WEIRD?!
OH NO...
OF COURSE NOT...
BUT IT'S JUST...
YOU'RE KIND OF LIKE THE PERSON I LOVE...
PERSON YOU LOVE?!
GACK
RINA! YOU'VE FALLEN IN LOVE WITH SOMEONE?!
NO WAY!!
OH, STOP IT.
YOU KNOW...

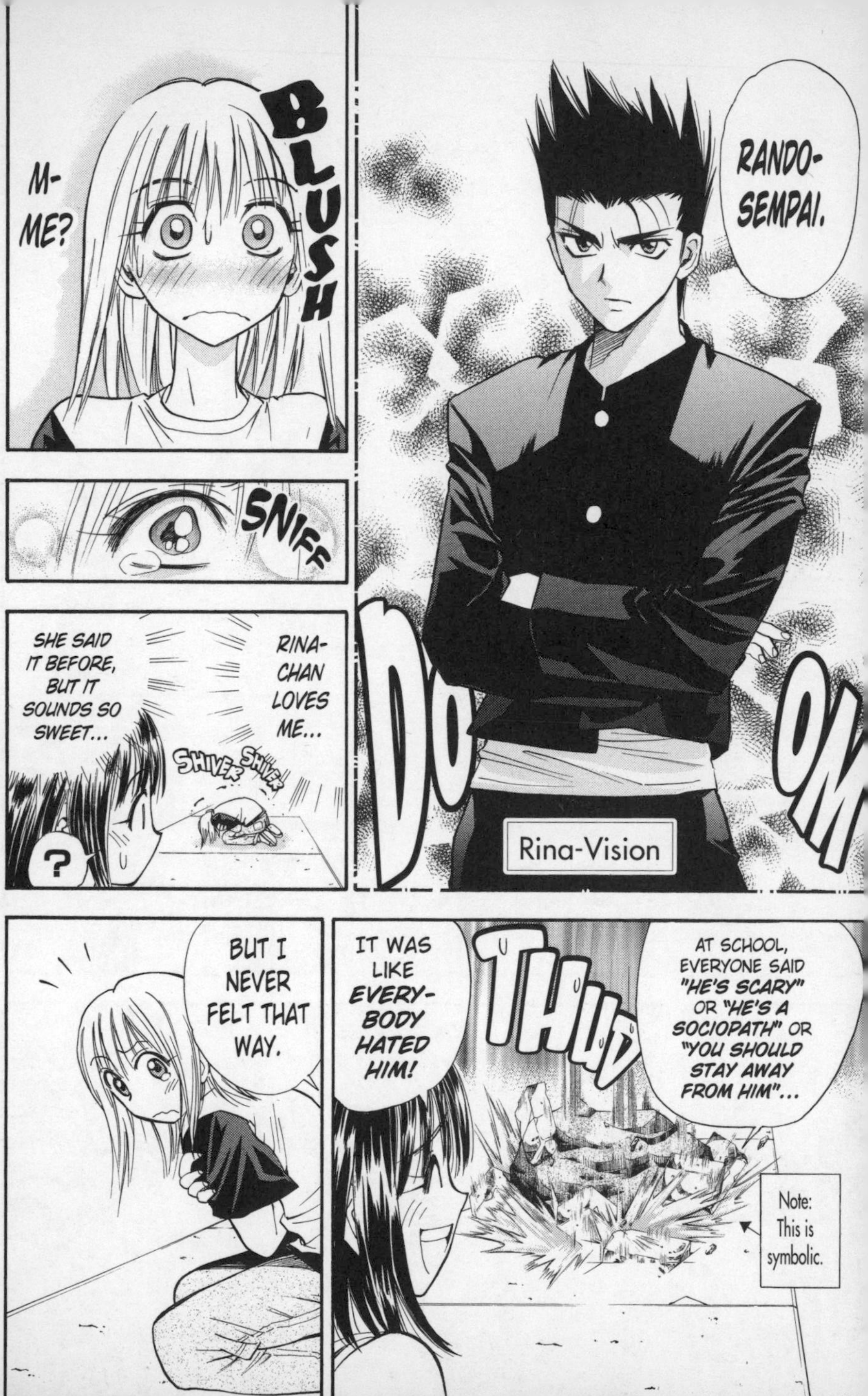
RANDO-SEMPAI.
DOOM
Rina-Vision
M-ME?
BLUSH
SNIFF
RINA-CHAN LOVES ME...
SHE SAID IT BEFORE, BUT IT SOUNDS SO SWEET...
SHIVER SHIVER
?
AT SCHOOL, EVERYONE SAID "HE'S SCARY" OR "HE'S A SOCIOPATH" OR "YOU SHOULD STAY AWAY FROM HIM"...
THUD
IT WAS LIKE EVERYBODY HATED HIM!
Note: This is symbolic.
BUT I NEVER FELT THAT WAY.

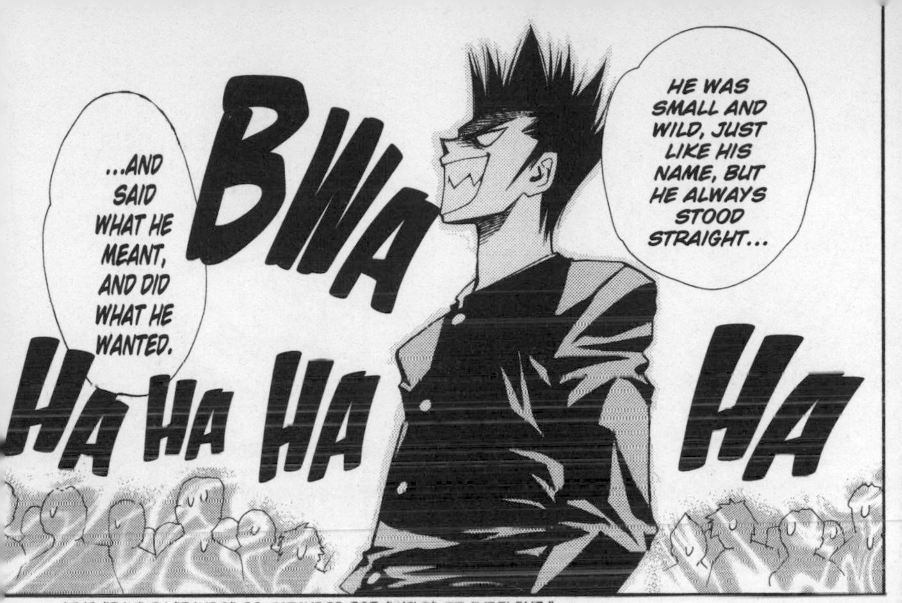
HE WAS SMALL AND WILD, JUST LIKE HIS NAME, BUT HE ALWAYS STOOD STRAIGHT...
BWA
...AND SAID WHAT HE MEANT, AND DID WHAT HE WANTED.
HA HA HA HA HA

*THE "RAN" IN "RANDO" IS JAPANESE FOR "WILD" OR "VIOLENT."

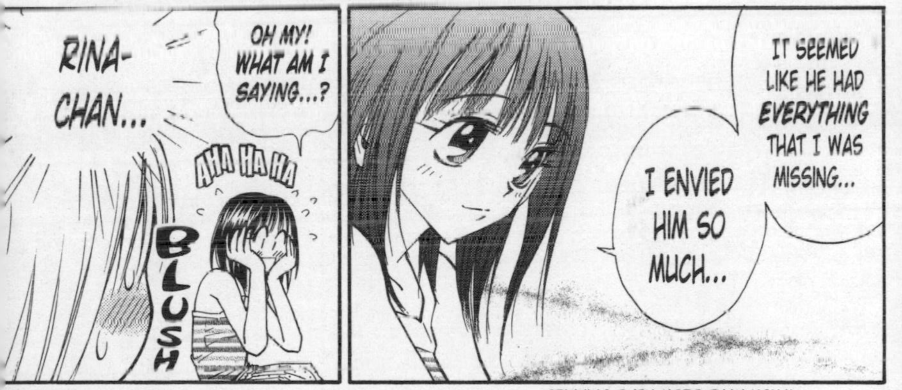
IT SEEMED LIKE HE HAD EVERYTHING THAT I WAS MISSING...
I ENVIED HIM SO MUCH...
OH MY! WHAT AM I SAYING...?
RINA-CHAN...
AHA HA HA
BLUSH

SPINNING EVEN MORE THAN USUAL

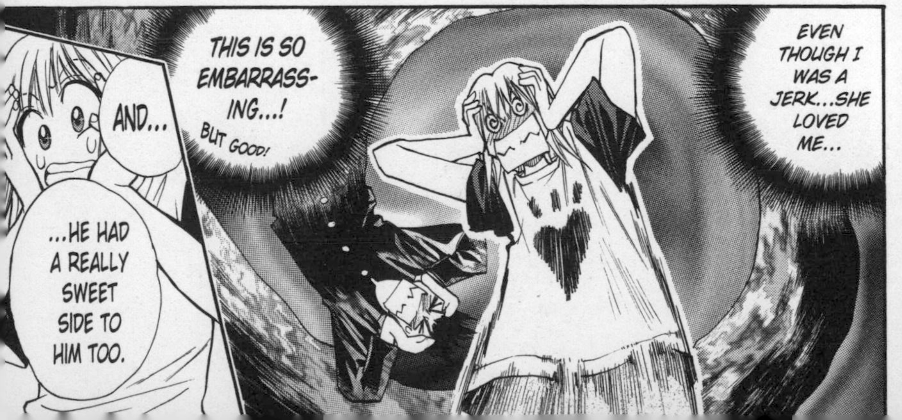
EVEN THOUGH I WAS A JERK...SHE LOVED ME...
THIS IS SO EMBARRASSING...!
BUT GOOD!
AND...
...HE HAD A REALLY SWEET SIDE TO HIM TOO.

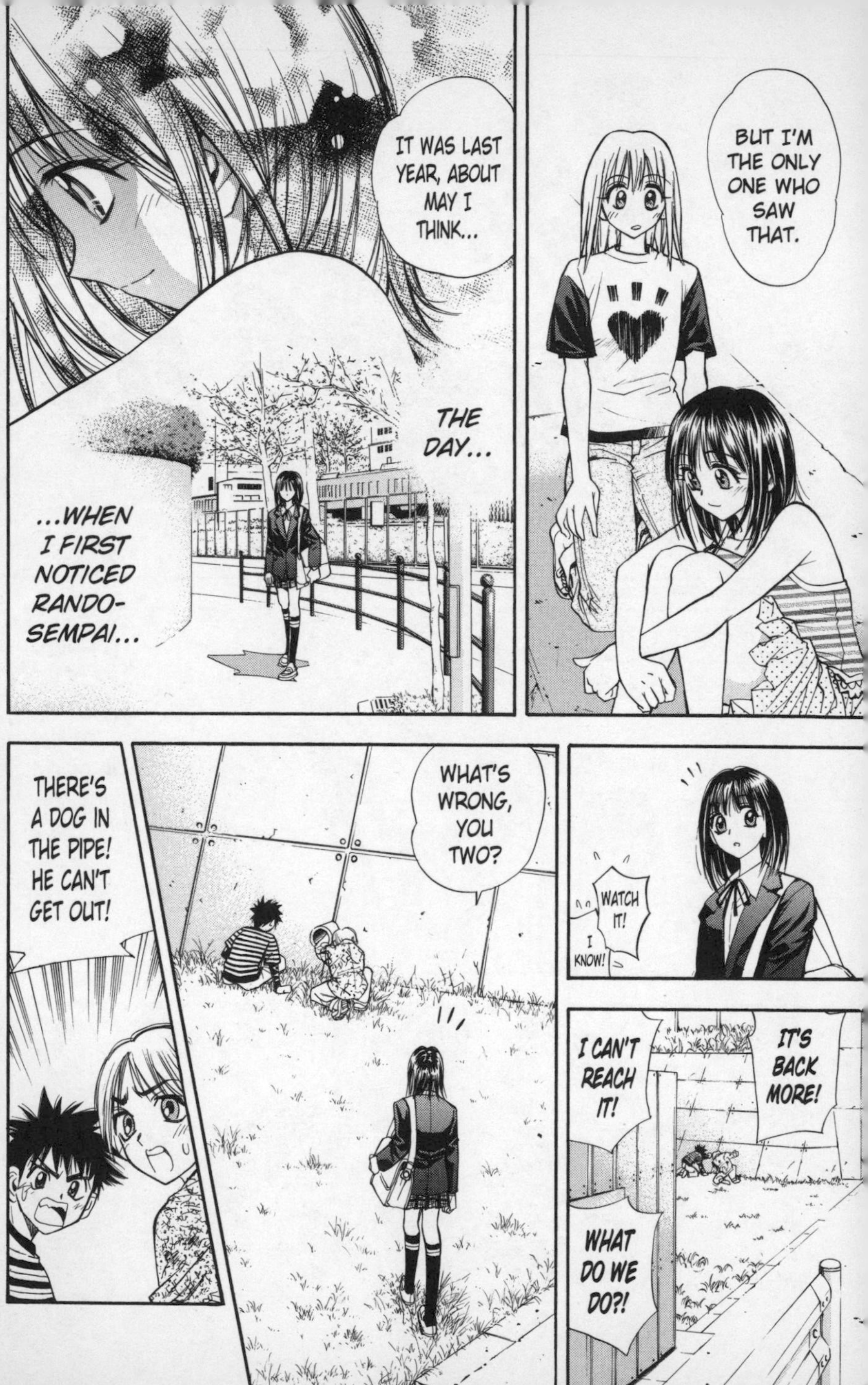
BUT I'M THE ONLY ONE WHO SAW THAT.
IT WAS LAST YEAR, ABOUT MAY I THINK...
THE DAY...
...WHEN I FIRST NOTICED RANDO-SEMPAI...
WATCH IT!
I KNOW!
IT'S BACK MORE!
I CAN'T REACH IT!
WHAT DO WE DO?!
WHAT'S WRONG, YOU TWO?
THERE'S A DOG IN THE PIPE! HE CAN'T GET OUT!

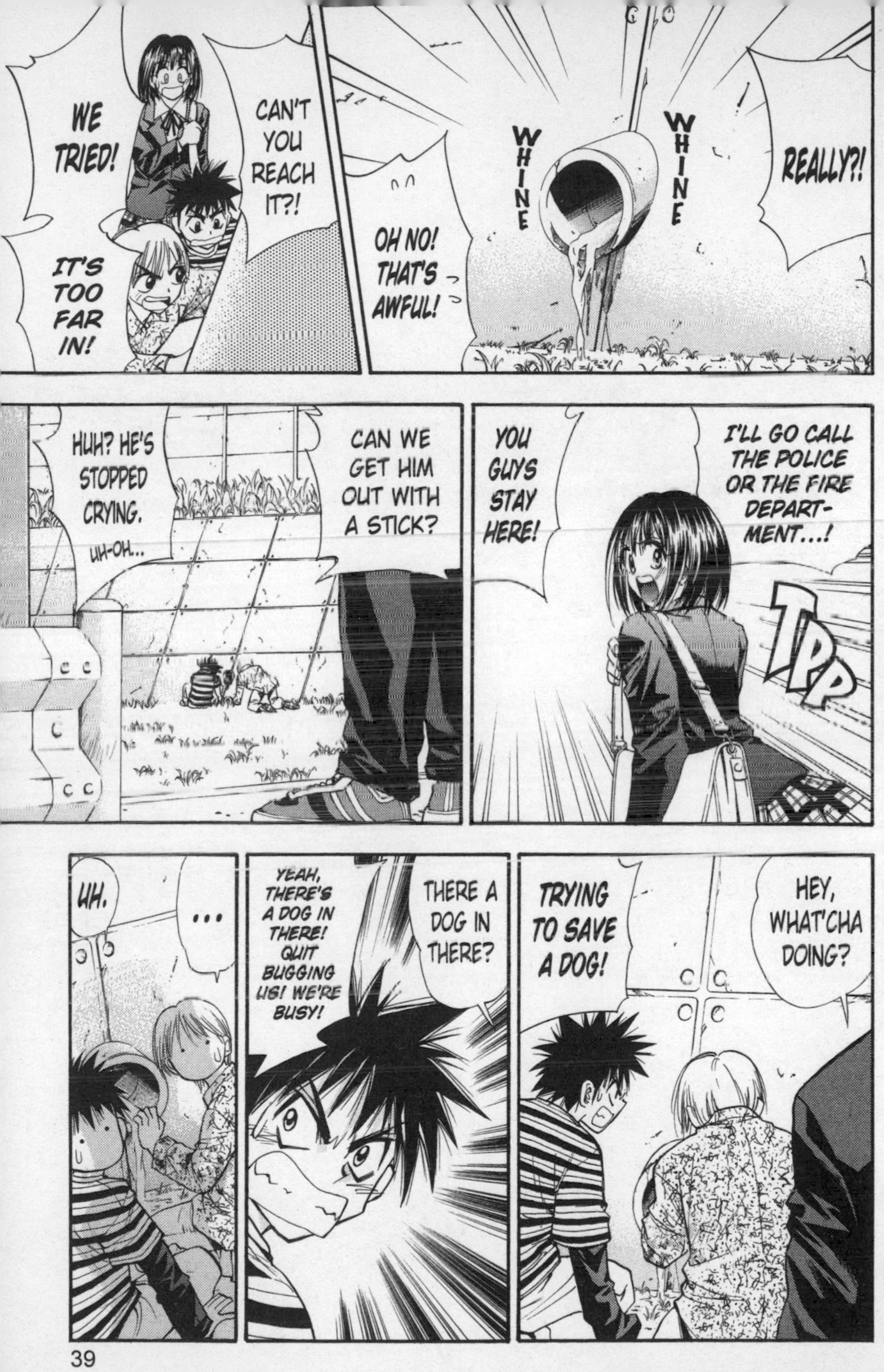
REALLY?!
WHINE
WHINE
OH NO! THAT'S AWFUL!
CAN'T YOU REACH IT?!
WE TRIED!
IT'S TOO FAR IN!
I'LL GO CALL THE POLICE OR THE FIRE DEPART-MENT...!
YOU GUYS STAY HERE!
TPP
CAN WE GET HIM OUT WITH A STICK?
HUH? HE'S STOPPED CRYING.
UH-OH...
HEY, WHAT'CHA DOING?
TRYING TO SAVE A DOG!
THERE A DOG IN THERE?
YEAH, THERE'S A DOG IN THERE! QUIT BUGGING US! WE'RE BUSY!
...
UH.

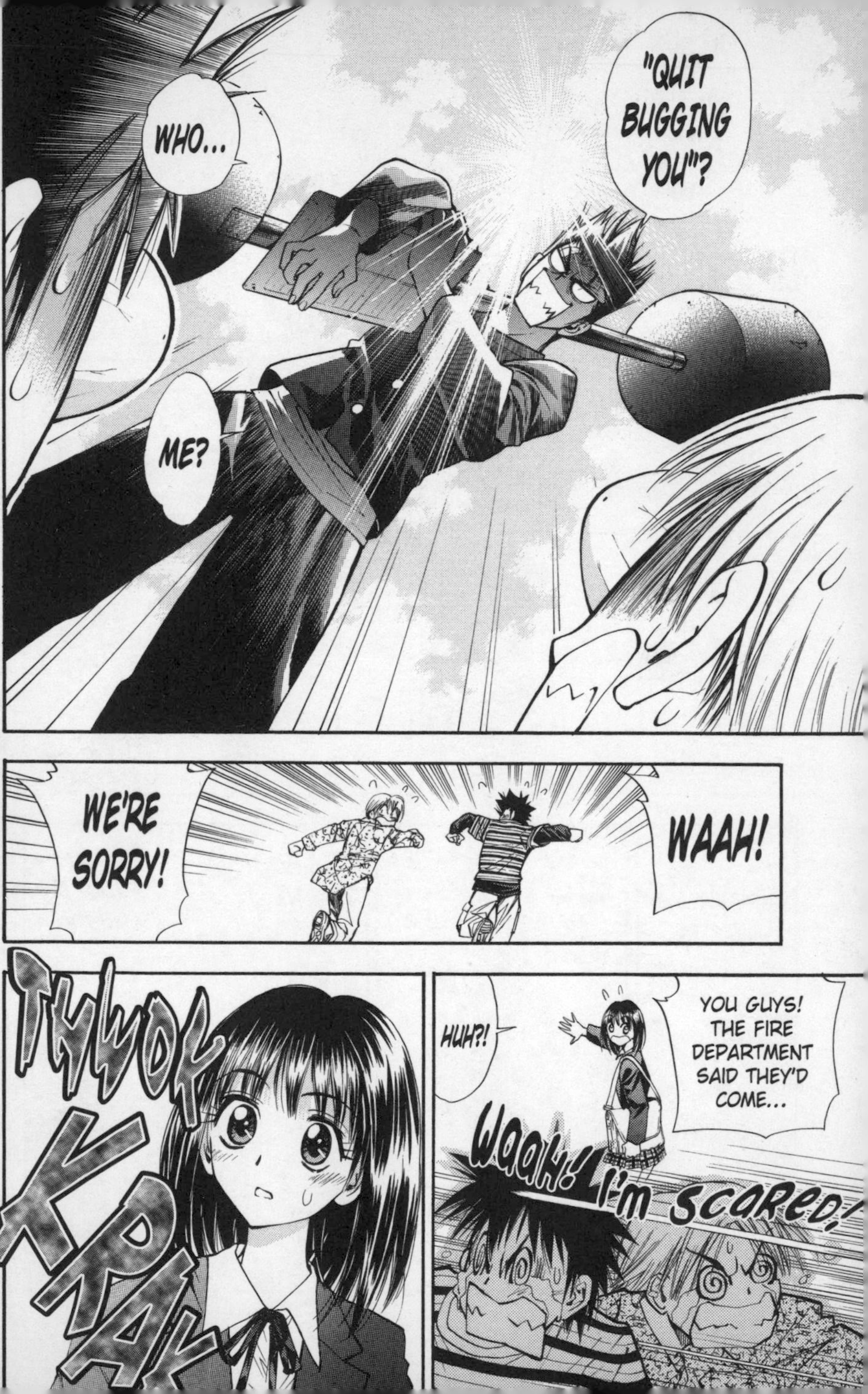
"QUIT BUGGING YOU"?
WHO...
ME?
WAAH!
WE'RE SORRY!
YOU GUYS! THE FIRE DEPARTMENT SAID THEY'D COME...
HUH?!
WAAH! I'm SCARED!
THWOK
KRAK

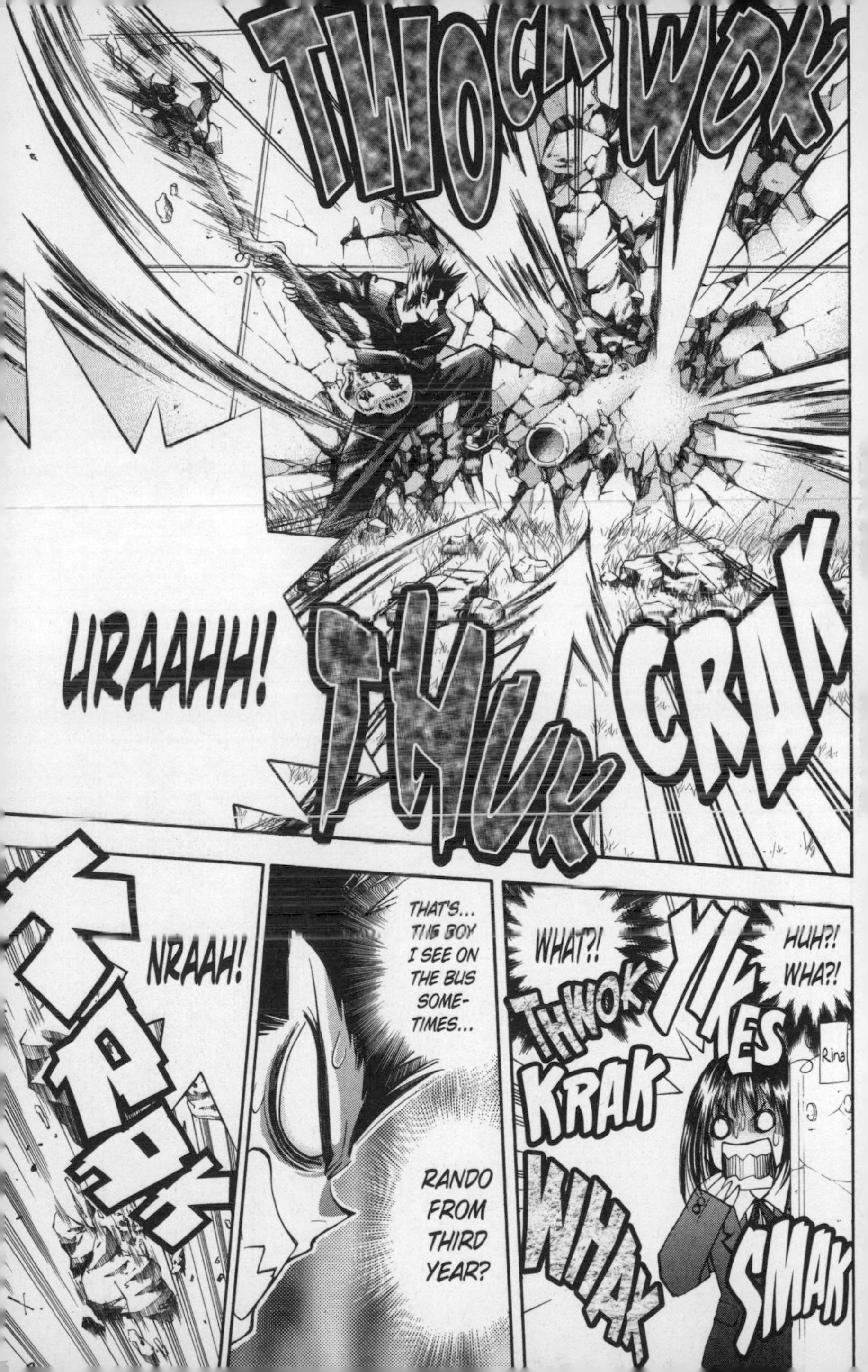
THWOCK WOK
CRAK
THUK
URAAHH!
HUH?! WHA?!
WHAT?!
YIKES
THWOK
KRAK
Rina
WHAK
SMAK
THAT'S... THE BOY I SEE ON THE BUS SOME-TIMES...
RANDO FROM THIRD YEAR?
NRAAH!

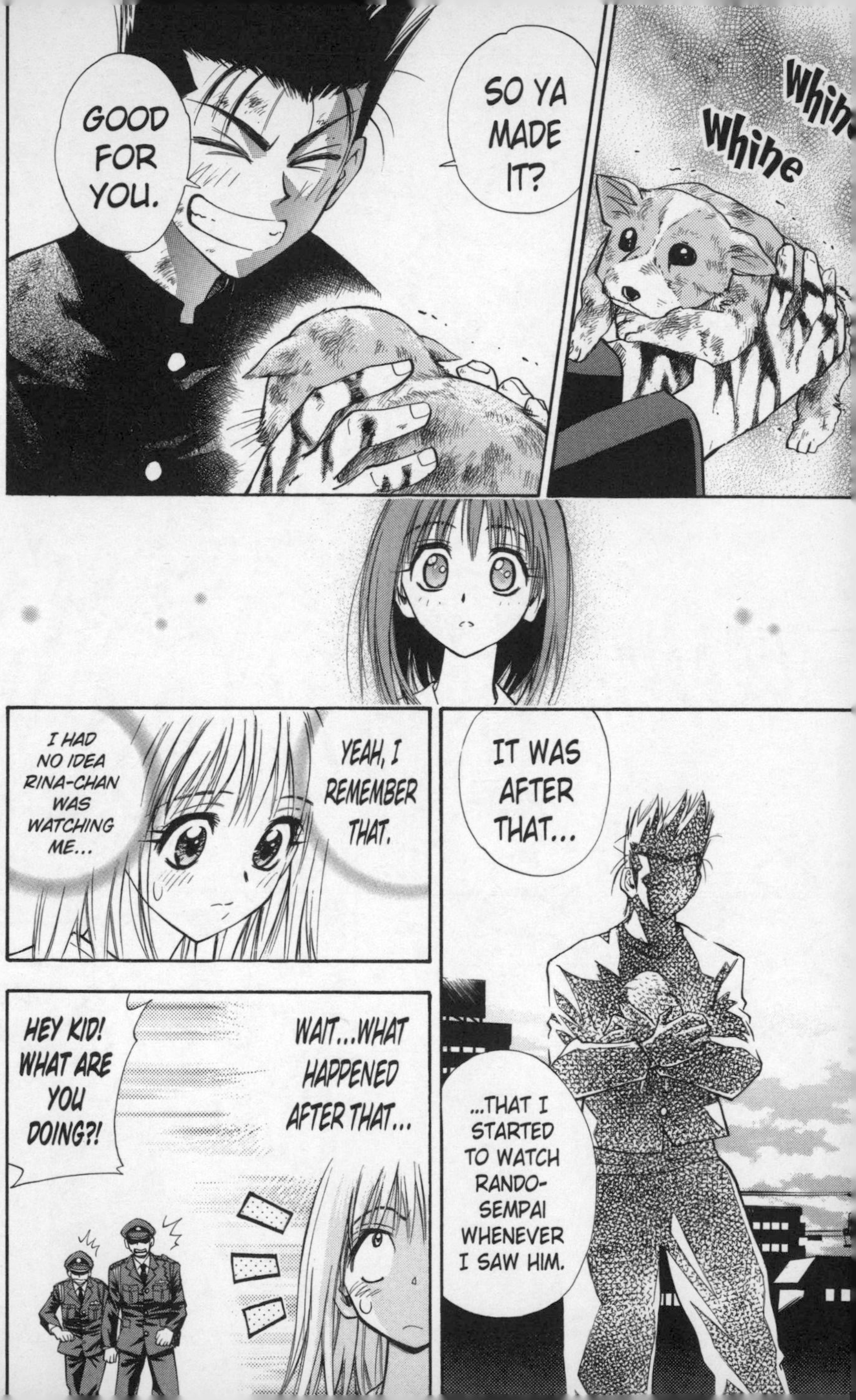
Whine
Whine
SO YA MADE IT?
GOOD FOR YOU.
IT WAS AFTER THAT...
...THAT I STARTED TO WATCH RANDO-SEMPAI WHENEVER I SAW HIM.
YEAH, I REMEMBER THAT.
I HAD NO IDEA RINA-CHAN WAS WATCHING ME...
WAIT...WHAT HAPPENED AFTER THAT...
HEY KID! WHAT ARE YOU DOING?!

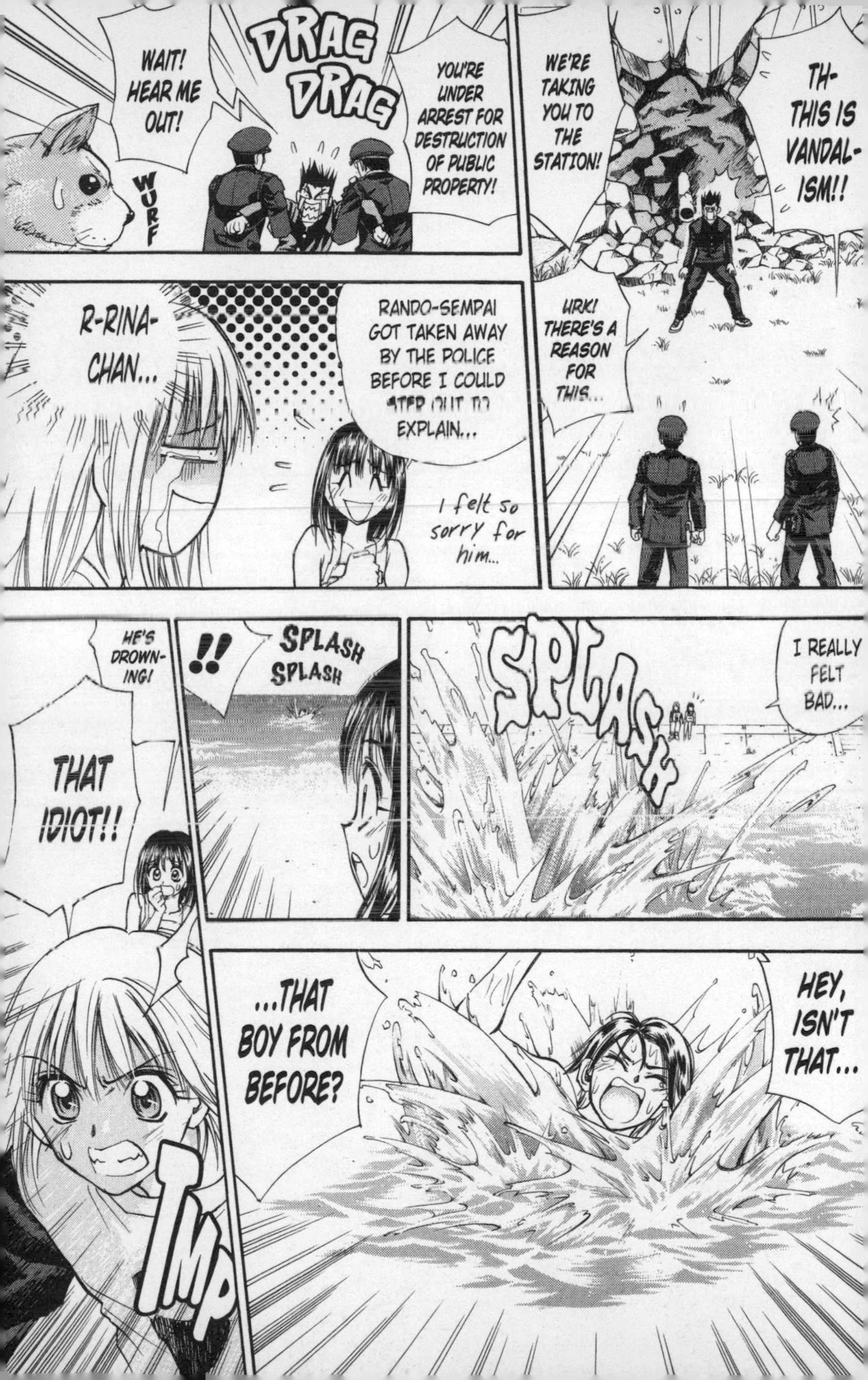
TH- THIS IS VANDAL-ISM!!
WE'RE TAKING YOU TO THE STATION!
URK! THERE'S A REASON FOR THIS...
YOU'RE UNDER ARREST FOR DESTRUCTION OF PUBLIC PROPERTY!
DRAG DRAG
WAIT! HEAR ME OUT!
WURF
RANDO-SEMPAI GOT TAKEN AWAY BY THE POLICE BEFORE I COULD STEP OUT TO EXPLAIN...
I felt so sorry for him...
R-RINA-CHAN...
I REALLY FELT BAD...
SPLASH
SPLASH SPLASH
!!
HE'S DROWNING!
THAT IDIOT!!
HEY, ISN'T THAT...
...THAT BOY FROM BEFORE?
TMP

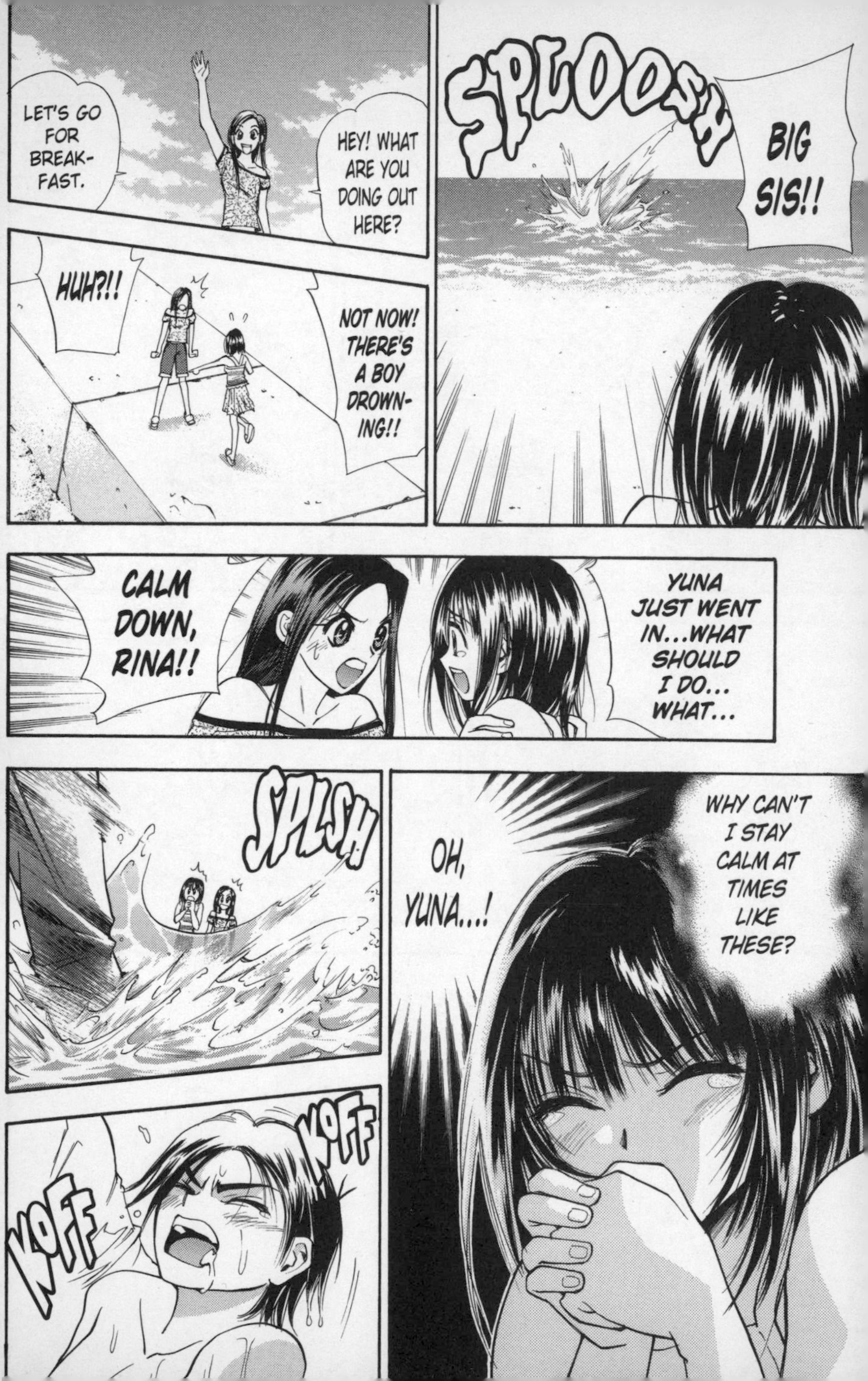
SPLOOSH
BIG SIS!!
HEY! WHAT ARE YOU DOING OUT HERE?
LET'S GO FOR BREAK-FAST.
NOT NOW! THERE'S A BOY DROWN-ING!!
HUH?!!
YUNA JUST WENT IN...WHAT SHOULD I DO... WHAT...
CALM DOWN, RINA!!
WHY CAN'T I STAY CALM AT TIMES LIKE THESE?
OH, YUNA...!
SPLSH
KOFF
KOFF

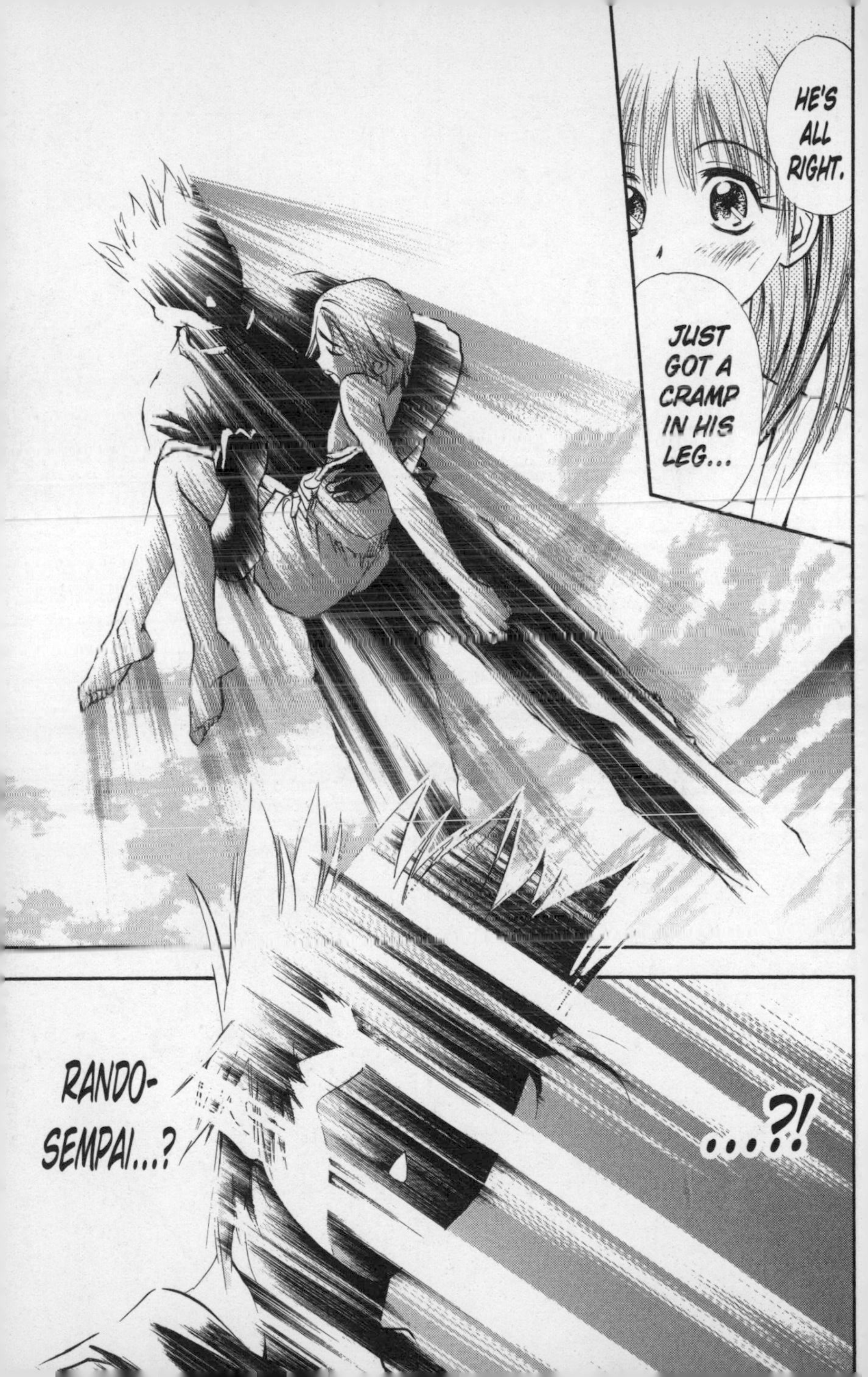
HE'S ALL RIGHT.
JUST GOT A CRAMP IN HIS LEG...
...?!
RANDO-SEMPAI...?

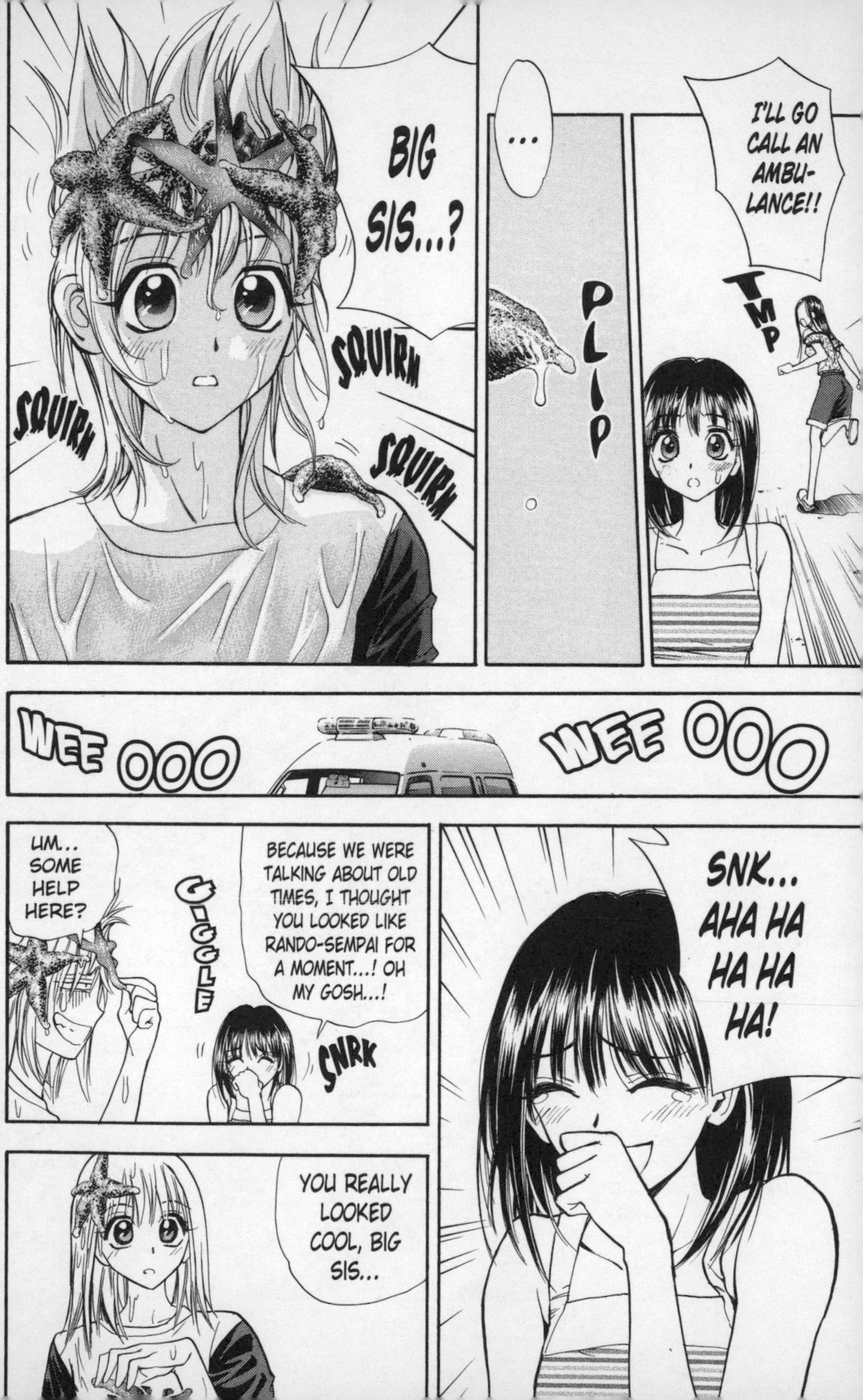
I'LL GO CALL AN AMBULANCE!!
TMP
...
PLIP
BIG SIS...?
SQUIRM
SQUIRM
SQUIRM
WEE OOO
WEE OOO
SNK... AHA HA HA HA HA!
BECAUSE WE WERE TALKING ABOUT OLD TIMES, I THOUGHT YOU LOOKED LIKE RANDO-SEMPAI FOR A MOMENT...! OH MY GOSH...!
SNRK
GIGGLE
UM... SOME HELP HERE?
YOU REALLY LOOKED COOL, BIG SIS...

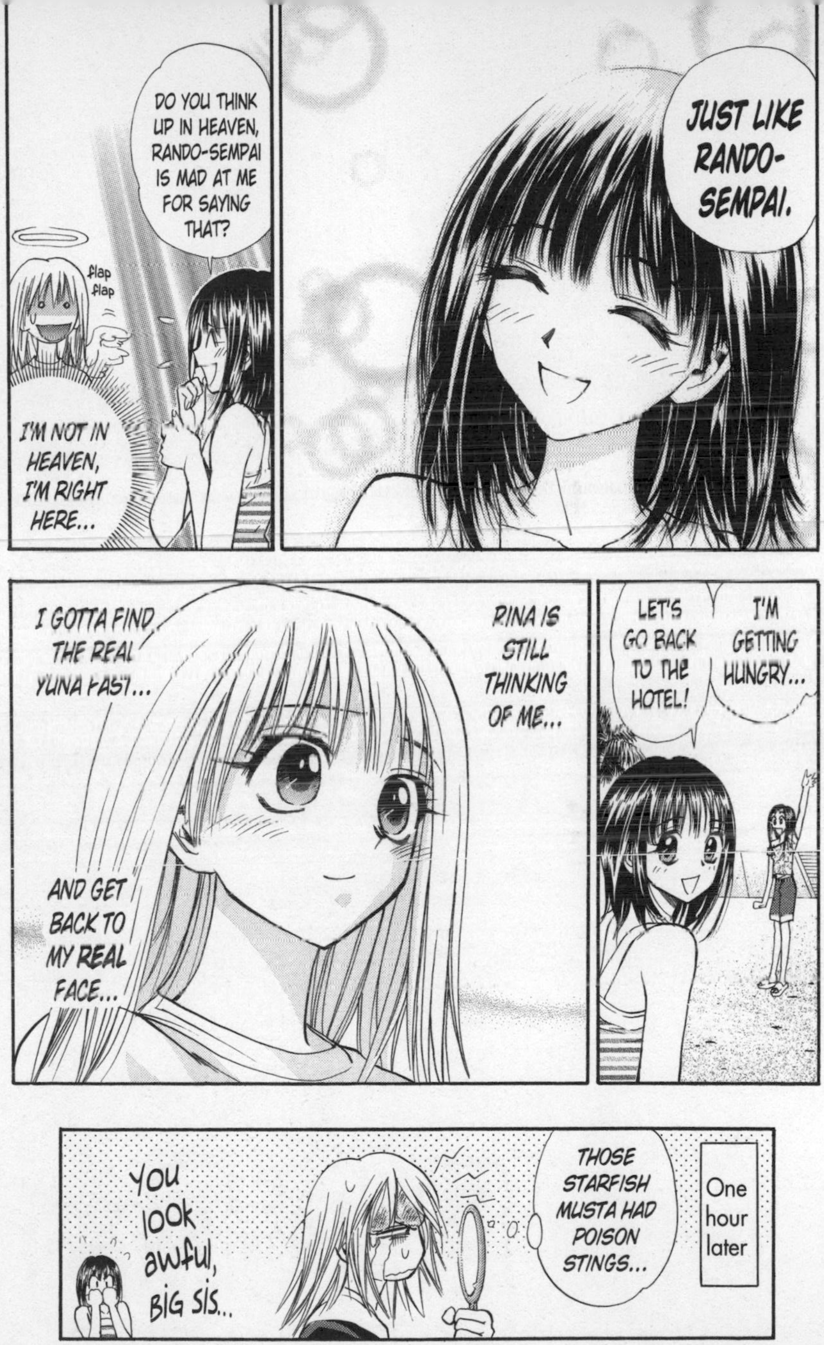
JUST LIKE RANDO-SEMPAI.
DO YOU THINK UP IN HEAVEN, RANDO-SEMPAI IS MAD AT ME FOR SAYING THAT?
flap flap
I'M NOT IN HEAVEN, I'M RIGHT HERE...
I'M GETTING HUNGRY...
LET'S GO BACK TO THE HOTEL!
RINA IS STILL THINKING OF ME...
I GOTTA FIND THE REAL YUNA FAST...
AND GET BACK TO MY REAL FACE...
One hour later
THOSE STARFISH MUSTA HAD POISON STINGS...
You look awful, big sis...

Pretty Face

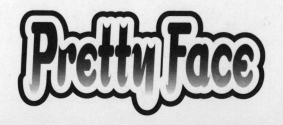

Chapter 11: The Terror of Yukie

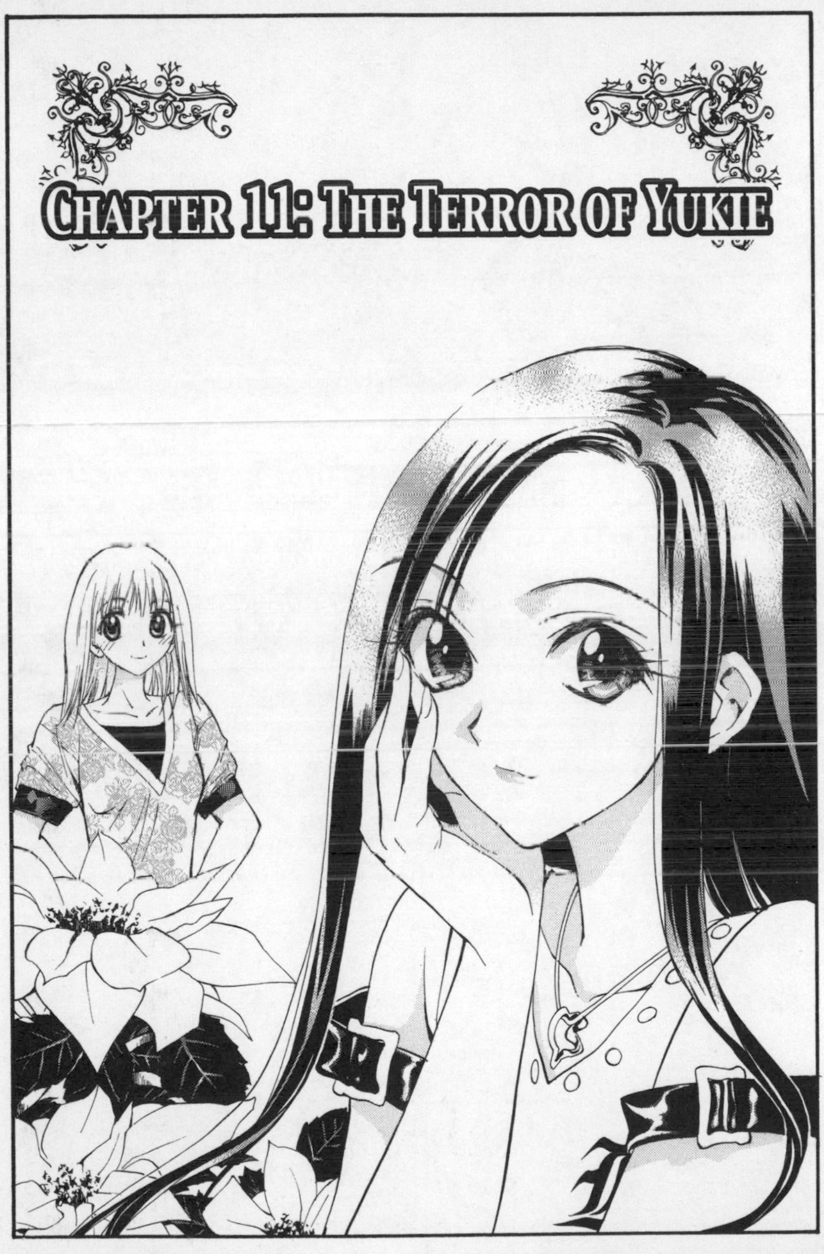

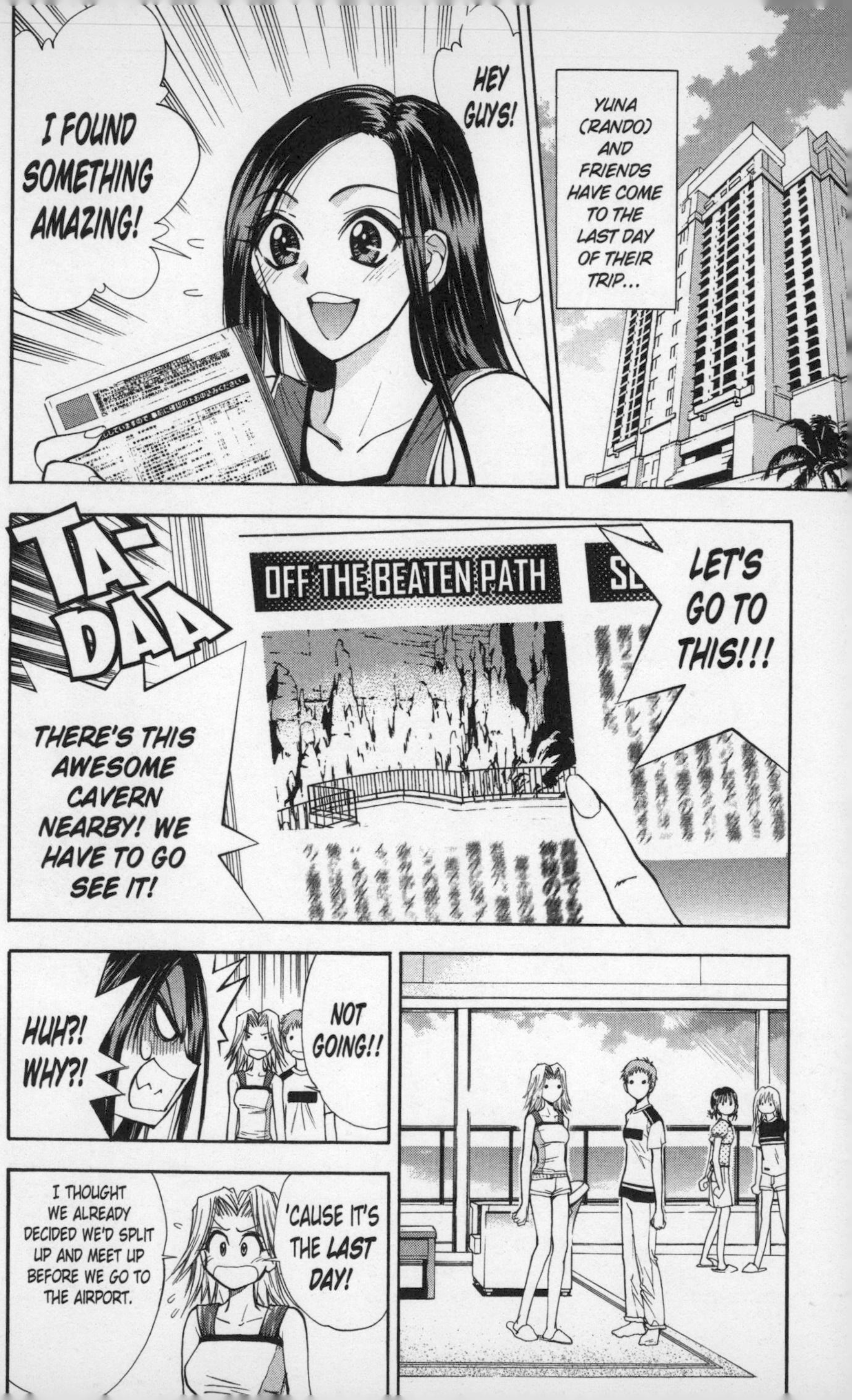

YUNA (RANDO) AND FRIENDS HAVE COME TO THE LAST DAY OF THEIR TRIP...
HEY GUYS!
I FOUND SOMETHING AMAZING!
LET'S GO TO THIS!!!
OFF THE BEATEN PATH
TA-DAA
THERE'S THIS AWESOME CAVERN NEARBY! WE HAVE TO GO SEE IT!
NOT GOING!!
HUH?! WHY?!
'CAUSE IT'S THE LAST DAY!
I THOUGHT WE ALREADY DECIDED WE'D SPLIT UP AND MEET UP BEFORE WE GO TO THE AIRPORT.

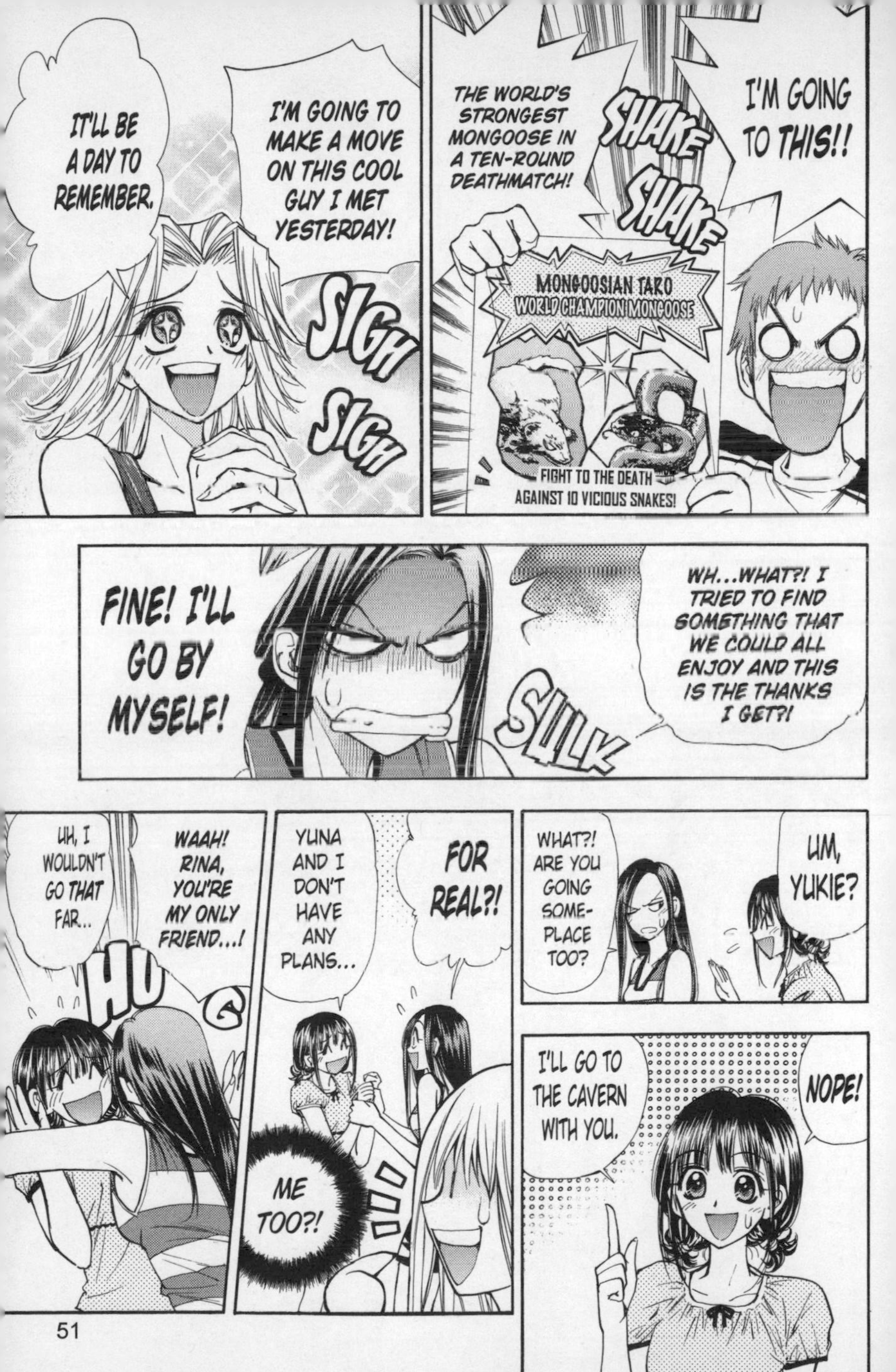
I'M GOING TO THIS!!
SHAKE SHAKE
THE WORLD'S STRONGEST MONGOOSE IN A TEN-ROUND DEATHMATCH!
MONGOOSIAN TARO
WORLD CHAMPION MONGOOSE
FIGHT TO THE DEATH AGAINST 10 VICIOUS SNAKES!
I'M GOING TO MAKE A MOVE ON THIS COOL GUY I MET YESTERDAY!
IT'LL BE A DAY TO REMEMBER.
SIGH SIGH
WH...WHAT?! I TRIED TO FIND SOMETHING THAT WE COULD ALL ENJOY AND THIS IS THE THANKS I GET?!
SULK
FINE! I'LL GO BY MYSELF!
UM, YUKIE?
WHAT?! ARE YOU GOING SOME-PLACE TOO?
NOPE!
I'LL GO TO THE CAVERN WITH YOU.
FOR REAL?!
YUNA AND I DON'T HAVE ANY PLANS...
ME TOO?!
WAAH! RINA, YOU'RE MY ONLY FRIEND...!
UH, I WOULDN'T GO THAT FAR...
HUG

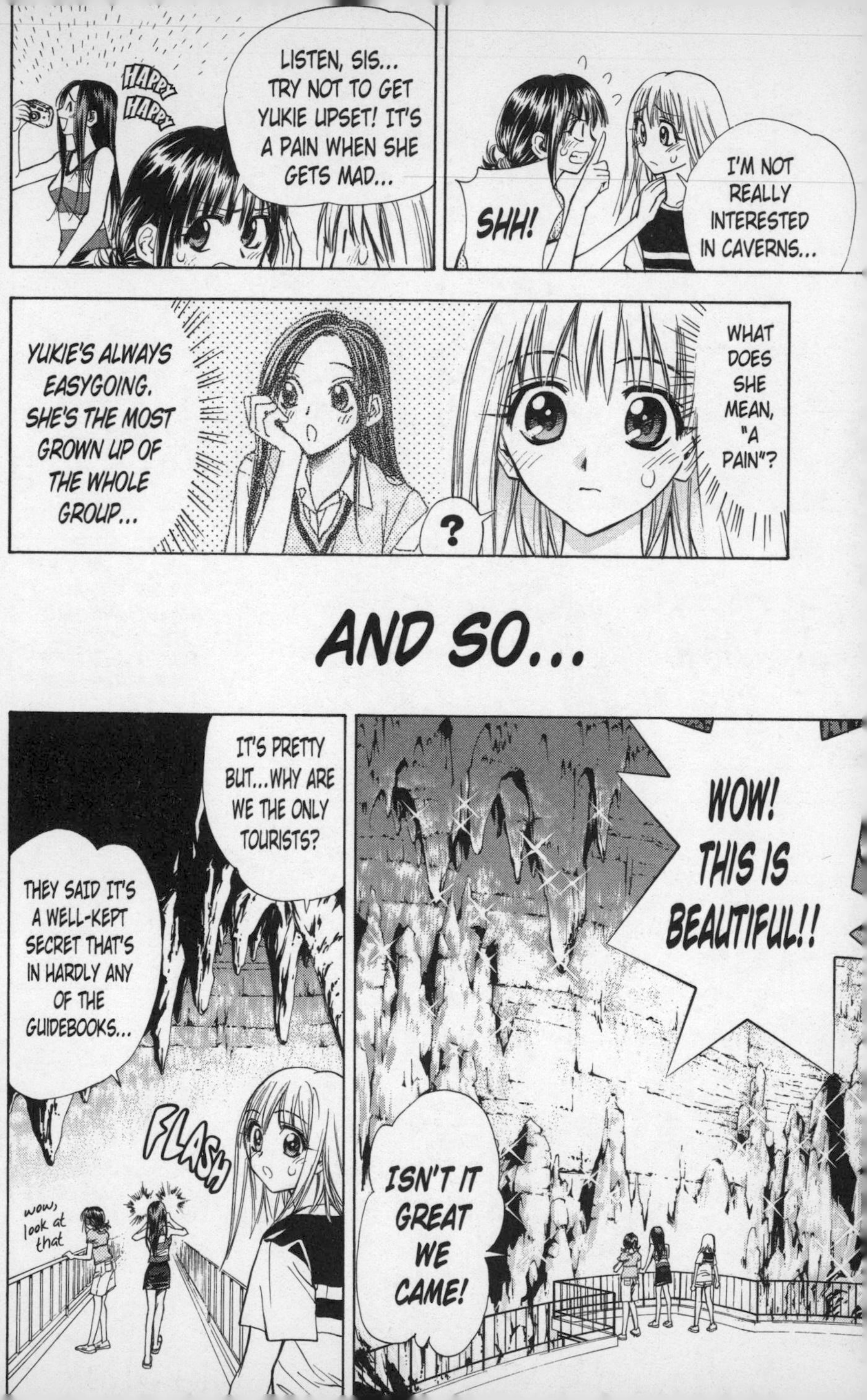
I'M NOT REALLY INTERESTED IN CAVERNS...
SHH!
LISTEN, SIS... TRY NOT TO GET YUKIE UPSET! IT'S A PAIN WHEN SHE GETS MAD...
HAPPY HAPPY
WHAT DOES SHE MEAN, "A PAIN"?
?
YUKIE'S ALWAYS EASYGOING. SHE'S THE MOST GROWN UP OF THE WHOLE GROUP...
AND SO...
WOW! THIS IS BEAUTIFUL!!
ISN'T IT GREAT WE CAME!
IT'S PRETTY BUT...WHY ARE WE THE ONLY TOURISTS?
THEY SAID IT'S A WELL-KEPT SECRET THAT'S IN HARDLY ANY OF THE GUIDEBOOKS...
FLASH
wow, look at that

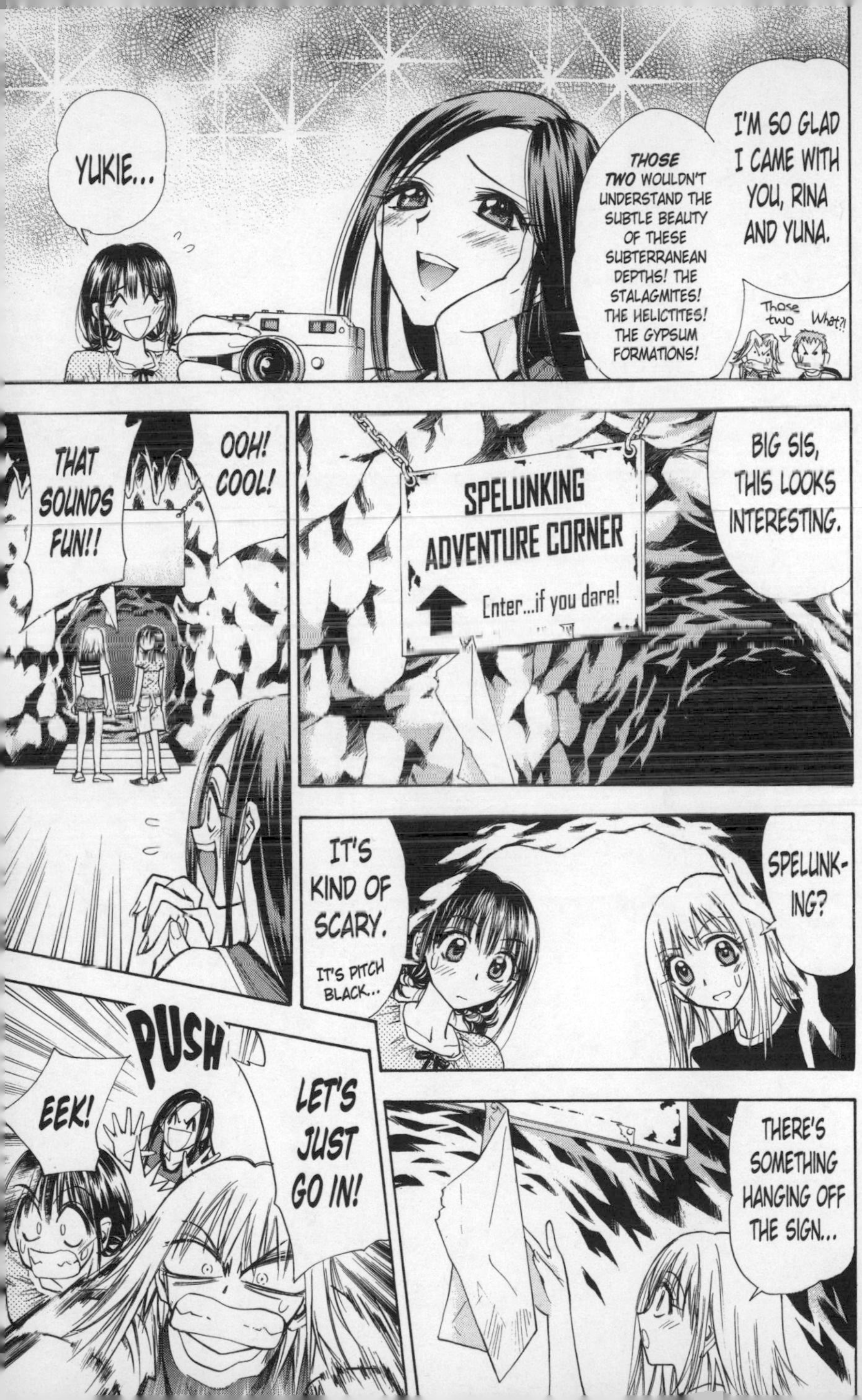
I'M SO GLAD I CAME WITH YOU, RINA AND YUNA.
THOSE TWO WOULDN'T UNDERSTAND THE SUBTLE BEAUTY OF THESE SUBTERRANEAN DEPTHS! THE STALAGMITES! THE HELICTITES! THE GYPSUM FORMATIONS!
Those two
What?!
YUKIE...
BIG SIS, THIS LOOKS INTERESTING.
SPELUNKING ADVENTURE CORNER
Enter...if you dare!
OOH! COOL!
THAT SOUNDS FUN!!
SPELUNK-ING?
IT'S KIND OF SCARY.
IT'S PITCH BLACK...
THERE'S SOMETHING HANGING OFF THE SIGN...
PUSH
LET'S JUST GO IN!
EEK!

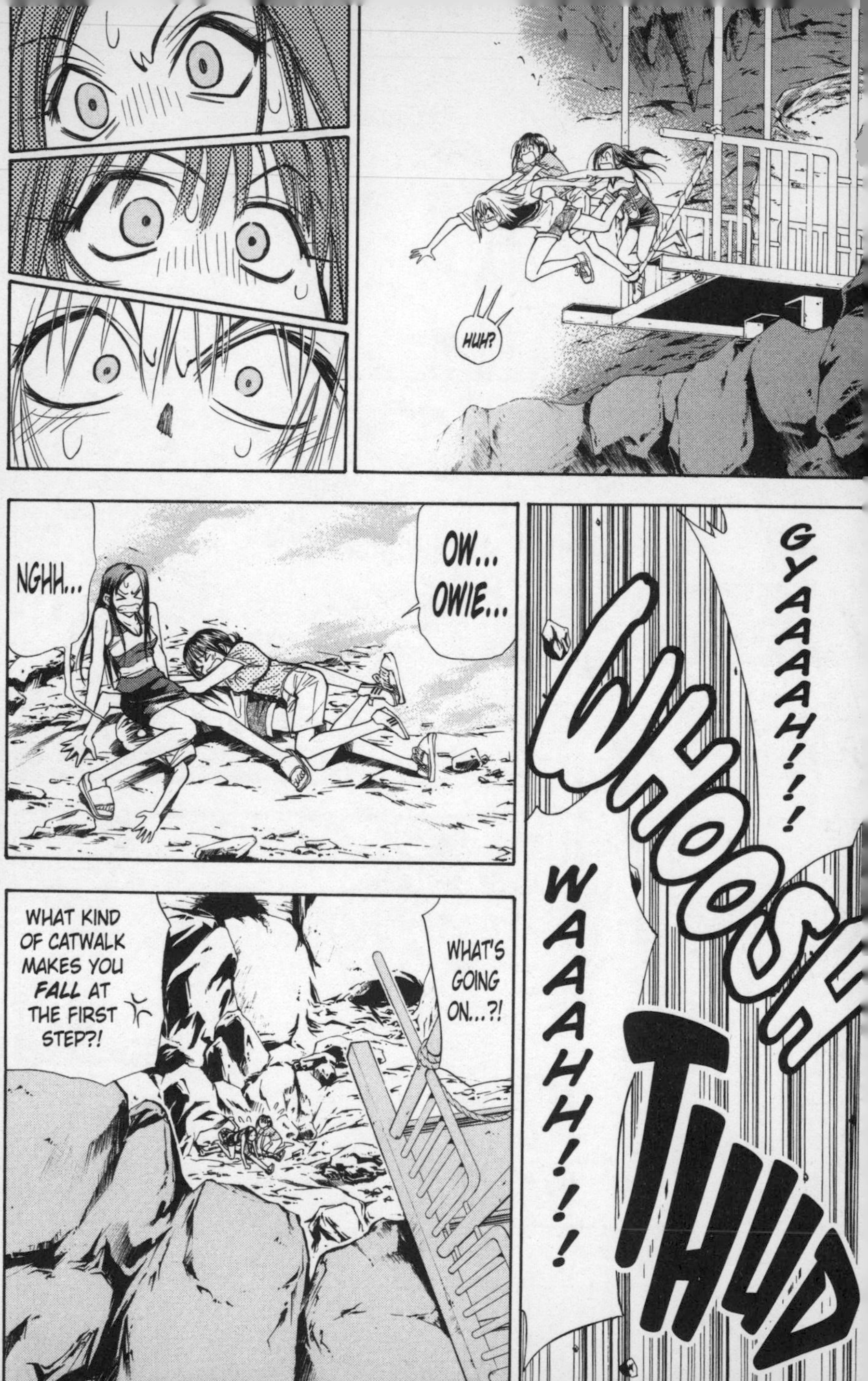
HUH?
GYAAAAH!!!
WHOOSH
WAAAAHH!!!
THUD
OW... OWIE...
NGHH...
WHAT'S GOING ON...?!
WHAT KIND OF CATWALK MAKES YOU FALL AT THE FIRST STEP?!

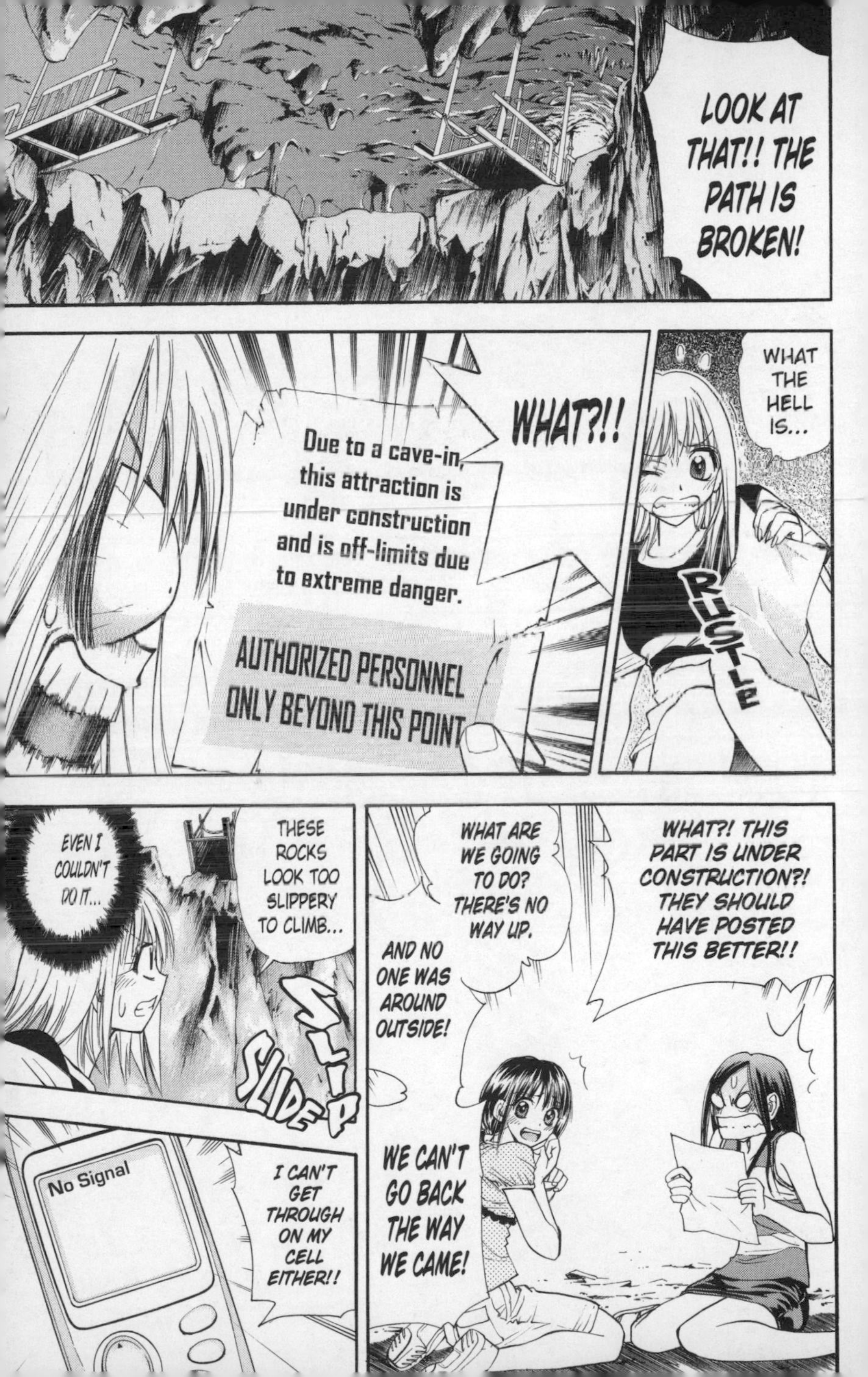

LOOK AT THAT!! THE PATH IS BROKEN!
WHAT THE HELL IS...
RUSTLE
WHAT?!!
Due to a cave-in, this attraction is under construction and is off-limits due to extreme danger.
AUTHORIZED PERSONNEL ONLY BEYOND THIS POINT
WHAT?! THIS PART IS UNDER CONSTRUCTION?! THEY SHOULD HAVE POSTED THIS BETTER!!
WHAT ARE WE GOING TO DO? THERE'S NO WAY UP.
AND NO ONE WAS AROUND OUTSIDE!
WE CAN'T GO BACK THE WAY WE CAME!
THESE ROCKS LOOK TOO SLIPPERY TO CLIMB...
EVEN I COULDN'T DO IT...
SLIP
SLIDE
No Signal
I CAN'T GET THROUGH ON MY CELL EITHER!!

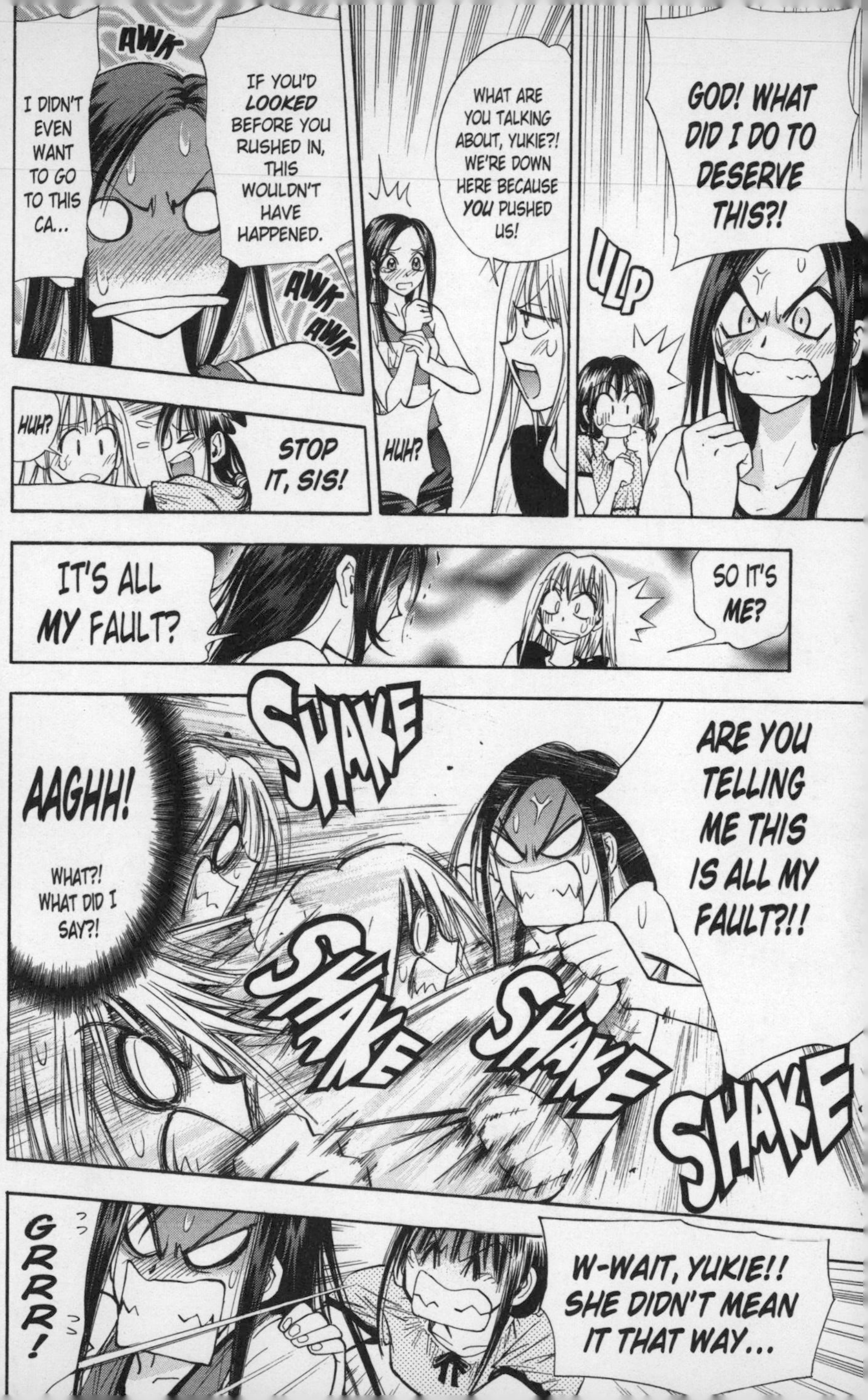
GOD! WHAT DID I DO TO DESERVE THIS?!
ULP
WHAT ARE YOU TALKING ABOUT, YUKIE?! WE'RE DOWN HERE BECAUSE YOU PUSHED US!
HUH?
AWK
IF YOU'D LOOKED BEFORE YOU RUSHED IN, THIS WOULDN'T HAVE HAPPENED.
I DIDN'T EVEN WANT TO GO TO THIS CA...
AWK
AWK
AWK
STOP IT, SIS!
HUH?
SO IT'S ME?
IT'S ALL MY FAULT?
SHAKE
ARE YOU TELLING ME THIS IS ALL MY FAULT?!!
AAGHH!
WHAT?! WHAT DID I SAY?!
SHAKE
SHAKE
SHAKE
W-WAIT, YUKIE!! SHE DIDN'T MEAN IT THAT WAY...
GRRR!

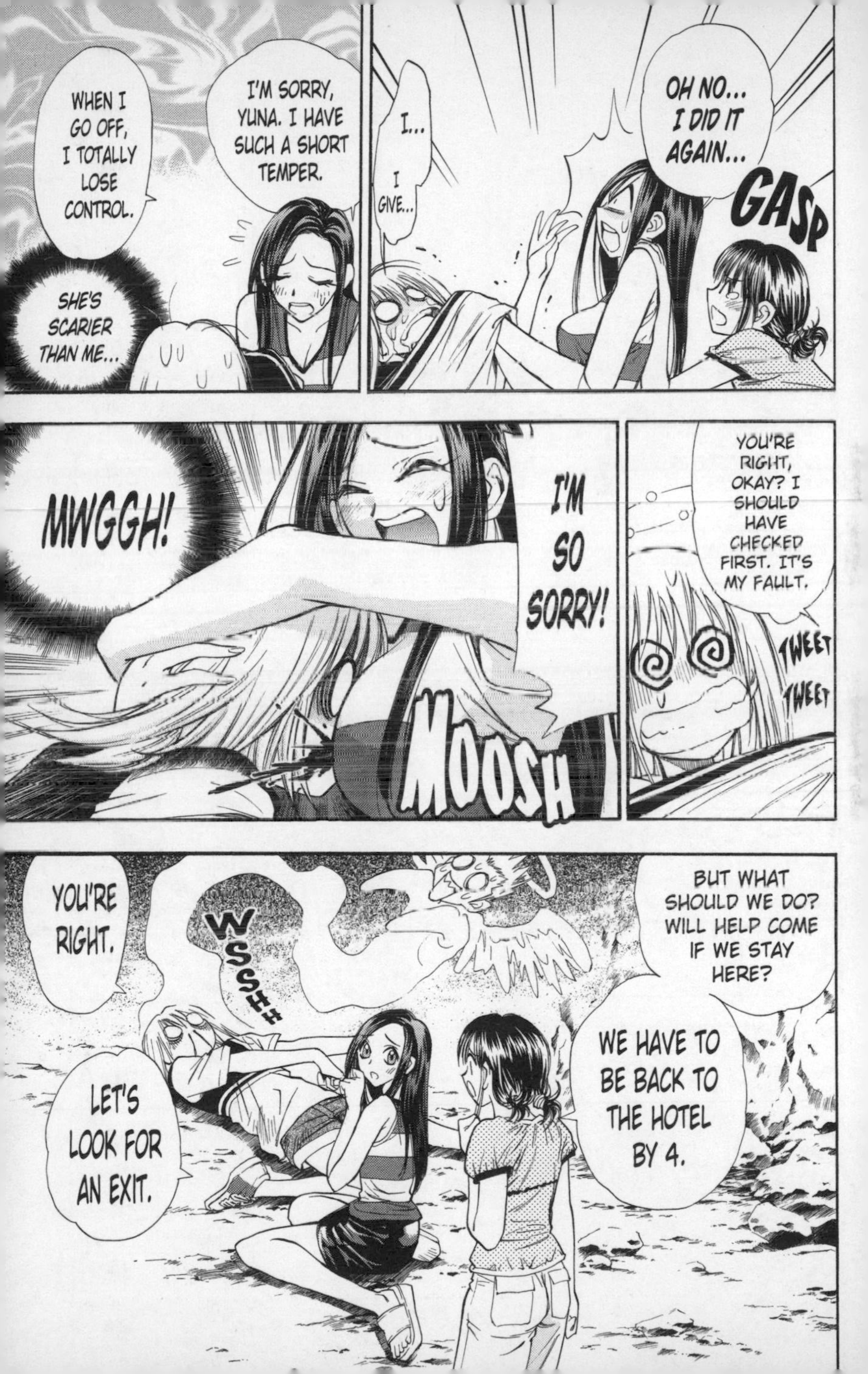
OH NO... I DID IT AGAIN...
GASP
I...
I GIVE...
I'M SORRY, YUNA. I HAVE SUCH A SHORT TEMPER.
WHEN I GO OFF, I TOTALLY LOSE CONTROL.
SHE'S SCARIER THAN ME...
YOU'RE RIGHT, OKAY? I SHOULD HAVE CHECKED FIRST. IT'S MY FAULT.
TWEET
TWEET
I'M SO SORRY!
MWGGH!
MOOSH
BUT WHAT SHOULD WE DO? WILL HELP COME IF WE STAY HERE?
YOU'RE RIGHT.
WSSHH
WE HAVE TO BE BACK TO THE HOTEL BY 4.
LET'S LOOK FOR AN EXIT.

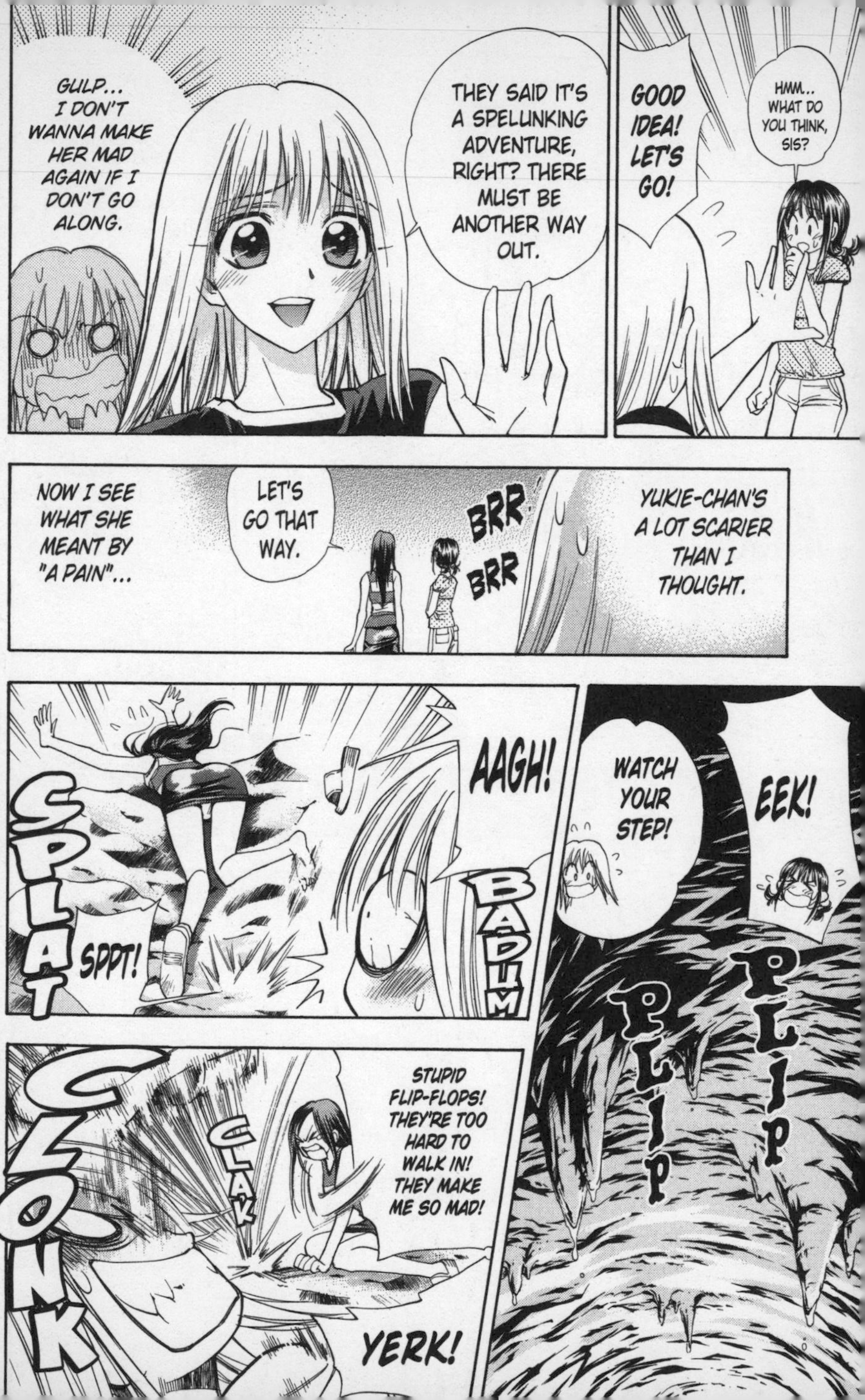
HMM... WHAT DO YOU THINK, SIS?
GOOD IDEA! LET'S GO!
THEY SAID IT'S A SPELUNKING ADVENTURE, RIGHT? THERE MUST BE ANOTHER WAY OUT.
GULP... I DON'T WANNA MAKE HER MAD AGAIN IF I DON'T GO ALONG.
YUKIE-CHAN'S A LOT SCARIER THAN I THOUGHT.
BRR BRR
LET'S GO THAT WAY.
NOW I SEE WHAT SHE MEANT BY "A PAIN"...
EEK!
WATCH YOUR STEP!
PLIP PLIP
AAGH!
BADUM
SPPT!
SPLAT
STUPID FLIP-FLOPS! THEY'RE TOO HARD TO WALK IN! THEY MAKE ME SO MAD!
CLAK
YERK!
CLONK

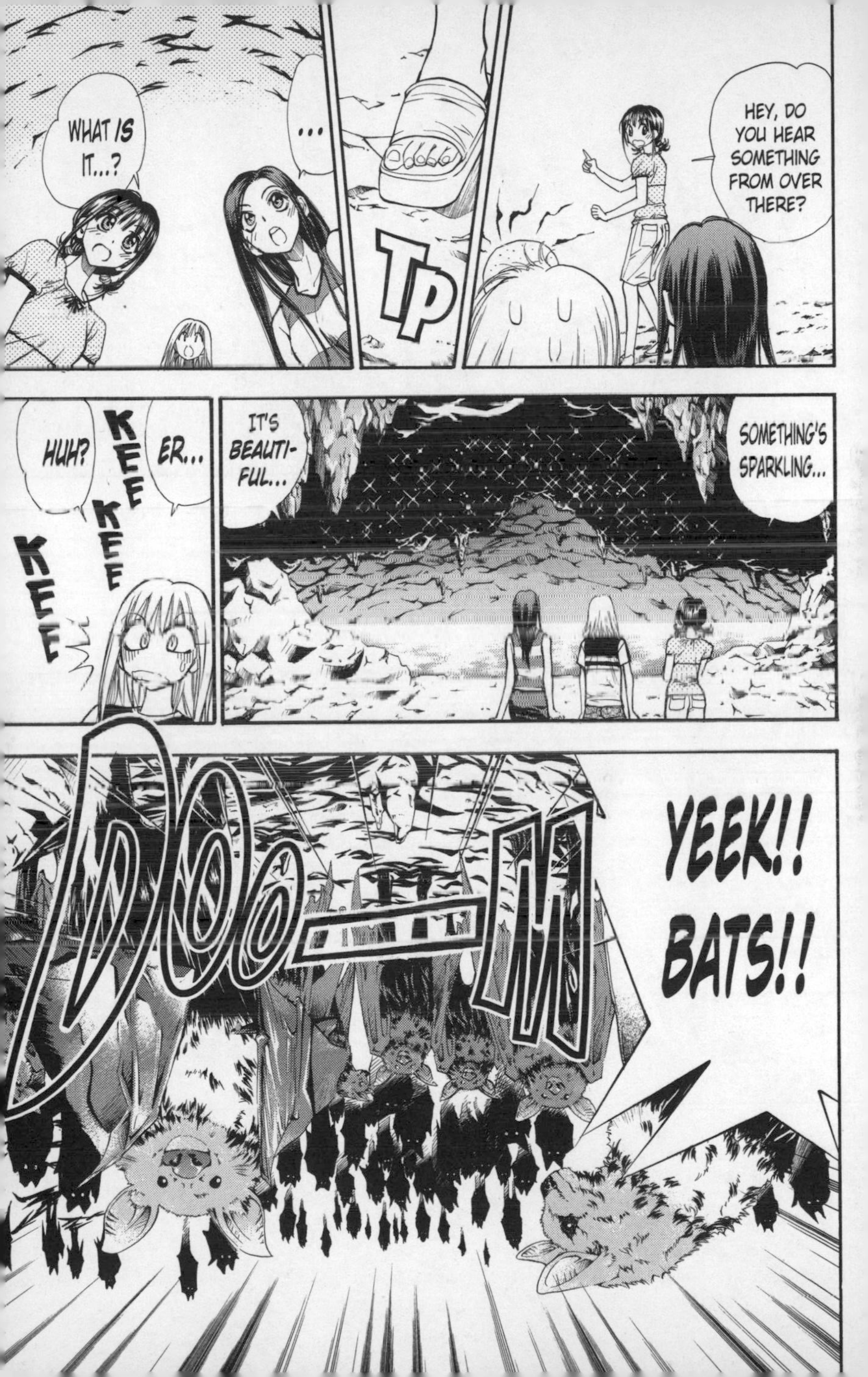
HEY, DO YOU HEAR SOMETHING FROM OVER THERE?
Tp
...
WHAT IS IT...?
SOMETHING'S SPARKLING...
IT'S BEAUTI-FUL...
ER...
KEE
KEE
KEE
HUH?
YEEK!! BATS!!
DOOO--M

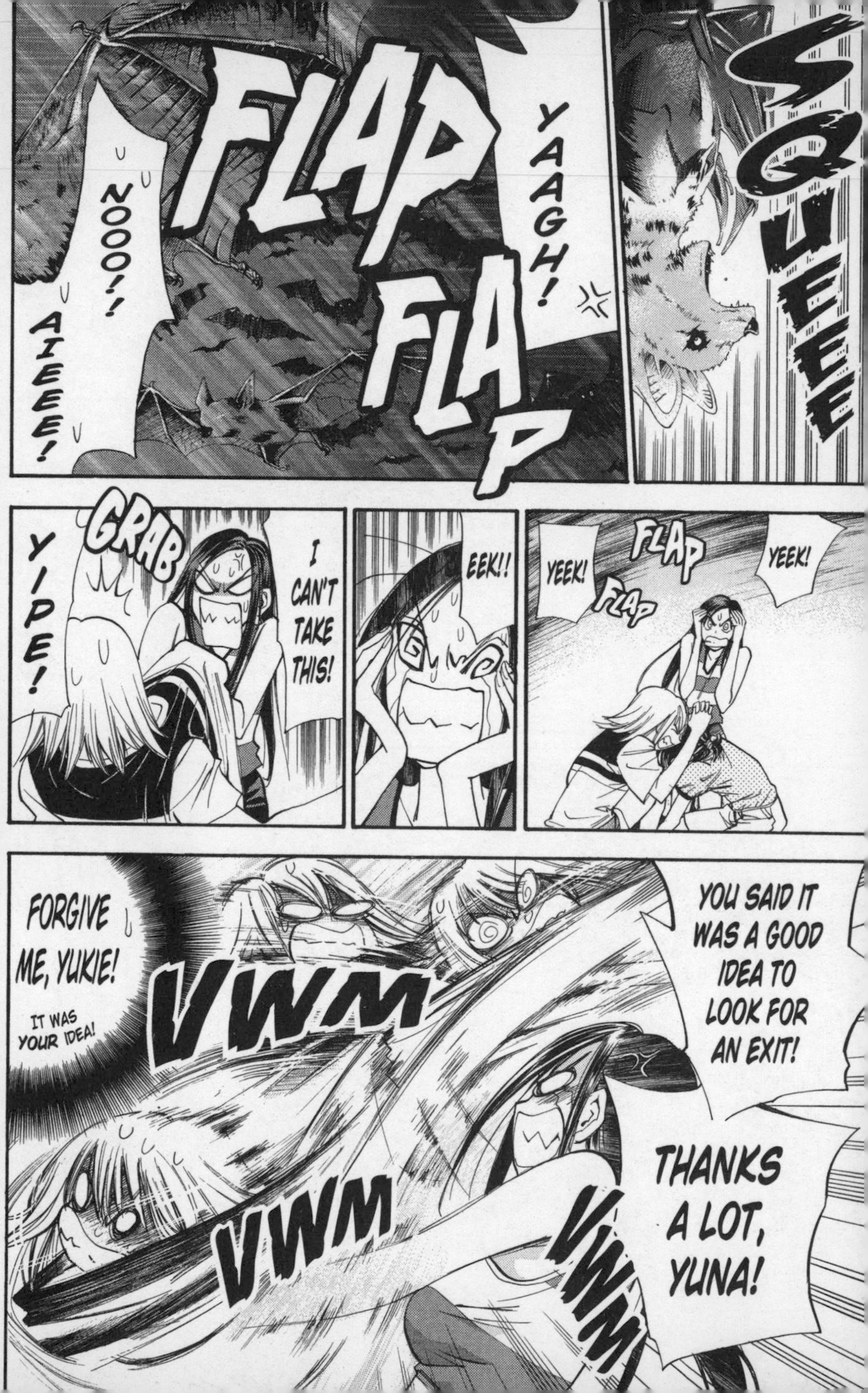
SQUEEEE
YAAAGH!
FLAP
FLAP
NOOO!!
AIEEEE!
YEEK!
FLAP
YEEK!
FLAP
EEK!!
I CAN'T TAKE THIS!
GRAB
YIPE!
YOU SAID IT WAS A GOOD IDEA TO LOOK FOR AN EXIT!
THANKS A LOT, YUNA!
VWM
FORGIVE ME, YUKIE!
IT WAS YOUR IDEA!
VWM
VWM

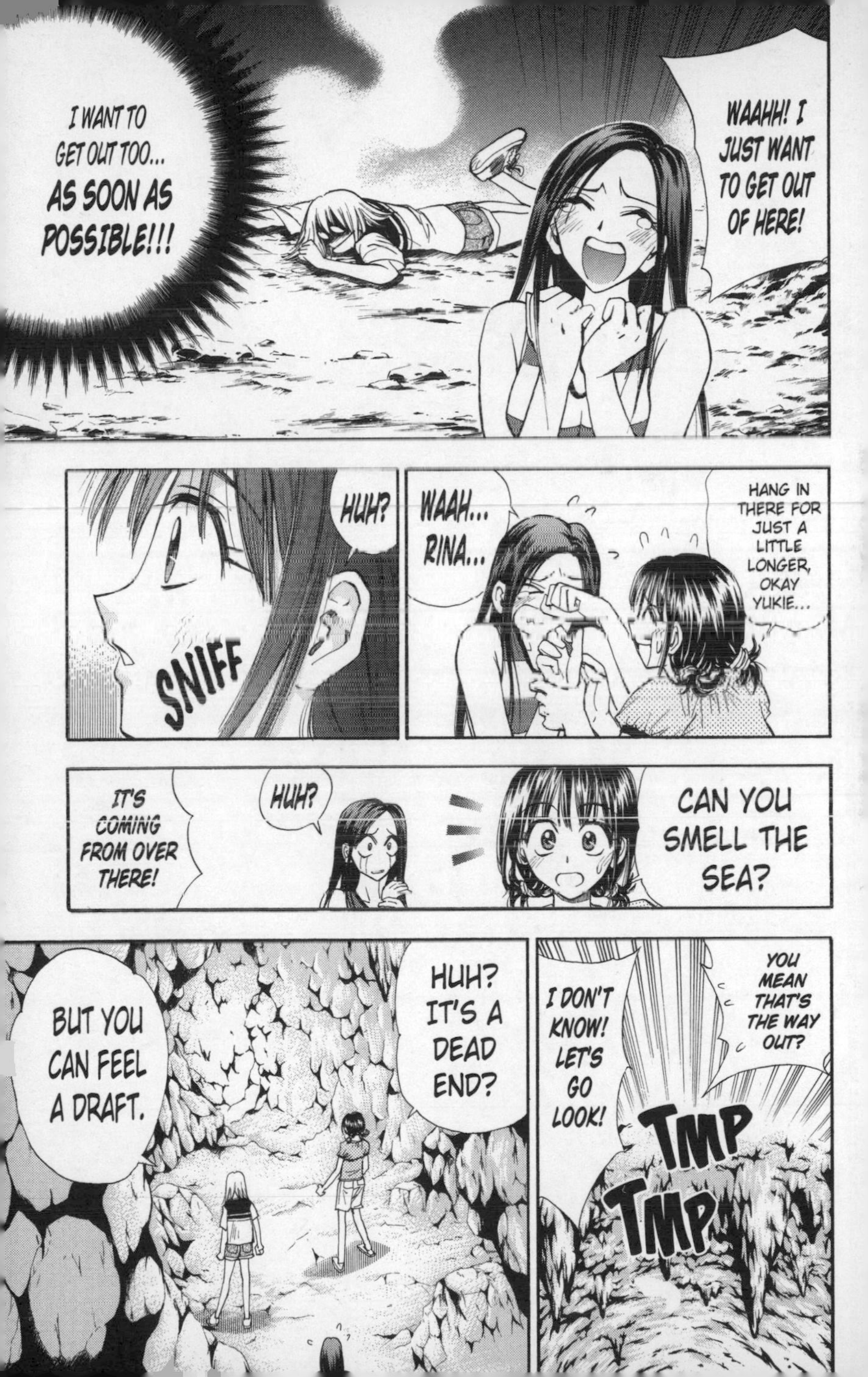
WAAHH! I JUST WANT TO GET OUT OF HERE!
I WANT TO GET OUT TOO... AS SOON AS POSSIBLE!!!
HANG IN THERE FOR JUST A LITTLE LONGER, OKAY YUKIE...
WAAH... RINA...
HUH?
SNIFF
CAN YOU SMELL THE SEA?
HUH?
IT'S COMING FROM OVER THERE!
YOU MEAN THAT'S THE WAY OUT?
I DON'T KNOW! LET'S GO LOOK!
TMP
TMP
HUH? IT'S A DEAD END?
BUT YOU CAN FEEL A DRAFT.

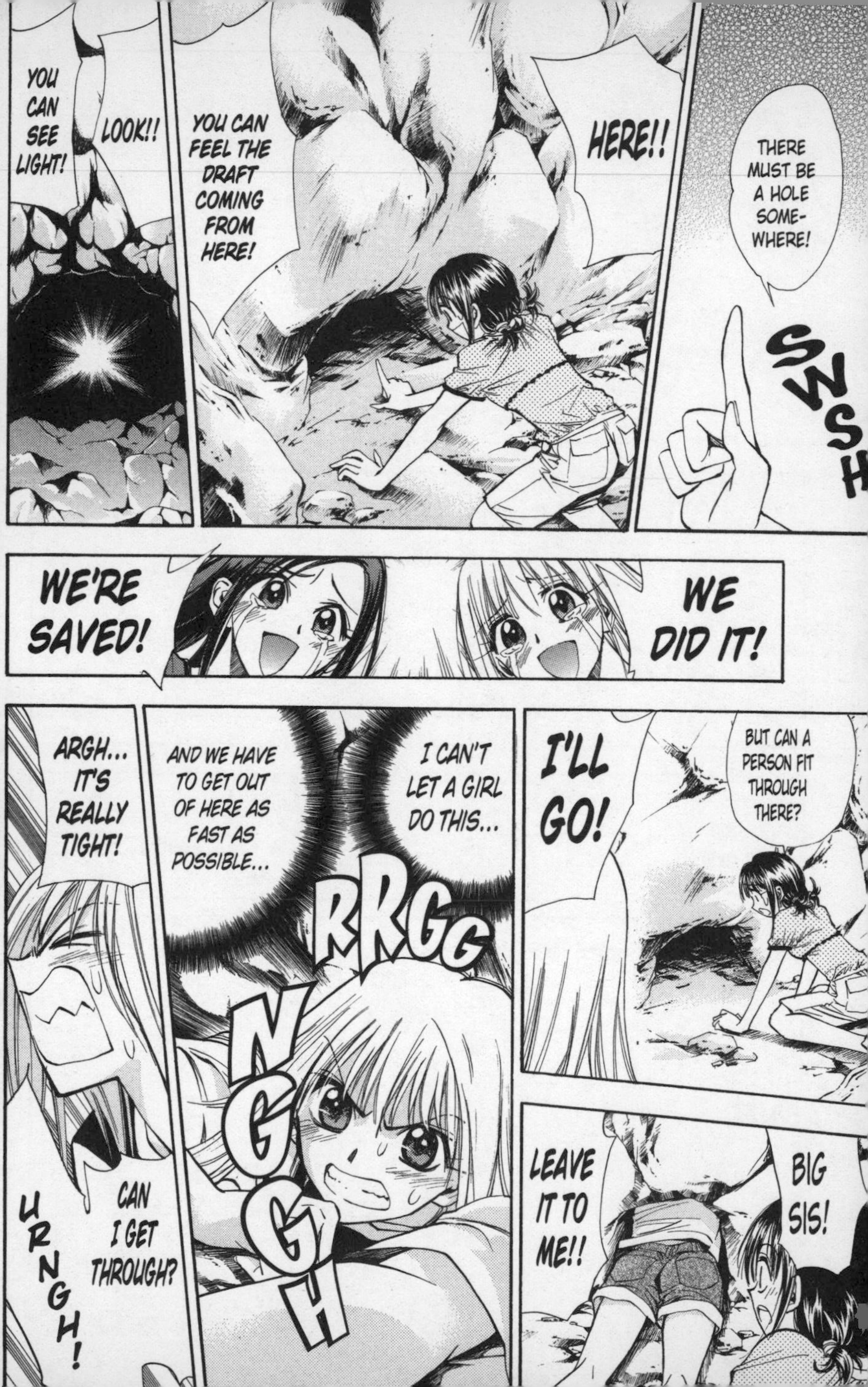
THERE MUST BE A HOLE SOME-WHERE!
SWSH
HERE!!
YOU CAN FEEL THE DRAFT COMING FROM HERE!
LOOK!!
YOU CAN SEE LIGHT!
WE DID IT!
WE'RE SAVED!
BUT CAN A PERSON FIT THROUGH THERE?
I'LL GO!
BIG SIS!
LEAVE IT TO ME!!
I CAN'T LET A GIRL DO THIS...
AND WE HAVE TO GET OUT OF HERE AS FAST AS POSSIBLE...
RRGG
NGGH
ARGH... IT'S REALLY TIGHT!
CAN I GET THROUGH?
URNGH!

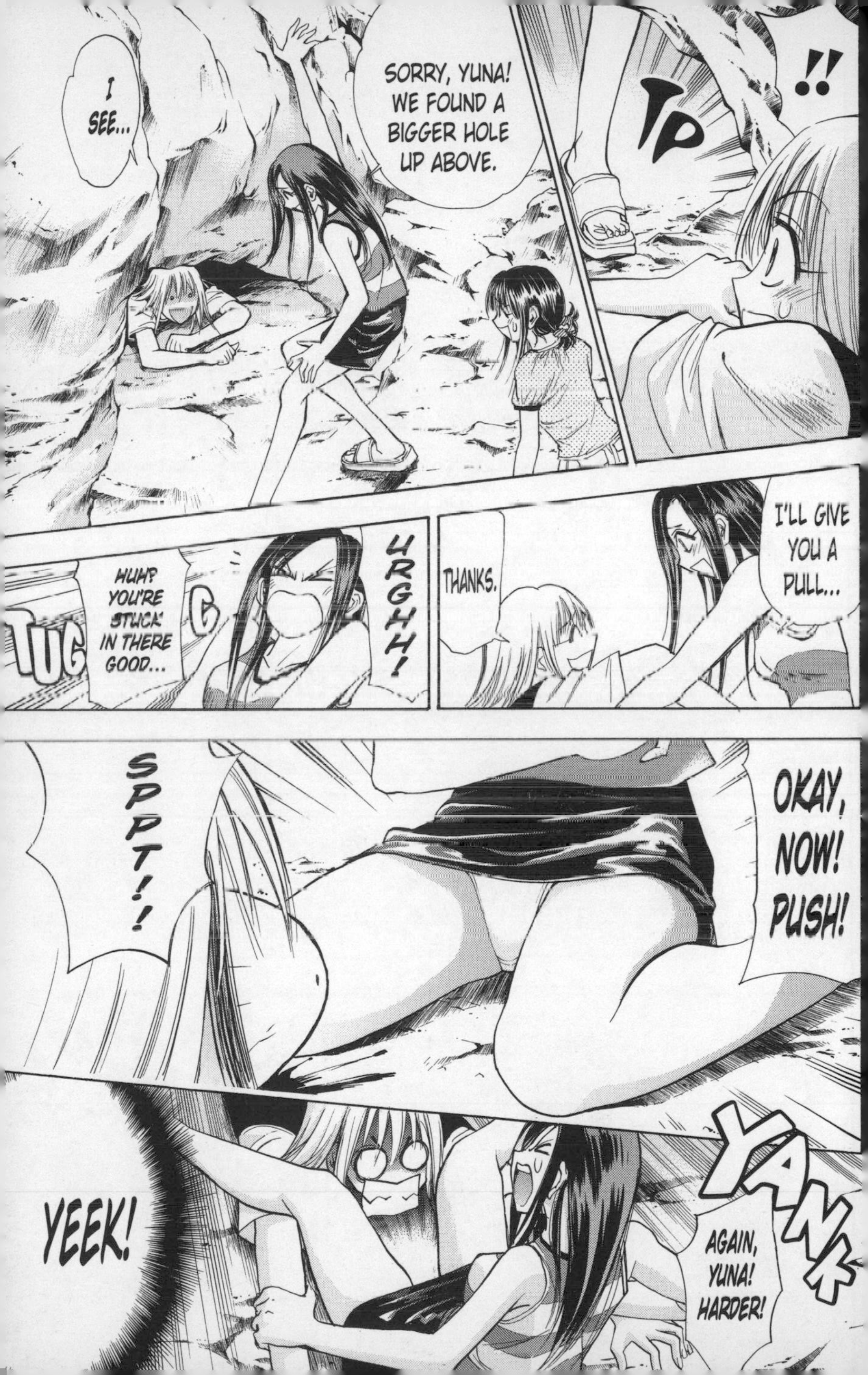
!!
TP
SORRY, YUNA! WE FOUND A BIGGER HOLE UP ABOVE.
I SEE...
I'LL GIVE YOU A PULL...
THANKS.
URGHH!
HUH? YOU'RE STUCK IN THERE GOOD...
TUG
OKAY, NOW! PUSH!
SPPT!!
YANK
AGAIN, YUNA! HARDER!
YEEK!

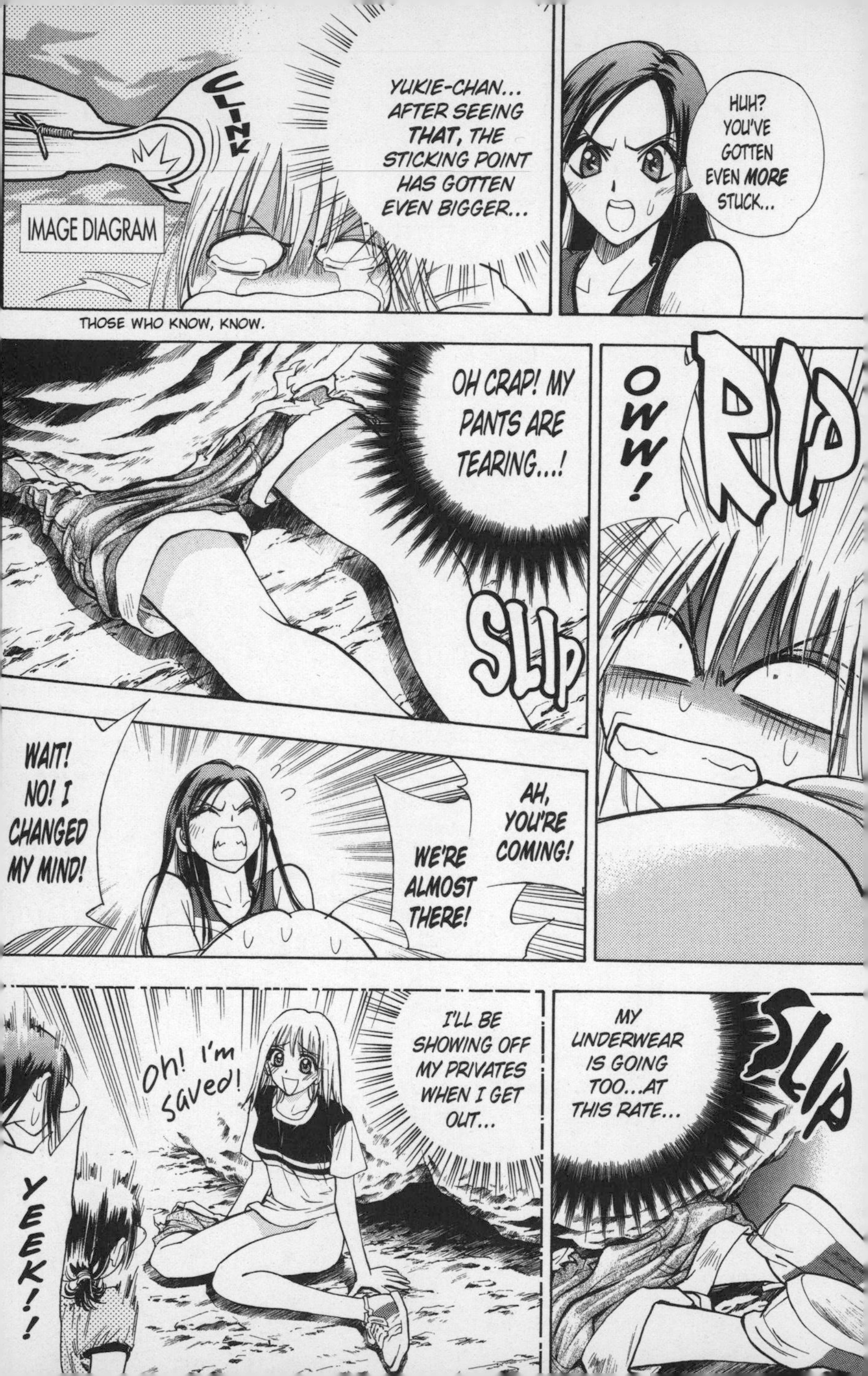
HUH? YOU'VE GOTTEN EVEN MORE STUCK...
YUKIE-CHAN... AFTER SEEING THAT, THE STICKING POINT HAS GOTTEN EVEN BIGGER...
CLINK
IMAGE DIAGRAM
THOSE WHO KNOW, KNOW.
RIP
OWW!
OH CRAP! MY PANTS ARE TEARING...!
SLIP
AH, YOU'RE COMING!
WE'RE ALMOST THERE!
WAIT! NO! I CHANGED MY MIND!
SLIP
MY UNDERWEAR IS GOING TOO...AT THIS RATE...
I'LL BE SHOWING OFF MY PRIVATES WHEN I GET OUT...
Oh! I'm saved!
YEEK!!

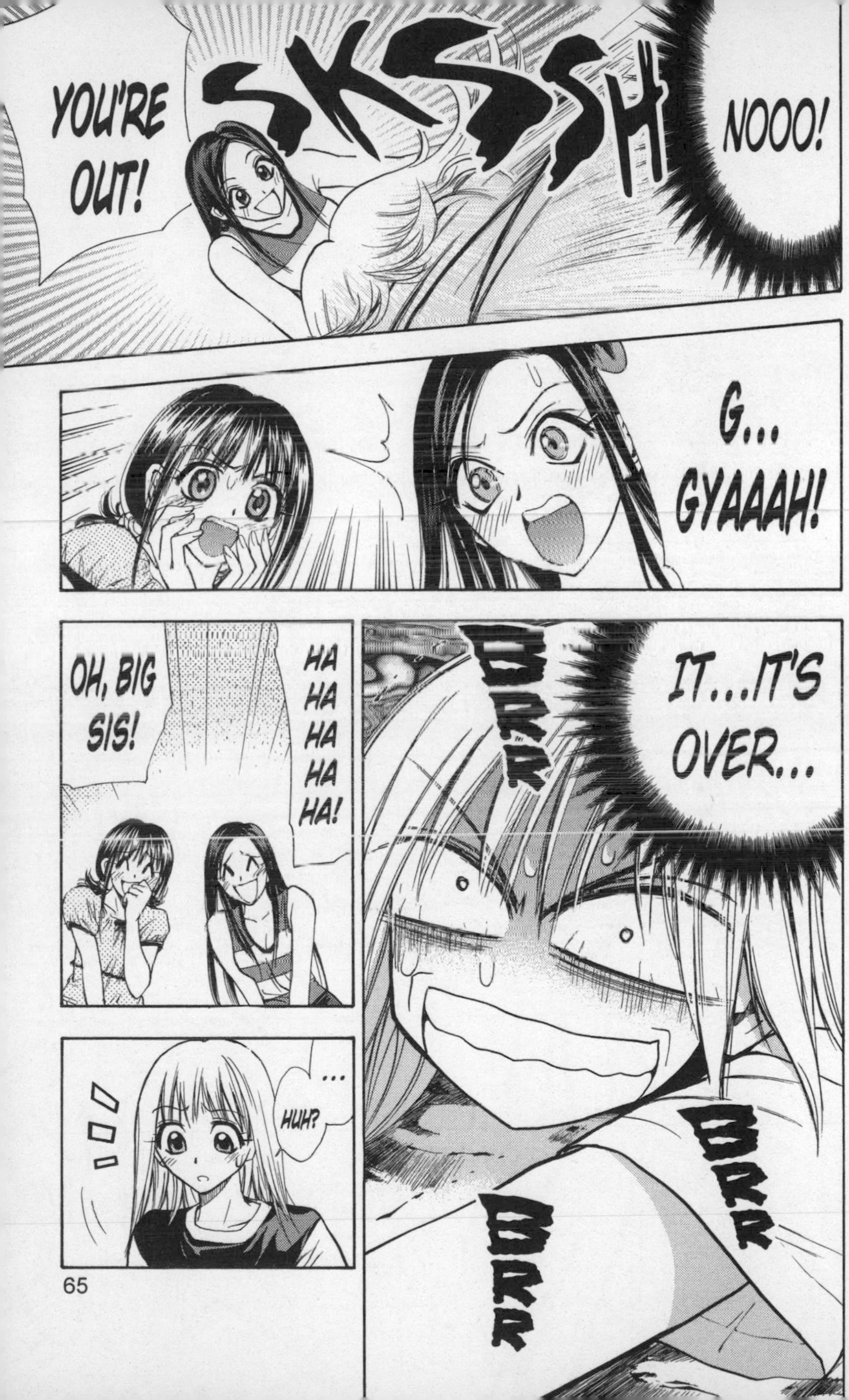
NOOO!
SKSSH
YOU'RE OUT!
G... GYAAAH!
IT...IT'S OVER...
BRR
BRR
BRR
HA HA HA HA HA!
OH, BIG SIS!
... HUH?

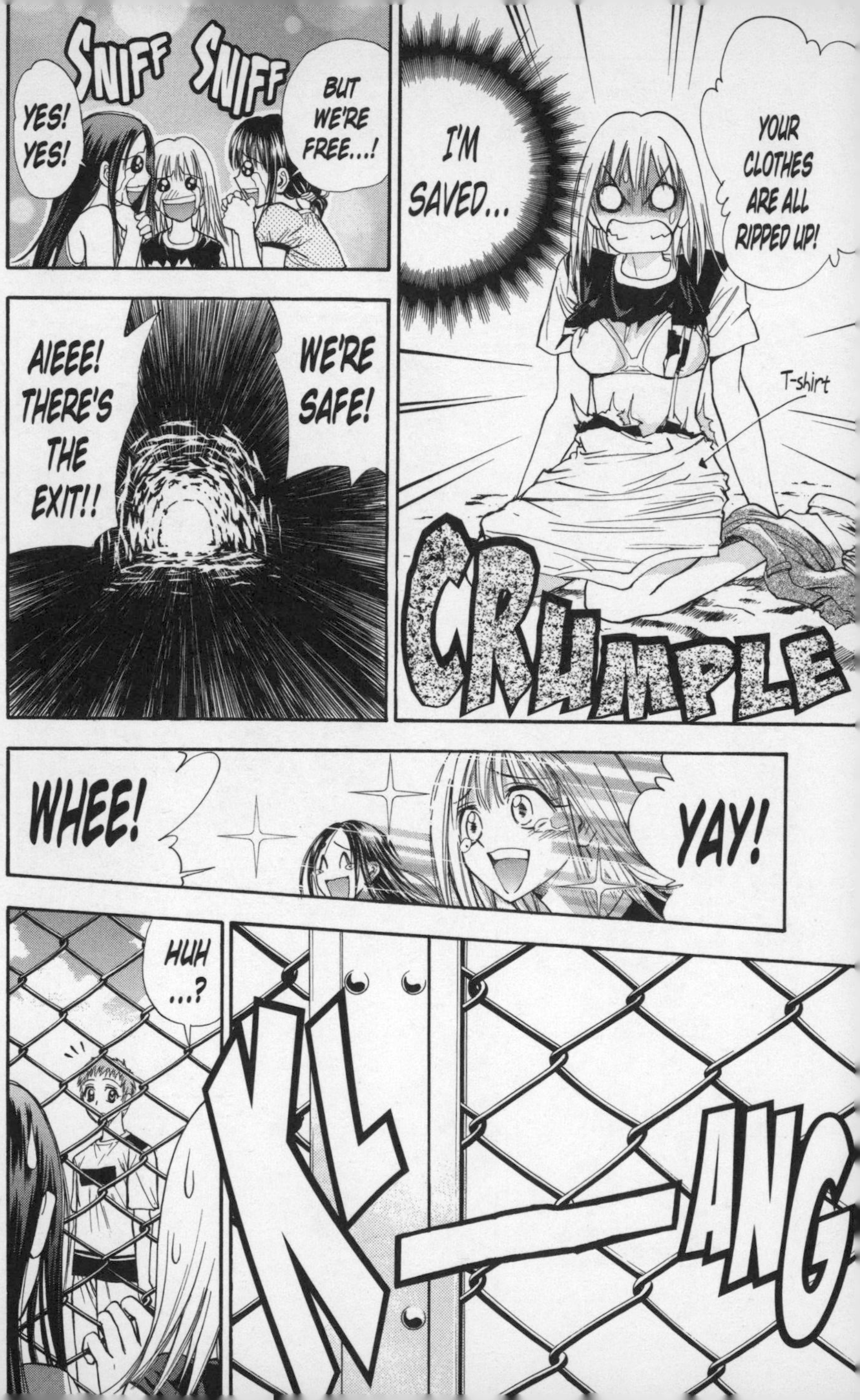
YOUR CLOTHES ARE ALL RIPPED UP!
I'M SAVED...
T-shirt
CRUMPLE
SNIFF SNIFF
BUT WE'RE FREE...!
YES! YES!
WE'RE SAFE!
AIEEE! THERE'S THE EXIT!!
YAY!
WHEE!
KL—ANG
HUH ...?

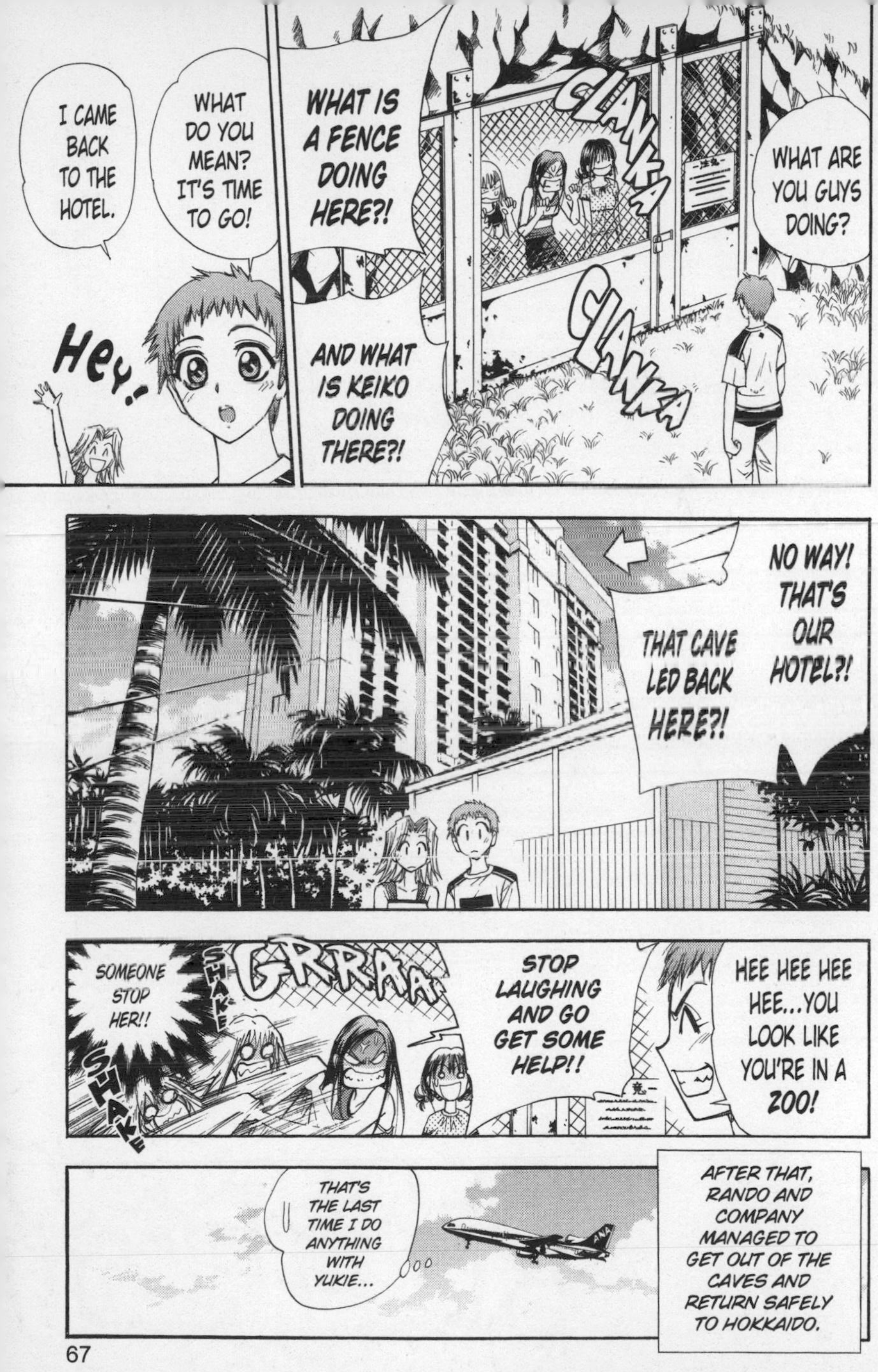
WHAT ARE YOU GUYS DOING?
CLANKA
CLANKA
WHAT IS A FENCE DOING HERE?!
AND WHAT IS KEIKO DOING THERE?!
WHAT DO YOU MEAN? IT'S TIME TO GO!
I CAME BACK TO THE HOTEL.
HEY!
NO WAY! THAT'S OUR HOTEL?!
THAT CAVE LED BACK HERE?!
HEE HEE HEE HEE...YOU LOOK LIKE YOU'RE IN A ZOO!
STOP LAUGHING AND GO GET SOME HELP!!
GRRRAA
SHAKE
SHAKE
SOMEONE STOP HER!!
SHAKE
AFTER THAT, RANDO AND COMPANY MANAGED TO GET OUT OF THE CAVES AND RETURN SAFELY TO HOKKAIDO.
THAT'S THE LAST TIME I DO ANYTHING WITH YUKIE...

Pretty Face

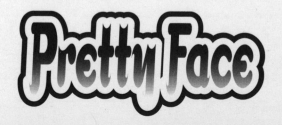

Chapter 12: The Summer Job Scheme

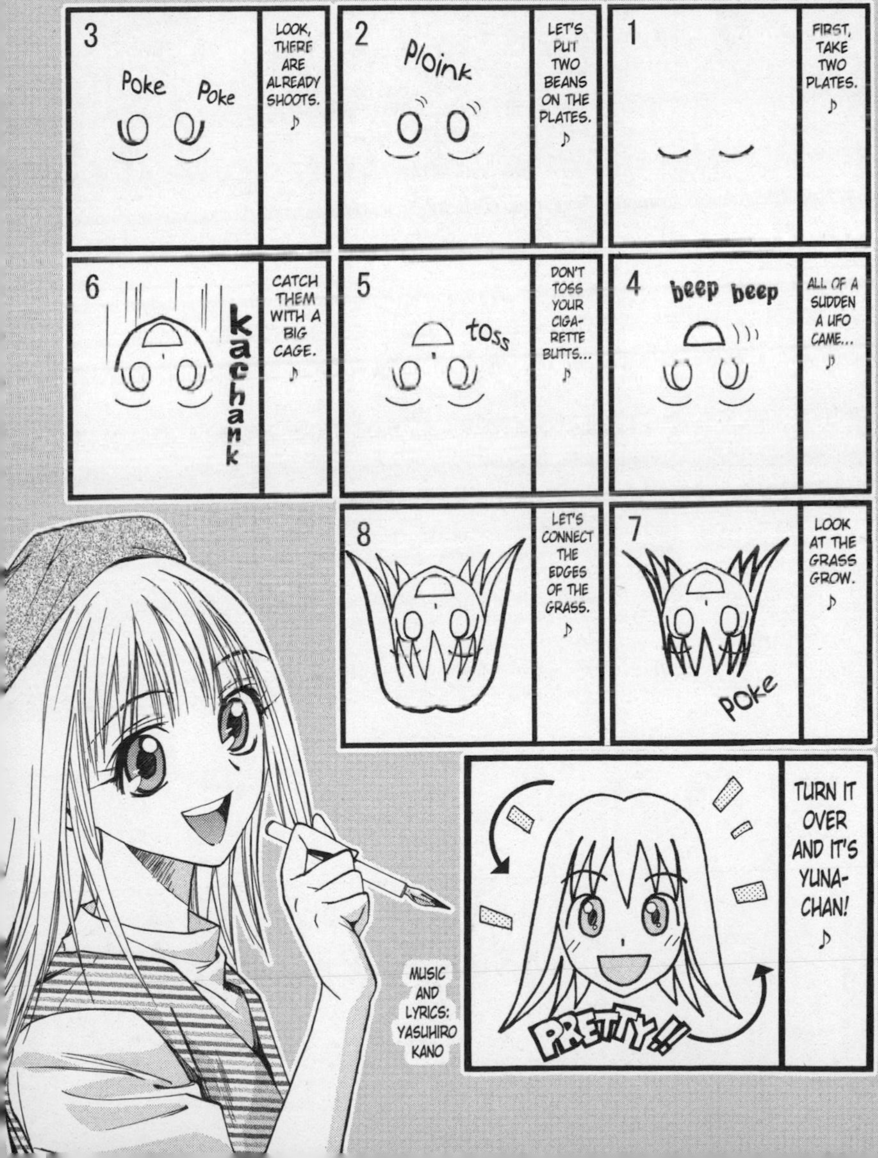
1
FIRST, TAKE TWO PLATES. ♪
2
LET'S PUT TWO BEANS ON THE PLATES. ♪
Ploink
3
LOOK, THERE ARE ALREADY SHOOTS. ♪
Poke
Poke
4
ALL OF A SUDDEN A UFO CAME... ♪
beep beep
5
DON'T TOSS YOUR CIGA-RETTE BUTTS... ♪
toss
6
CATCH THEM WITH A BIG CAGE. ♪
kachank
7
LOOK AT THE GRASS GROW. ♪
Poke
8
LET'S CONNECT THE EDGES OF THE GRASS. ♪
TURN IT OVER AND IT'S YUNA-CHAN! ♪
PRETTY!!
MUSIC AND LYRICS: YASUHIRO KANO

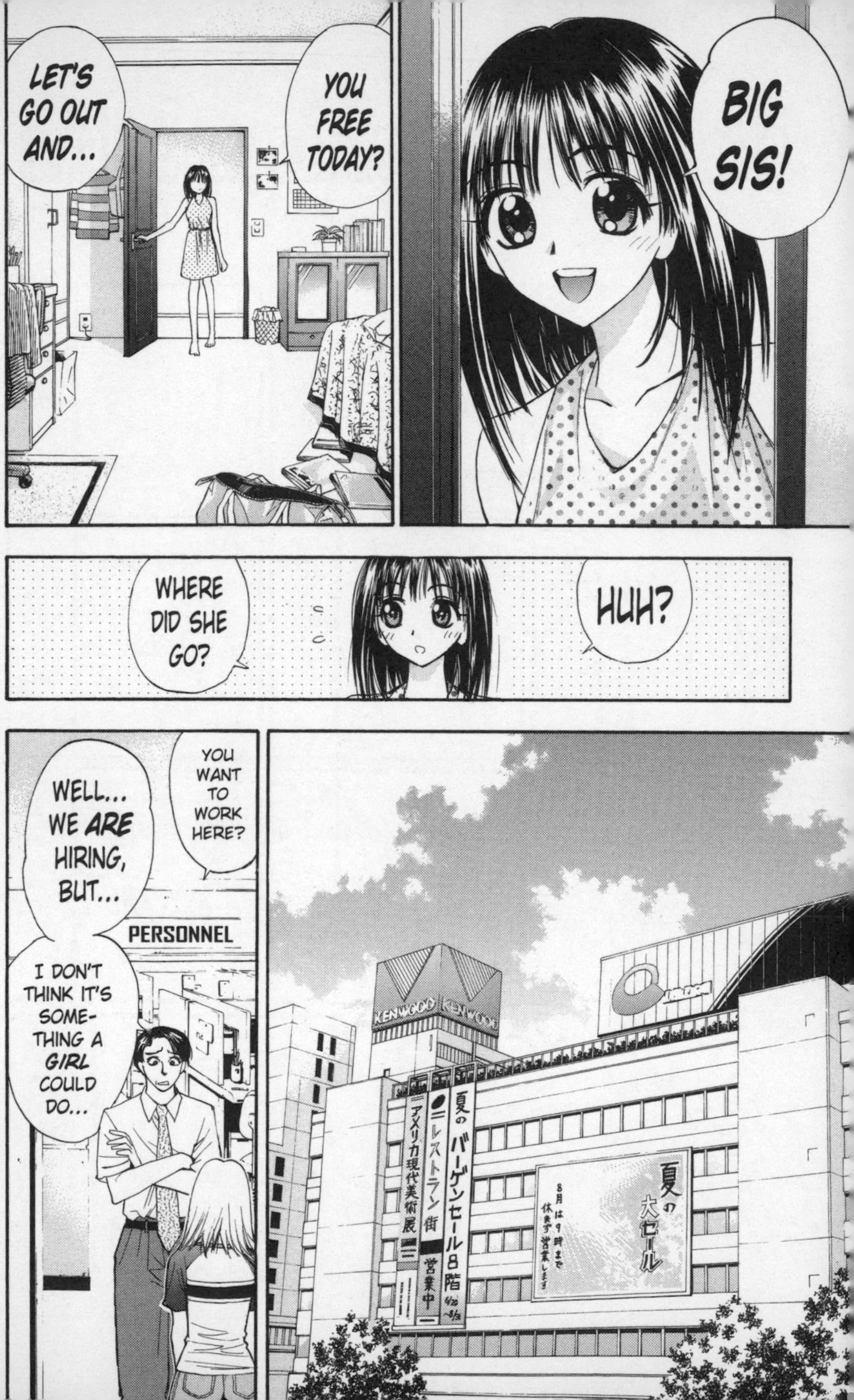
BIG SIS!
YOU FREE TODAY?
LET'S GO OUT AND...
HUH?
WHERE DID SHE GO?
KENWOOD KENWOOD
夏のバーゲンセール8階
レストラン街 営業中
アメリカ現代美術展
夏の大セール
8月は9時まで休まず営業します
YOU WANT TO WORK HERE?
WELL... WE *ARE* HIRING, BUT...
PERSONNEL
I DON'T THINK IT'S SOME-THING A *GIRL* COULD DO...

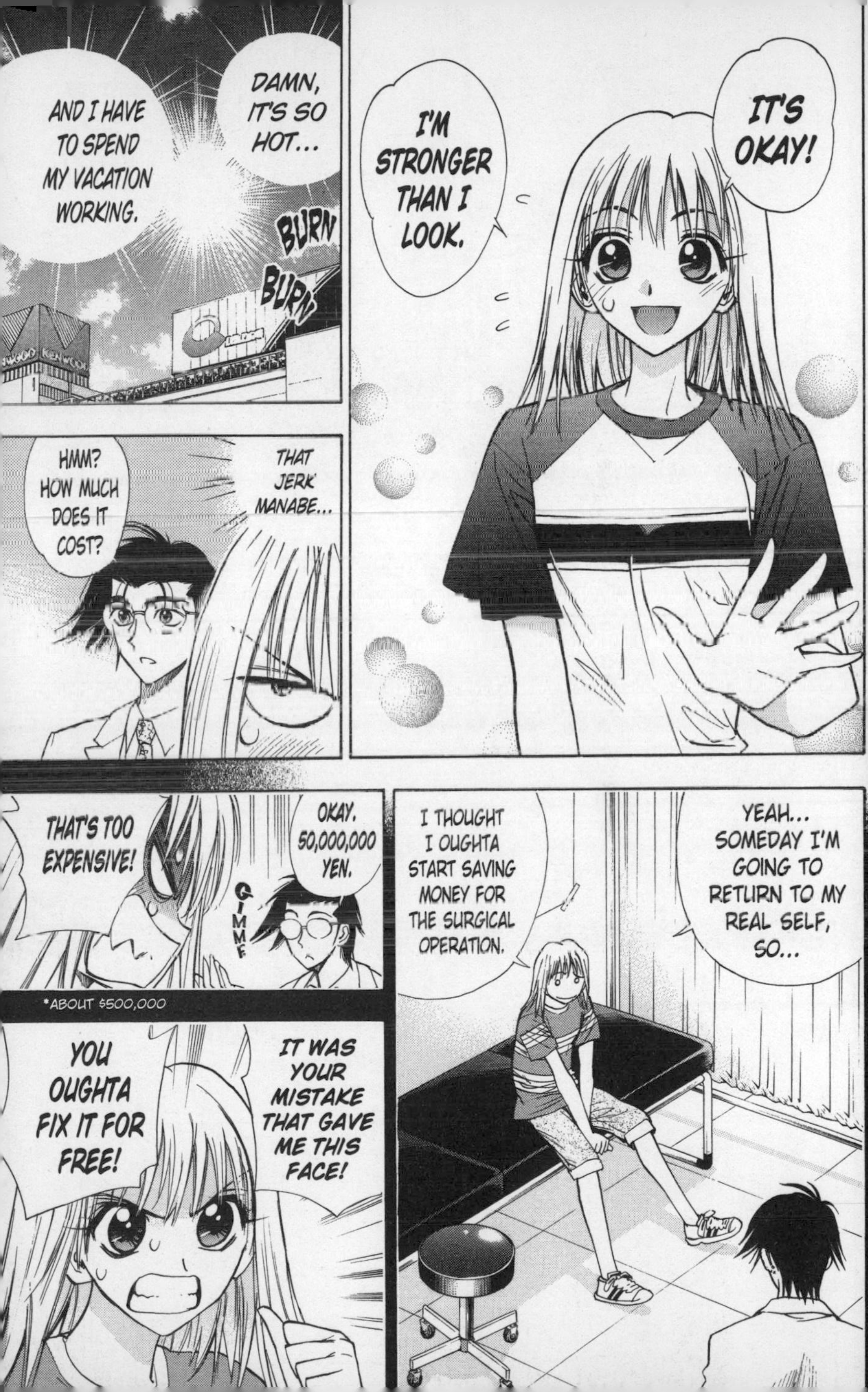
IT'S OKAY!
I'M STRONGER THAN I LOOK.
DAMN, IT'S SO HOT...
AND I HAVE TO SPEND MY VACATION WORKING.
BURN
BURN
THAT JERK MANABE...
HMM? HOW MUCH DOES IT COST?
YEAH... SOMEDAY I'M GOING TO RETURN TO MY REAL SELF, SO...
I THOUGHT I OUGHTA START SAVING MONEY FOR THE SURGICAL OPERATION.
OKAY. 50,000,000 YEN.
GIMMF
THAT'S TOO EXPENSIVE!
*ABOUT $500,000
IT WAS YOUR MISTAKE THAT GAVE ME THIS FACE!
YOU OUGHTA FIX IT FOR FREE!

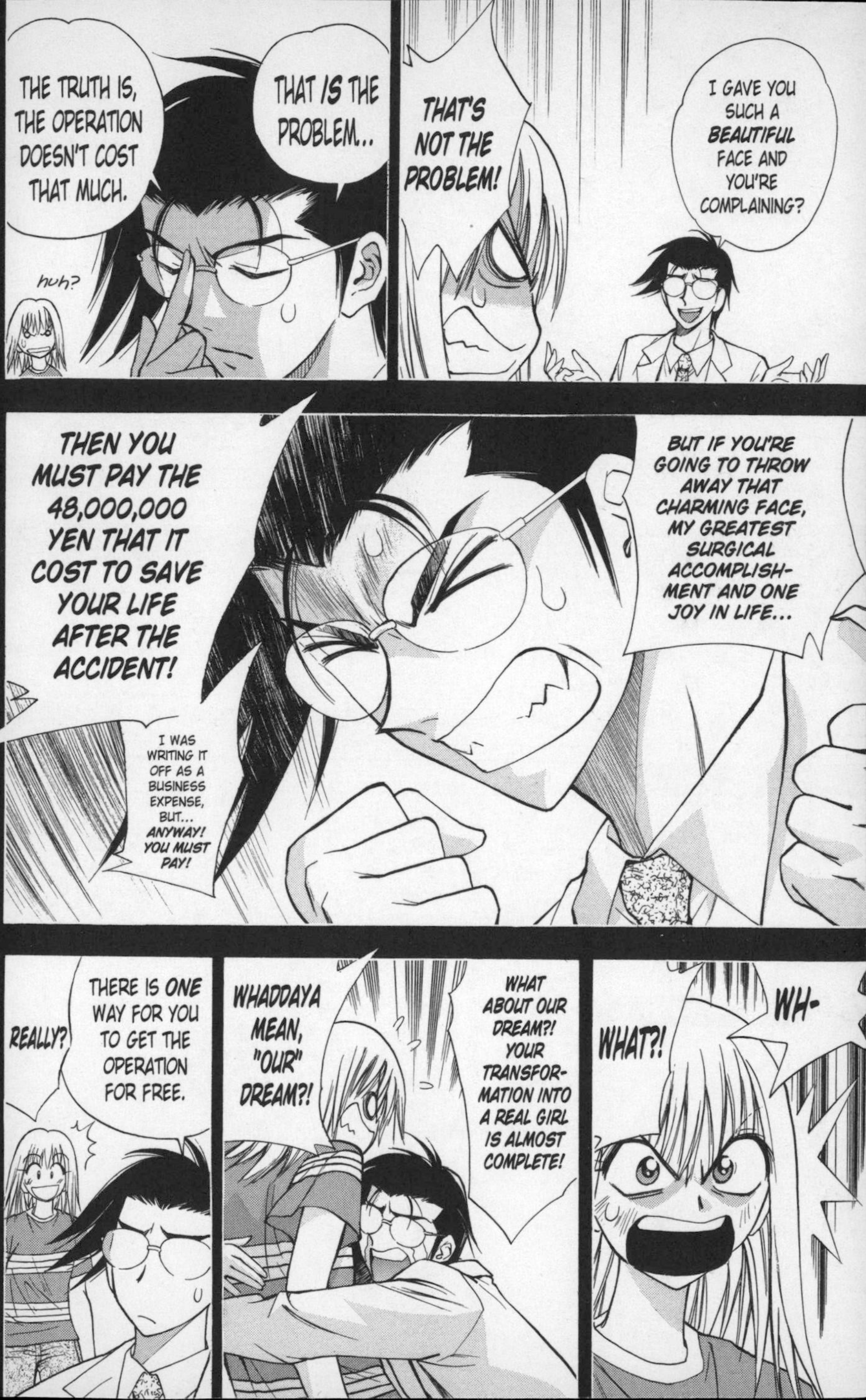
I GAVE YOU SUCH A BEAUTIFUL FACE AND YOU'RE COMPLAINING?
THAT'S NOT THE PROBLEM!
THAT IS THE PROBLEM...
THE TRUTH IS, THE OPERATION DOESN'T COST THAT MUCH.
huh?
BUT IF YOU'RE GOING TO THROW AWAY THAT CHARMING FACE, MY GREATEST SURGICAL ACCOMPLISH-MENT AND ONE JOY IN LIFE...
THEN YOU MUST PAY THE 48,000,000 YEN THAT IT COST TO SAVE YOUR LIFE AFTER THE ACCIDENT!
I WAS WRITING IT OFF AS A BUSINESS EXPENSE, BUT... ANYWAY! YOU MUST PAY!
WH-
WHAT?!
WHAT ABOUT OUR DREAM?! YOUR TRANSFOR-MATION INTO A REAL GIRL IS ALMOST COMPLETE!
WHADDAYA MEAN, "OUR" DREAM?!
THERE IS ONE WAY FOR YOU TO GET THE OPERATION FOR FREE.
REALLY?

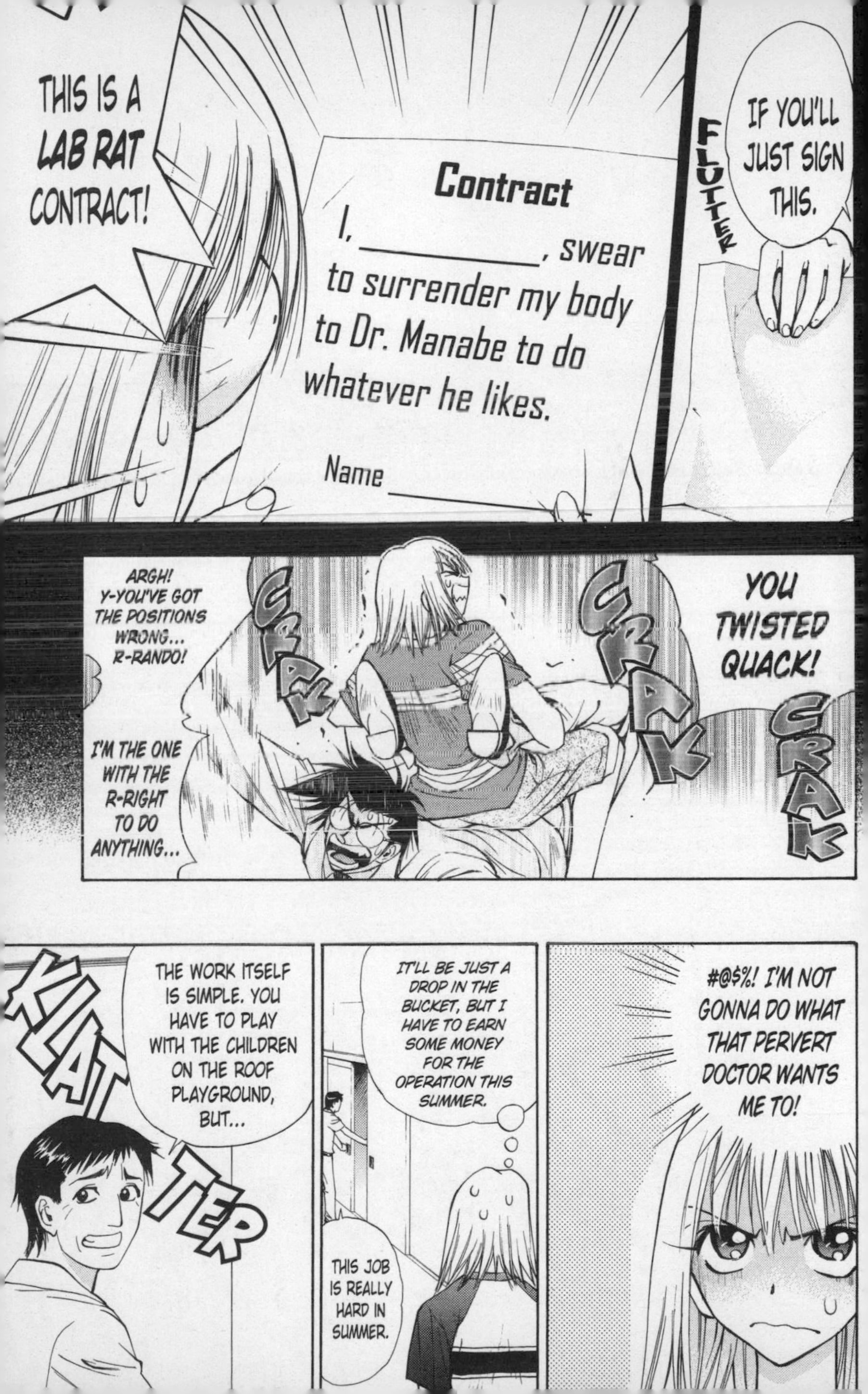
IF YOU'LL JUST SIGN THIS.
FLUTTER
THIS IS A LAB RAT CONTRACT!
Contract
I, __________, swear to surrender my body to Dr. Manabe to do whatever he likes.
Name __________
YOU TWISTED QUACK!
CRAK
CRAK
CRAK
ARGH! Y-YOU'VE GOT THE POSITIONS WRONG... R-RANDO!
I'M THE ONE WITH THE R-RIGHT TO DO ANYTHING...
#@$%! I'M NOT GONNA DO WHAT THAT PERVERT DOCTOR WANTS ME TO!
IT'LL BE JUST A DROP IN THE BUCKET, BUT I HAVE TO EARN SOME MONEY FOR THE OPERATION THIS SUMMER.
THIS JOB IS REALLY HARD IN SUMMER.
THE WORK ITSELF IS SIMPLE. YOU HAVE TO PLAY WITH THE CHILDREN ON THE ROOF PLAYGROUND, BUT...
KLATTER

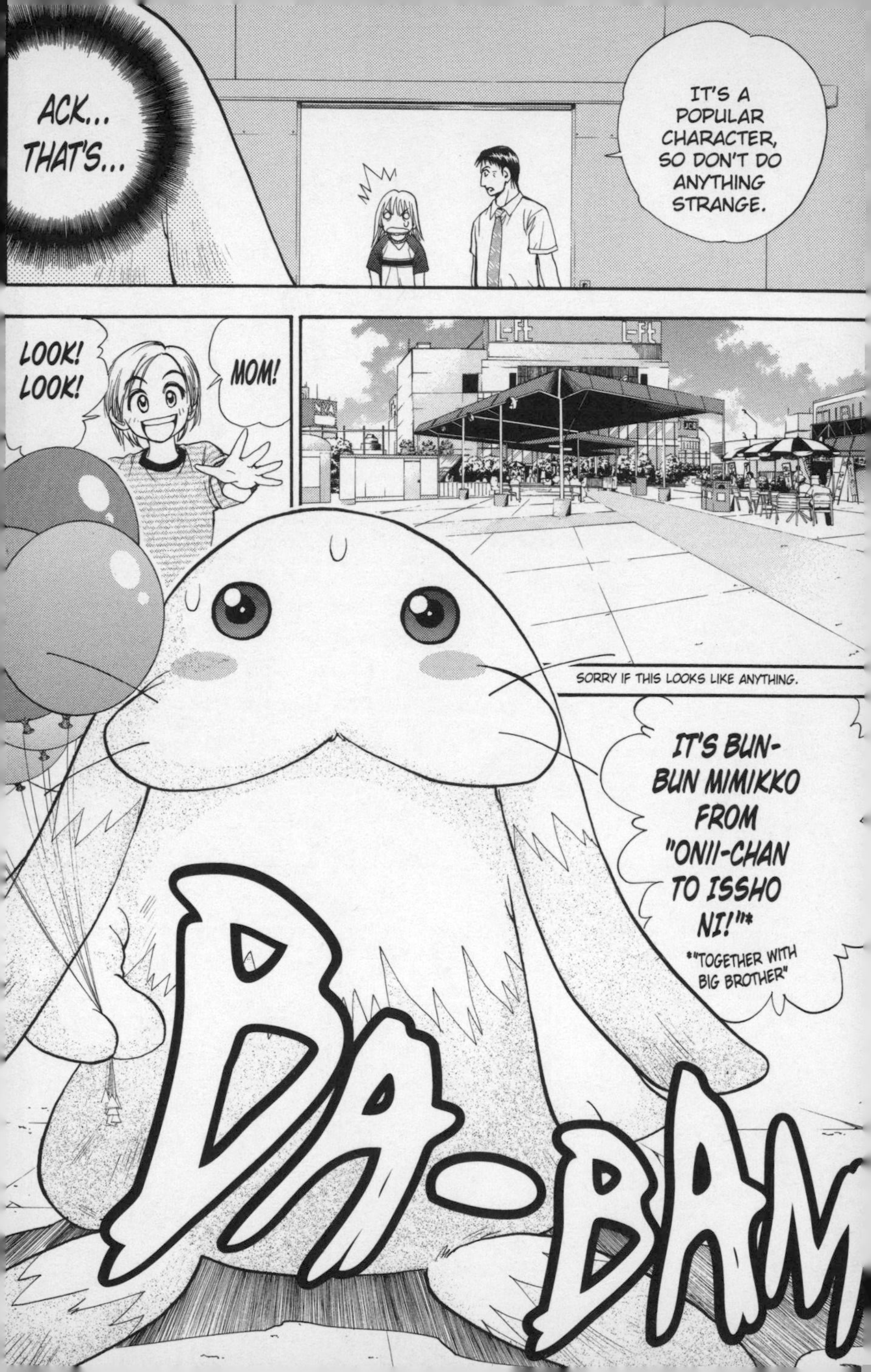
IT'S A POPULAR CHARACTER, SO DON'T DO ANYTHING STRANGE.
ACK... THAT'S...
SORRY IF THIS LOOKS LIKE ANYTHING.
MOM!
LOOK! LOOK!
IT'S BUN-BUN MIMIKKO FROM "ONII-CHAN TO ISSHO NI!"*
*"TOGETHER WITH BIG BROTHER"
DA-BAM

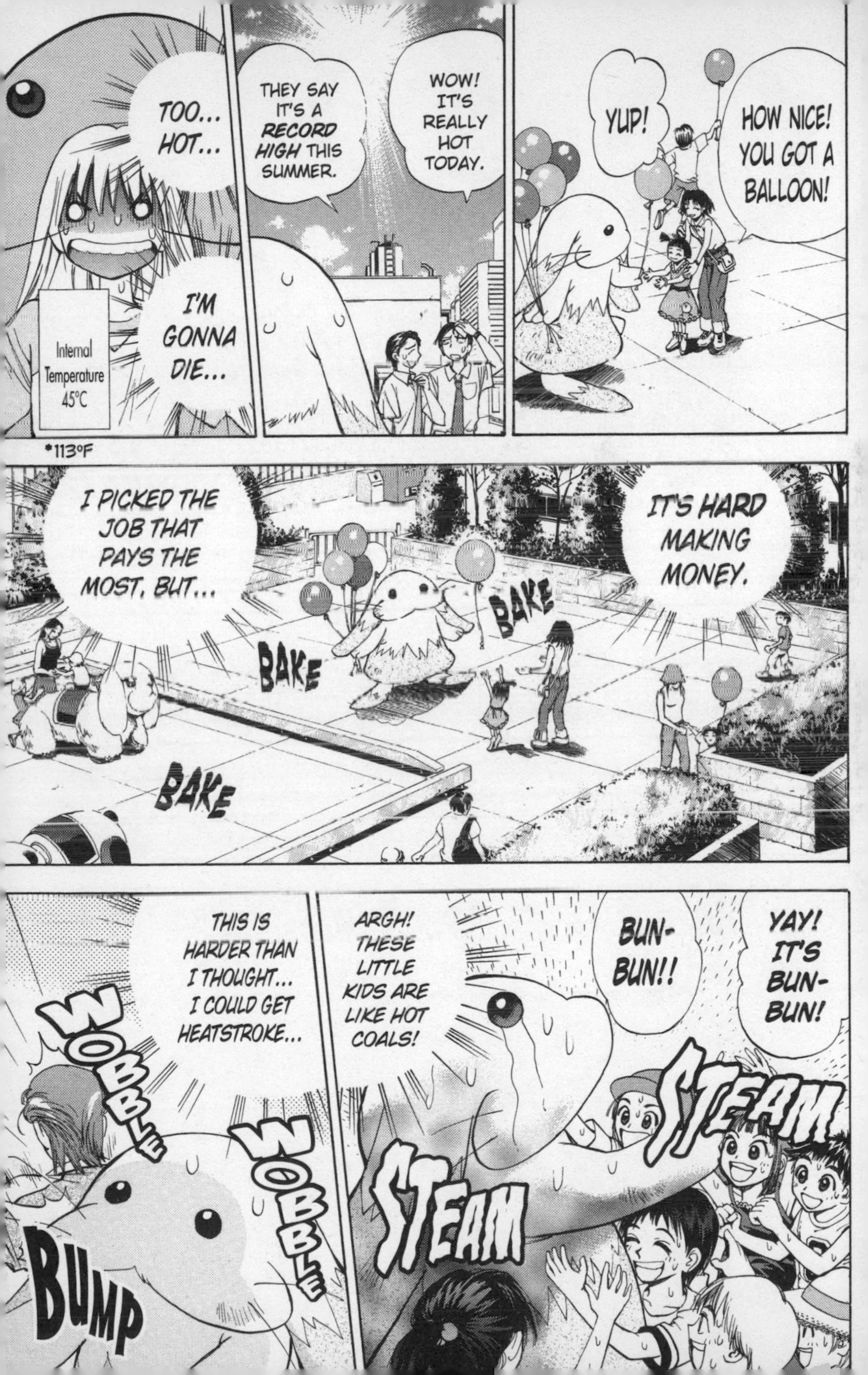
HOW NICE! YOU GOT A BALLOON!
YUP!
WOW! IT'S REALLY HOT TODAY.
THEY SAY IT'S A RECORD HIGH THIS SUMMER.
TOO... HOT...
I'M GONNA DIE...
Internal Temperature 45°C
*113°F
IT'S HARD MAKING MONEY.
I PICKED THE JOB THAT PAYS THE MOST, BUT...
BAKE
BAKE
BAKE
YAY! IT'S BUN-BUN!
BUN-BUN!!
ARGH! THESE LITTLE KIDS ARE LIKE HOT COALS!
STEAM
STEAM
THIS IS HARDER THAN I THOUGHT... I COULD GET HEATSTROKE...
WOBBLE
WOBBLE
BUMP

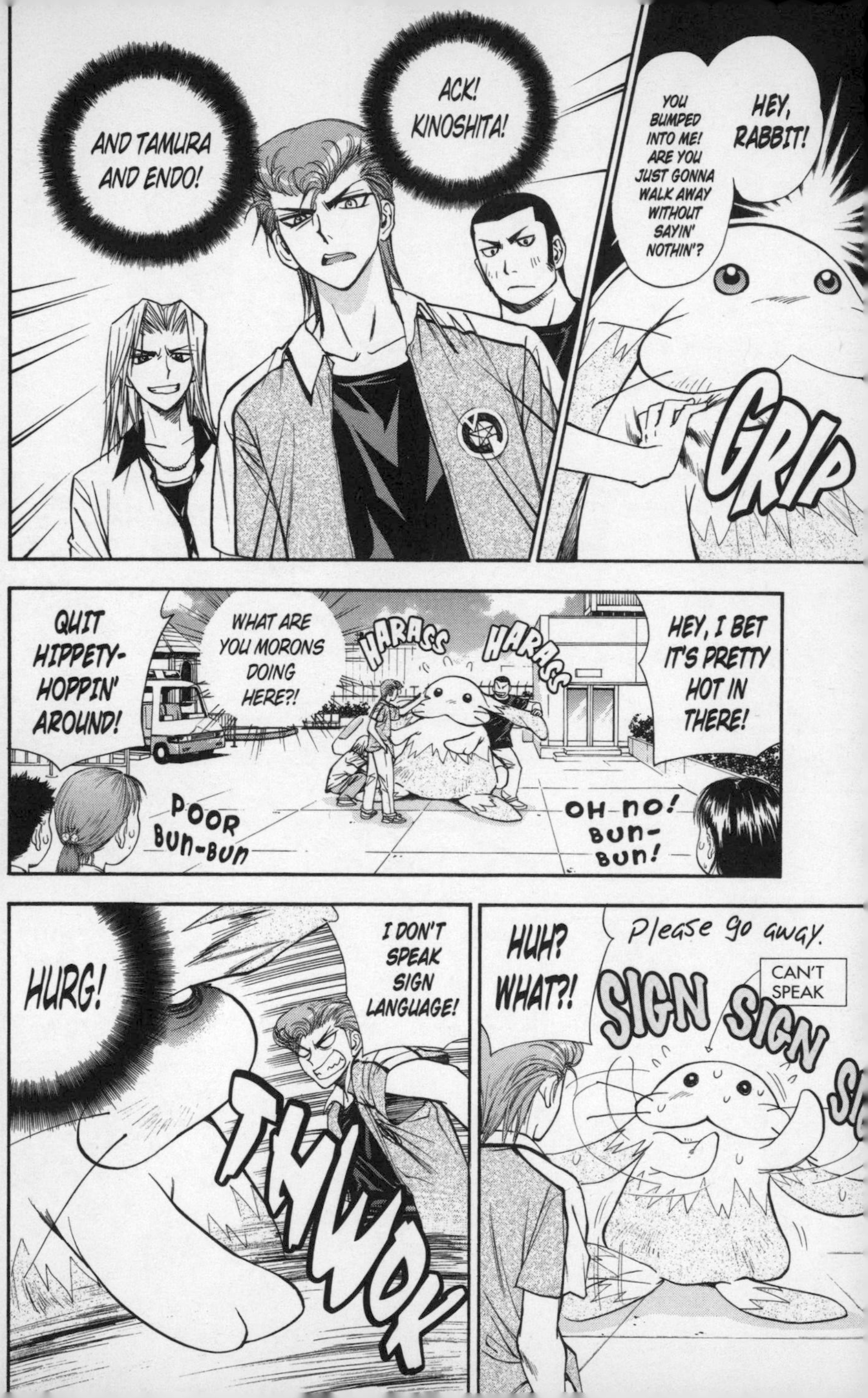
HEY, RABBIT!
YOU BUMPED INTO ME! ARE YOU JUST GONNA WALK AWAY WITHOUT SAYIN' NOTHIN'?
GRIP
ACK! KINOSHITA!
AND TAMURA AND ENDO!
HEY, I BET IT'S PRETTY HOT IN THERE!
HARASS
HARASS
WHAT ARE YOU MORONS DOING HERE?!
QUIT HIPPETY-HOPPIN' AROUND!
OH NO! BUN-BUN!
POOR BUN-BUN
Please go away.
HUH? WHAT?!
CAN'T SPEAK
SIGN SIGN
I DON'T SPEAK SIGN LANGUAGE!
HURG!
THWOK

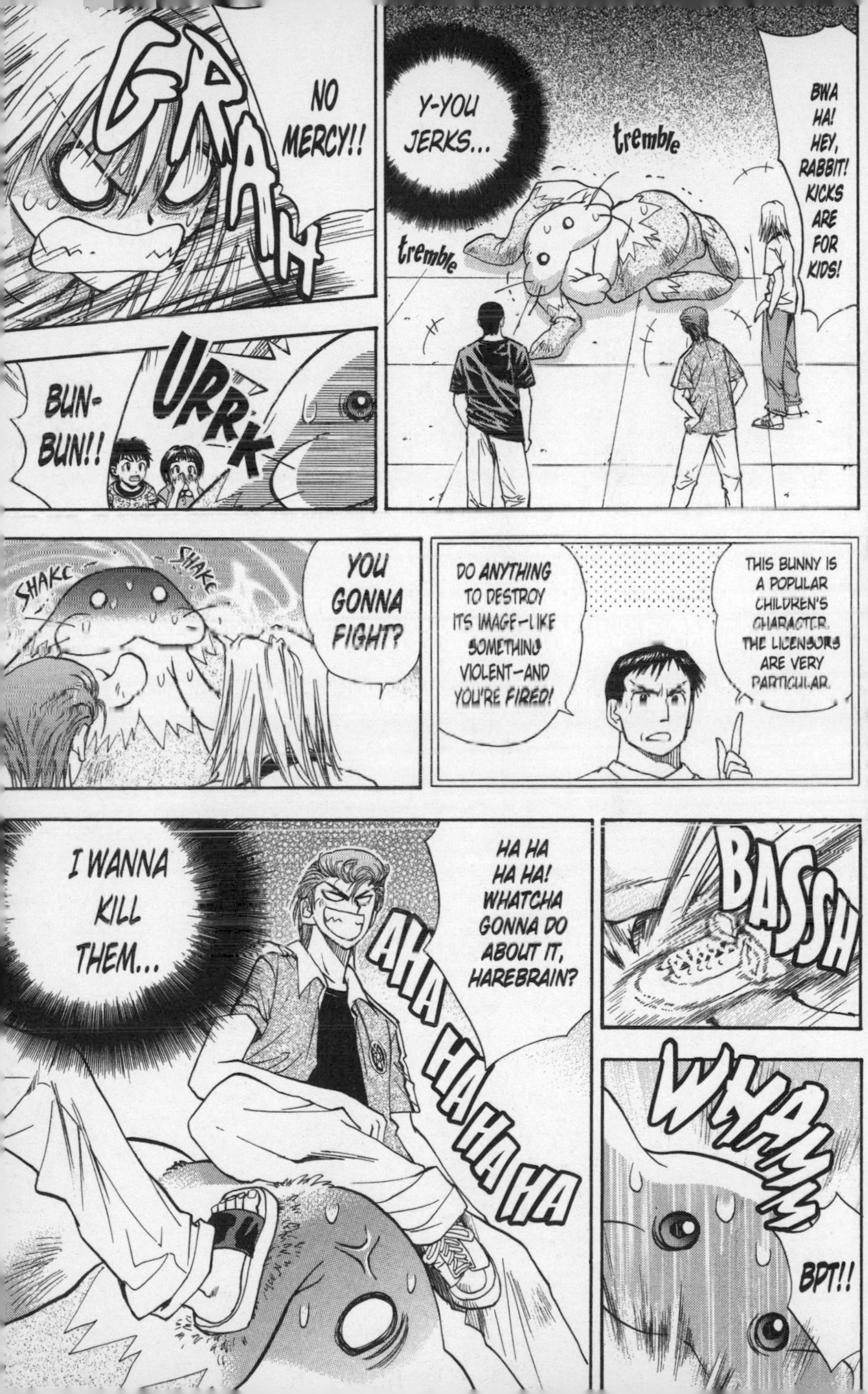
BWA HA! HEY, RABBIT! KICKS ARE FOR KIDS!
tremble
Y-YOU JERKS...
tremble
NO MERCY!!
GRAAH
URRK
BUN-BUN!!
THIS BUNNY IS A POPULAR CHILDREN'S CHARACTER. THE LICENSORS ARE VERY PARTICULAR.
DO ANYTHING TO DESTROY ITS IMAGE—LIKE SOMETHING VIOLENT—AND YOU'RE FIRED!
SHAKE
SHAKE
YOU GONNA FIGHT?
BASSH
WHAM
BPT!!
HA HA HA HA! WHATCHA GONNA DO ABOUT IT, HAREBRAIN?
AHA HA HA HA HA
I WANNA KILL THEM...

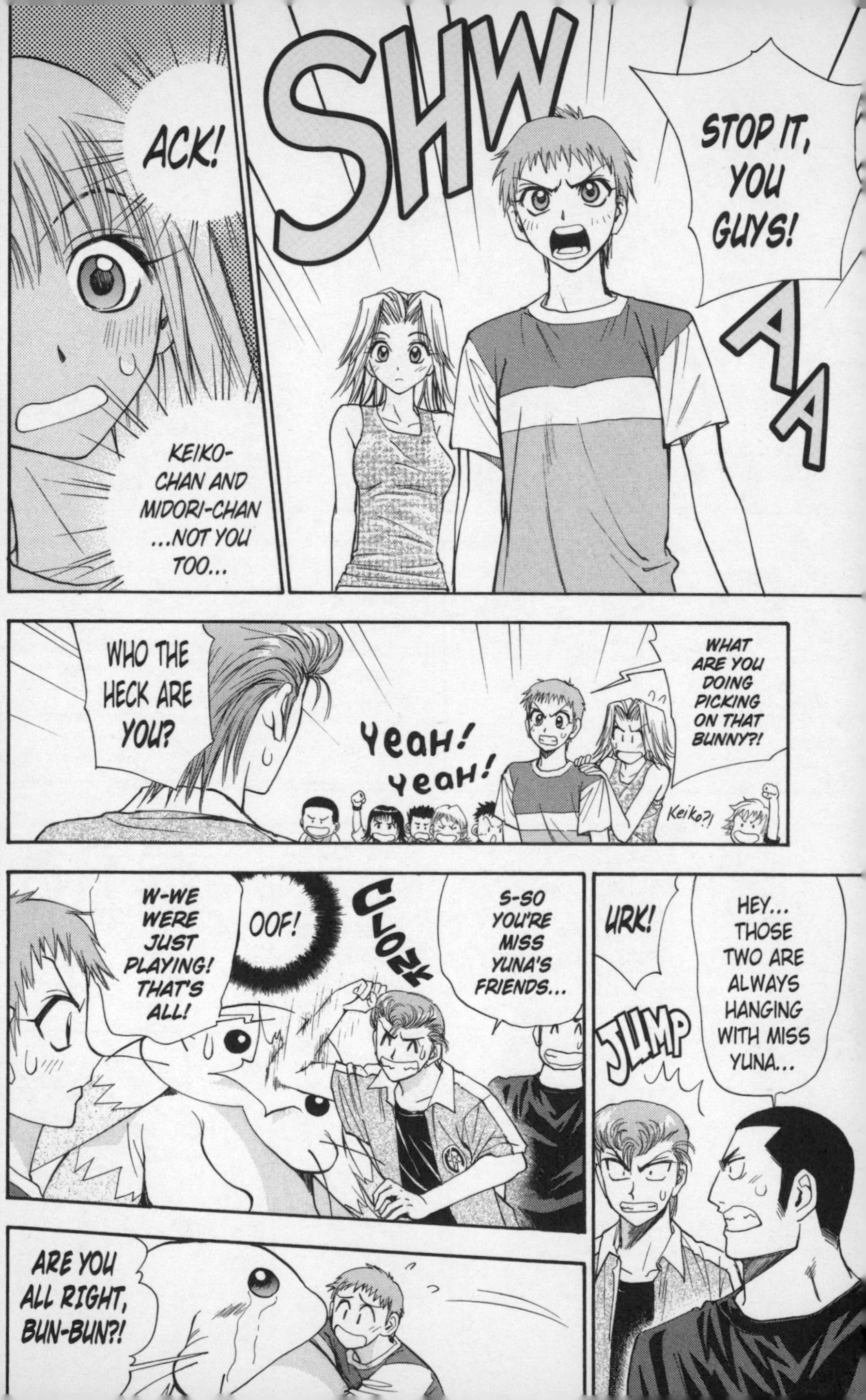
STOP IT, YOU GUYS!
SHW
AA
ACK!
KEIKO-CHAN AND MIDORI-CHAN ...NOT YOU TOO...
WHAT ARE YOU DOING PICKING ON THAT BUNNY?!
Keiko?!
Yeah! yeah!
WHO THE HECK ARE YOU?
HEY... THOSE TWO ARE ALWAYS HANGING WITH MISS YUNA...
URK!
JUMP
S-SO YOU'RE MISS YUNA'S FRIENDS...
CLONK
OOF!
W-WE WERE JUST PLAYING! THAT'S ALL!
ARE YOU ALL RIGHT, BUN-BUN?!

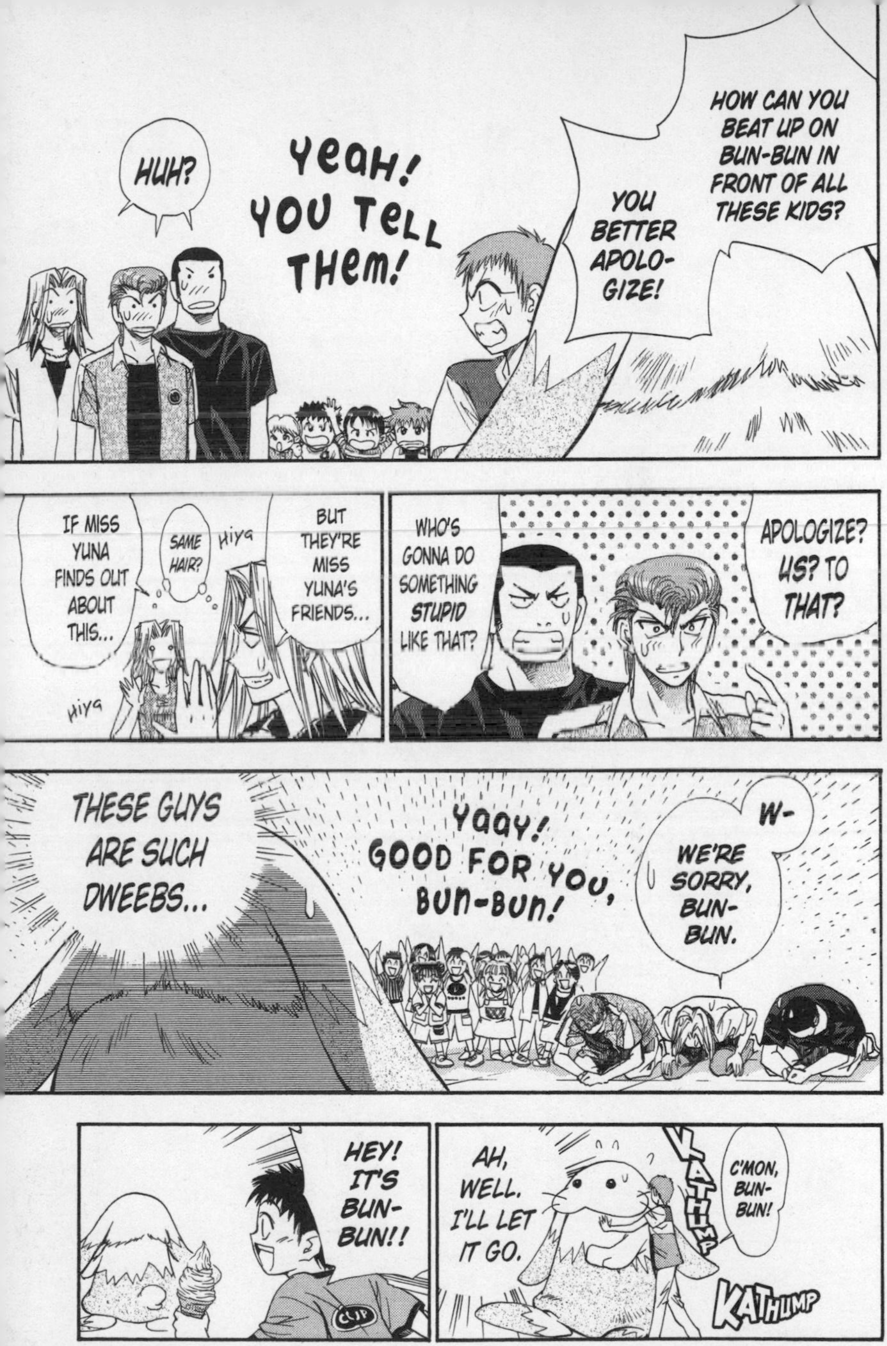
HOW CAN YOU BEAT UP ON BUN-BUN IN FRONT OF ALL THESE KIDS?
YOU BETTER APOLOGIZE!
Yeah! YOU TELL THEM!
HUH?
APOLOGIZE? US? TO THAT?
WHO'S GONNA DO SOMETHING STUPID LIKE THAT?
BUT THEY'RE MISS YUNA'S FRIENDS...
Hiya
SAME HAIR?
IF MISS YUNA FINDS OUT ABOUT THIS...
Hiya
W- WE'RE SORRY, BUN-BUN.
Yaay! GOOD FOR YOU, BUN-BUN!
THESE GUYS ARE SUCH DWEEBS...
C'MON, BUN-BUN!
KATHUMP
AH, WELL. I'LL LET IT GO.
KATHUMP
HEY! IT'S BUN-BUN!!

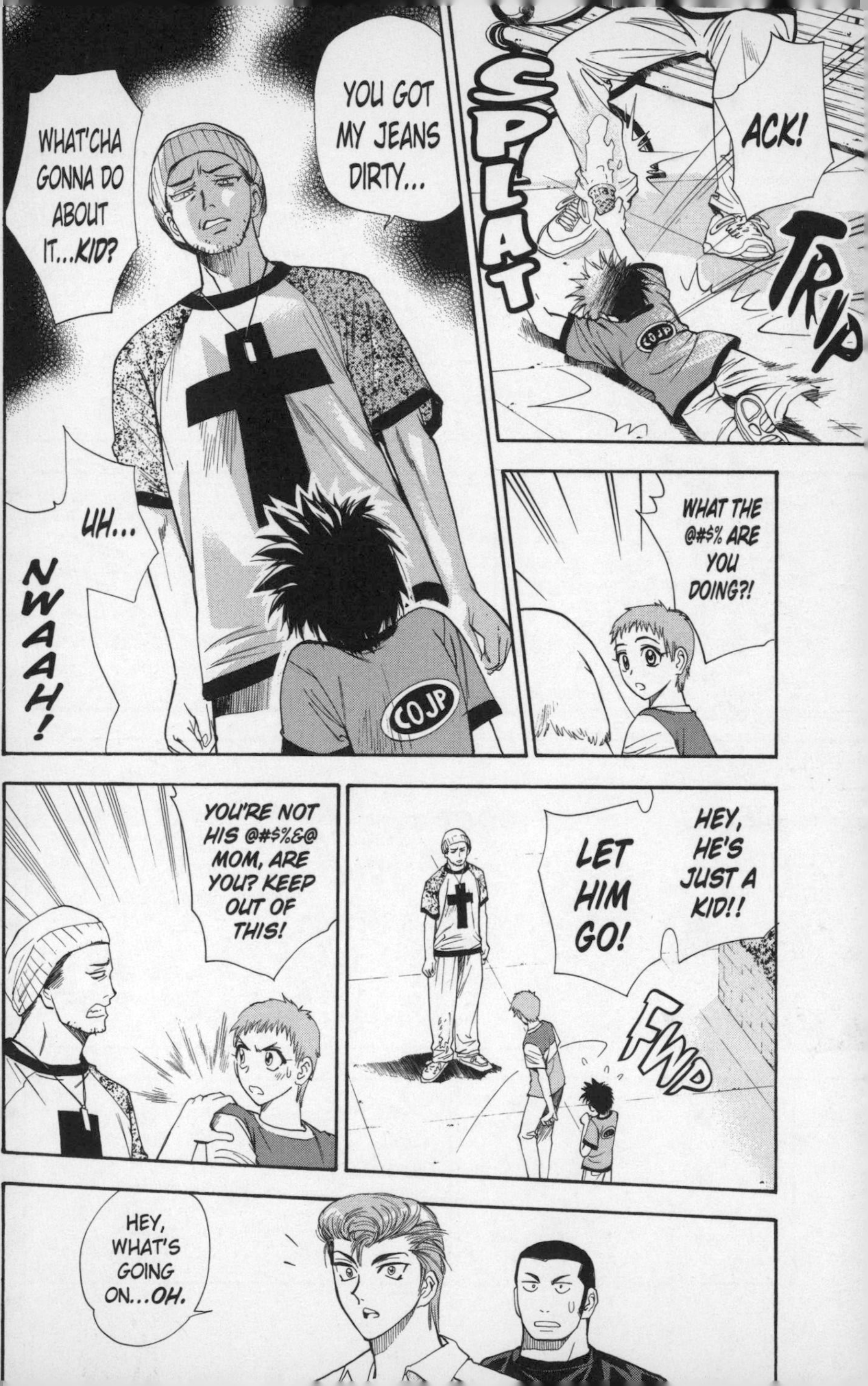
ACK!
TRIP
SPLAT
WHAT THE @#$% ARE YOU DOING?!
YOU GOT MY JEANS DIRTY...
WHAT'CHA GONNA DO ABOUT IT...KID?
UH...
NWAAAH!
HEY, HE'S JUST A KID!!
LET HIM GO!
FWIP
YOU'RE NOT HIS @#$%&@ MOM, ARE YOU? KEEP OUT OF THIS!
HEY, WHAT'S GOING ON...OH.

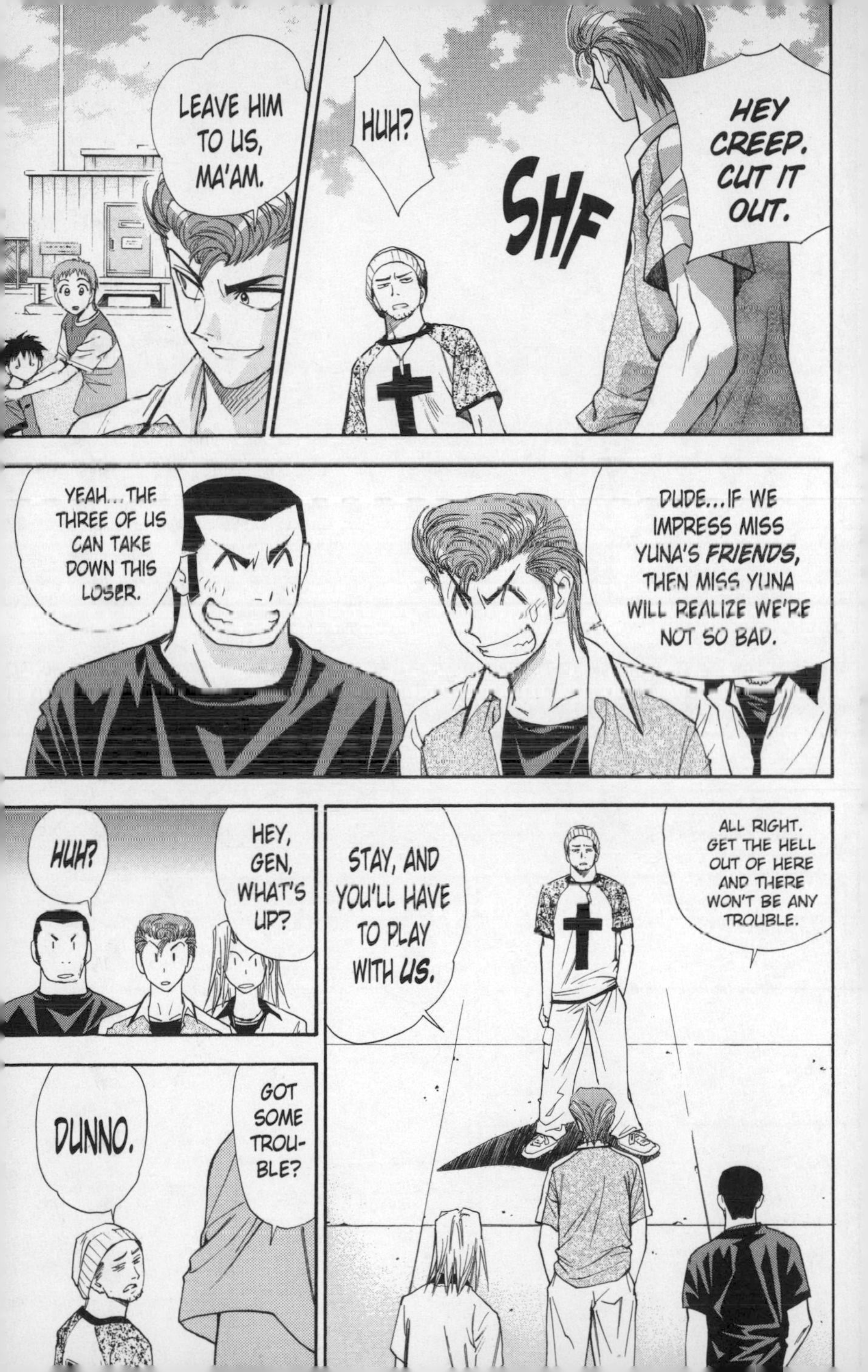
HEY CREEP. CUT IT OUT.
SHF
HUH?
LEAVE HIM TO US, MA'AM.
DUDE...IF WE IMPRESS MISS YUNA'S FRIENDS, THEN MISS YUNA WILL REALIZE WE'RE NOT SO BAD.
YEAH...THE THREE OF US CAN TAKE DOWN THIS LOSER.
ALL RIGHT. GET THE HELL OUT OF HERE AND THERE WON'T BE ANY TROUBLE.
STAY, AND YOU'LL HAVE TO PLAY WITH US.
HEY, GEN, WHAT'S UP?
HUH?
GOT SOME TROU-BLE?
DUNNO.

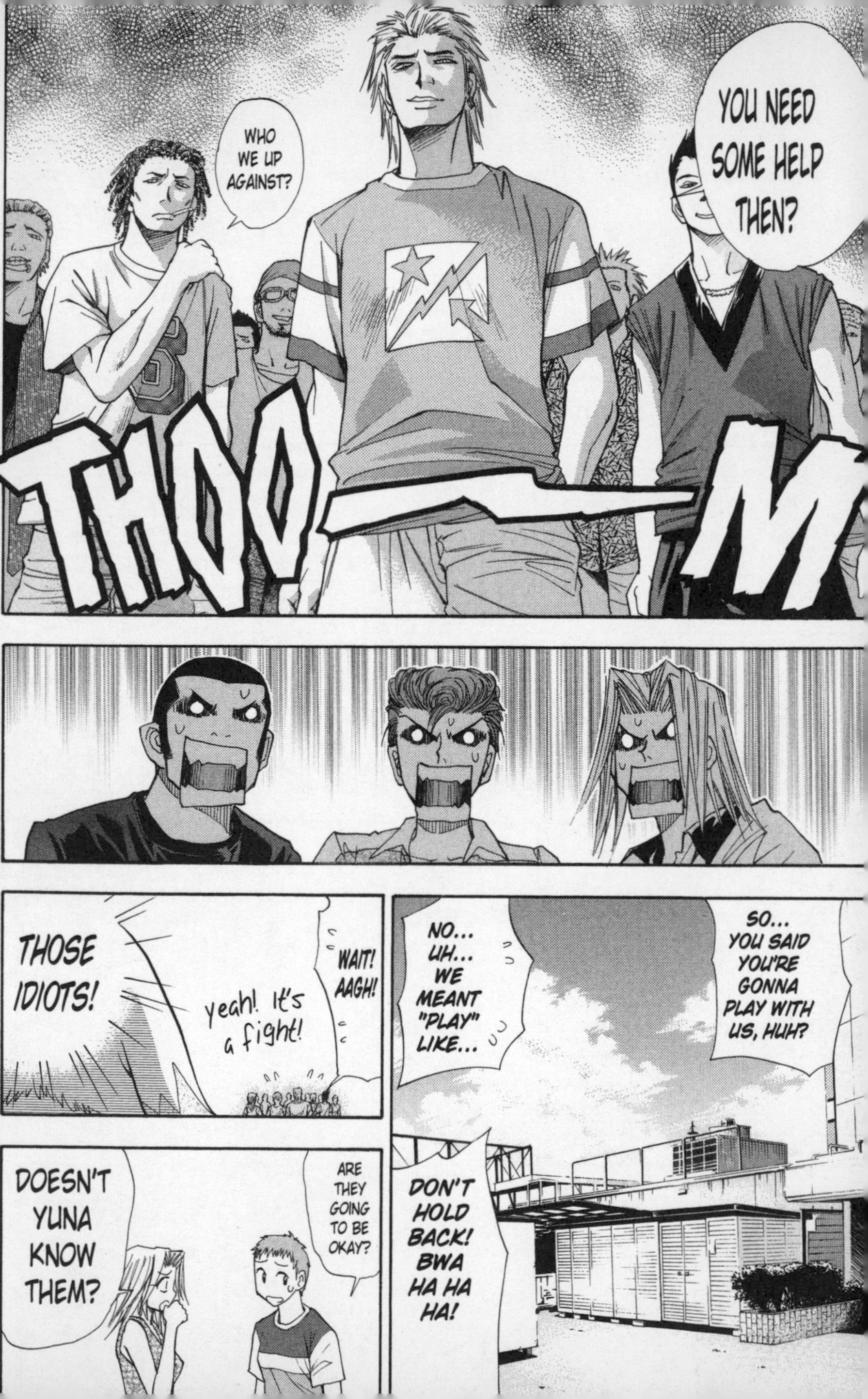
YOU NEED SOME HELP THEN?
WHO WE UP AGAINST?
THOO—M
SO... YOU SAID YOU'RE GONNA PLAY WITH US, HUH?
NO... UH... WE MEANT "PLAY" LIKE...
DON'T HOLD BACK! BWA HA HA HA!
WAIT! AAGH!
yeah! It's a fight!
THOSE IDIOTS!
ARE THEY GOING TO BE OKAY?
DOESN'T YUNA KNOW THEM?

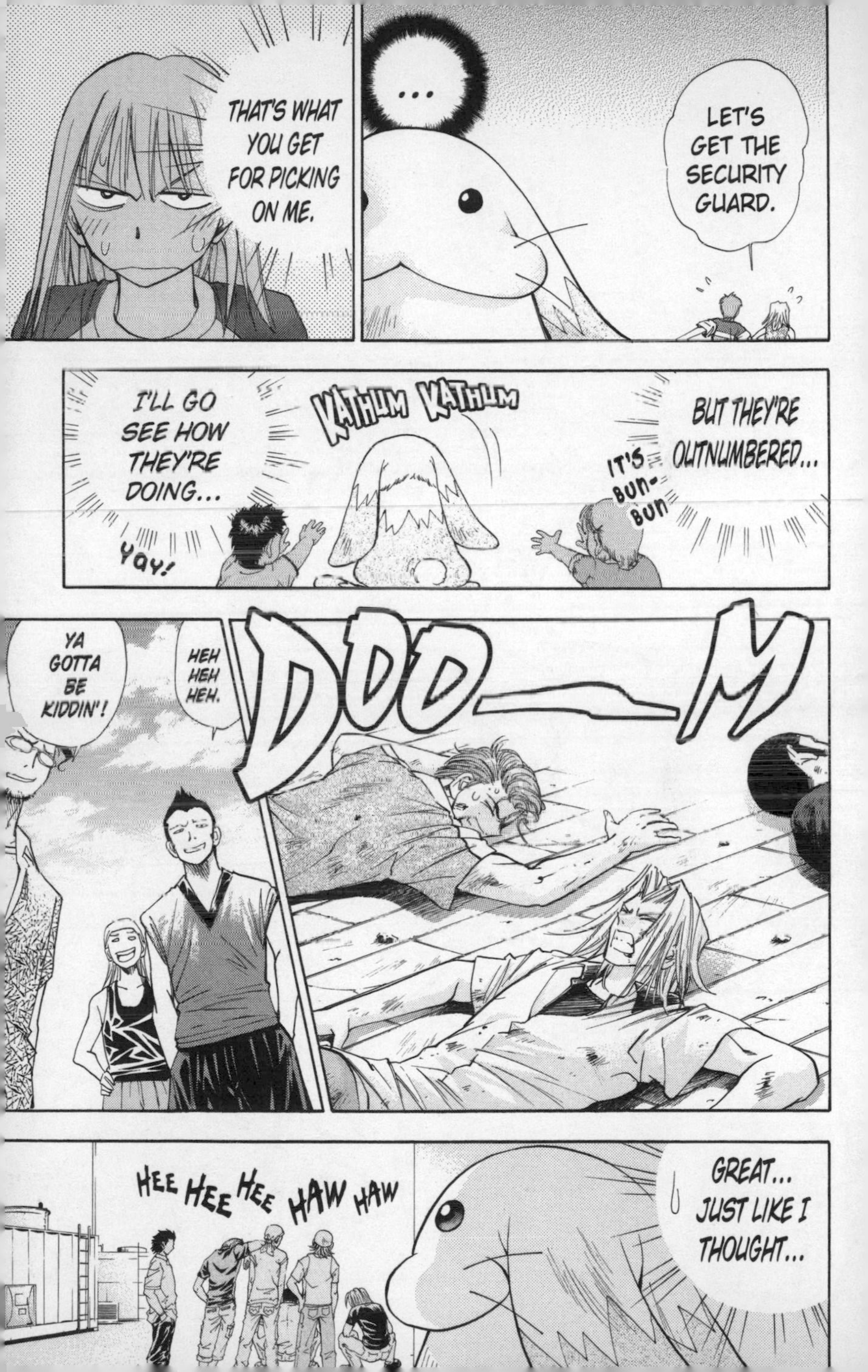
LET'S GET THE SECURITY GUARD.
...
THAT'S WHAT YOU GET FOR PICKING ON ME.
BUT THEY'RE OUTNUMBERED...
IT'S BUN-BUN
KATHUM KATHUM
I'LL GO SEE HOW THEY'RE DOING...
YAY!
DOO—M
HEH HEH HEH.
YA GOTTA BE KIDDIN'!
GREAT... JUST LIKE I THOUGHT...
HEE HEE HEE HAW HAW

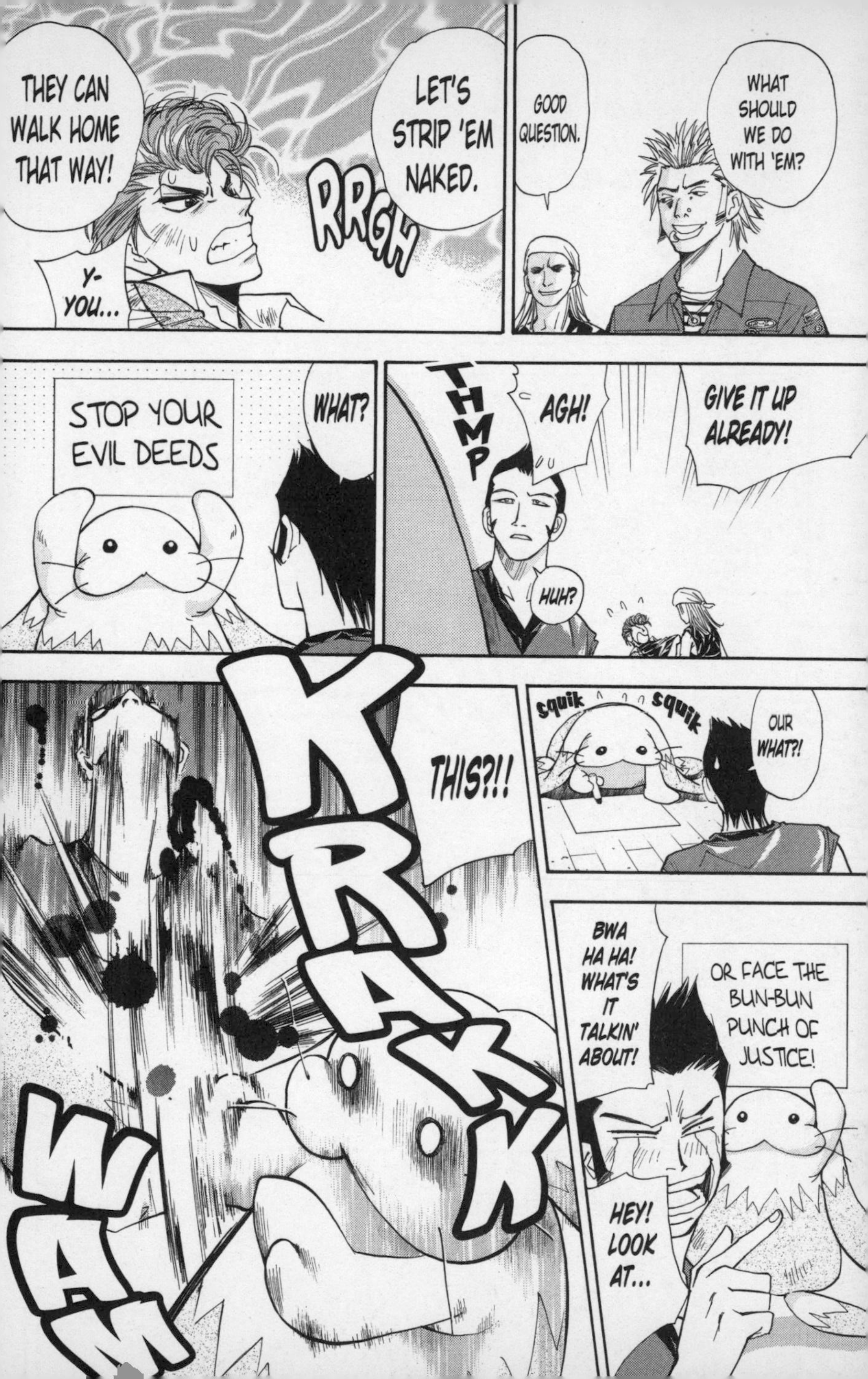
WHAT SHOULD WE DO WITH 'EM?
GOOD QUESTION.
LET'S STRIP 'EM NAKED.
RRGH
THEY CAN WALK HOME THAT WAY!
Y-YOU...
GIVE IT UP ALREADY!
AGH!
THMP
HUH?
WHAT?
STOP YOUR EVIL DEEDS
OUR WHAT?!
squik
squik
OR FACE THE BUN-BUN PUNCH OF JUSTICE!
BWA HA HA! WHAT'S IT TALKIN' ABOUT!
HEY! LOOK AT...
THIS?!!
KRAKK
WHAM

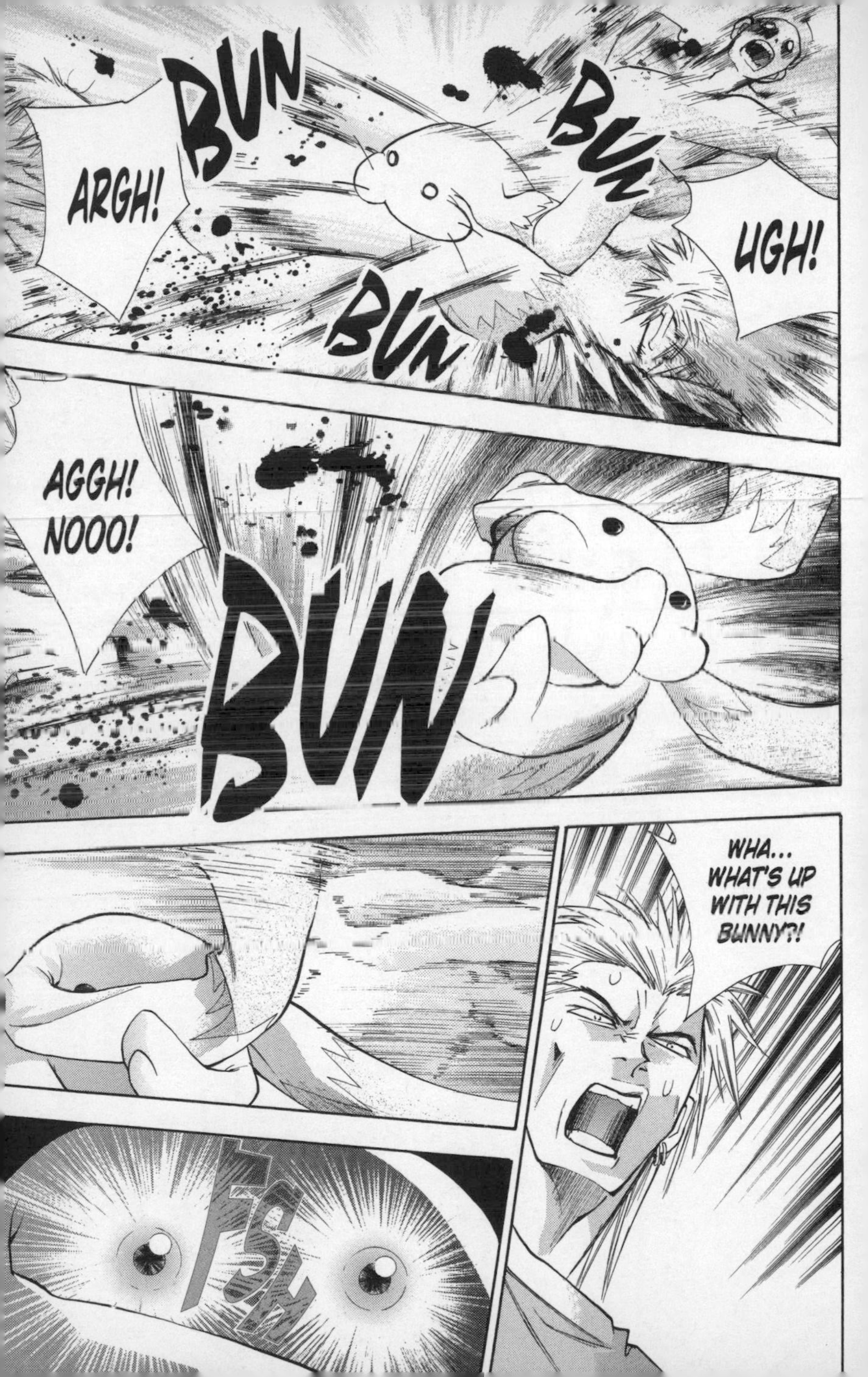
BUN
UGH!
BUN
ARGH!
BUN
BUN
AGGH! NOOO!
WHA... WHAT'S UP WITH THIS BUNNY?!
FSH

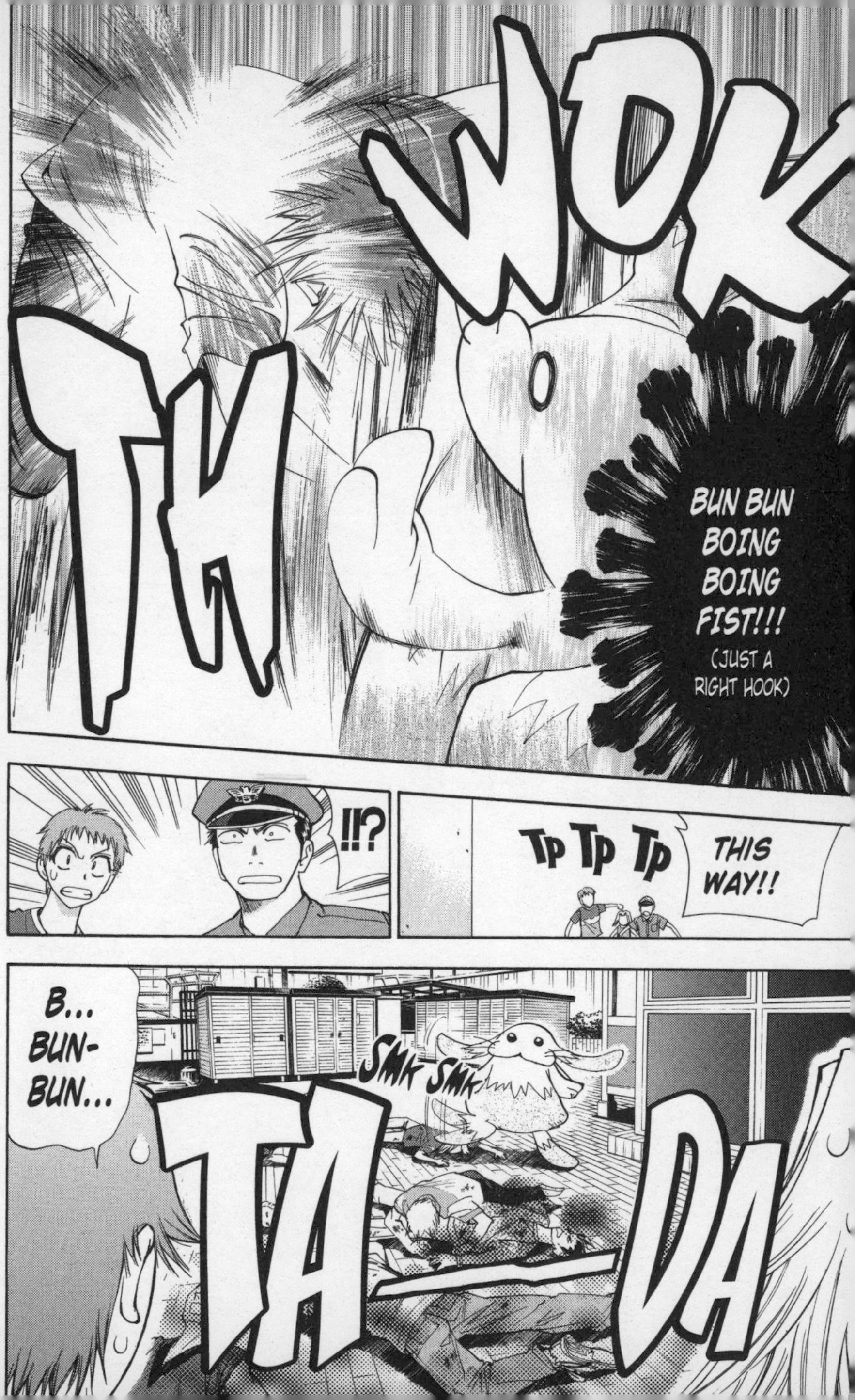
TH WOK
BUN BUN BOING BOING FIST!!!
(JUST A RIGHT HOOK)
THIS WAY!!
Tp Tp Tp
!!?
TA DA
SMK SMK
B... BUN-BUN...

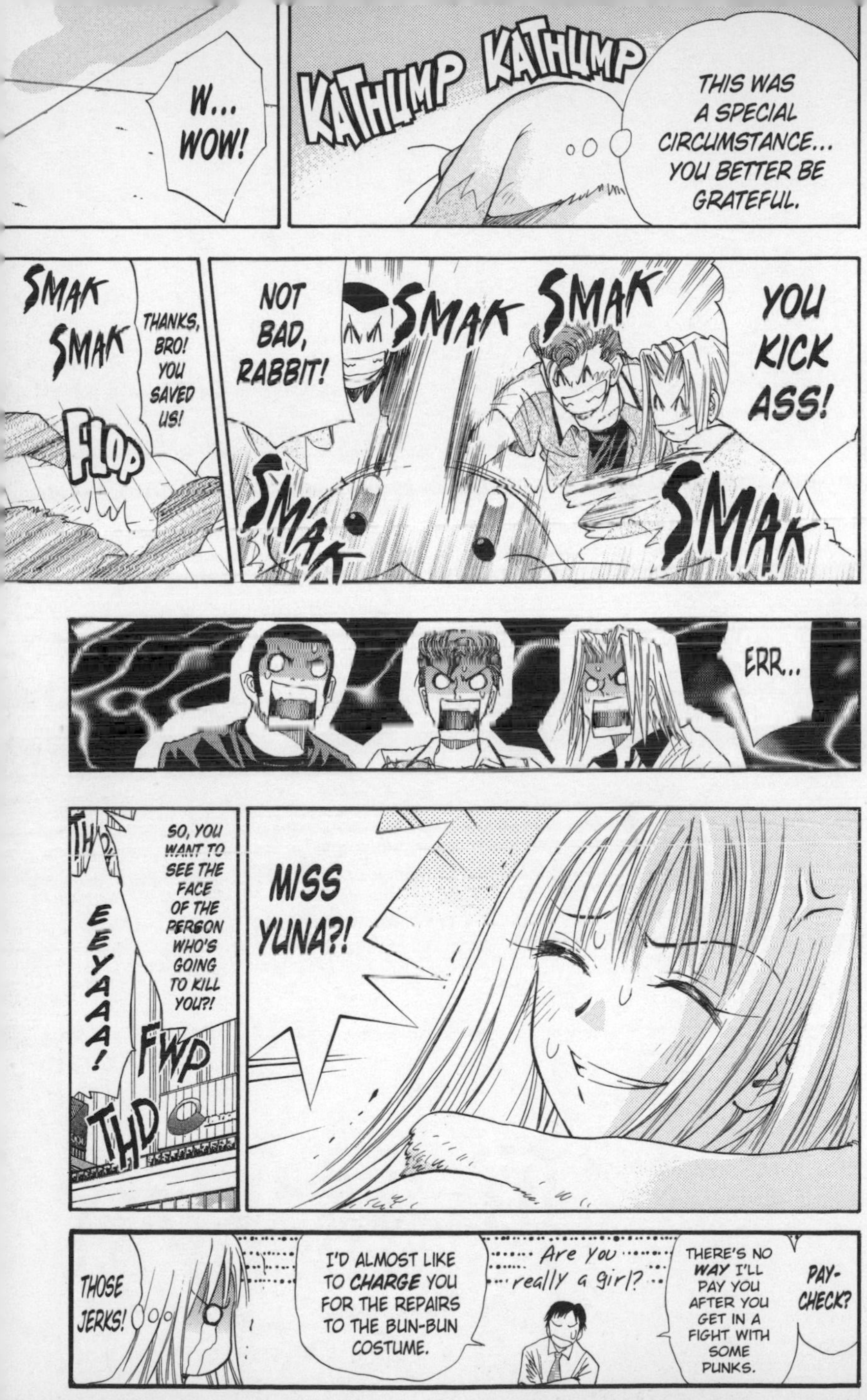

KATHUMP KATHUMP
THIS WAS A SPECIAL CIRCUMSTANCE... YOU BETTER BE GRATEFUL.
W... WOW!
YOU KICK ASS!
SMAK
SMAK
NOT BAD, RABBIT!
SMAK
SMAK
THANKS, BRO! YOU SAVED US!
SMAK
SMAK
FLOP
ERR...
MISS YUNA?!
SO, YOU WANT TO SEE THE FACE OF THE PERSON WHO'S GOING TO KILL YOU?!
EEYAAAA!
FWP
THD
PAY-CHECK?
THERE'S NO WAY I'LL PAY YOU AFTER YOU GET IN A FIGHT WITH SOME PUNKS.
Are you really a girl?
I'D ALMOST LIKE TO CHARGE YOU FOR THE REPAIRS TO THE BUN-BUN COSTUME.
THOSE JERKS!

Pretty Face

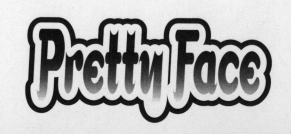

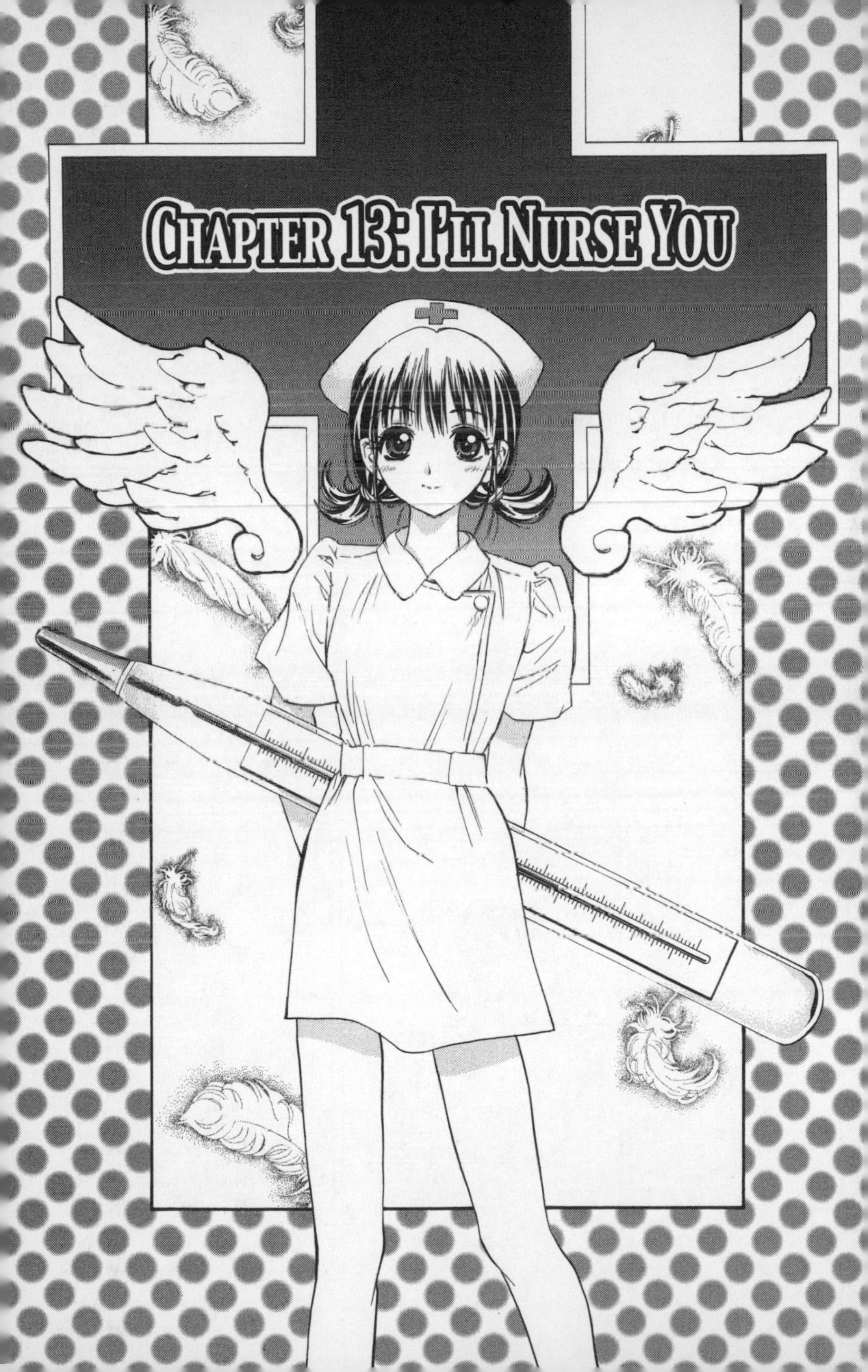
Chapter 13: I'll Nurse You

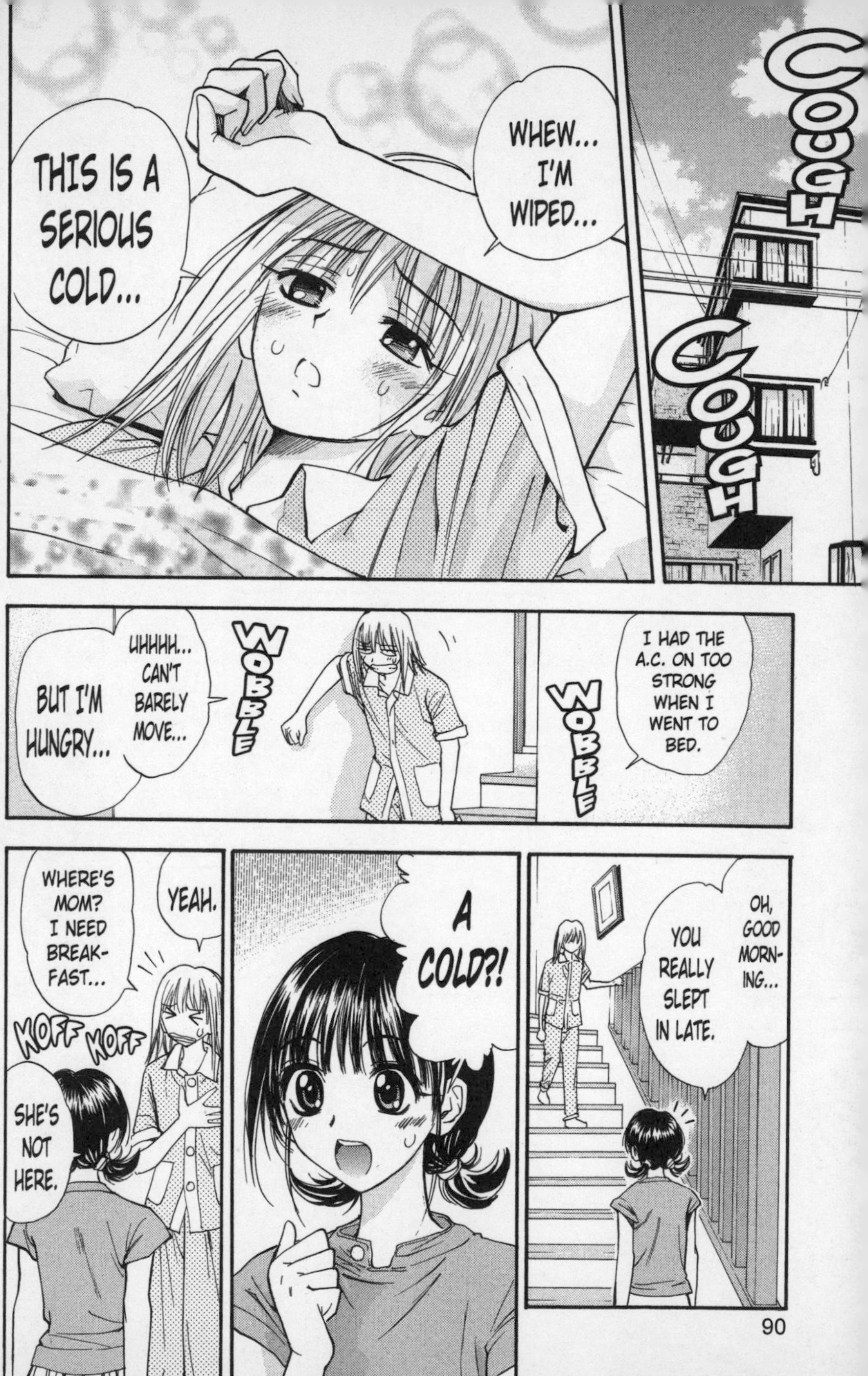
COUGH COUGH
COUGH COUGH
WHEW... I'M WIPED...
THIS IS A SERIOUS COLD...
I HAD THE A.C. ON TOO STRONG WHEN I WENT TO BED.
WOBBLE
WOBBLE
UHHHH... CAN'T BARELY MOVE...
BUT I'M HUNGRY...
OH, GOOD MORN-ING...
YOU REALLY SLEPT IN LATE.
A COLD?!
YEAH.
WHERE'S MOM? I NEED BREAK-FAST...
KOFF KOFF
SHE'S NOT HERE.

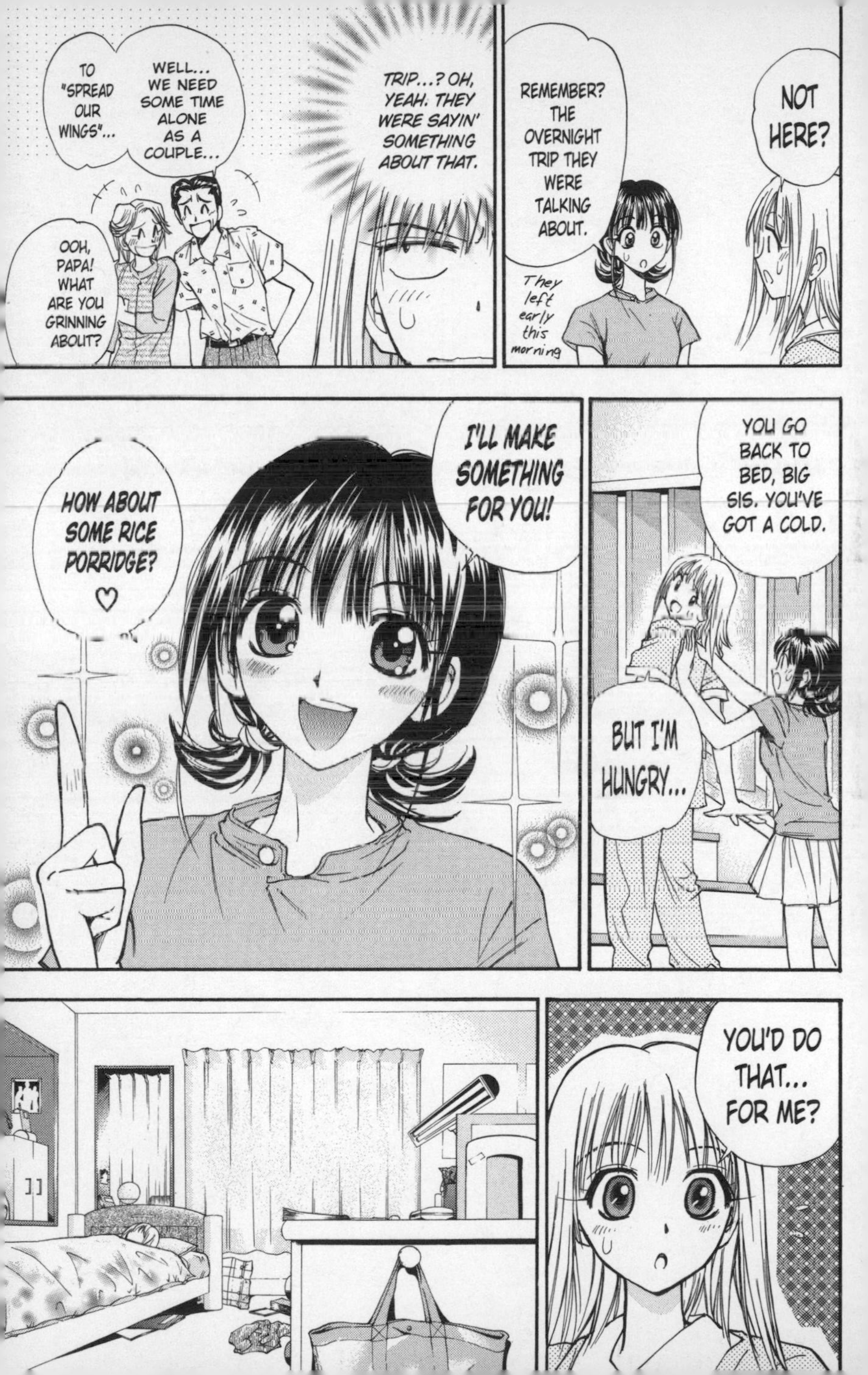
NOT HERE?
REMEMBER? THE OVERNIGHT TRIP THEY WERE TALKING ABOUT.
They left early this morning
TRIP...? OH, YEAH. THEY WERE SAYIN' SOMETHING ABOUT THAT.
WELL... WE NEED SOME TIME ALONE AS A COUPLE...
TO "SPREAD OUR WINGS"...
OOH, PAPA! WHAT ARE YOU GRINNING ABOUT?
YOU GO BACK TO BED, BIG SIS. YOU'VE GOT A COLD.
BUT I'M HUNGRY...
I'LL MAKE SOMETHING FOR YOU!
HOW ABOUT SOME RICE PORRIDGE? ♡
YOU'D DO THAT... FOR ME?

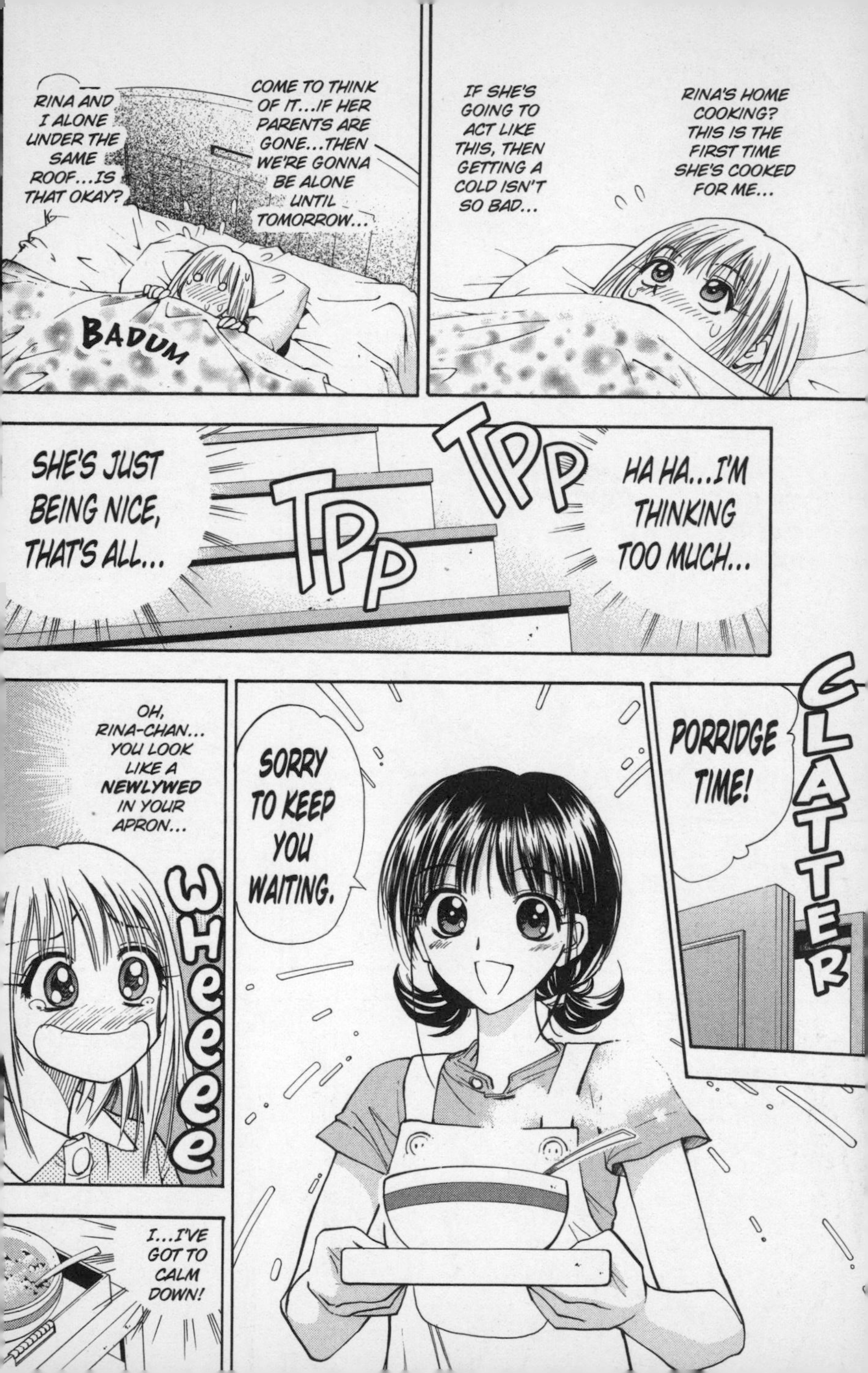
RINA'S HOME COOKING? THIS IS THE FIRST TIME SHE'S COOKED FOR ME...
IF SHE'S GOING TO ACT LIKE THIS, THEN GETTING A COLD ISN'T SO BAD...
COME TO THINK OF IT...IF HER PARENTS ARE GONE...THEN WE'RE GONNA BE ALONE UNTIL TOMORROW...
RINA AND I ALONE UNDER THE SAME ROOF...IS THAT OKAY?
BADUM
HA HA...I'M THINKING TOO MUCH...
TPP
TPP
SHE'S JUST BEING NICE, THAT'S ALL...
PORRIDGE TIME!
CLATTER
SORRY TO KEEP YOU WAITING.
OH, RINA-CHAN... YOU LOOK LIKE A NEWLYWED IN YOUR APRON...
WHEEEE
I...I'VE GOT TO CALM DOWN!

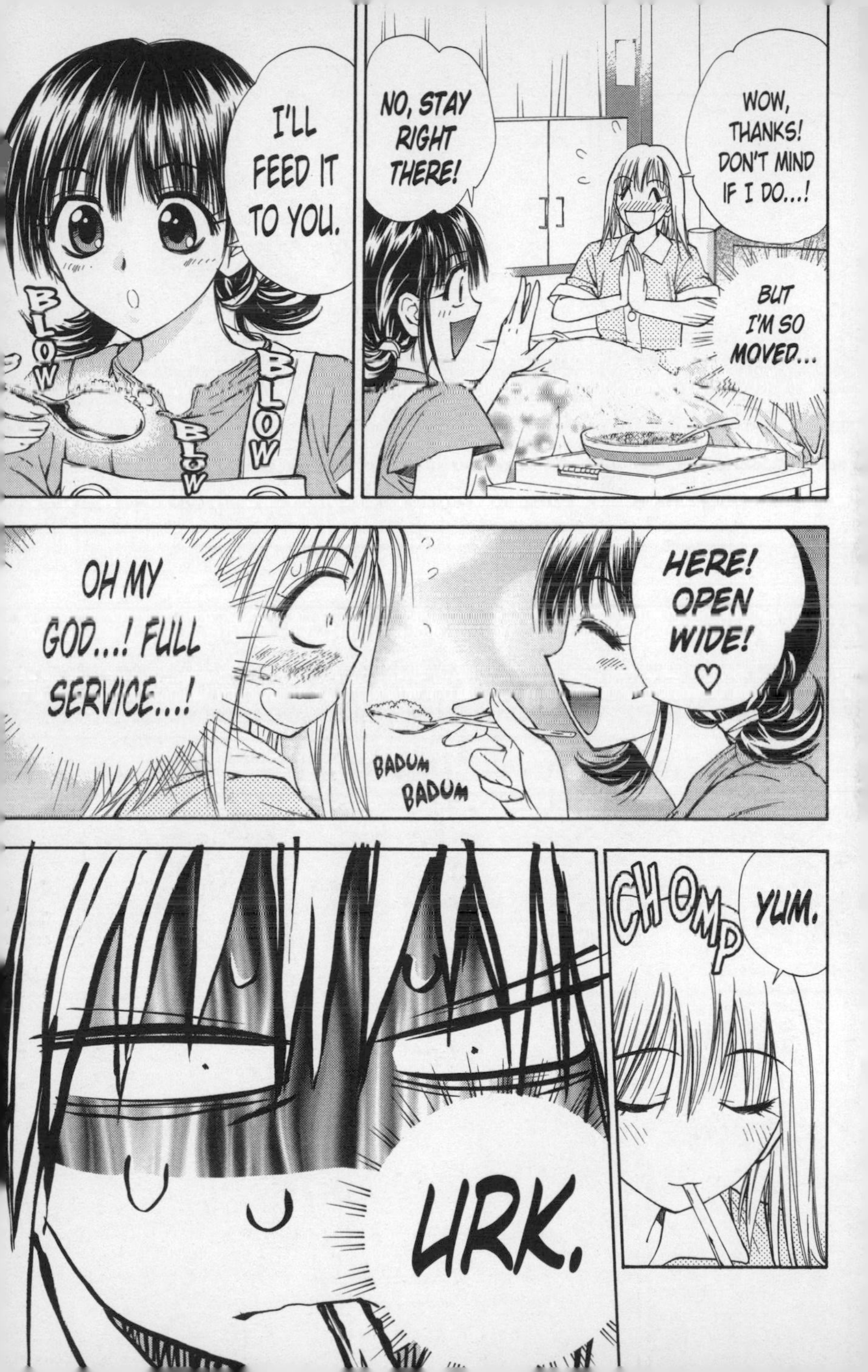
WOW, THANKS! DON'T MIND IF I DO...!
BUT I'M SO MOVED...
NO, STAY RIGHT THERE!
I'LL FEED IT TO YOU.
BLOW
BLOW
BLOW
HERE! OPEN WIDE! ♥
BADUM BADUM
OH MY GOD...! FULL SERVICE...!
CHOMP
YUM.
URK.

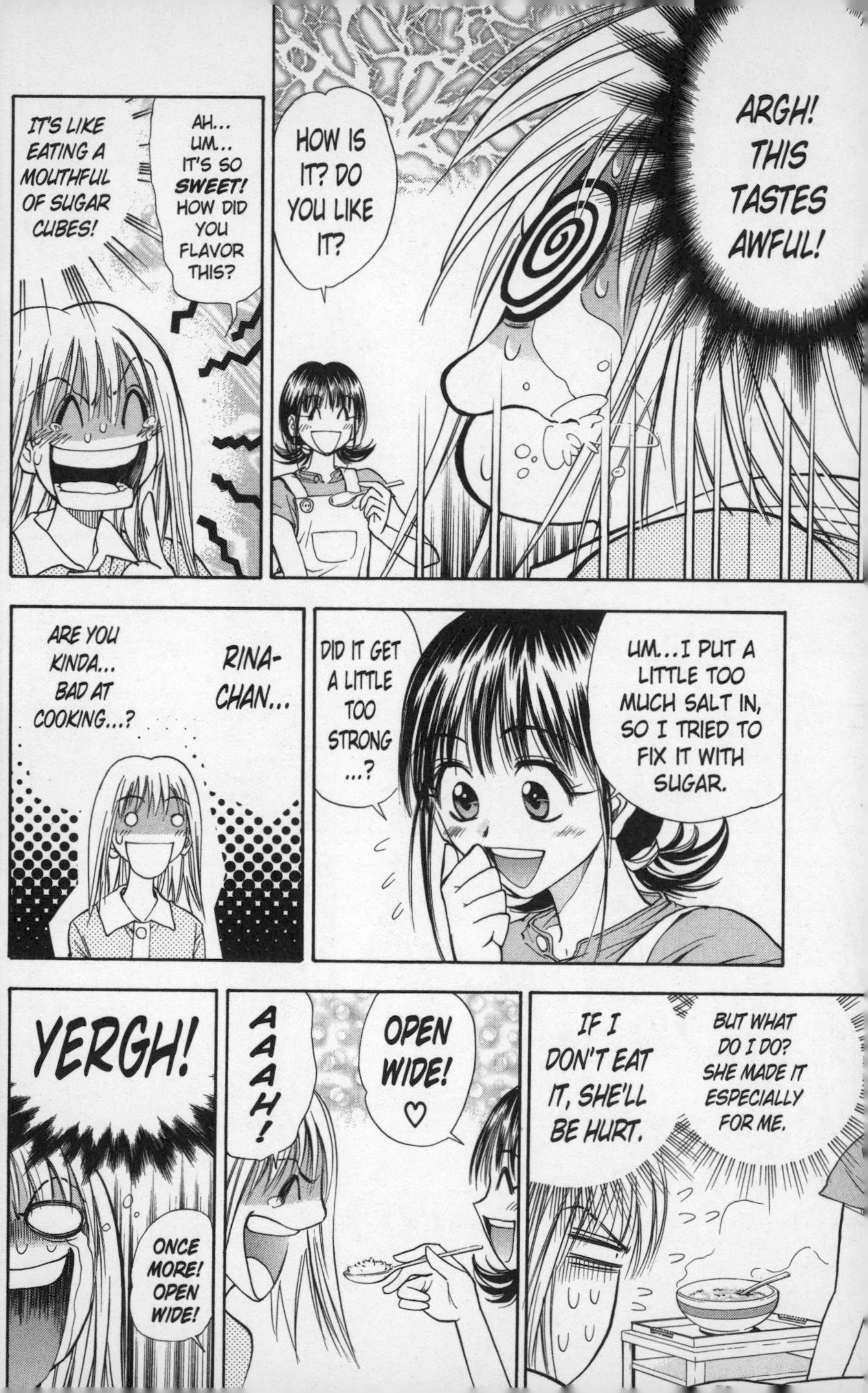
ARGH! THIS TASTES AWFUL!
HOW IS IT? DO YOU LIKE IT?
AH... UM... IT'S SO SWEET! HOW DID YOU FLAVOR THIS?
IT'S LIKE EATING A MOUTHFUL OF SUGAR CUBES!
UM...I PUT A LITTLE TOO MUCH SALT IN, SO I TRIED TO FIX IT WITH SUGAR.
DID IT GET A LITTLE TOO STRONG ...?
RINA-CHAN...
ARE YOU KINDA... BAD AT COOKING...?
BUT WHAT DO I DO? SHE MADE IT ESPECIALLY FOR ME.
IF I DON'T EAT IT, SHE'LL BE HURT.
OPEN WIDE! ♥
AAAH!
YERGH!
ONCE MORE! OPEN WIDE!

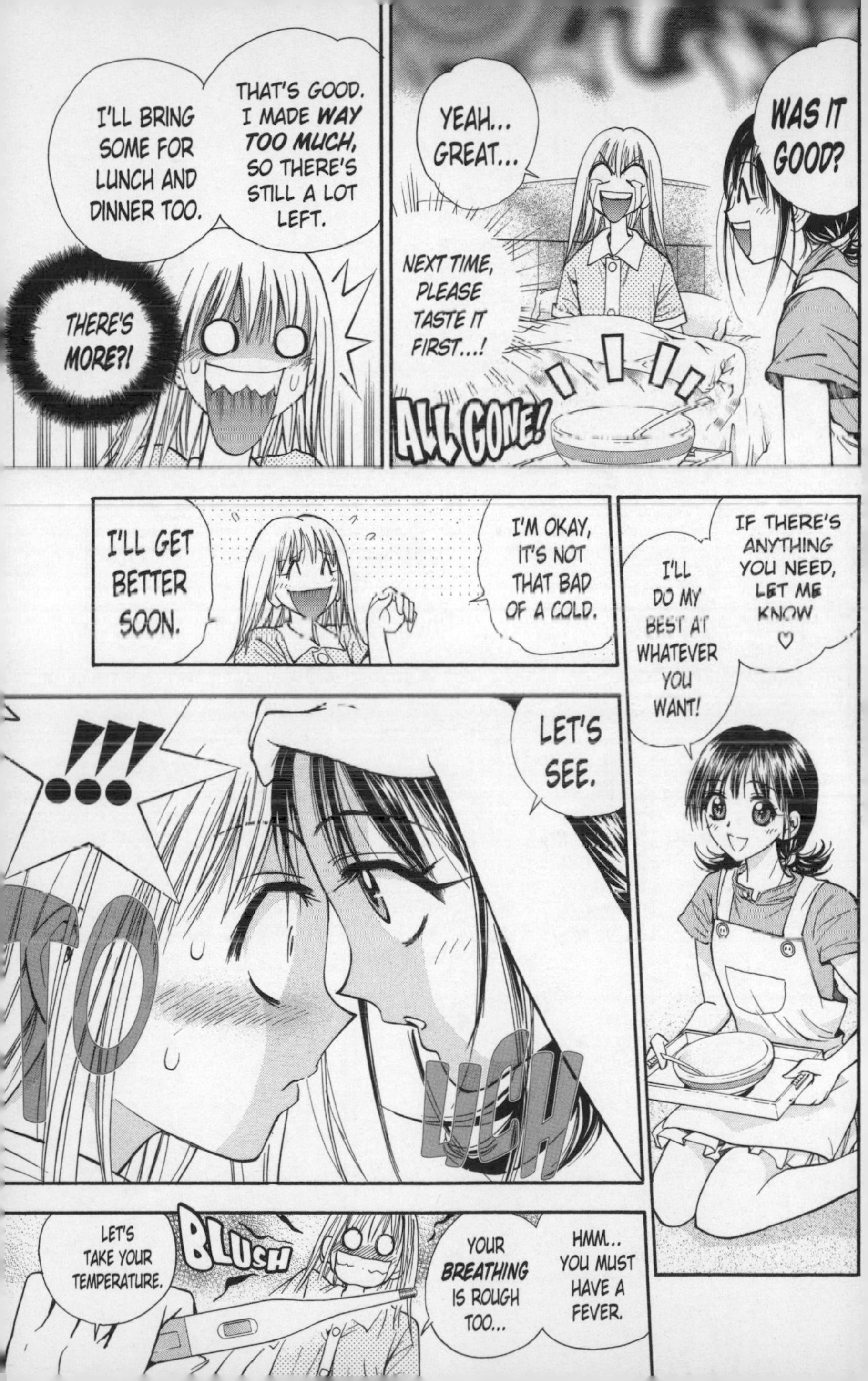
WAS IT GOOD?
YEAH... GREAT...
NEXT TIME, PLEASE TASTE IT FIRST...!
ALL GONE!
THAT'S GOOD. I MADE *WAY TOO MUCH,* SO THERE'S STILL A LOT LEFT.
I'LL BRING SOME FOR LUNCH AND DINNER TOO.
THERE'S MORE?!
IF THERE'S ANYTHING YOU NEED, LET ME KNOW ♡
I'LL DO MY BEST AT WHATEVER YOU WANT!
I'M OKAY, IT'S NOT THAT BAD OF A COLD.
I'LL GET BETTER SOON.
LET'S SEE.
...!!!
TOUCH
HMM... YOU MUST HAVE A FEVER.
YOUR *BREATHING* IS ROUGH TOO...
BLUSH
LET'S TAKE YOUR TEMPERATURE.

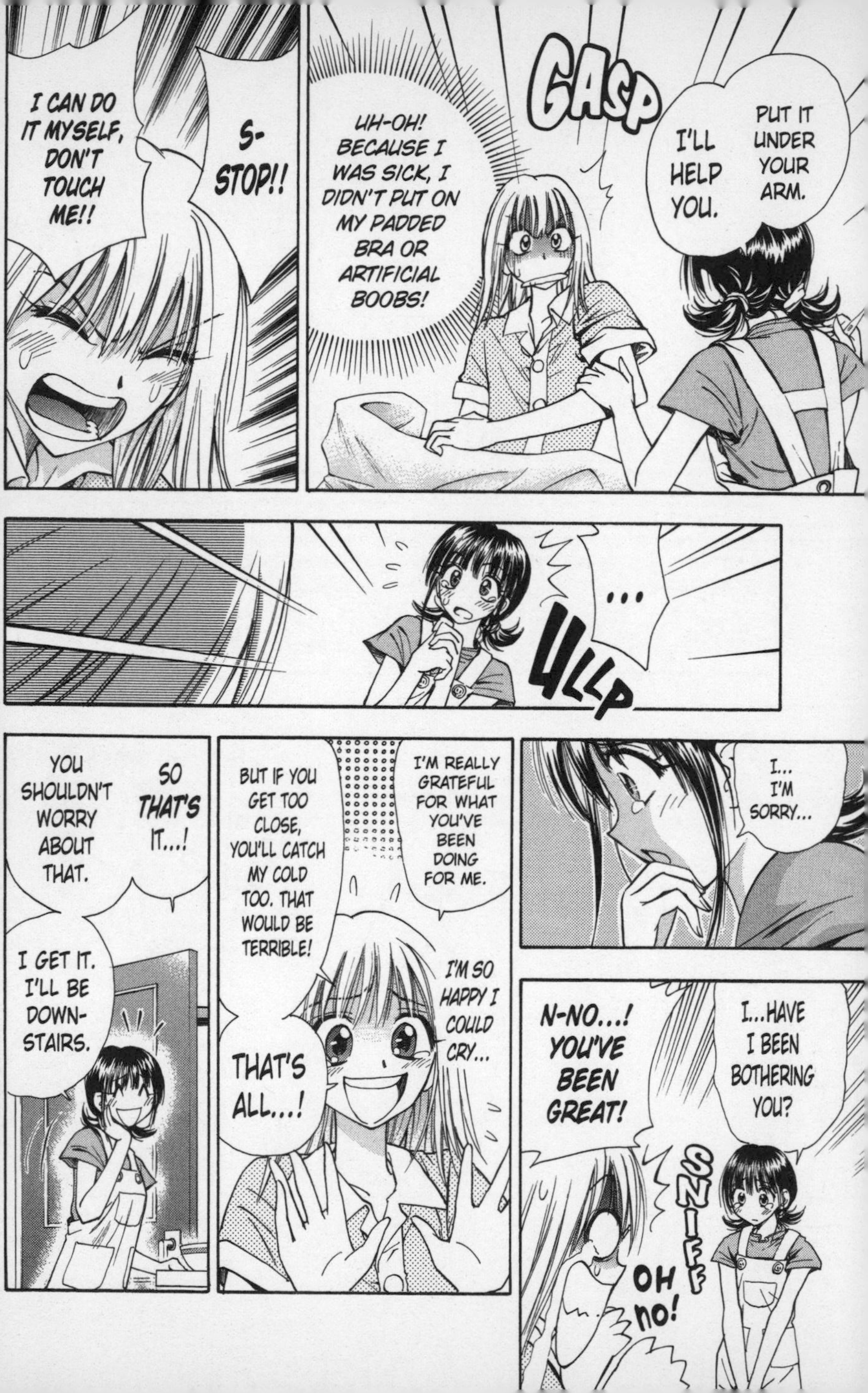

I'LL HELP YOU. PUT IT UNDER YOUR ARM.
GASP
UH-OH! BECAUSE I WAS SICK, I DIDN'T PUT ON MY PADDED BRA OR ARTIFICIAL BOOBS!
S-STOP!!
I CAN DO IT MYSELF, DON'T TOUCH ME!!
...
ULLP
I... I'M SORRY...
I...HAVE I BEEN BOTHERING YOU?
SNIFF
N-NO...! YOU'VE BEEN GREAT!
OH no!
I'M REALLY GRATEFUL FOR WHAT YOU'VE BEEN DOING FOR ME.
BUT IF YOU GET TOO CLOSE, YOU'LL CATCH MY COLD TOO. THAT WOULD BE TERRIBLE!
I'M SO HAPPY I COULD CRY...
THAT'S ALL...!
SO THAT'S IT...!
YOU SHOULDN'T WORRY ABOUT THAT.
I GET IT. I'LL BE DOWN-STAIRS.

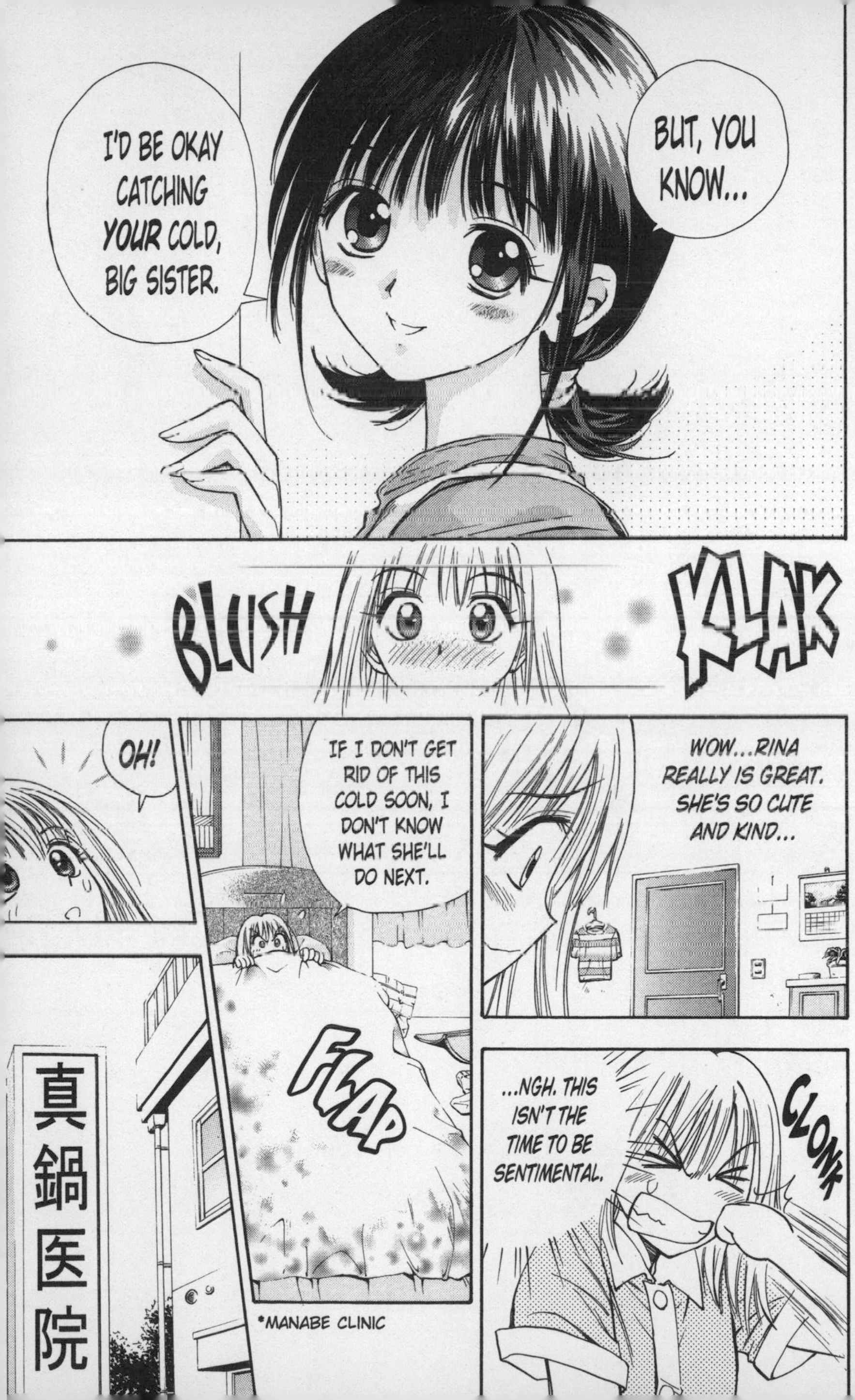
BUT, YOU KNOW...
I'D BE OKAY CATCHING YOUR COLD, BIG SISTER.
KLAK
BLUSH
WOW...RINA REALLY IS GREAT. SHE'S SO CUTE AND KIND...
CLONK
...NGH. THIS ISN'T THE TIME TO BE SENTIMENTAL.
IF I DON'T GET RID OF THIS COLD SOON, I DON'T KNOW WHAT SHE'LL DO NEXT.
FLAP
OH!
真鍋医院
*MANABE CLINIC

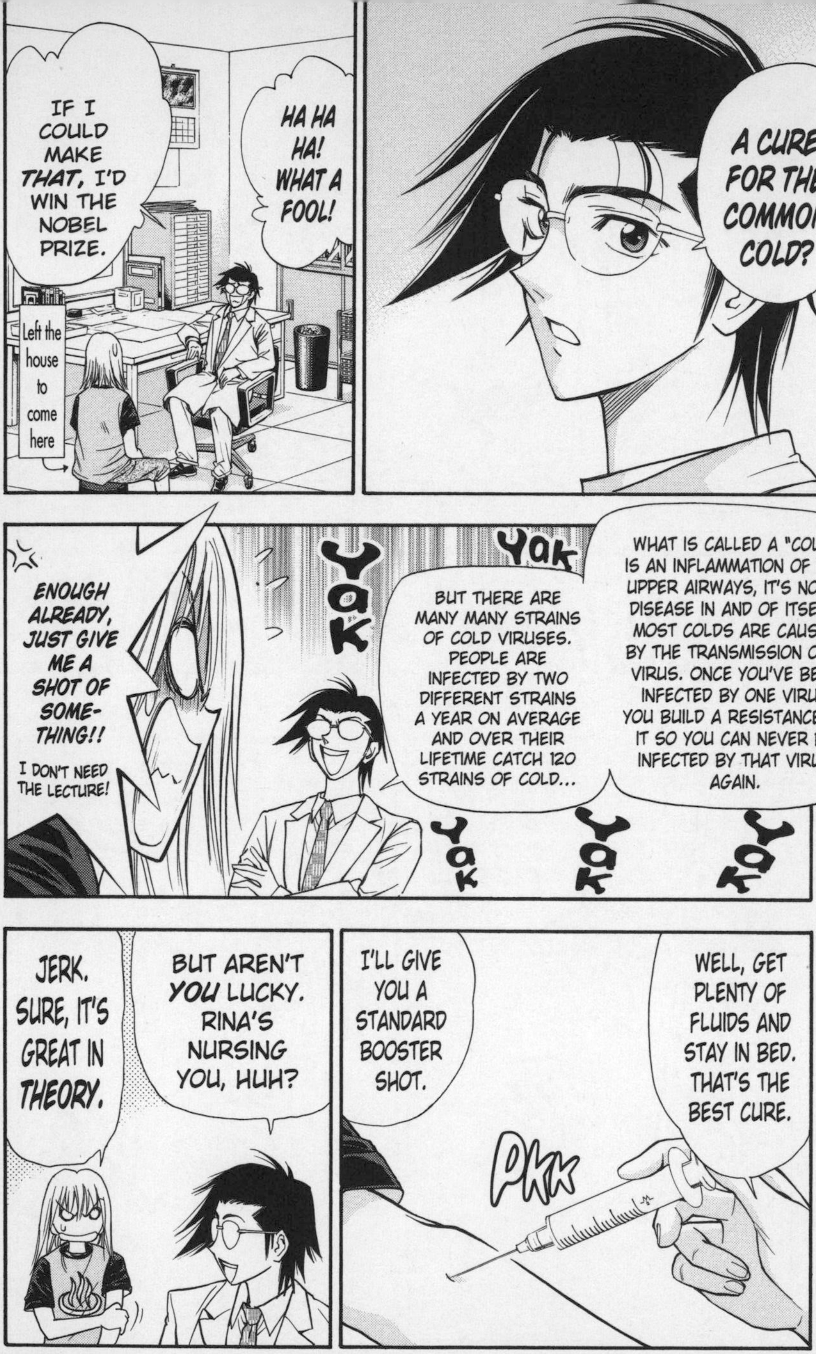
A CURE FOR THE COMMON COLD?
HA HA HA! WHAT A FOOL!
IF I COULD MAKE THAT, I'D WIN THE NOBEL PRIZE.
Left the house to come here
WHAT IS CALLED A "COLD" IS AN INFLAMMATION OF THE UPPER AIRWAYS, IT'S NOT A DISEASE IN AND OF ITSELF. MOST COLDS ARE CAUSED BY THE TRANSMISSION OF A VIRUS. ONCE YOU'VE BEEN INFECTED BY ONE VIRUS YOU BUILD A RESISTANCE TO IT SO YOU CAN NEVER BE INFECTED BY THAT VIRUS AGAIN.
Yak
BUT THERE ARE MANY MANY STRAINS OF COLD VIRUSES. PEOPLE ARE INFECTED BY TWO DIFFERENT STRAINS A YEAR ON AVERAGE AND OVER THEIR LIFETIME CATCH 120 STRAINS OF COLD...
Yak
Yak
Yak
Yak
ENOUGH ALREADY, JUST GIVE ME A SHOT OF SOME-THING!!
I DON'T NEED THE LECTURE!
WELL, GET PLENTY OF FLUIDS AND STAY IN BED. THAT'S THE BEST CURE.
I'LL GIVE YOU A STANDARD BOOSTER SHOT.
Pkk
BUT AREN'T YOU LUCKY. RINA'S NURSING YOU, HUH?
JERK. SURE, IT'S GREAT IN THEORY.

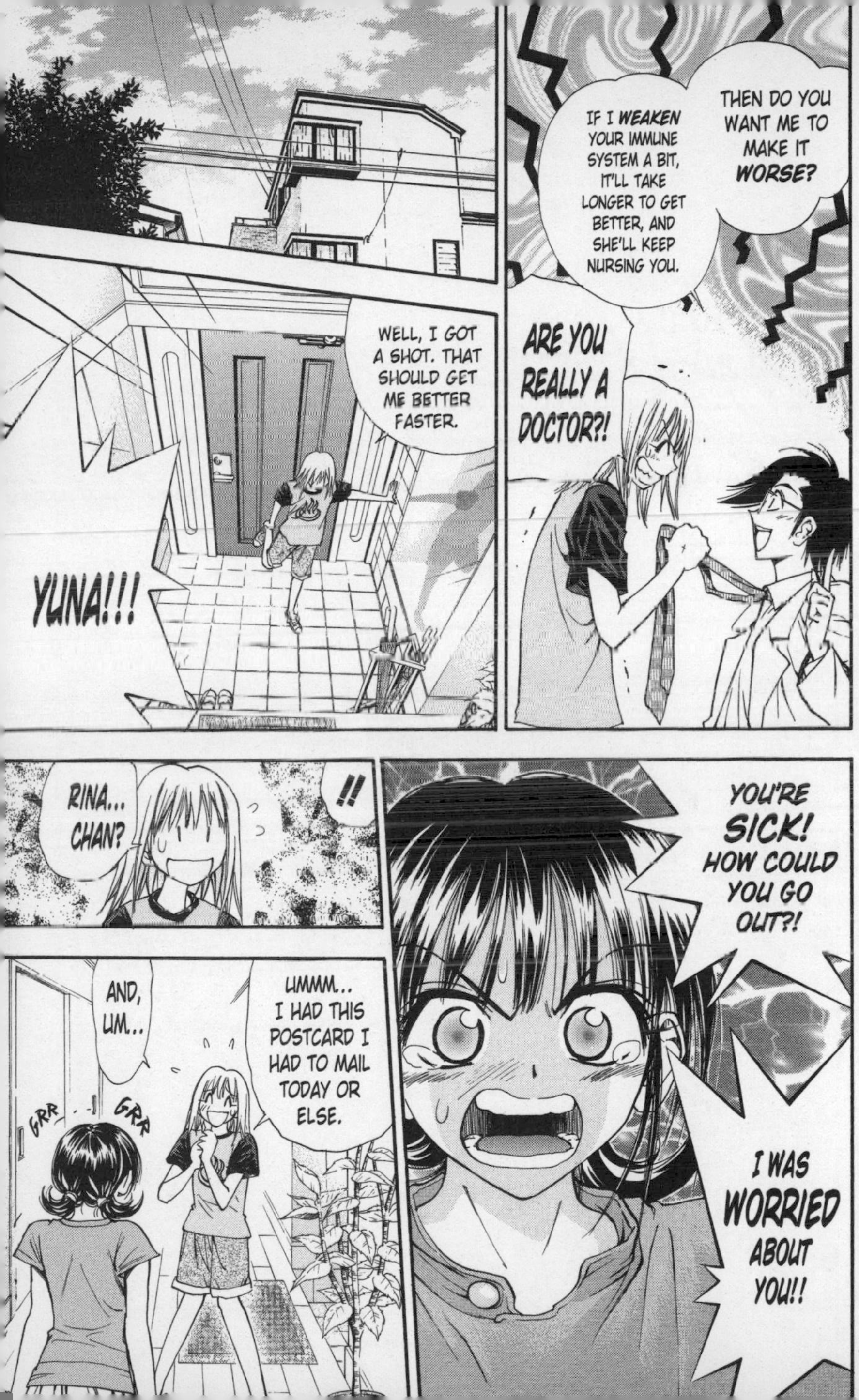
THEN DO YOU WANT ME TO MAKE IT WORSE?
IF I WEAKEN YOUR IMMUNE SYSTEM A BIT, IT'LL TAKE LONGER TO GET BETTER, AND SHE'LL KEEP NURSING YOU.
ARE YOU REALLY A DOCTOR?!
WELL, I GOT A SHOT. THAT SHOULD GET ME BETTER FASTER.
YUNA!!!
YOU'RE SICK! HOW COULD YOU GO OUT?!
I WAS WORRIED ABOUT YOU!!
!!
RINA... CHAN?
UMMM... I HAD THIS POSTCARD I HAD TO MAIL TODAY OR ELSE.
AND, UM...
GRR
GRR

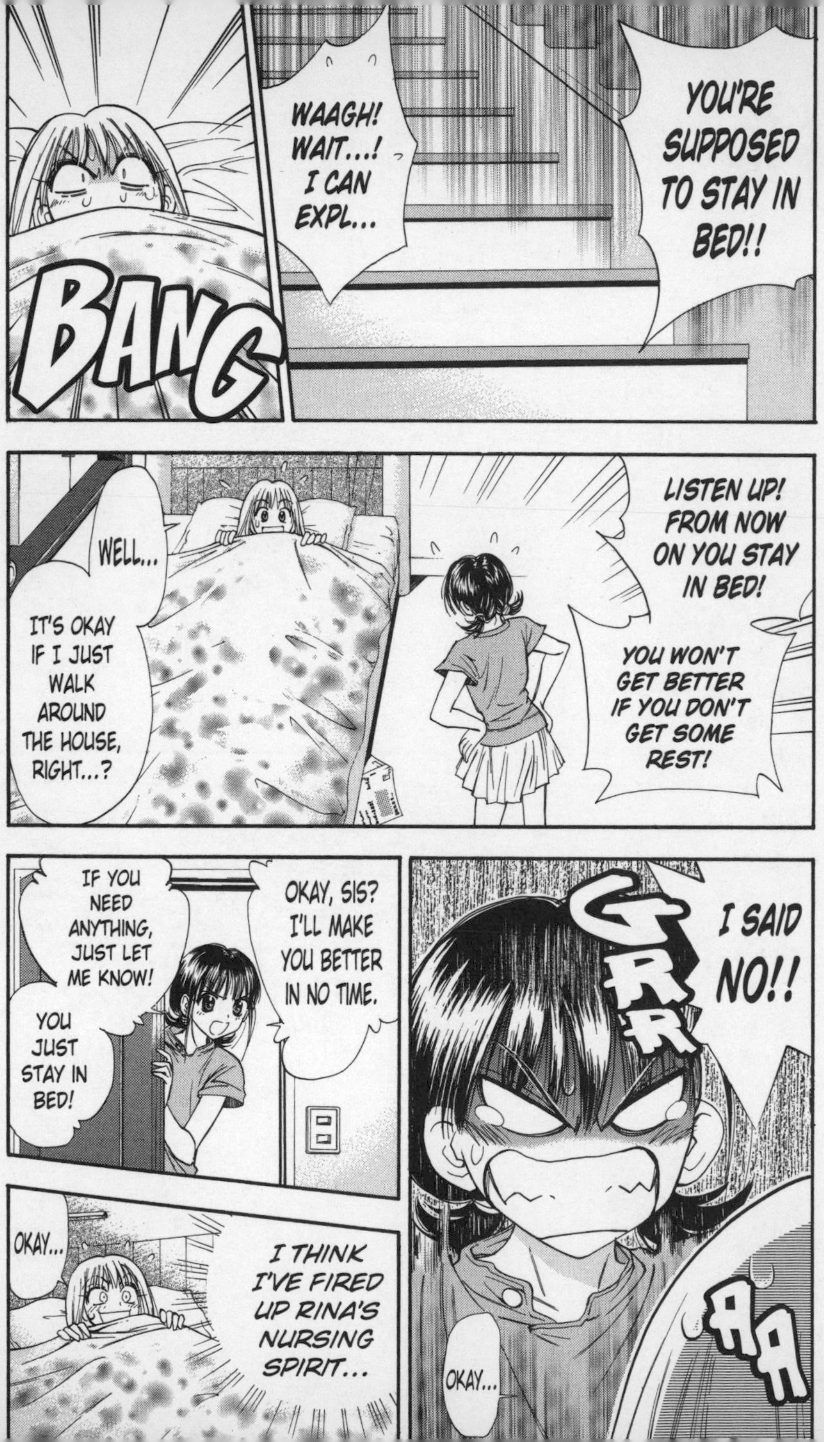
YOU'RE SUPPOSED TO STAY IN BED!!
WAAGH! WAIT...! I CAN EXPL...
BANG
LISTEN UP! FROM NOW ON YOU STAY IN BED!
YOU WON'T GET BETTER IF YOU DON'T GET SOME REST!
WELL...
IT'S OKAY IF I JUST WALK AROUND THE HOUSE, RIGHT...?
GRR
I SAID NO!!
AA
OKAY...
OKAY, SIS? I'LL MAKE YOU BETTER IN NO TIME.
IF YOU NEED ANYTHING, JUST LET ME KNOW!
YOU JUST STAY IN BED!
I THINK I'VE FIRED UP RINA'S NURSING SPIRIT...
OKAY...

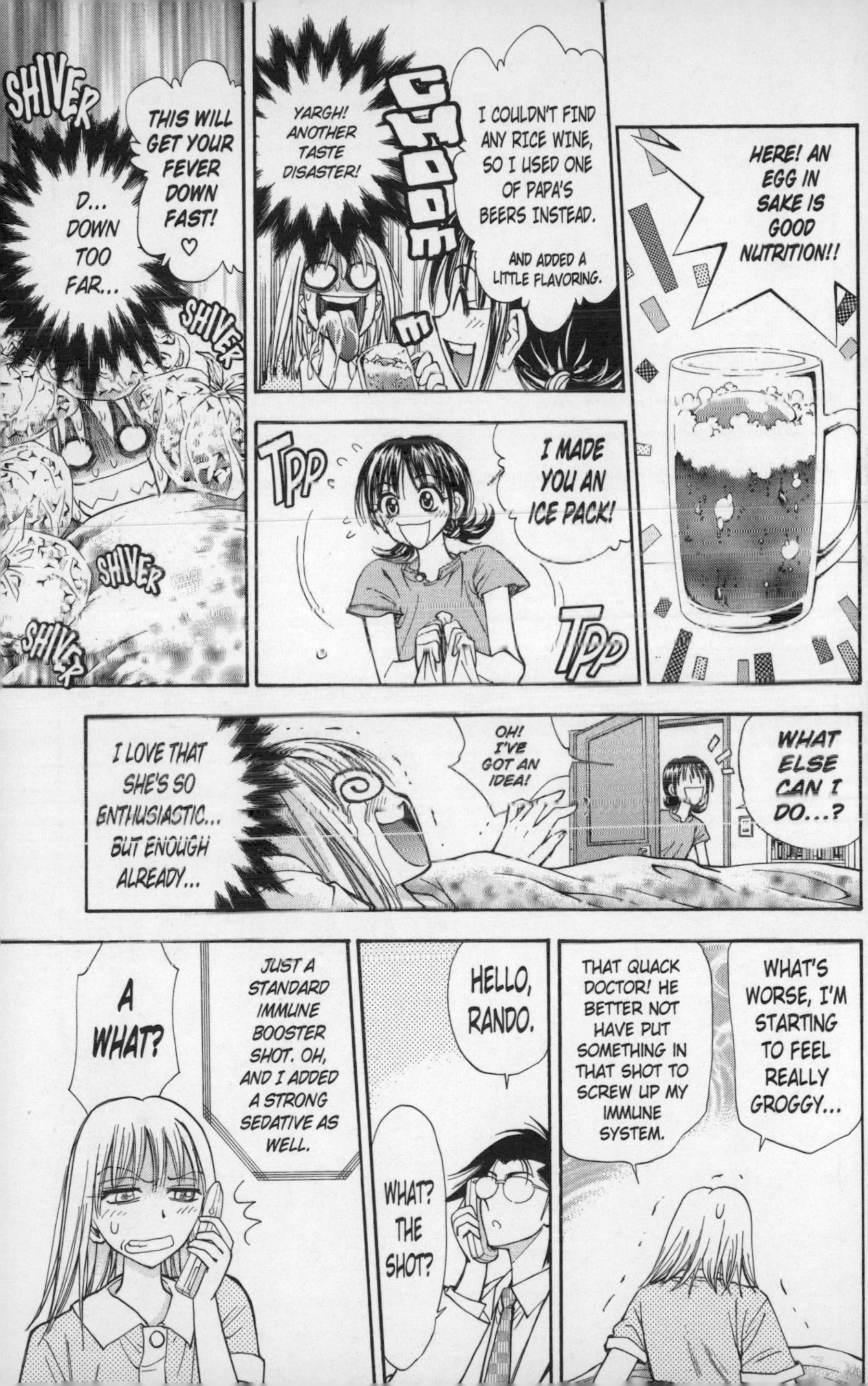
HERE! AN EGG IN SAKE IS GOOD NUTRITION!!
I COULDN'T FIND ANY RICE WINE, SO I USED ONE OF PAPA'S BEERS INSTEAD.
AND ADDED A LITTLE FLAVORING.
CHOOM
YARGH! ANOTHER TASTE DISASTER!
I MADE YOU AN ICE PACK!
TPP
TPP
SHIVER
THIS WILL GET YOUR FEVER DOWN FAST! ♡
D... DOWN TOO FAR...
SHIVER
SHIVER
SHIVER
WHAT ELSE CAN I DO...?
OH! I'VE GOT AN IDEA!
I LOVE THAT SHE'S SO ENTHUSIASTIC... BUT ENOUGH ALREADY...
WHAT'S WORSE, I'M STARTING TO FEEL REALLY GROGGY...
THAT QUACK DOCTOR! HE BETTER NOT HAVE PUT SOMETHING IN THAT SHOT TO SCREW UP MY IMMUNE SYSTEM.
HELLO, RANDO.
WHAT? THE SHOT?
JUST A STANDARD IMMUNE BOOSTER SHOT. OH, AND I ADDED A STRONG SEDATIVE AS WELL.
A WHAT?

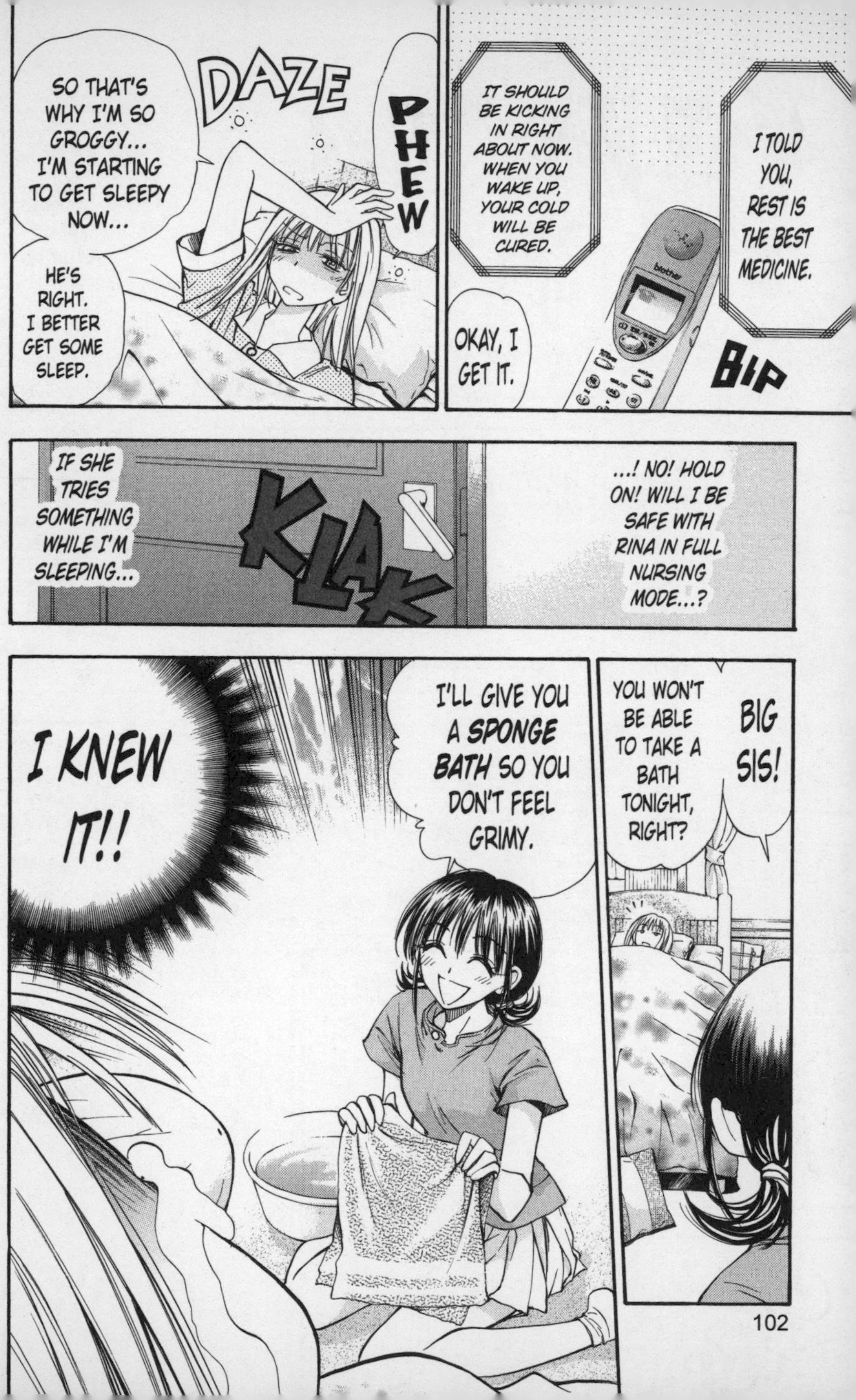
I TOLD YOU, REST IS THE BEST MEDICINE.
IT SHOULD BE KICKING IN RIGHT ABOUT NOW. WHEN YOU WAKE UP, YOUR COLD WILL BE CURED.
OKAY, I GET IT.
BIP
PHEW
DAZE
SO THAT'S WHY I'M SO GROGGY... I'M STARTING TO GET SLEEPY NOW...
HE'S RIGHT. I BETTER GET SOME SLEEP.
...! NO! HOLD ON! WILL I BE SAFE WITH RINA IN FULL NURSING MODE...?
KLAK
IF SHE TRIES SOMETHING WHILE I'M SLEEPING...
BIG SIS!
YOU WON'T BE ABLE TO TAKE A BATH TONIGHT, RIGHT?
I'LL GIVE YOU A **SPONGE BATH** SO YOU DON'T FEEL GRIMY.
I KNEW IT!!

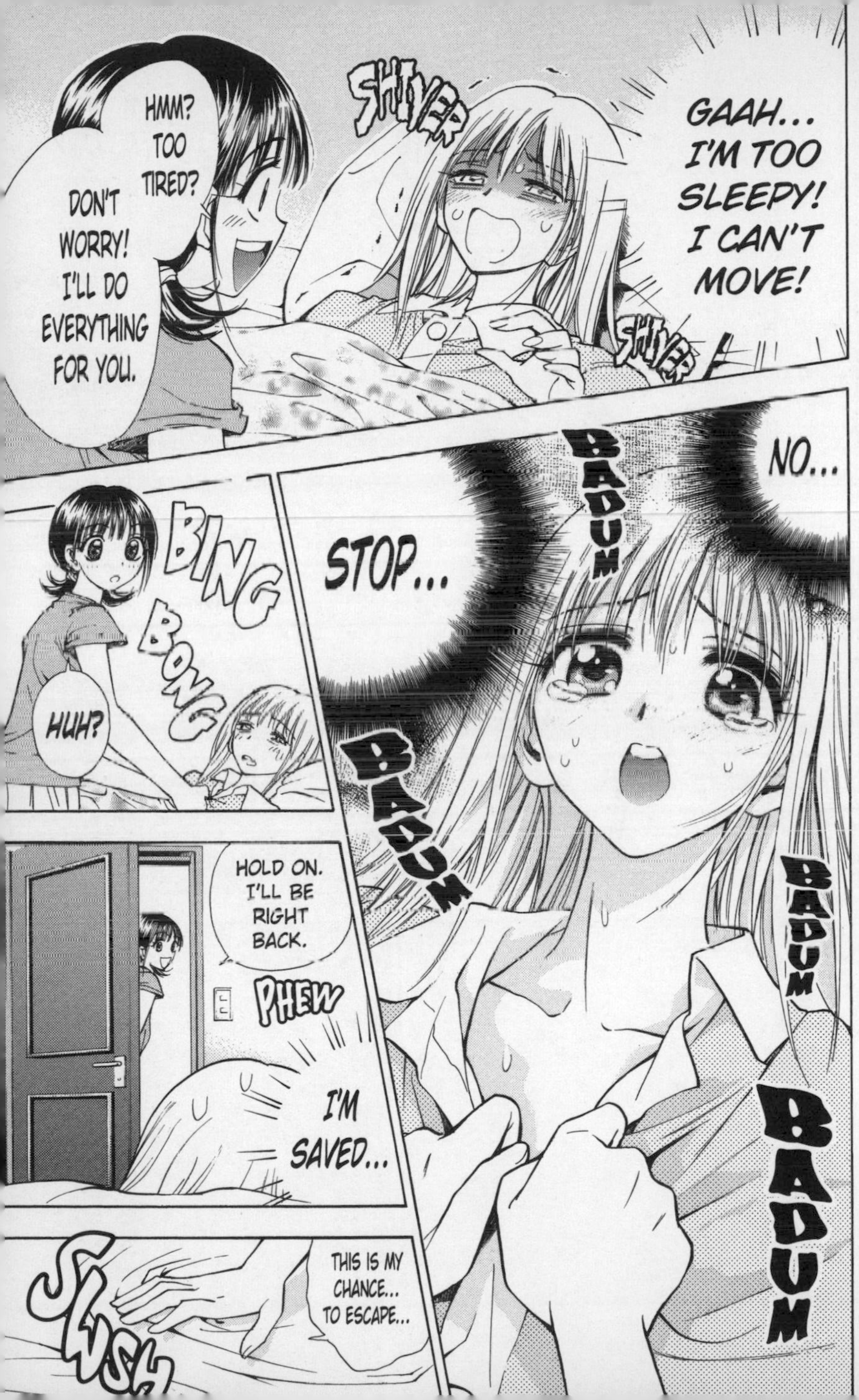
GAAH... I'M TOO SLEEPY! I CAN'T MOVE!
SHIVER
SHIVER
HMM? TOO TIRED?
DON'T WORRY! I'LL DO EVERYTHING FOR YOU.
NO...
BADUM
STOP...
BADUM
BADUM
BADUM
BING BONG
HUH?
HOLD ON. I'LL BE RIGHT BACK.
PHEW
I'M SAVED...
THIS IS MY CHANCE... TO ESCAPE...
SLUSH

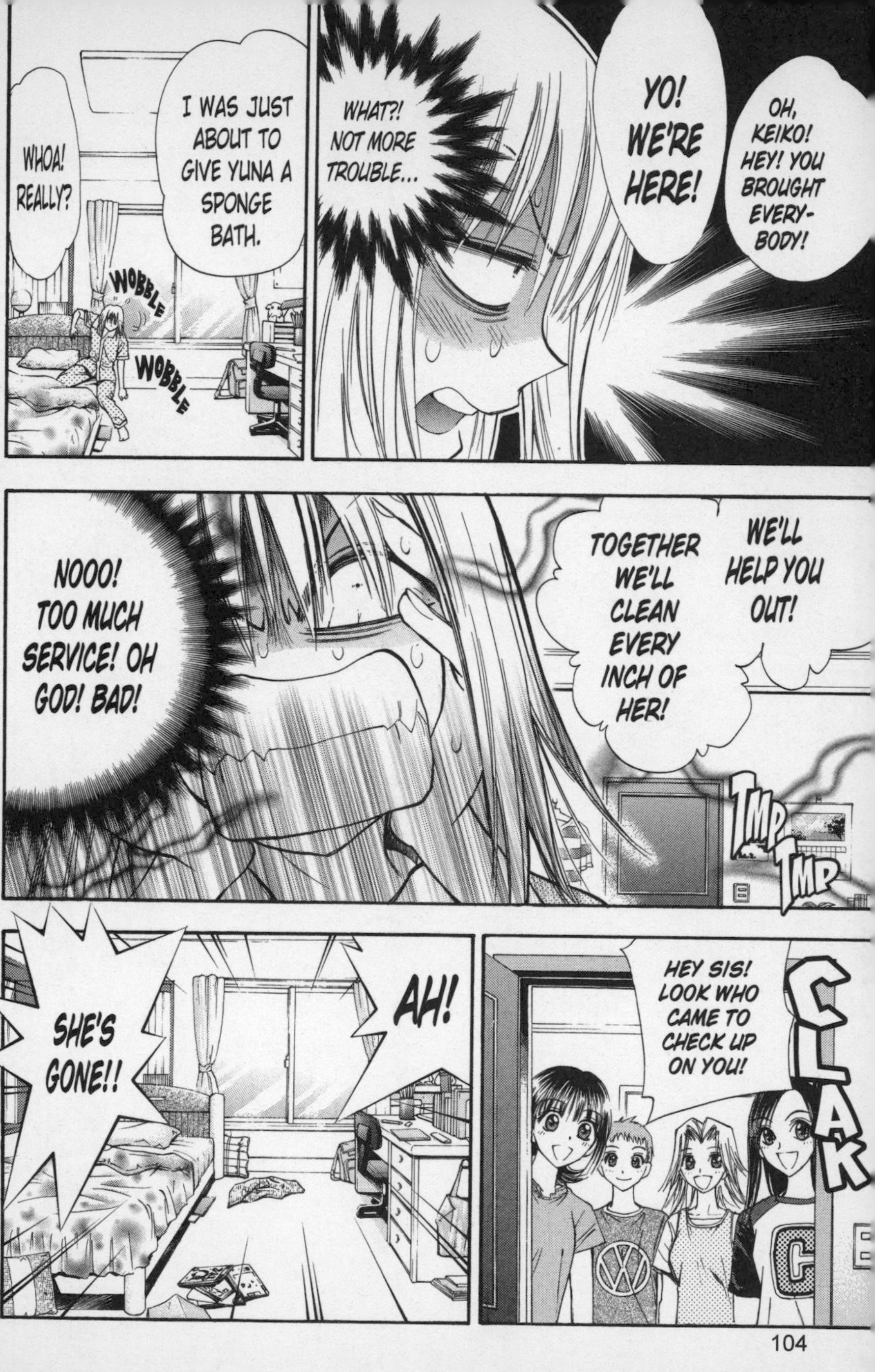
OH, KEIKO! HEY! YOU BROUGHT EVERY-BODY!
YO! WE'RE HERE!
WHAT?! NOT MORE TROUBLE...
I WAS JUST ABOUT TO GIVE YUNA A SPONGE BATH.
WHOA! REALLY?
WOBBLE
WOBBLE
WE'LL HELP YOU OUT!
TOGETHER WE'LL CLEAN EVERY INCH OF HER!
NOOO! TOO MUCH SERVICE! OH GOD! BAD!
TMP
TMP
CLAK
HEY SIS! LOOK WHO CAME TO CHECK UP ON YOU!
AH!
SHE'S GONE!!

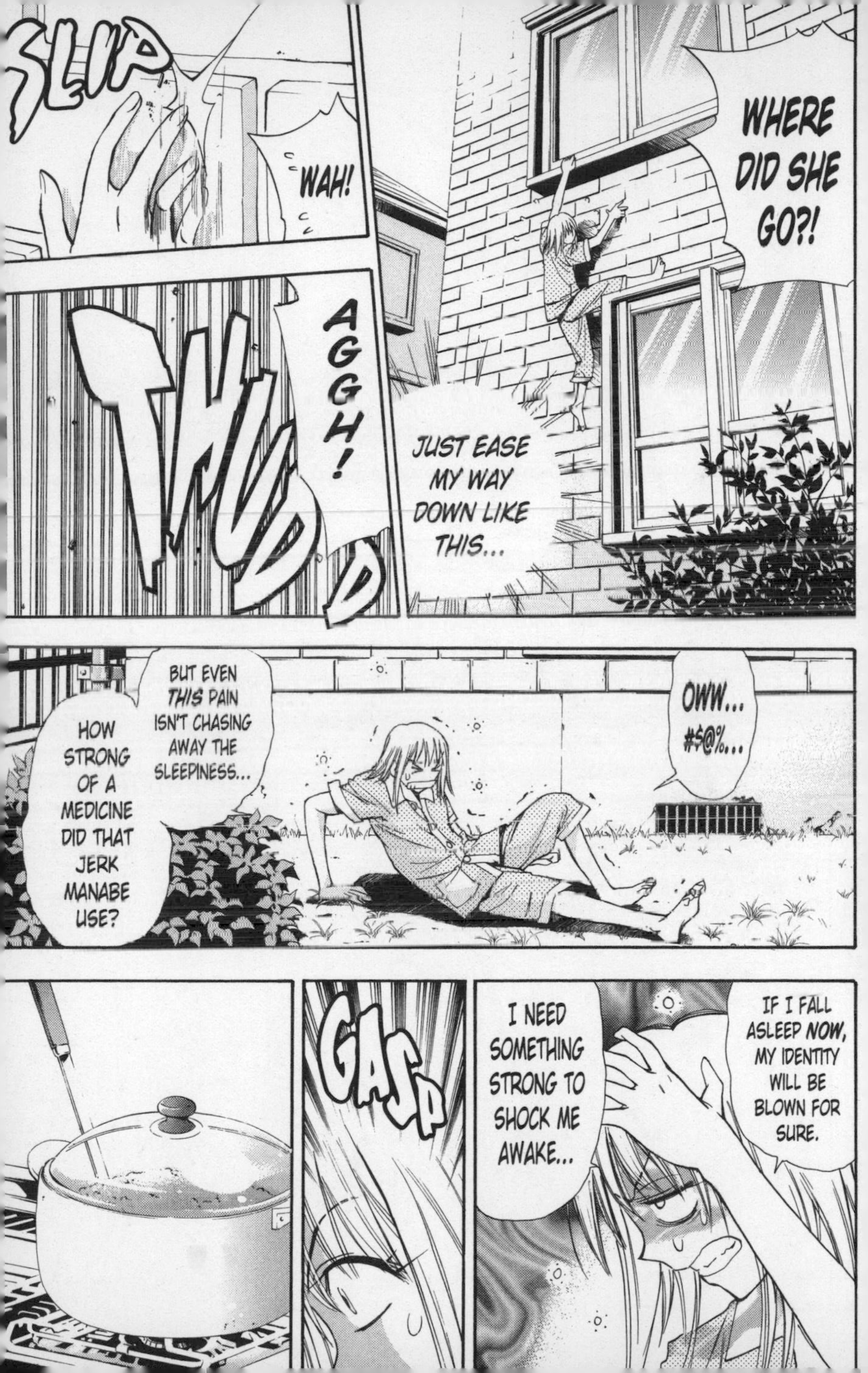
WHERE DID SHE GO?!
JUST EASE MY WAY DOWN LIKE THIS...
SLIP
WAH!
AGGH!
THUD
OWW... #$@%...
BUT EVEN *THIS* PAIN ISN'T CHASING AWAY THE SLEEPINESS...
HOW STRONG OF A MEDICINE DID THAT JERK MANABE USE?
IF I FALL ASLEEP *NOW*, MY IDENTITY WILL BE BLOWN FOR SURE.
I NEED SOMETHING STRONG TO SHOCK ME AWAKE...
GASP

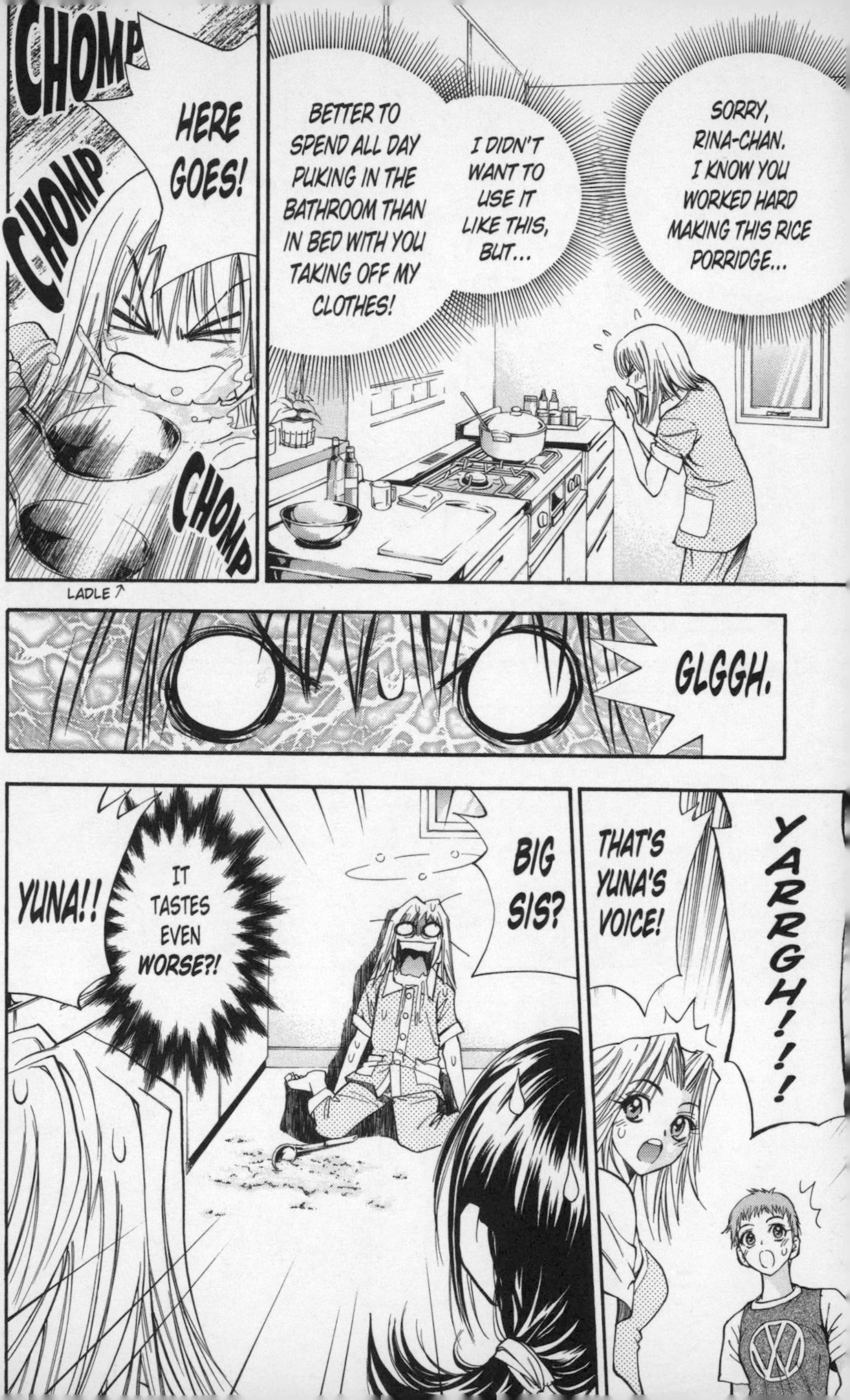
SORRY, RINA-CHAN. I KNOW YOU WORKED HARD MAKING THIS RICE PORRIDGE...
I DIDN'T WANT TO USE IT LIKE THIS, BUT...
BETTER TO SPEND ALL DAY PUKING IN THE BATHROOM THAN IN BED WITH YOU TAKING OFF MY CLOTHES!
HERE GOES!
CHOMP
CHOMP
CHOMP
LADLE
GLGGH.
YARRGH!!!
THAT'S YUNA'S VOICE!
BIG SIS?
IT TASTES EVEN WORSE?!
YUNA!!

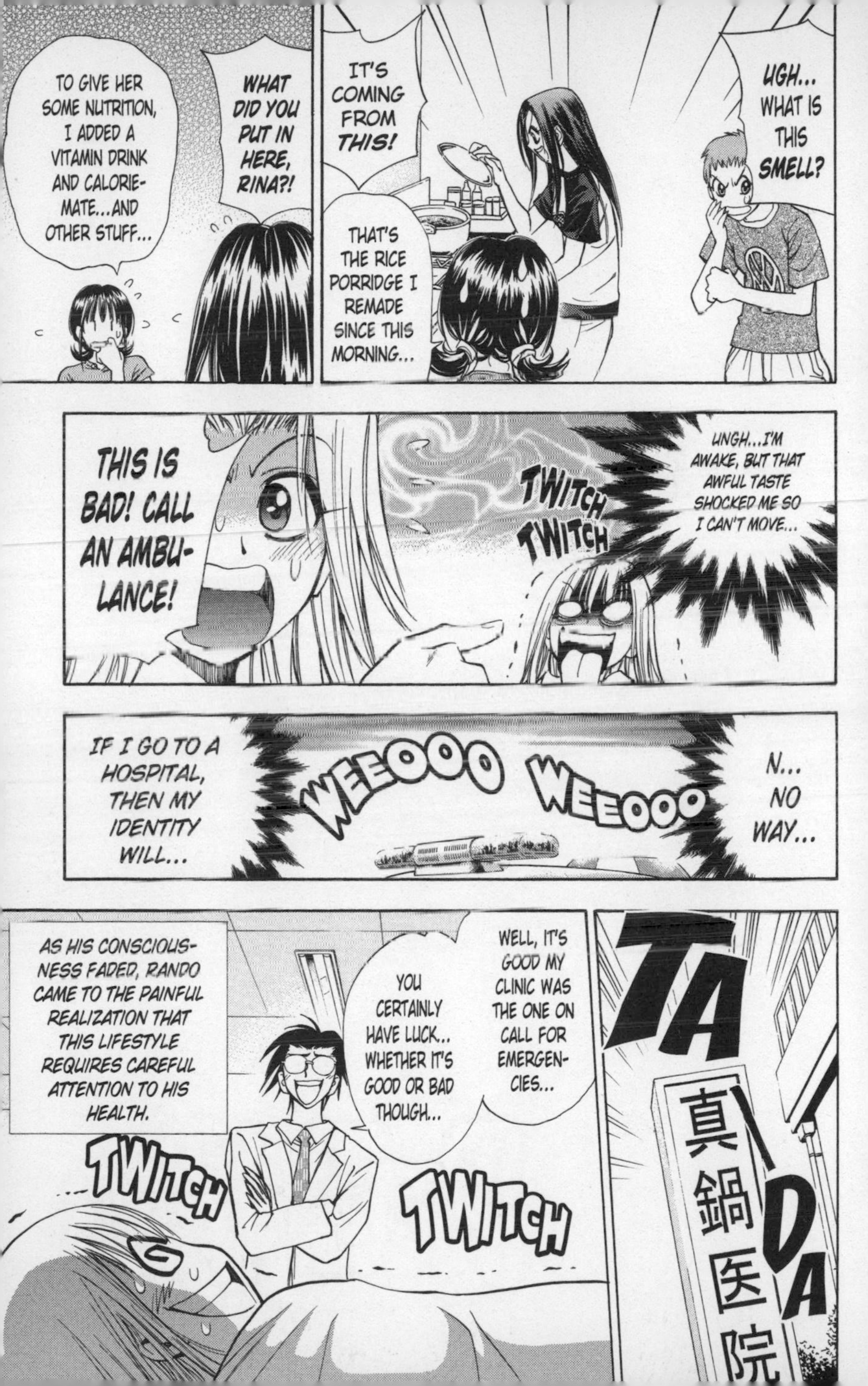
UGH... WHAT IS THIS SMELL?
IT'S COMING FROM THIS!
THAT'S THE RICE PORRIDGE I REMADE SINCE THIS MORNING...
WHAT DID YOU PUT IN HERE, RINA?!
TO GIVE HER SOME NUTRITION, I ADDED A VITAMIN DRINK AND CALORIE-MATE...AND OTHER STUFF...
UNGH...I'M AWAKE, BUT THAT AWFUL TASTE SHOCKED ME SO I CAN'T MOVE...
TWITCH TWITCH
THIS IS BAD! CALL AN AMBU-LANCE!
N... NO WAY...
WEEOOO WEEOOO
IF I GO TO A HOSPITAL, THEN MY IDENTITY WILL...
TA DA
真鍋医院
WELL, IT'S GOOD MY CLINIC WAS THE ONE ON CALL FOR EMERGEN-CIES...
YOU CERTAINLY HAVE LUCK... WHETHER IT'S GOOD OR BAD THOUGH...
AS HIS CONSCIOUS-NESS FADED, RANDO CAME TO THE PAINFUL REALIZATION THAT THIS LIFESTYLE REQUIRES CAREFUL ATTENTION TO HIS HEALTH.
TWITCH
TWITCH

Pretty Face

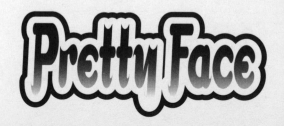

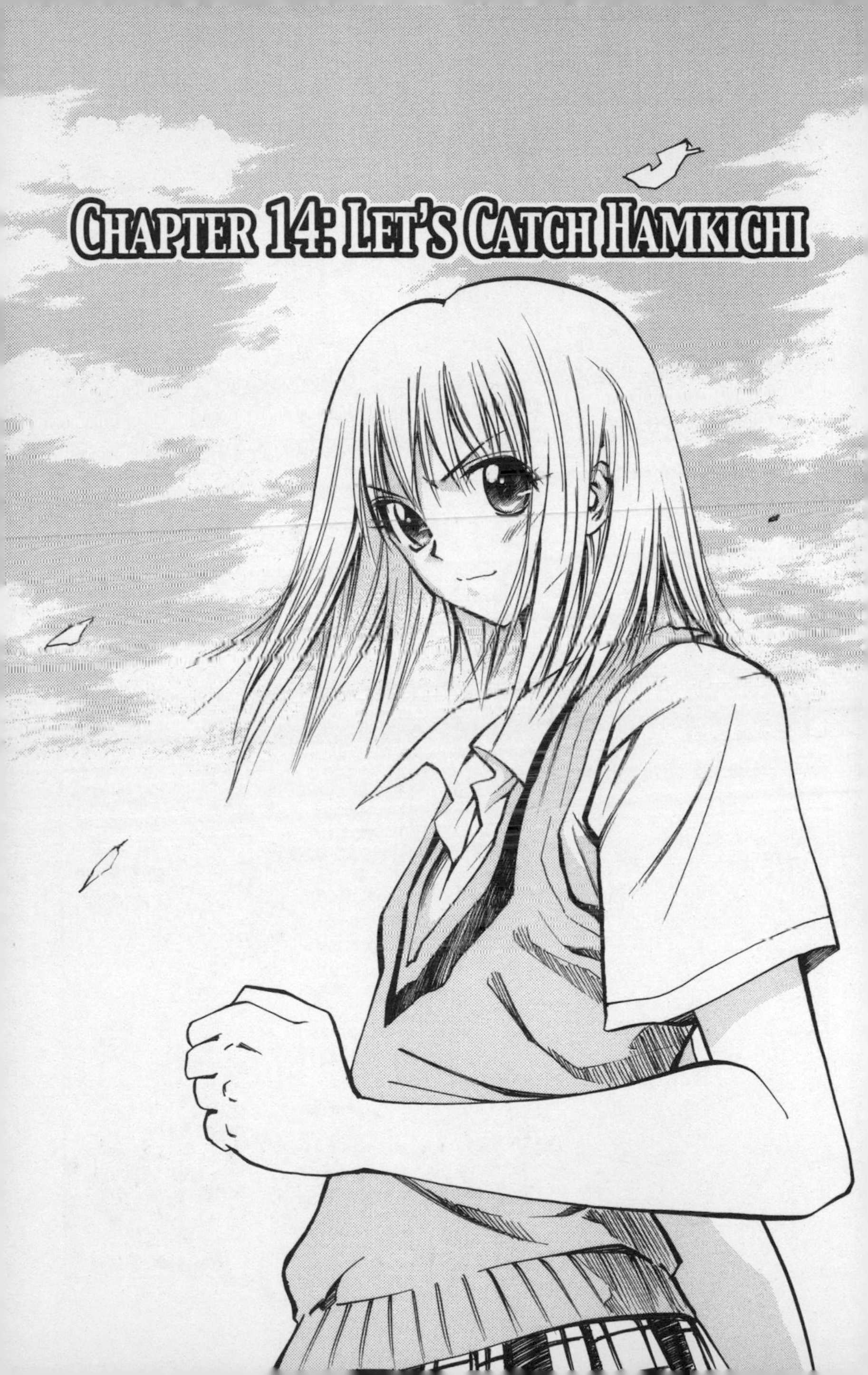
Chapter 14: Let's Catch Hamkichi

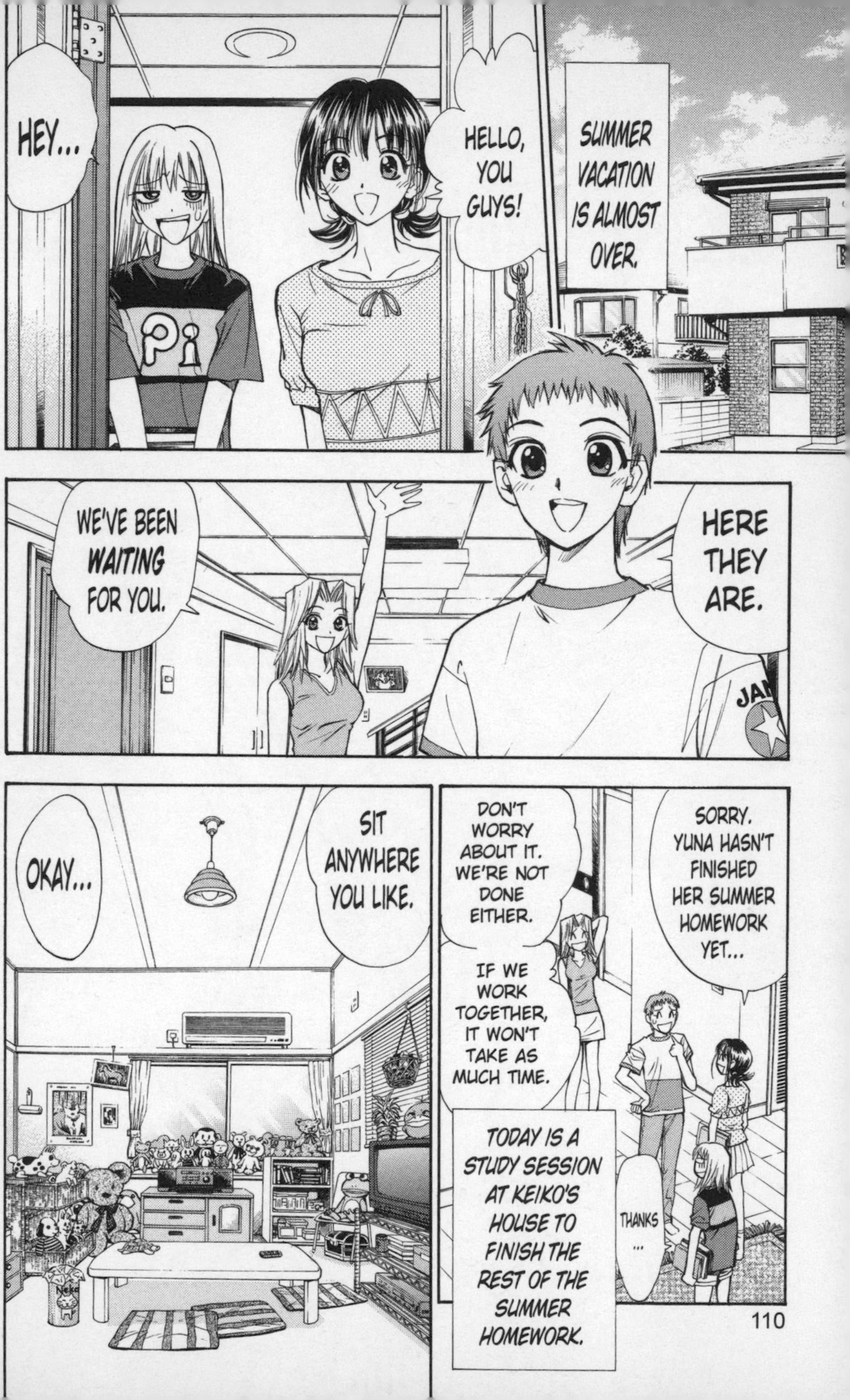
SUMMER VACATION IS ALMOST OVER.
HELLO, YOU GUYS!
HEY...
HERE THEY ARE.
WE'VE BEEN WAITING FOR YOU.
SORRY. YUNA HASN'T FINISHED HER SUMMER HOMEWORK YET...
DON'T WORRY ABOUT IT. WE'RE NOT DONE EITHER.
IF WE WORK TOGETHER, IT WON'T TAKE AS MUCH TIME.
THANKS...
TODAY IS A STUDY SESSION AT KEIKO'S HOUSE TO FINISH THE REST OF THE SUMMER HOMEWORK.
SIT ANYWHERE YOU LIKE.
OKAY...

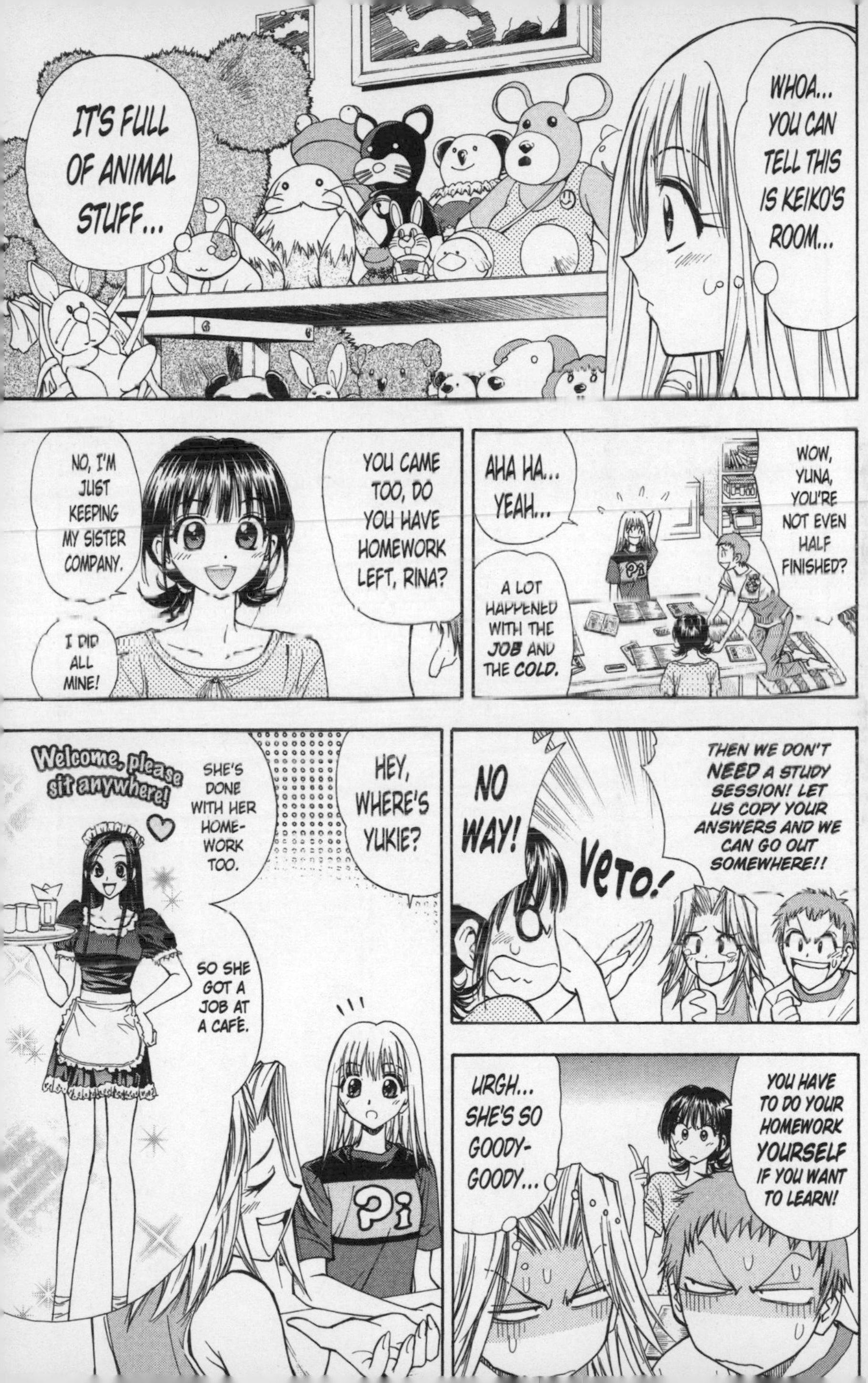
WHOA... YOU CAN TELL THIS IS KEIKO'S ROOM...
IT'S FULL OF ANIMAL STUFF...
WOW, YUNA, YOU'RE NOT EVEN HALF FINISHED?
AHA HA... YEAH...
A LOT HAPPENED WITH THE JOB AND THE COLD.
YOU CAME TOO, DO YOU HAVE HOMEWORK LEFT, RINA?
NO, I'M JUST KEEPING MY SISTER COMPANY.
I DID ALL MINE!
THEN WE DON'T NEED A STUDY SESSION! LET US COPY YOUR ANSWERS AND WE CAN GO OUT SOMEWHERE!!
NO WAY!
VETO!
YOU HAVE TO DO YOUR HOMEWORK YOURSELF IF YOU WANT TO LEARN!
URGH... SHE'S SO GOODY-GOODY...
HEY, WHERE'S YUKIE?
SHE'S DONE WITH HER HOME-WORK TOO.
Welcome, please sit anywhere!
SO SHE GOT A JOB AT A CAFÉ.

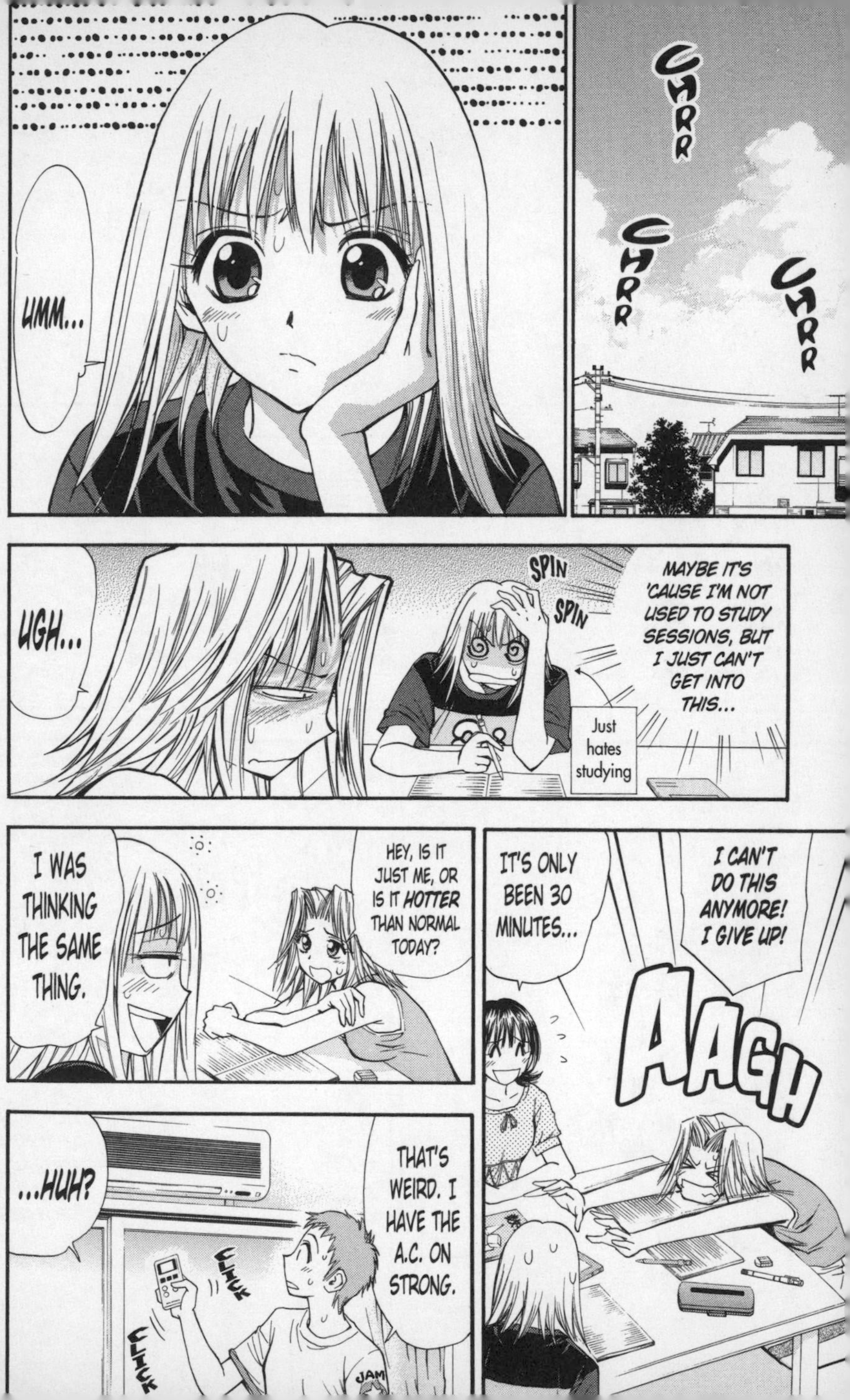
CHRR
CHRR
CHRR
UMM...
MAYBE IT'S 'CAUSE I'M NOT USED TO STUDY SESSIONS, BUT I JUST CAN'T GET INTO THIS...
SPIN
SPIN
Just hates studying
UGH...
I CAN'T DO THIS ANYMORE! I GIVE UP!
IT'S ONLY BEEN 30 MINUTES...
AAGH
HEY, IS IT JUST ME, OR IS IT *HOTTER* THAN NORMAL TODAY?
I WAS THINKING THE SAME THING.
THAT'S WEIRD. I HAVE THE A.C. ON STRONG.
CLICK
CLICK
...HUH?
JAM

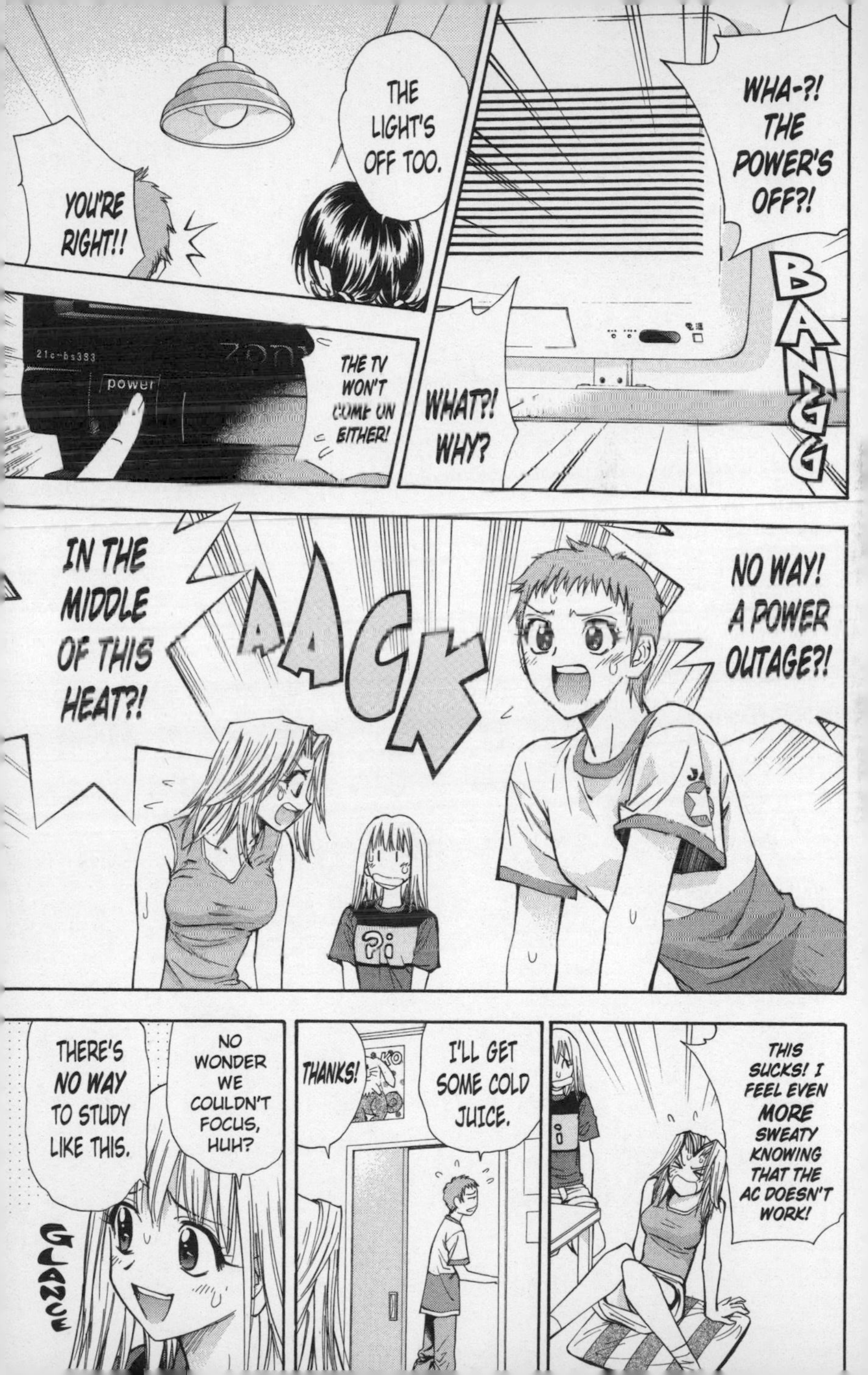
WHA-?! THE POWER'S OFF?!
BANGG
WHAT?! WHY?
THE LIGHT'S OFF TOO.
YOU'RE RIGHT!!
THE TV WON'T COME ON EITHER!
power
NO WAY! A POWER OUTAGE?!
AACK
IN THE MIDDLE OF THIS HEAT?!
THIS SUCKS! I FEEL EVEN MORE SWEATY KNOWING THAT THE AC DOESN'T WORK!
I'LL GET SOME COLD JUICE.
THANKS!
NO WONDER WE COULDN'T FOCUS, HUH?
THERE'S NO WAY TO STUDY LIKE THIS.
GLANCE

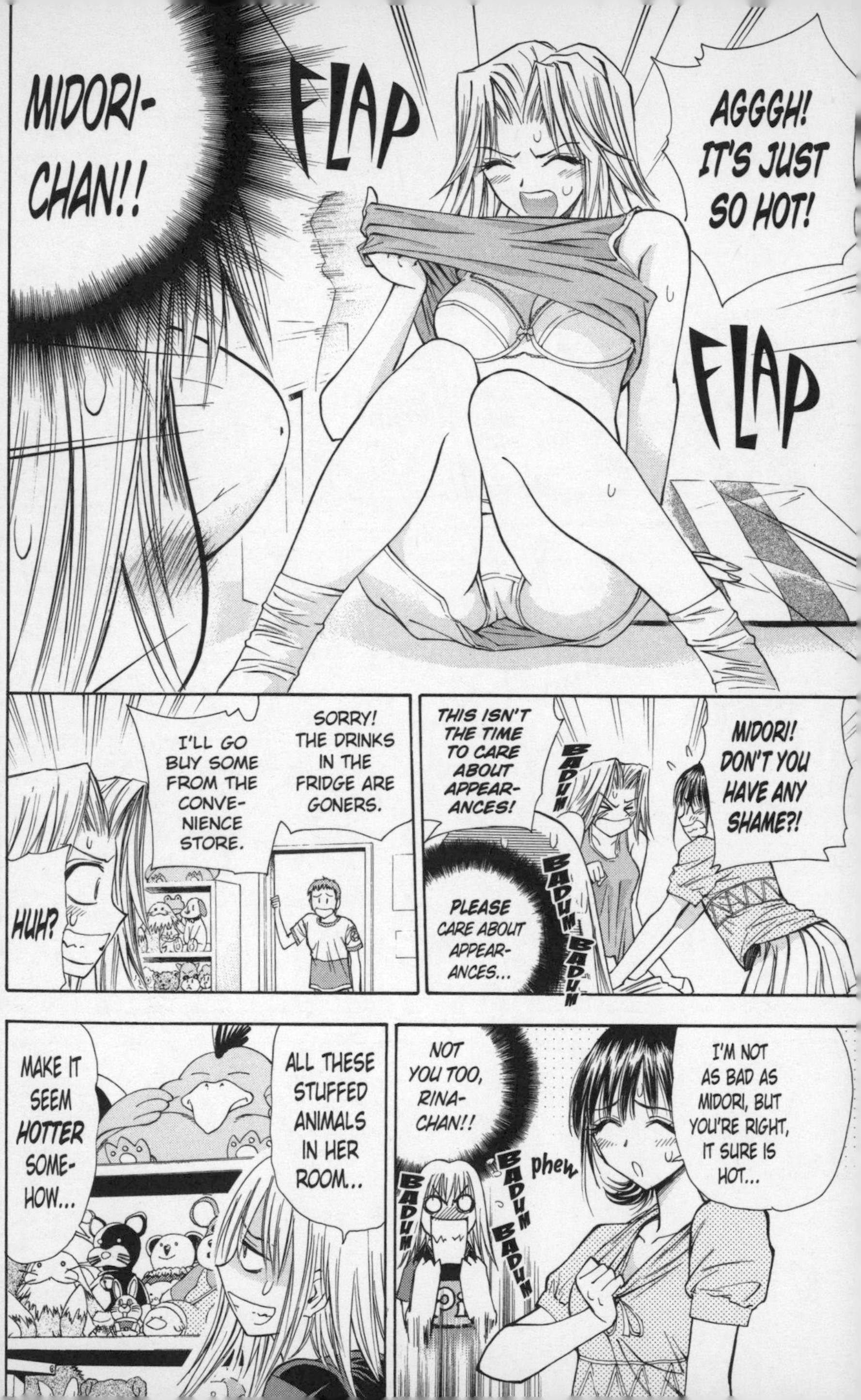
AGGGH! IT'S JUST SO HOT!
FLAP
FLAP
MIDORI-CHAN!!
MIDORI! DON'T YOU HAVE ANY SHAME?!
BADUM
THIS ISN'T THE TIME TO CARE ABOUT APPEARANCES!
BADUM BADUM BADUM
PLEASE CARE ABOUT APPEARANCES...
SORRY! THE DRINKS IN THE FRIDGE ARE GONERS.
I'LL GO BUY SOME FROM THE CONVENIENCE STORE.
HUH?
I'M NOT AS BAD AS MIDORI, BUT YOU'RE RIGHT, IT SURE IS HOT...
phew
BADUM BADUM
NOT YOU TOO, RINA-CHAN!!
BADUM
ALL THESE STUFFED ANIMALS IN HER ROOM...
MAKE IT SEEM HOTTER SOMEHOW...

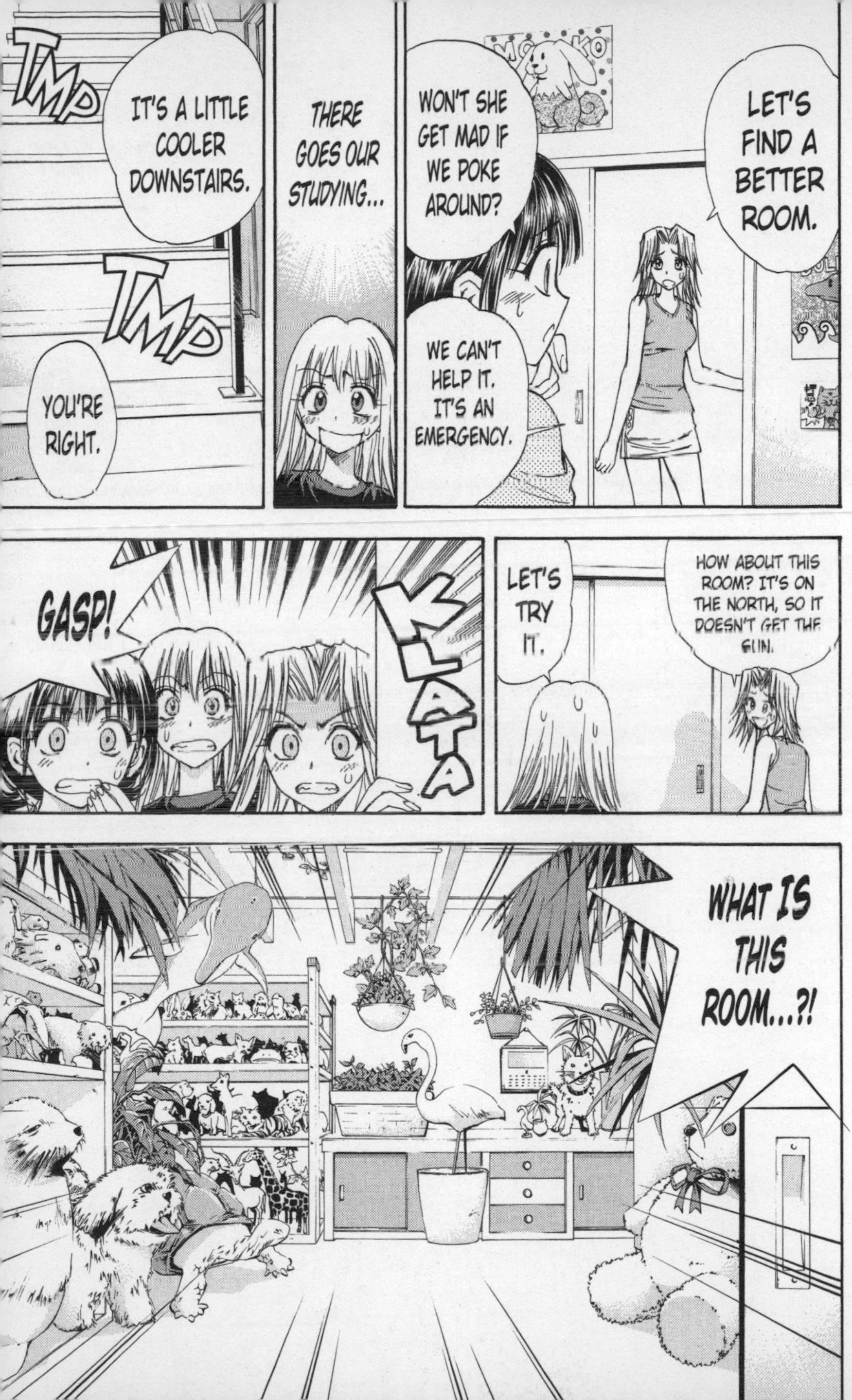
LET'S FIND A BETTER ROOM.
WON'T SHE GET MAD IF WE POKE AROUND?
WE CAN'T HELP IT. IT'S AN EMERGENCY.
THERE GOES OUR STUDYING...
TMP
IT'S A LITTLE COOLER DOWNSTAIRS.
TMP
YOU'RE RIGHT.
HOW ABOUT THIS ROOM? IT'S ON THE NORTH, SO IT DOESN'T GET THE SUN.
LET'S TRY IT.
KLATA
GASP!
WHAT IS THIS ROOM...?!

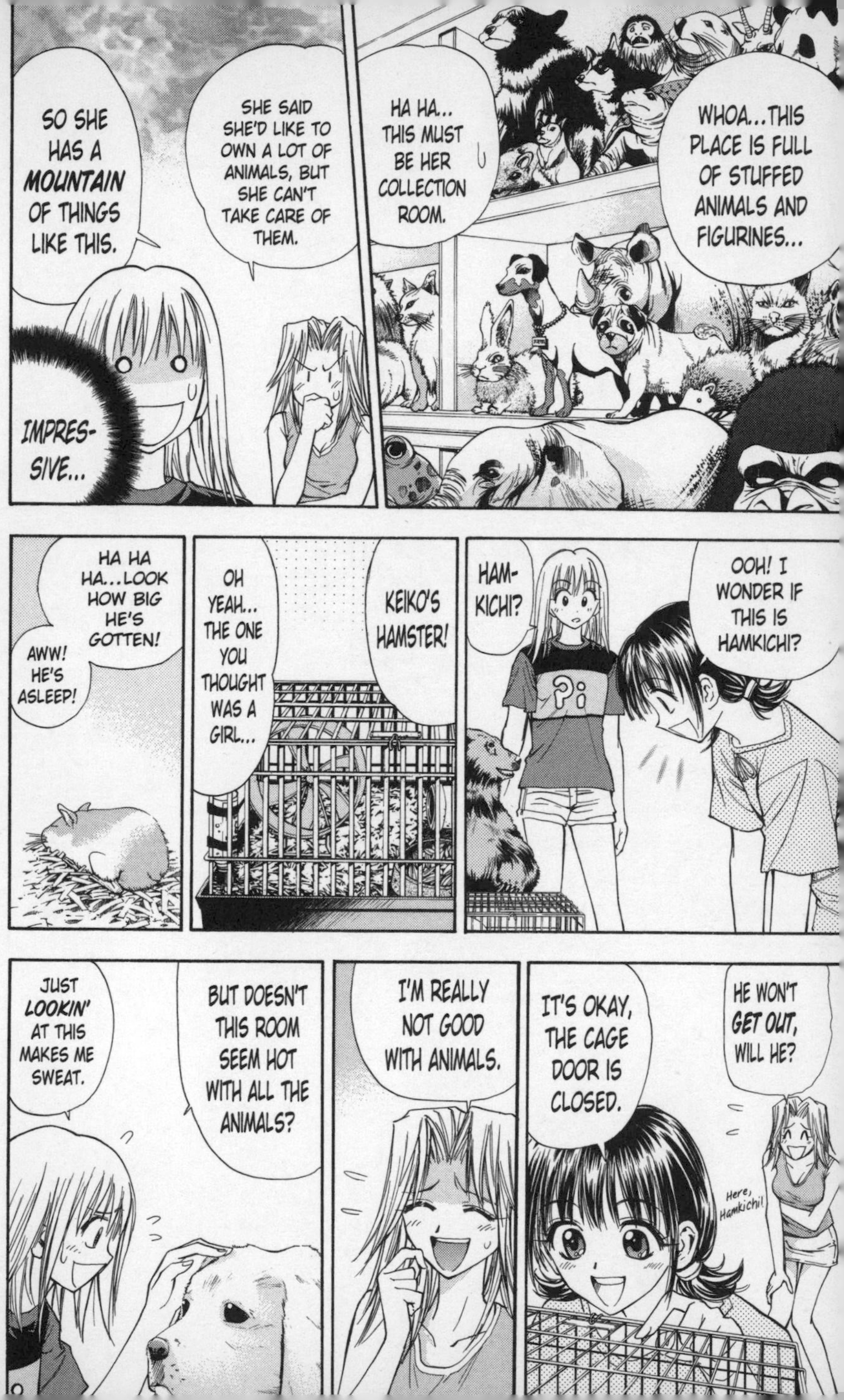
WHOA...THIS PLACE IS FULL OF STUFFED ANIMALS AND FIGURINES...
HA HA... THIS MUST BE HER COLLECTION ROOM.
SHE SAID SHE'D LIKE TO OWN A LOT OF ANIMALS, BUT SHE CAN'T TAKE CARE OF THEM.
SO SHE HAS A MOUNTAIN OF THINGS LIKE THIS.
IMPRES-SIVE...
OOH! I WONDER IF THIS IS HAMKICHI?
HAM-KICHI?
KEIKO'S HAMSTER!
OH YEAH... THE ONE YOU THOUGHT WAS A GIRL...
HA HA HA...LOOK HOW BIG HE'S GOTTEN!
AWW! HE'S ASLEEP!
HE WON'T GET OUT, WILL HE?
Here, Hamkichi!
IT'S OKAY, THE CAGE DOOR IS CLOSED.
I'M REALLY NOT GOOD WITH ANIMALS.
BUT DOESN'T THIS ROOM SEEM HOT WITH ALL THE ANIMALS?
JUST LOOKIN' AT THIS MAKES ME SWEAT.

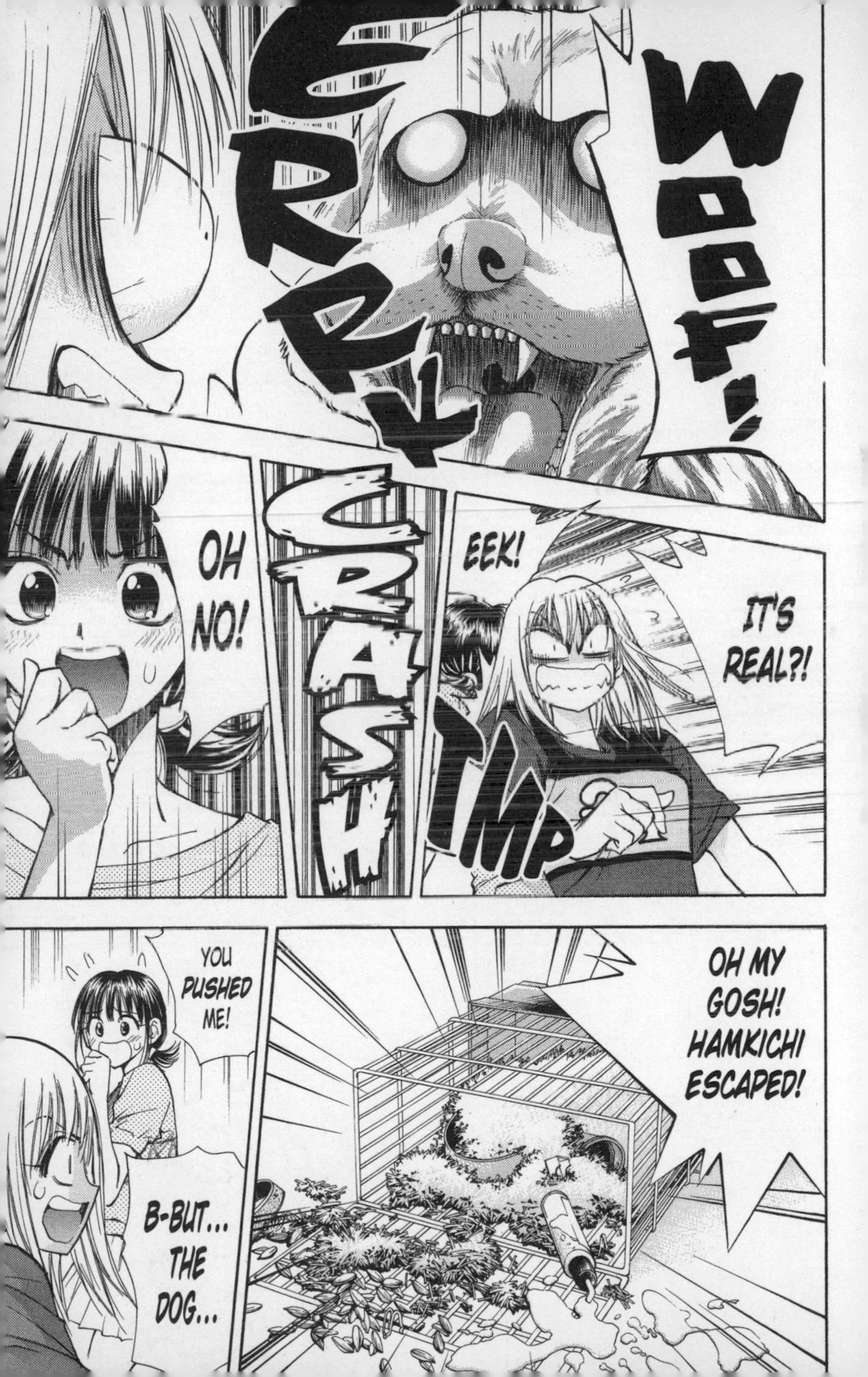
WOOF!!
GRRR
IT'S REAL?!
EEK!
TMP
CRASH
OH NO!
OH MY GOSH! HAMKICHI ESCAPED!
YOU PUSHED ME!
B-BUT... THE DOG...

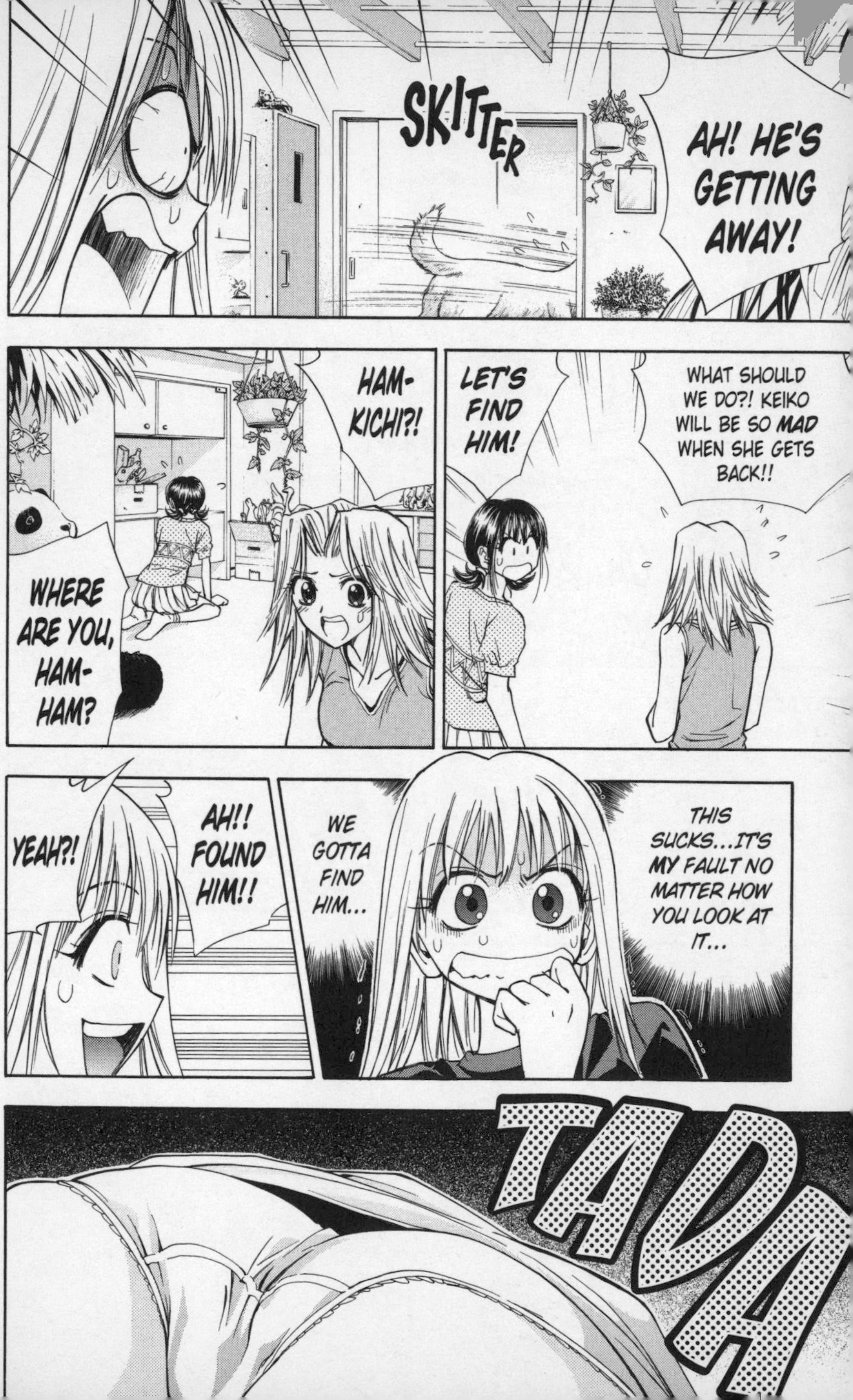
AH! HE'S GETTING AWAY!
SKITTER
WHAT SHOULD WE DO?! KEIKO WILL BE SO MAD WHEN SHE GETS BACK!!
LET'S FIND HIM!
HAM-KICHI?!
WHERE ARE YOU, HAM-HAM?
THIS SUCKS...IT'S MY FAULT NO MATTER HOW YOU LOOK AT IT...
WE GOTTA FIND HIM...
AH!! FOUND HIM!!
YEAH?!
TADA

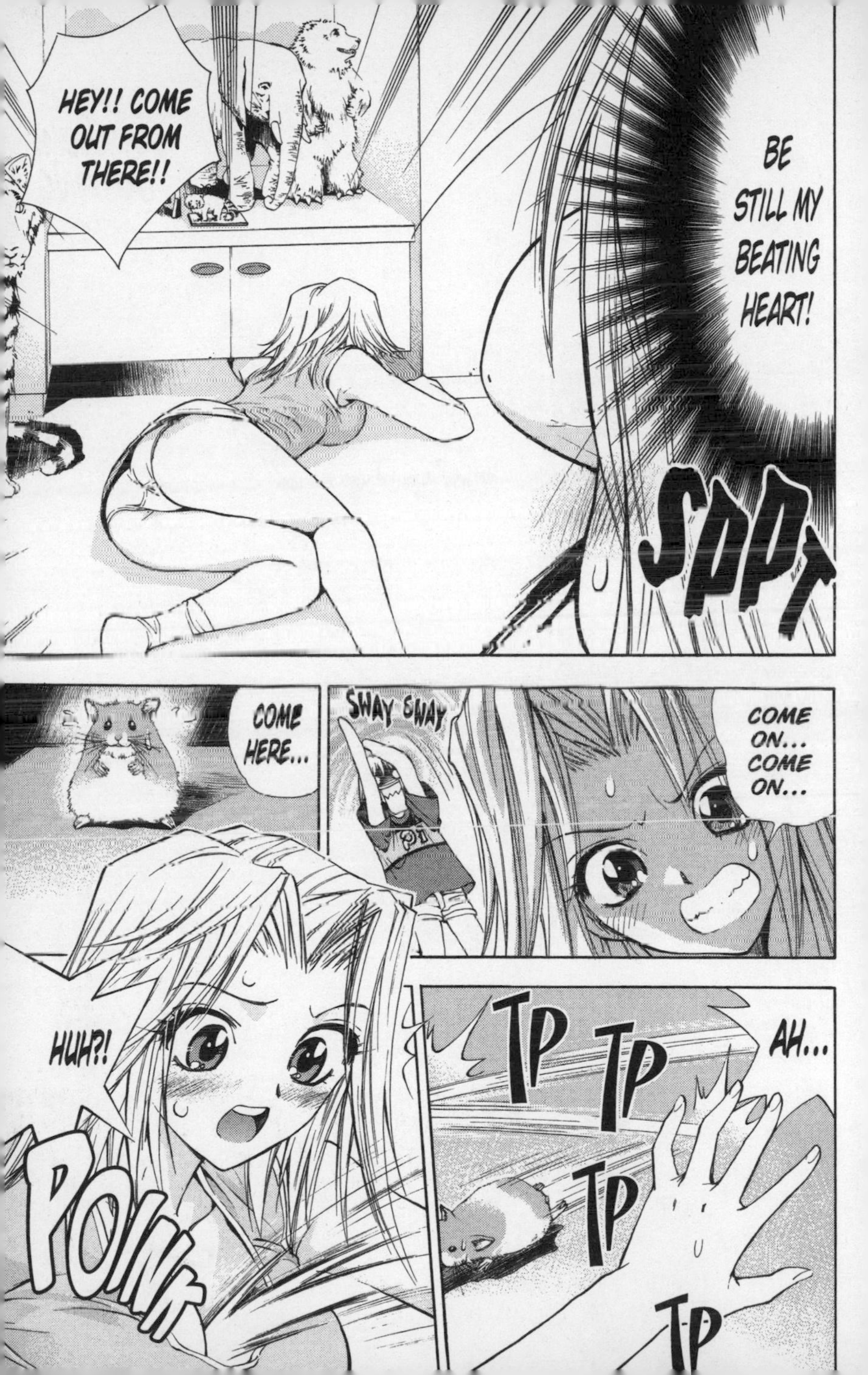
BE STILL MY BEATING HEART!
HEY!! COME OUT FROM THERE!!
SPPT
COME ON... COME ON...
SWAY SWAY
COME HERE...
AH...
TP TP
TP
TP
HUH?!
POINK

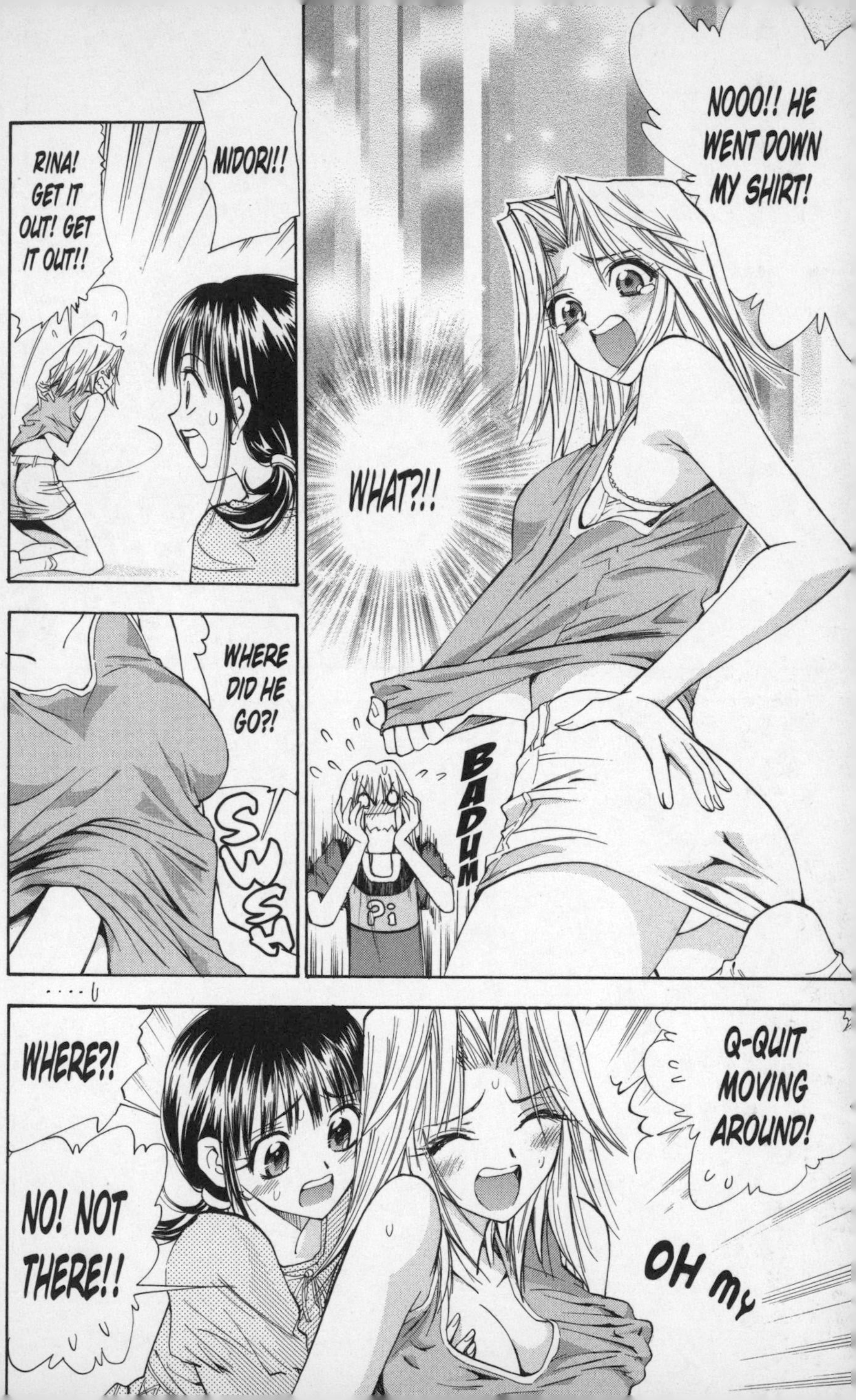
NOOO!! HE WENT DOWN MY SHIRT!
WHAT?!!
BADUM
MIDORI!!
RINA! GET IT OUT! GET IT OUT!!
WHERE DID HE GO?!
SWSH
....!
Q-QUIT MOVING AROUND!
OH my
WHERE?!
NO! NOT THERE!!

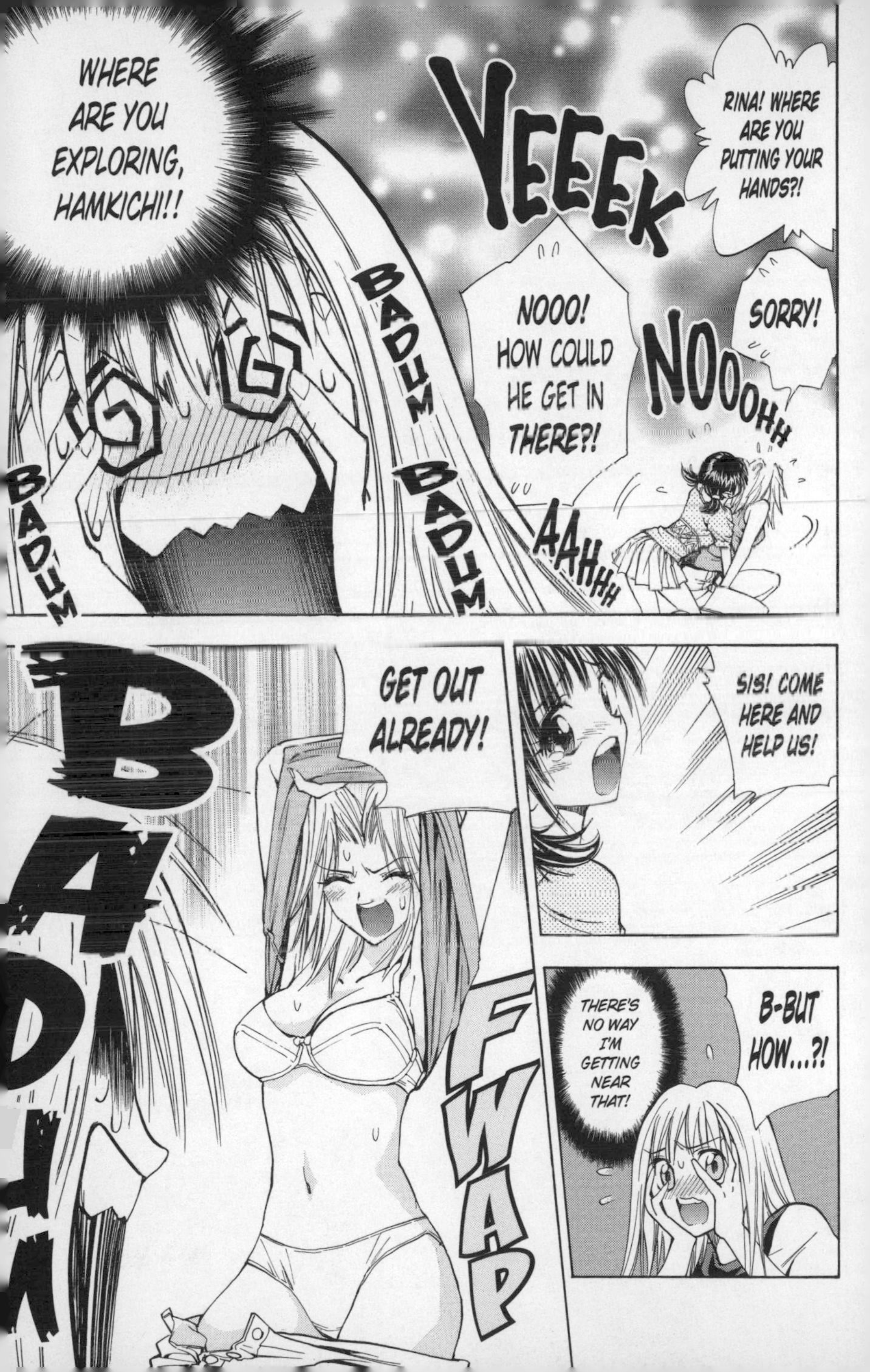
RINA! WHERE ARE YOU PUTTING YOUR HANDS?!
YEEEK
SORRY!
NOOOOHH
NOOO! HOW COULD HE GET IN THERE?!
AAHHHH
BADUM
BADUM
WHERE ARE YOU EXPLORING, HAMKICHI!!
BADUM
SIS! COME HERE AND HELP US!
B-BUT HOW...?!
THERE'S NO WAY I'M GETTING NEAR THAT!
GET OUT ALREADY!
FWAP
BAD

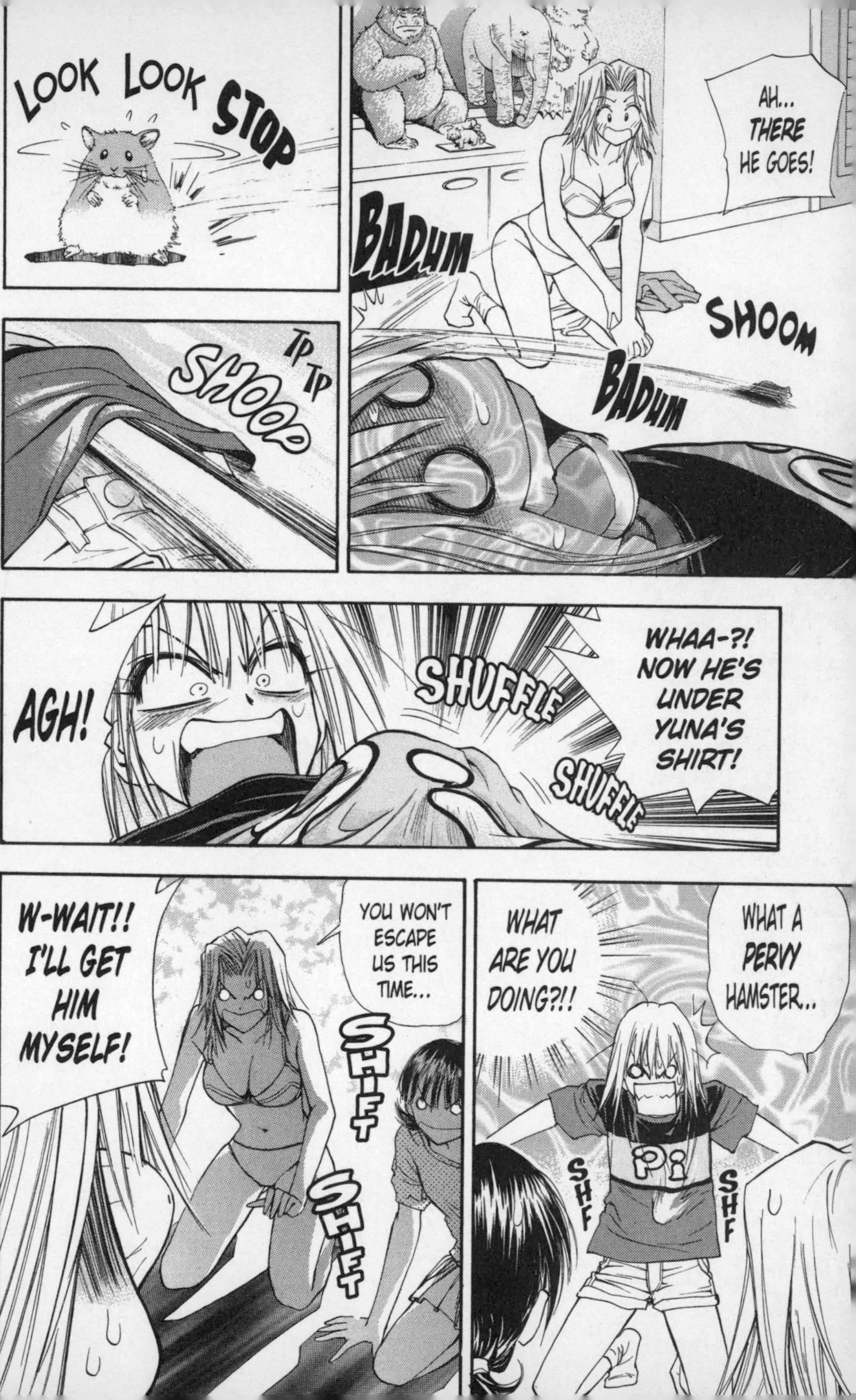
AH... THERE HE GOES!
BADUM
SHOOM
BADUM
LOOK LOOK STOP
TP TP
SHOOP
WHAA-?! NOW HE'S UNDER YUNA'S SHIRT!
SHUFFLE
SHUFFLE
AGH!
WHAT A PERVY HAMSTER...
WHAT ARE YOU DOING?!!
SHF
SHF
YOU WON'T ESCAPE US THIS TIME...
W-WAIT!! I'LL GET HIM MYSELF!
SHIFT
SHIFT

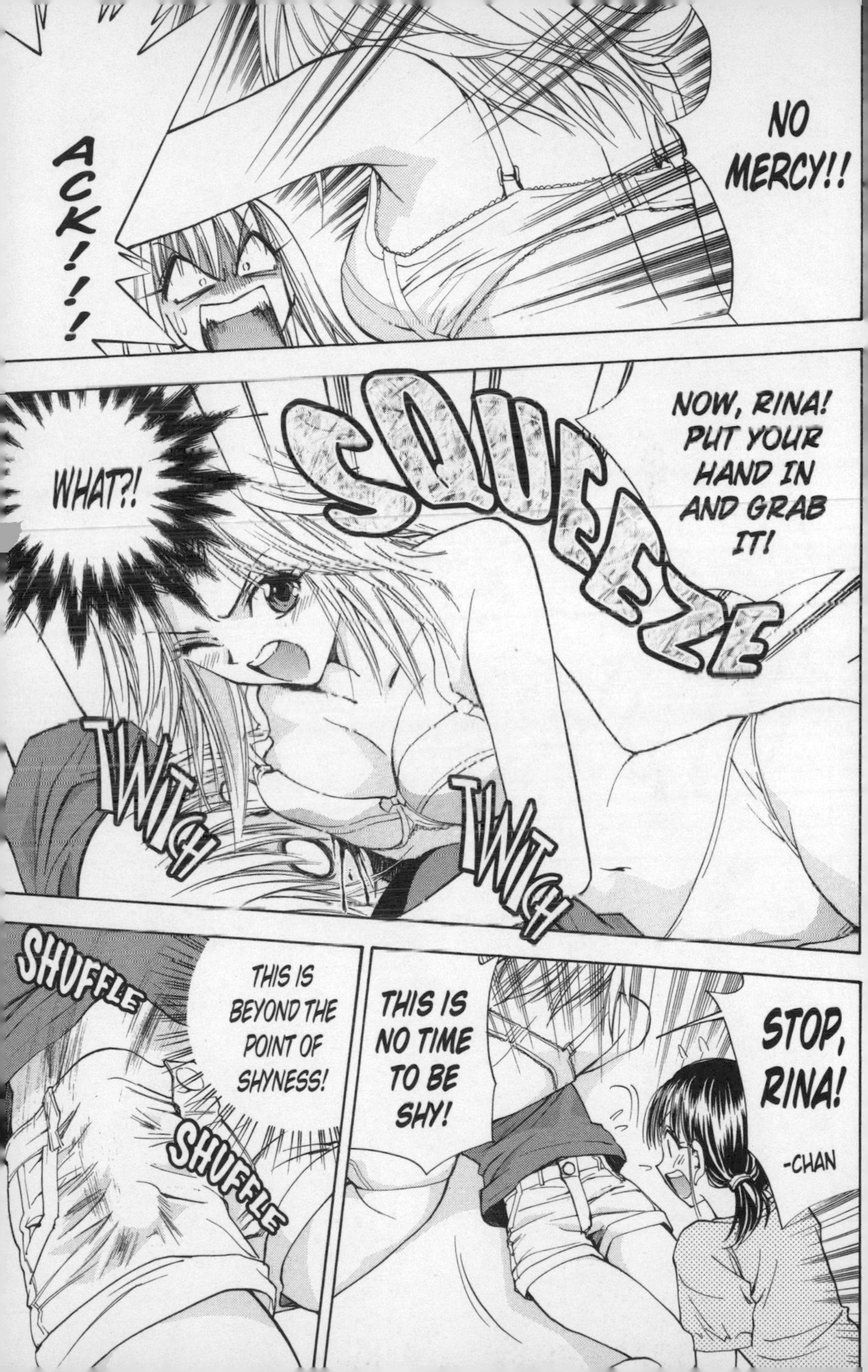
NO MERCY!!
ACK!!!
NOW, RINA! PUT YOUR HAND IN AND GRAB IT!
SQUEEZE
WHAT?!
TWITCH
TWITCH
STOP, RINA!
-CHAN
THIS IS NO TIME TO BE SHY!
THIS IS BEYOND THE POINT OF SHYNESS!
SHUFFLE
SHUFFLE

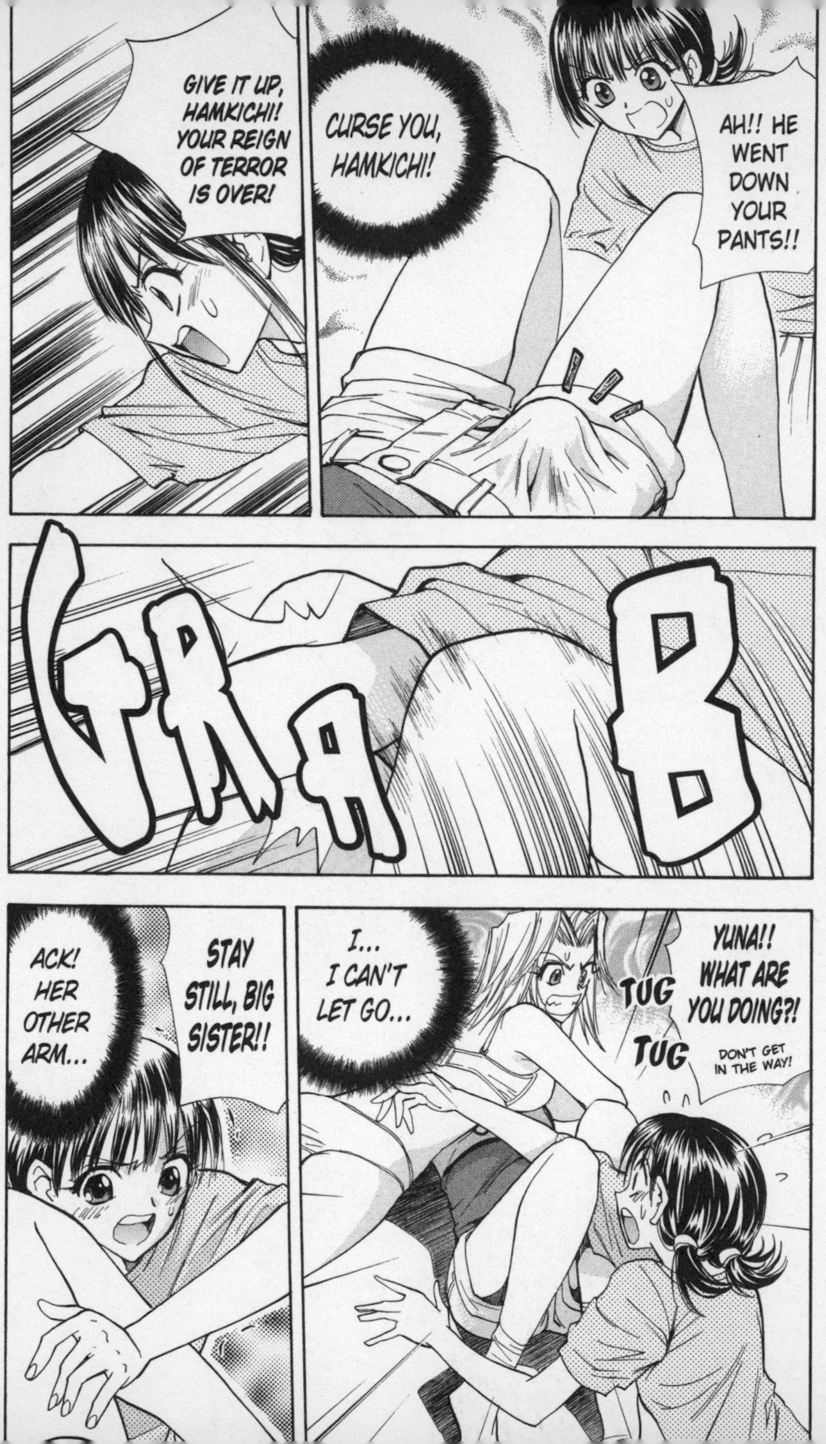
AH!! HE WENT DOWN YOUR PANTS!!
CURSE YOU, HAMKICHI!
GIVE IT UP, HAMKICHI! YOUR REIGN OF TERROR IS OVER!
GRAB
YUNA!! WHAT ARE YOU DOING?!
TUG TUG
DON'T GET IN THE WAY!
I... I CAN'T LET GO...
STAY STILL, BIG SISTER!!
ACK! HER OTHER ARM...

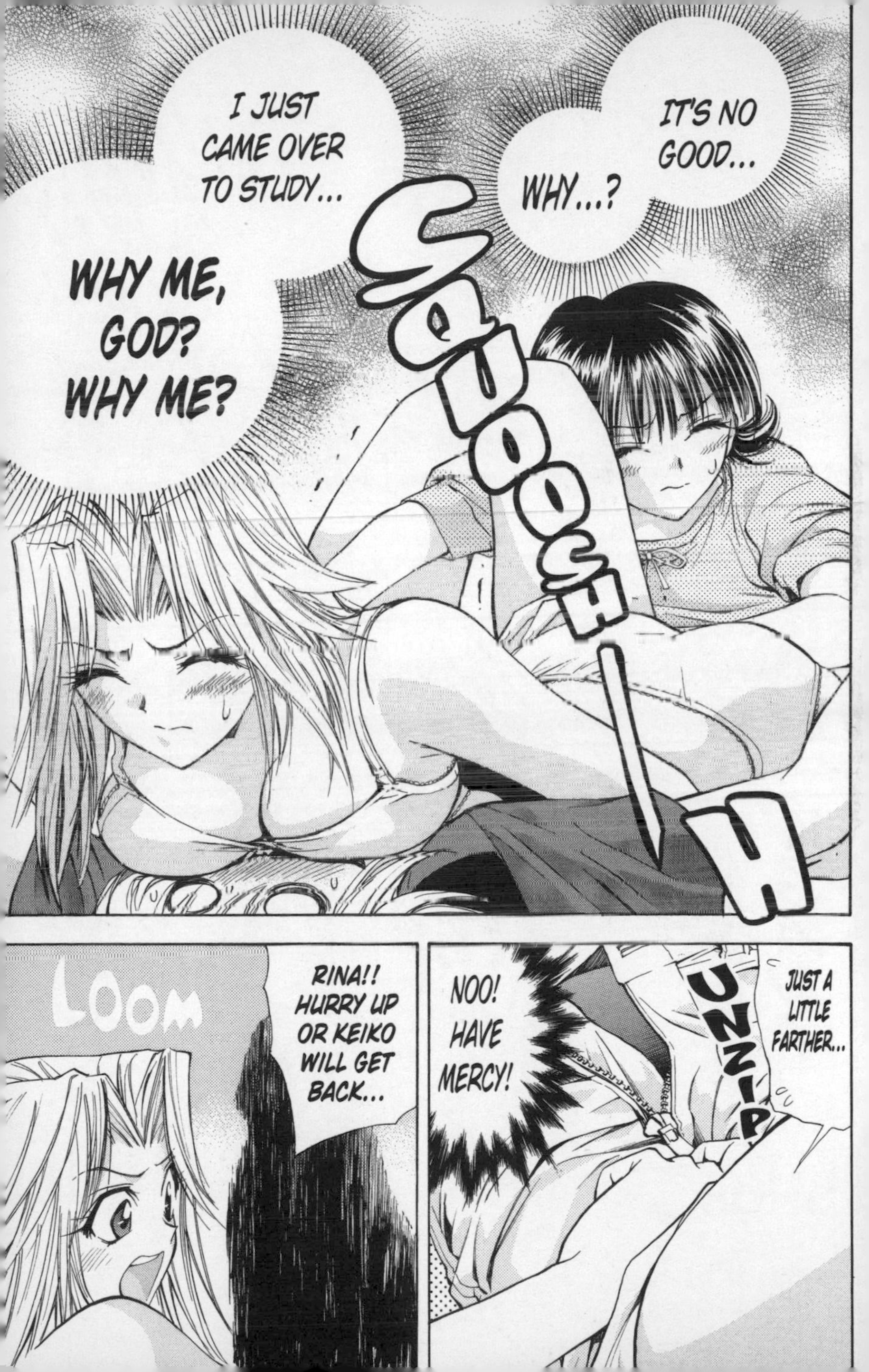
IT'S NO GOOD...
WHY...?
I JUST CAME OVER TO STUDY...
WHY ME, GOD? WHY ME?
JUST A LITTLE FARTHER...
UNZIP
NOO! HAVE MERCY!
RINA!! HURRY UP OR KEIKO WILL GET BACK...
LOOM

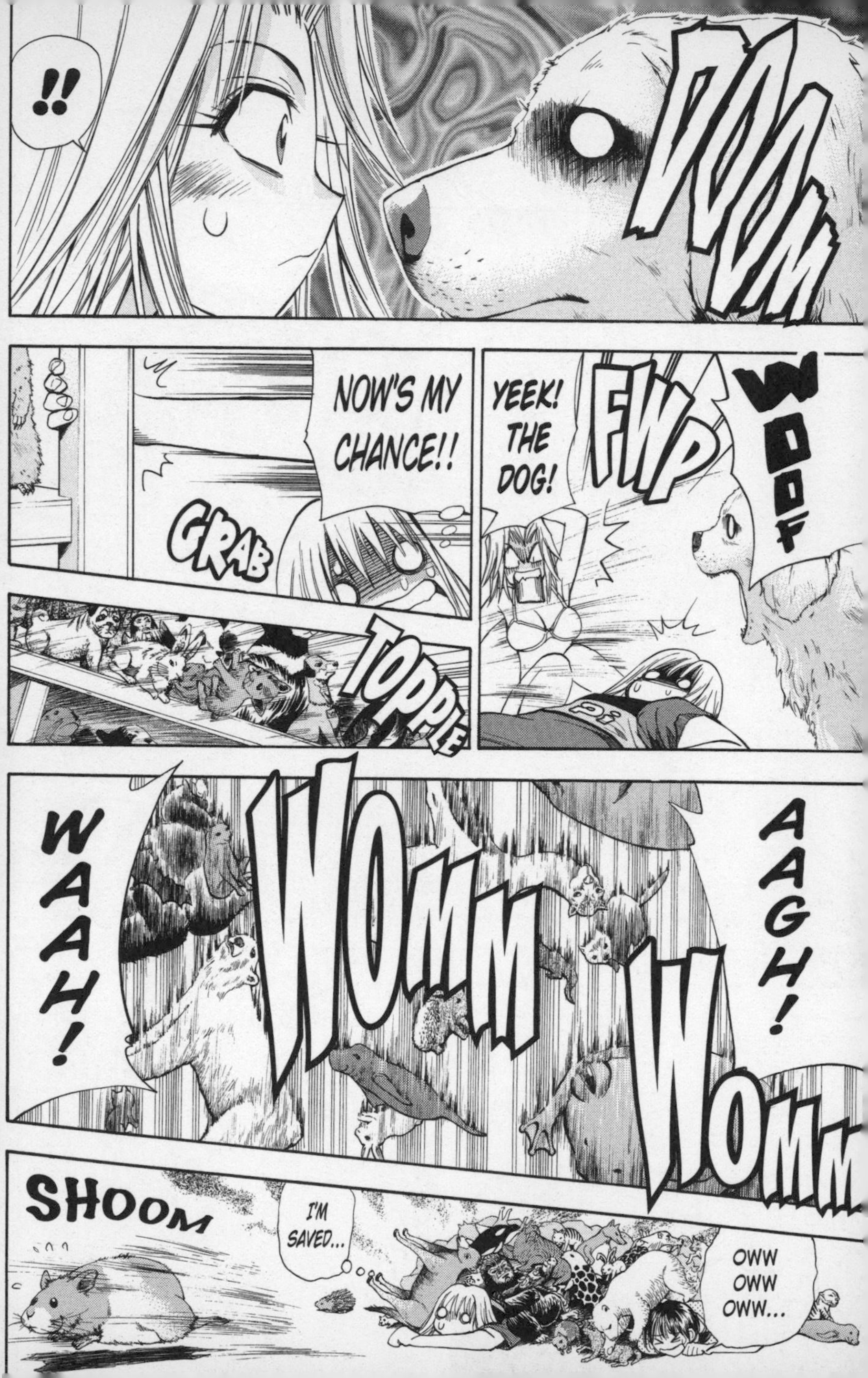
VOOM
!!
WOOF
FWP
YEEK! THE DOG!
NOW'S MY CHANCE!!
GRAB
TOPPLE
AAGH!
WOMM
WOMM
WAAH!
OWW OWW OWW...
I'M SAVED...
SHOOM

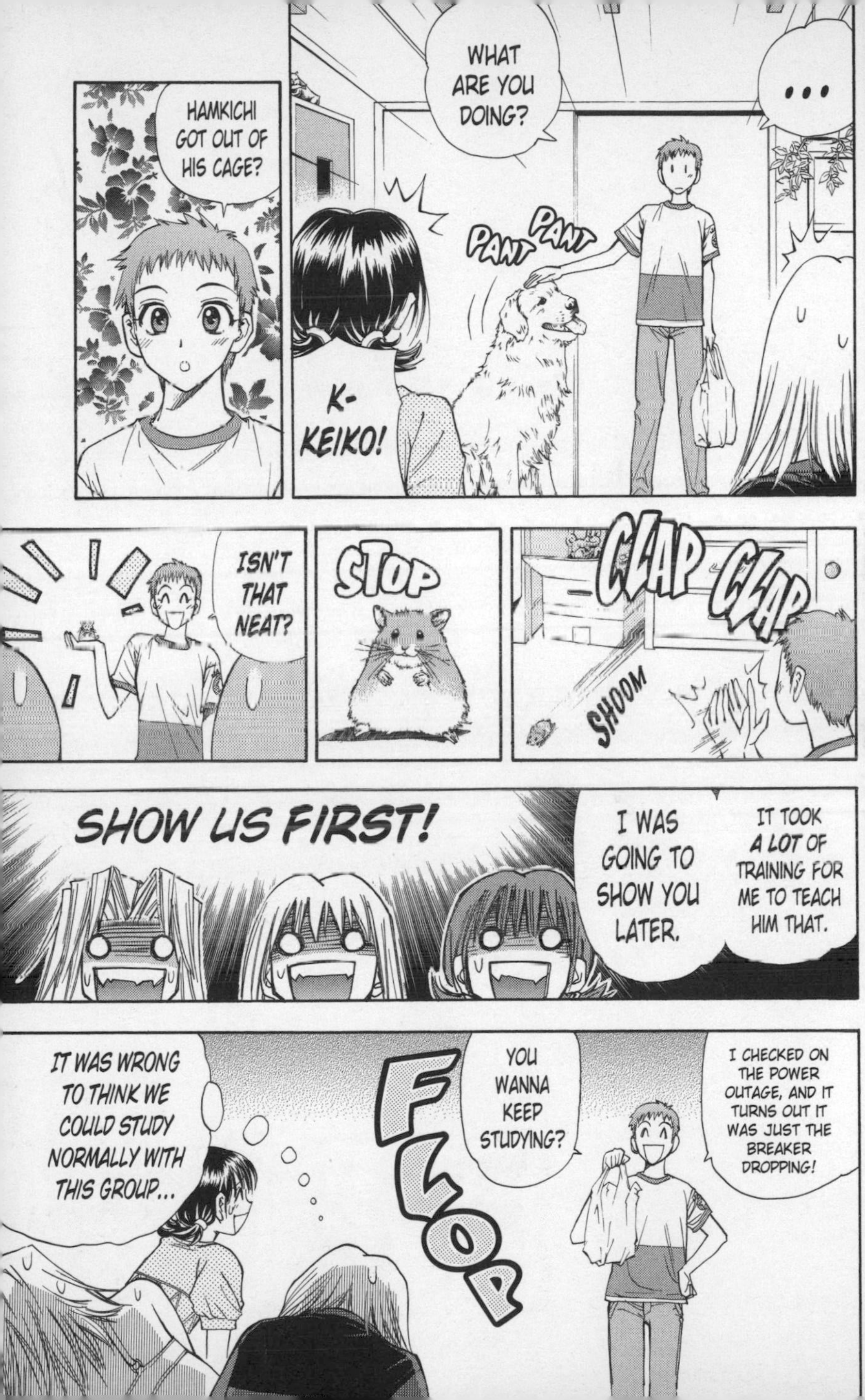
...
WHAT ARE YOU DOING?
PANT PANT
K-KEIKO!
HAMKICHI GOT OUT OF HIS CAGE?
CLAP CLAP
SHOOM
STOP
ISN'T THAT NEAT?
IT TOOK A LOT OF TRAINING FOR ME TO TEACH HIM THAT.
I WAS GOING TO SHOW YOU LATER.
SHOW US FIRST!
I CHECKED ON THE POWER OUTAGE, AND IT TURNS OUT IT WAS JUST THE BREAKER DROPPING!
YOU WANNA KEEP STUDYING?
FLOP
IT WAS WRONG TO THINK WE COULD STUDY NORMALLY WITH THIS GROUP...

Pretty Face

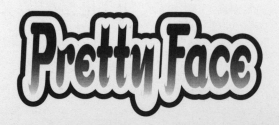

Chapter 15: Pretty Horror Face

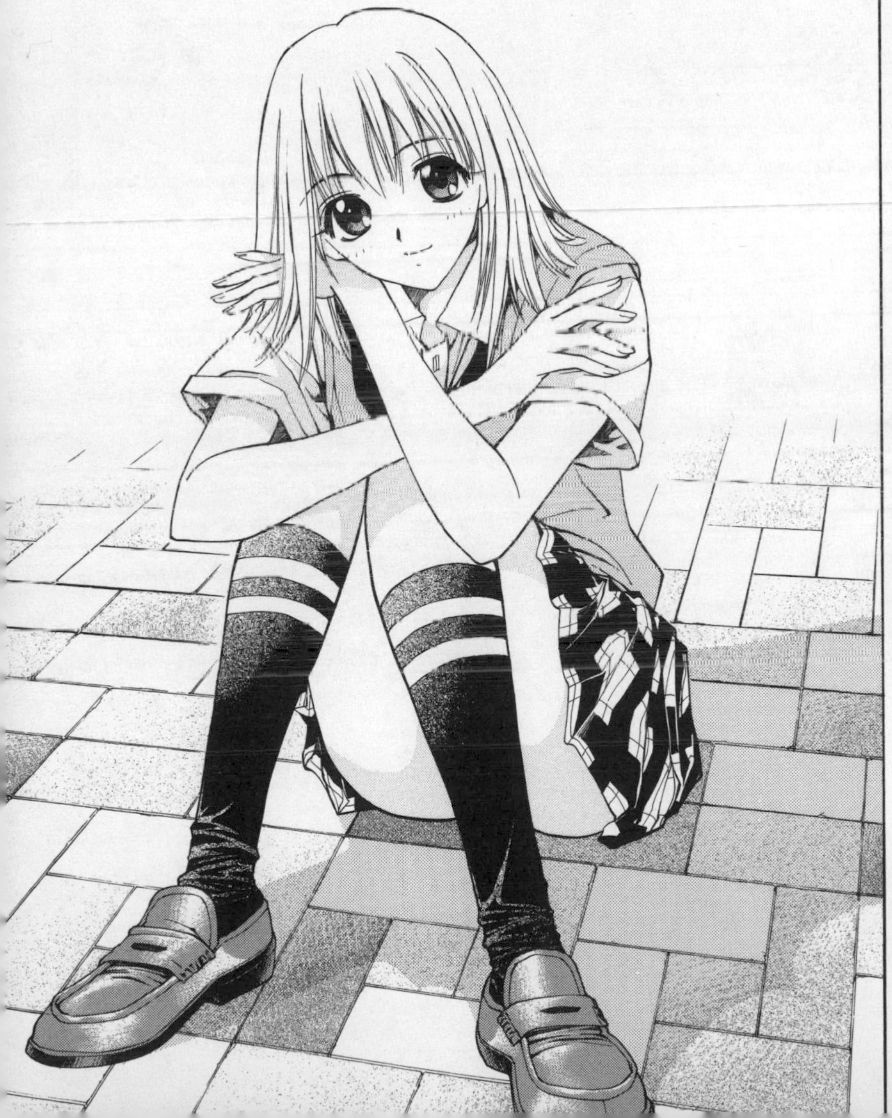

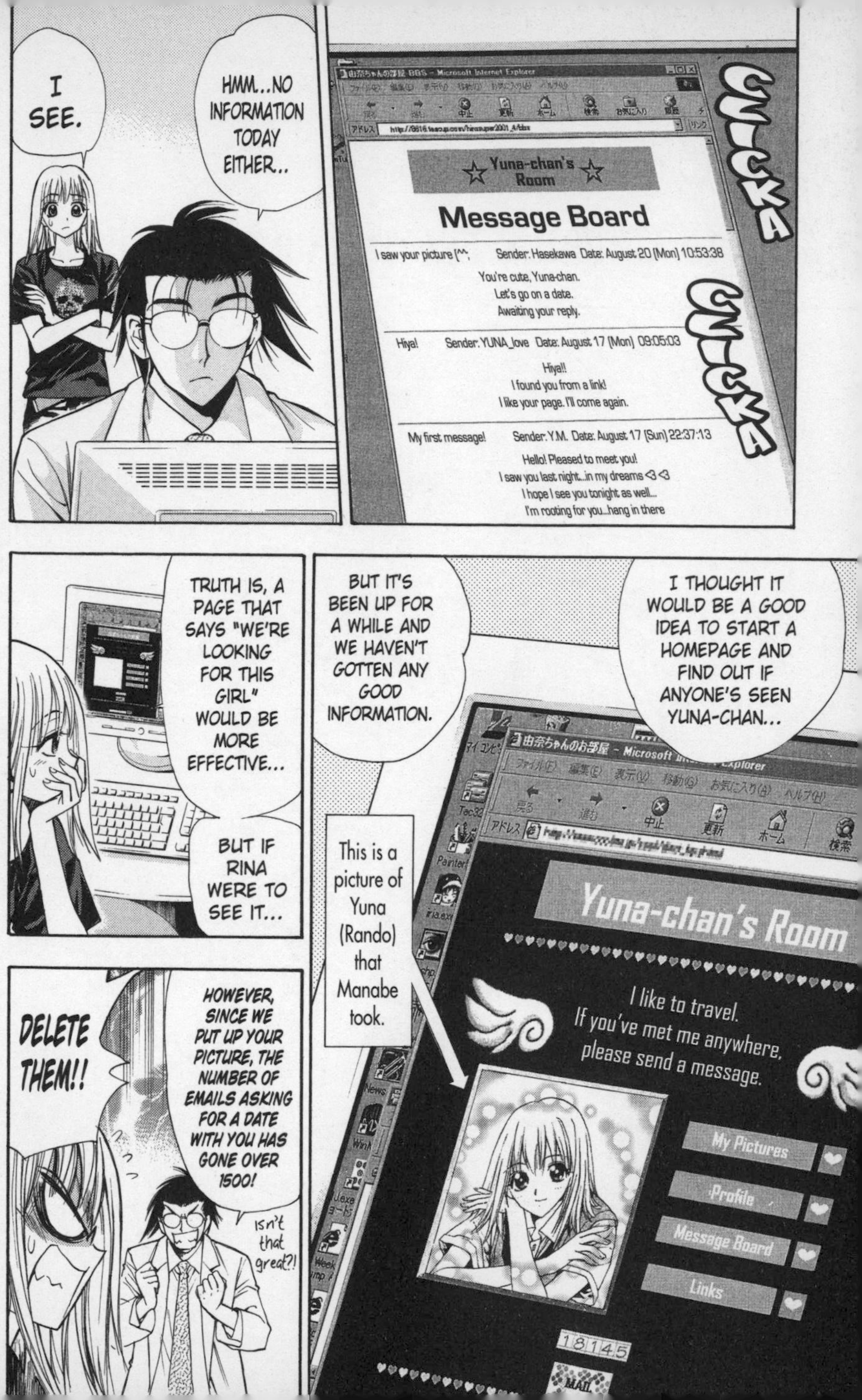

CLICKA
CLICKA
☆ Yuna-chan's Room ☆
Message Board
I saw your picture (^^; Sender: Hasekawa Date: August 20 (Mon) 10:53:38
You're cute, Yuna-chan.
Let's go on a date.
Awaiting your reply.
Hiya! Sender: YUNA_love Date: August 17 (Mon) 09:05:03
Hiya!!
I found you from a link!
I like your page. I'll come again.
My first message! Sender: Y.M. Date: August 17 (Sun) 22:37:13
Hello! Pleased to meet you!
I saw you last night...in my dreams <3 <3
I hope I see you tonight as well...
I'm rooting for you...hang in there
HMM...NO INFORMATION TODAY EITHER...
I SEE.
I THOUGHT IT WOULD BE A GOOD IDEA TO START A HOMEPAGE AND FIND OUT IF ANYONE'S SEEN YUNA-CHAN...
BUT IT'S BEEN UP FOR A WHILE AND WE HAVEN'T GOTTEN ANY GOOD INFORMATION.
This is a picture of Yuna (Rando) that Manabe took.
Yuna-chan's Room
I like to travel.
If you've met me anywhere,
please send a message.
My Pictures
Profile
Message Board
Links
18145
MAIL
TRUTH IS, A PAGE THAT SAYS "WE'RE LOOKING FOR THIS GIRL" WOULD BE MORE EFFECTIVE...
BUT IF RINA WERE TO SEE IT...
HOWEVER, SINCE WE PUT UP YOUR PICTURE, THE NUMBER OF EMAILS ASKING FOR A DATE WITH YOU HAS GONE OVER 1500!
Isn't that great?!
DELETE THEM!!

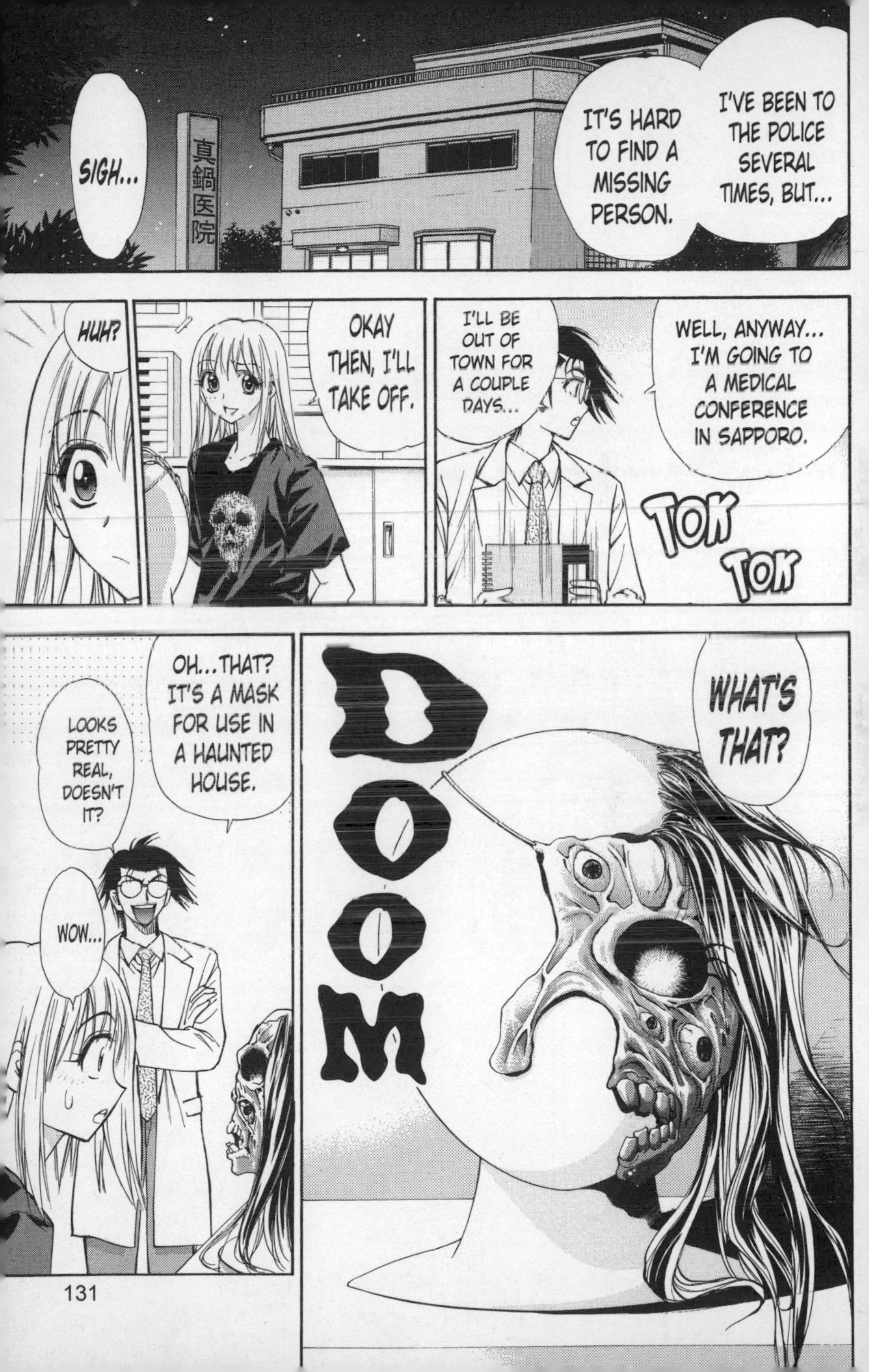
I'VE BEEN TO THE POLICE SEVERAL TIMES, BUT...
IT'S HARD TO FIND A MISSING PERSON.
真鍋医院
SIGH...
WELL, ANYWAY... I'M GOING TO A MEDICAL CONFERENCE IN SAPPORO.
I'LL BE OUT OF TOWN FOR A COUPLE DAYS...
TOK TOK
OKAY THEN, I'LL TAKE OFF.
HUH?
WHAT'S THAT?
DOOM
OH...THAT? IT'S A MASK FOR USE IN A HAUNTED HOUSE.
LOOKS PRETTY REAL, DOESN'T IT?
WOW...

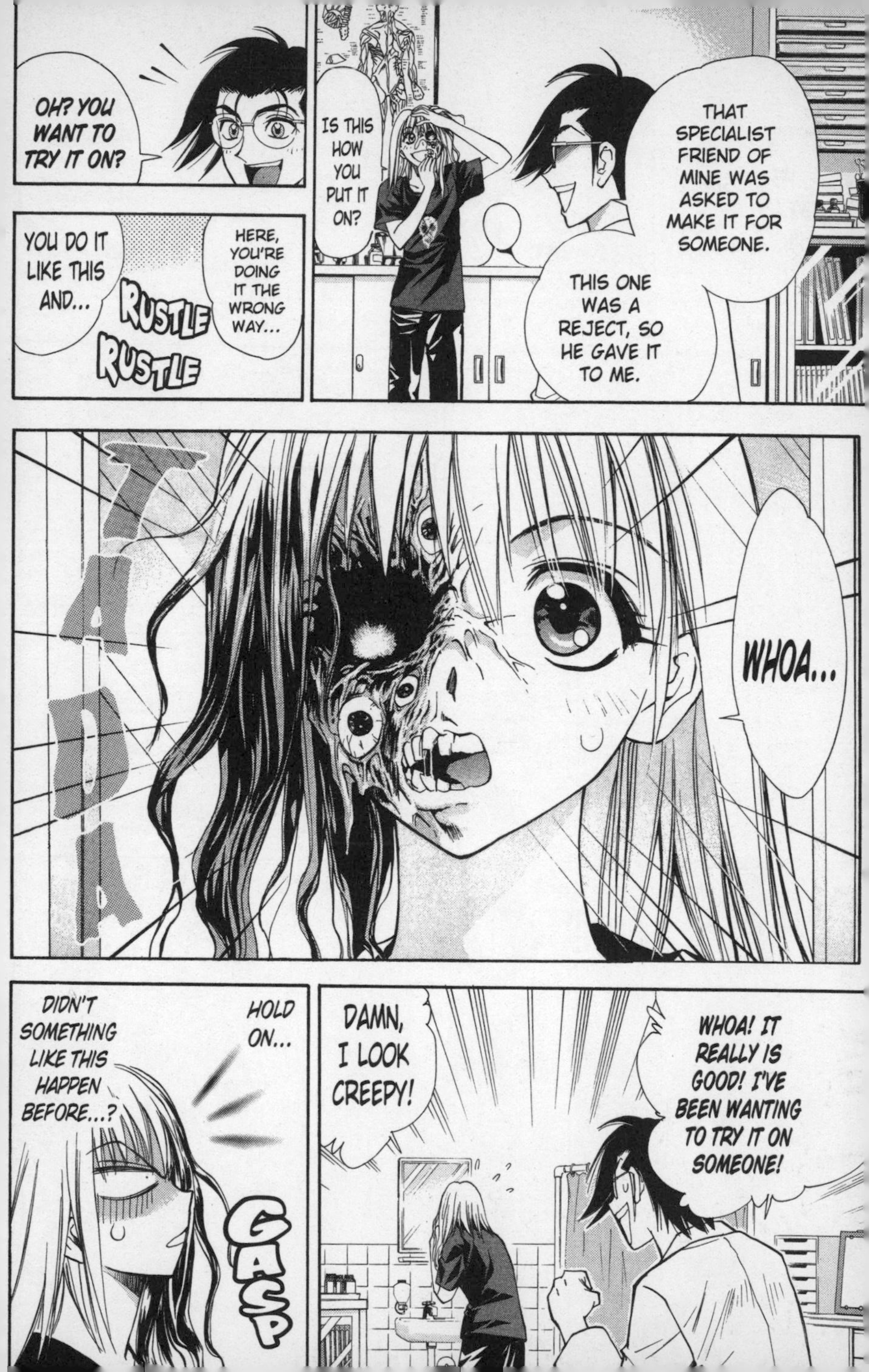
THAT SPECIALIST FRIEND OF MINE WAS ASKED TO MAKE IT FOR SOMEONE.
THIS ONE WAS A REJECT, SO HE GAVE IT TO ME.
IS THIS HOW YOU PUT IT ON?
OH? YOU WANT TO TRY IT ON?
HERE, YOU'RE DOING IT THE WRONG WAY...
YOU DO IT LIKE THIS AND...
RUSTLE
RUSTLE
WHOA...
WHOA! IT REALLY IS GOOD! I'VE BEEN WANTING TO TRY IT ON SOMEONE!
DAMN, I LOOK CREEPY!
HOLD ON...
DIDN'T SOMETHING LIKE THIS HAPPEN BEFORE...?
GASP

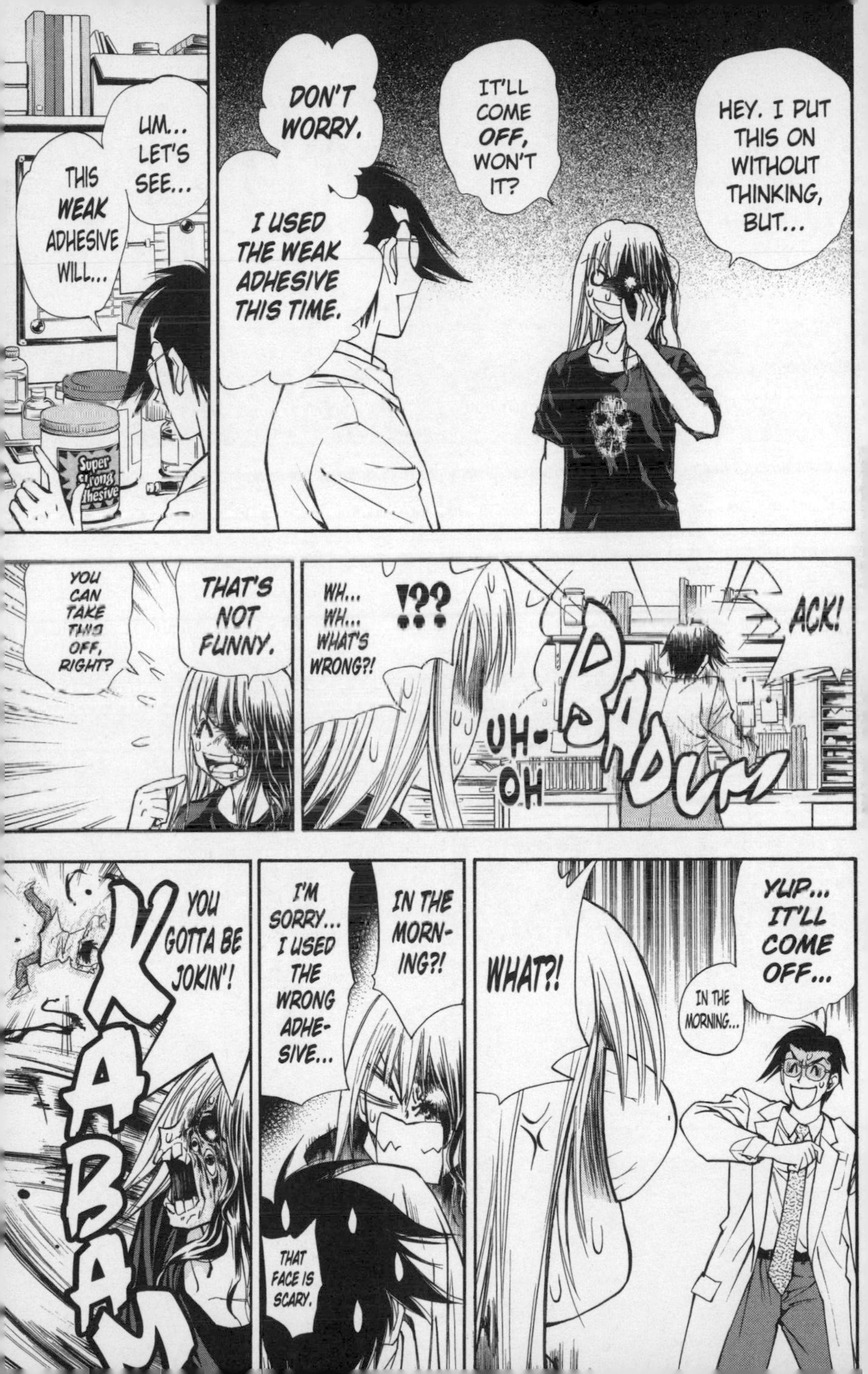
HEY. I PUT THIS ON WITHOUT THINKING, BUT...
IT'LL COME OFF, WON'T IT?
DON'T WORRY.
I USED THE WEAK ADHESIVE THIS TIME.
UM... LET'S SEE...
THIS WEAK ADHESIVE WILL...
Super Strong Adhesive
ACK!
BADUM
UH-OH
!??
WH... WH... WHAT'S WRONG?!
THAT'S NOT FUNNY.
YOU CAN TAKE THIS OFF, RIGHT?
YUP... IT'LL COME OFF...
IN THE MORNING...
WHAT?!
IN THE MORNING?!
I'M SORRY... I USED THE WRONG ADHESIVE...
THAT FACE IS SCARY.
YOU GOTTA BE JOKIN'!
KABAM

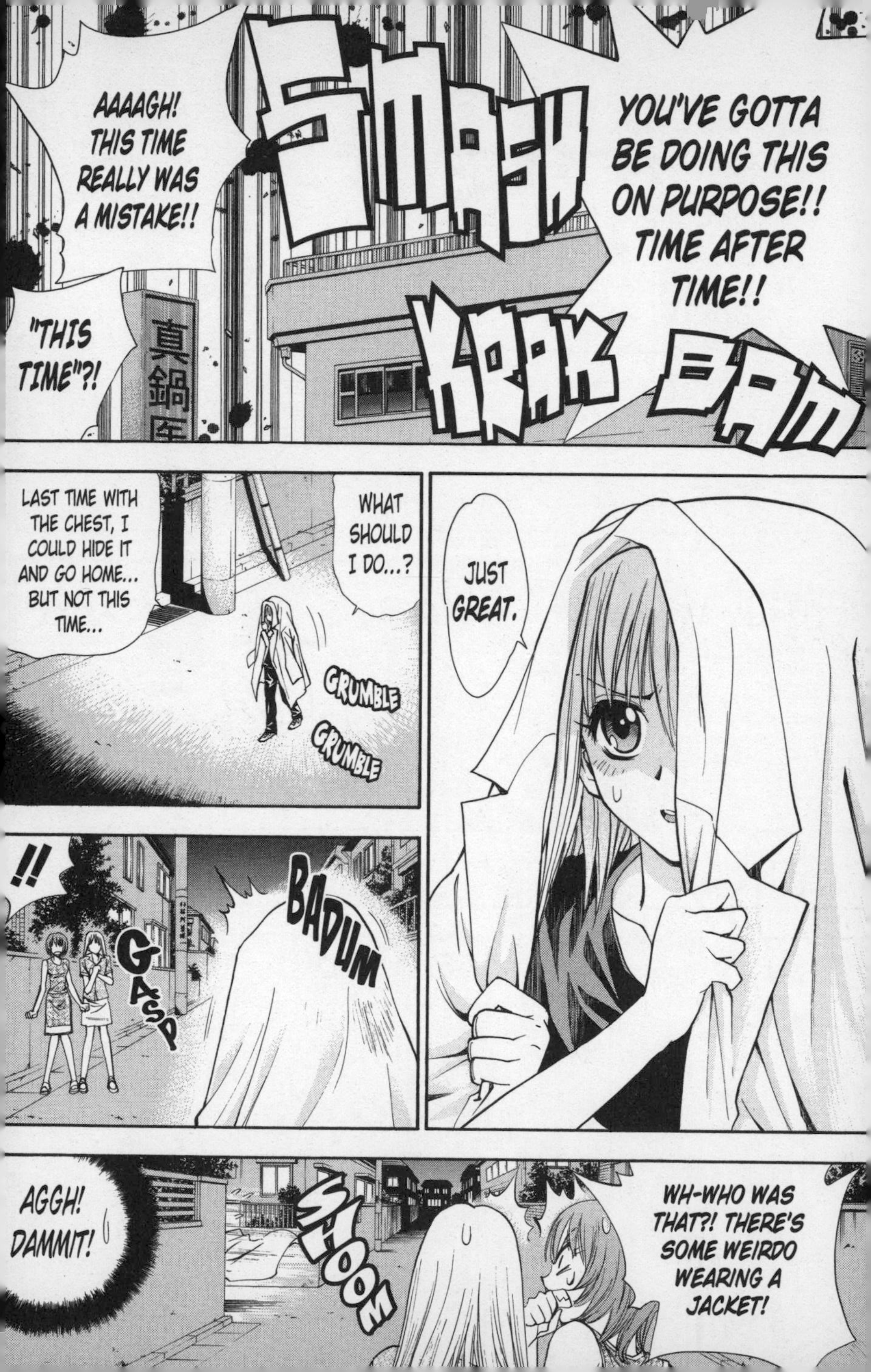
YOU'VE GOTTA BE DOING THIS ON PURPOSE!! TIME AFTER TIME!!
SMASH
AAAAGH! THIS TIME REALLY WAS A MISTAKE!!
BAM
KRAK
"THIS TIME"?!
JUST GREAT.
WHAT SHOULD I DO...?
LAST TIME WITH THE CHEST, I COULD HIDE IT AND GO HOME... BUT NOT THIS TIME...
GRUMBLE
GRUMBLE
BADUM
GASP
!!
WH-WHO WAS THAT?! THERE'S SOME WEIRDO WEARING A JACKET!
SHOOM
AGGH! DAMMIT!

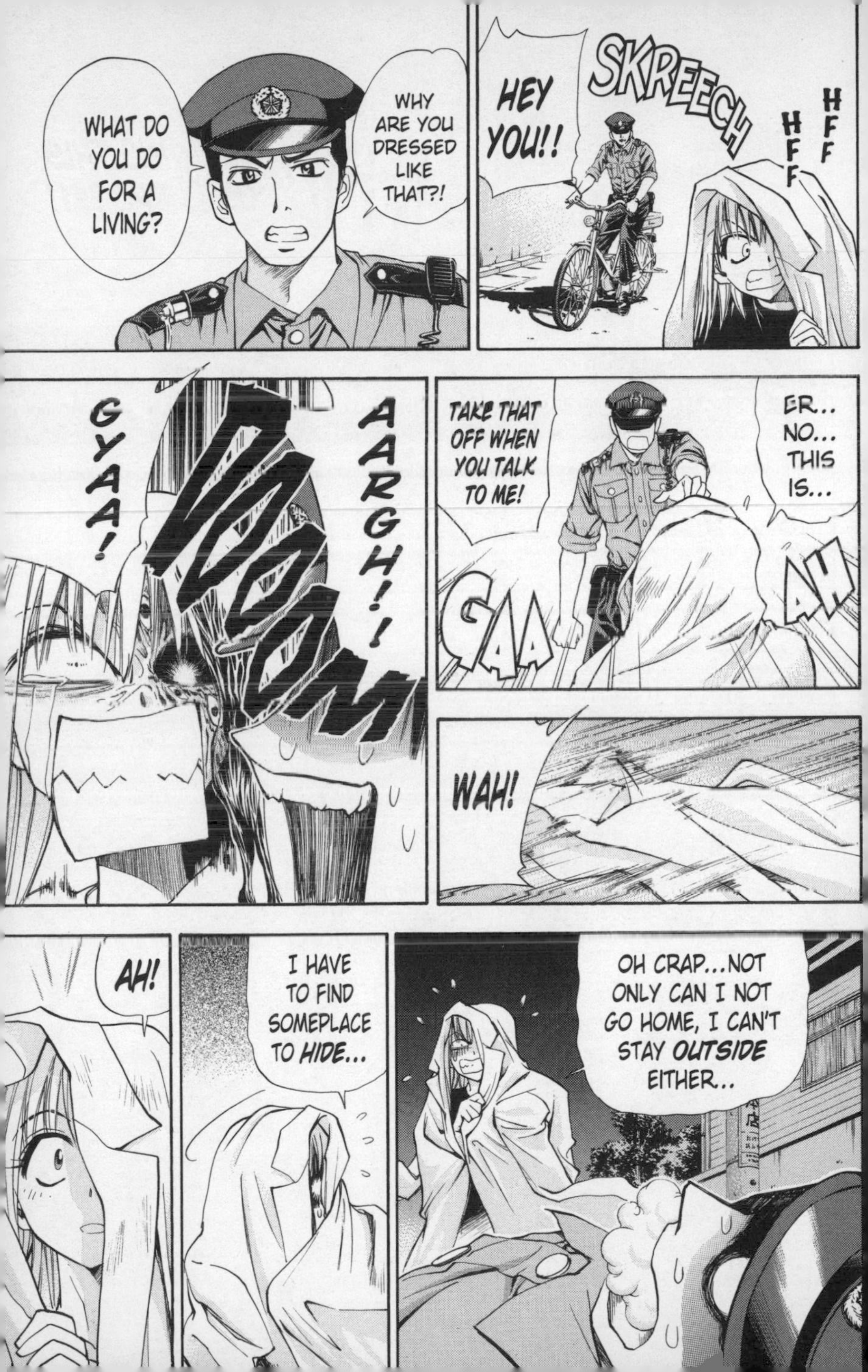
HEY YOU!!
SKREECH
HFF HFF
WHY ARE YOU DRESSED LIKE THAT?!
WHAT DO YOU DO FOR A LIVING?
ER... NO... THIS IS...
TAKE THAT OFF WHEN YOU TALK TO ME!
AH
GAA
WAH!
AARGH!!
VOOM!
GYAA!
OH CRAP...NOT ONLY CAN I NOT GO HOME, I CAN'T STAY OUTSIDE EITHER...
I HAVE TO FIND SOMEPLACE TO HIDE...
AH!

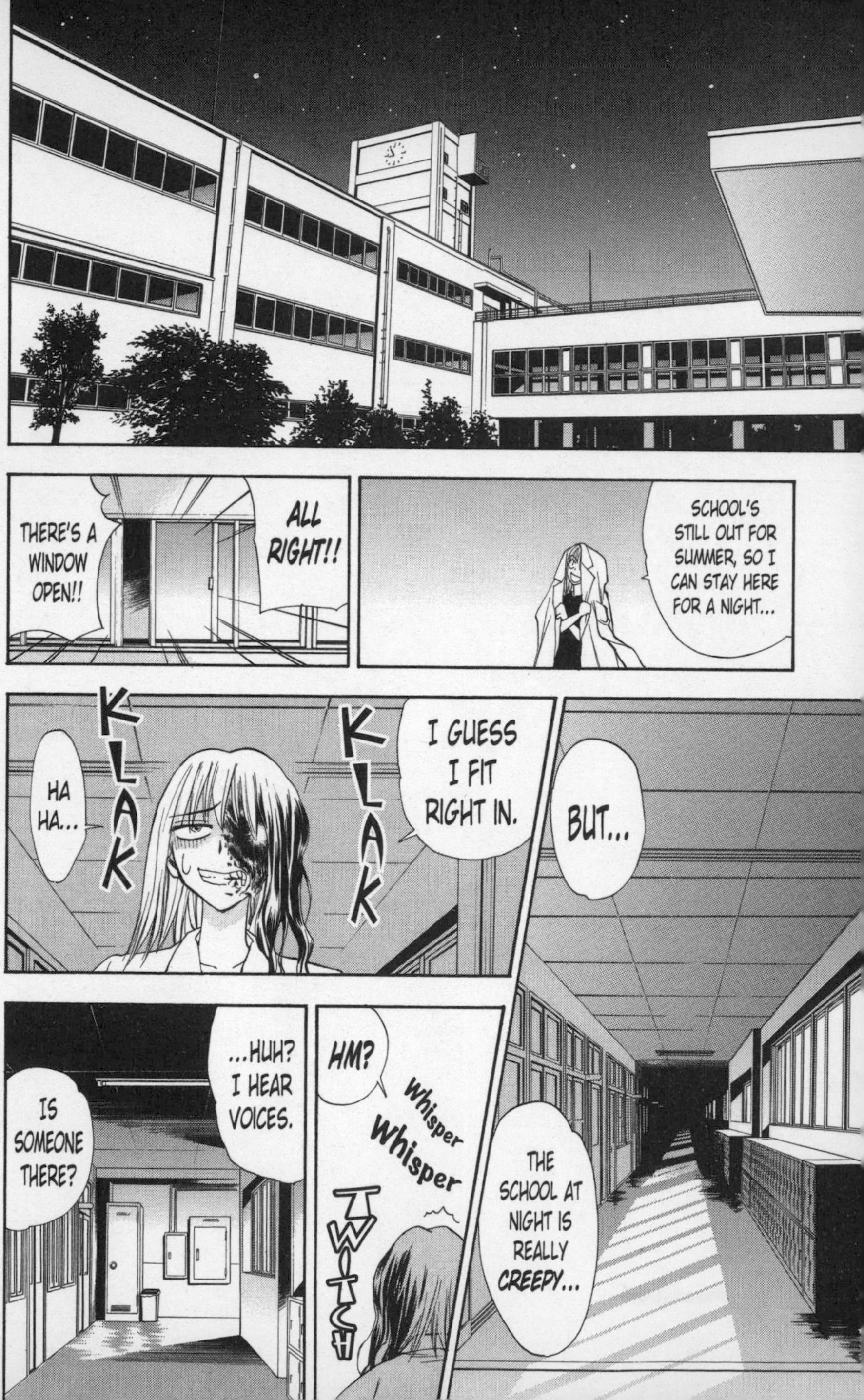
SCHOOL'S STILL OUT FOR SUMMER, SO I CAN STAY HERE FOR A NIGHT...
ALL RIGHT!!
THERE'S A WINDOW OPEN!!
KLAK
I GUESS I FIT RIGHT IN.
KLAK
HA HA...
BUT...
THE SCHOOL AT NIGHT IS REALLY CREEPY...
HM?
Whisper
Whisper
TWITCH
...HUH? I HEAR VOICES.
IS SOMEONE THERE?

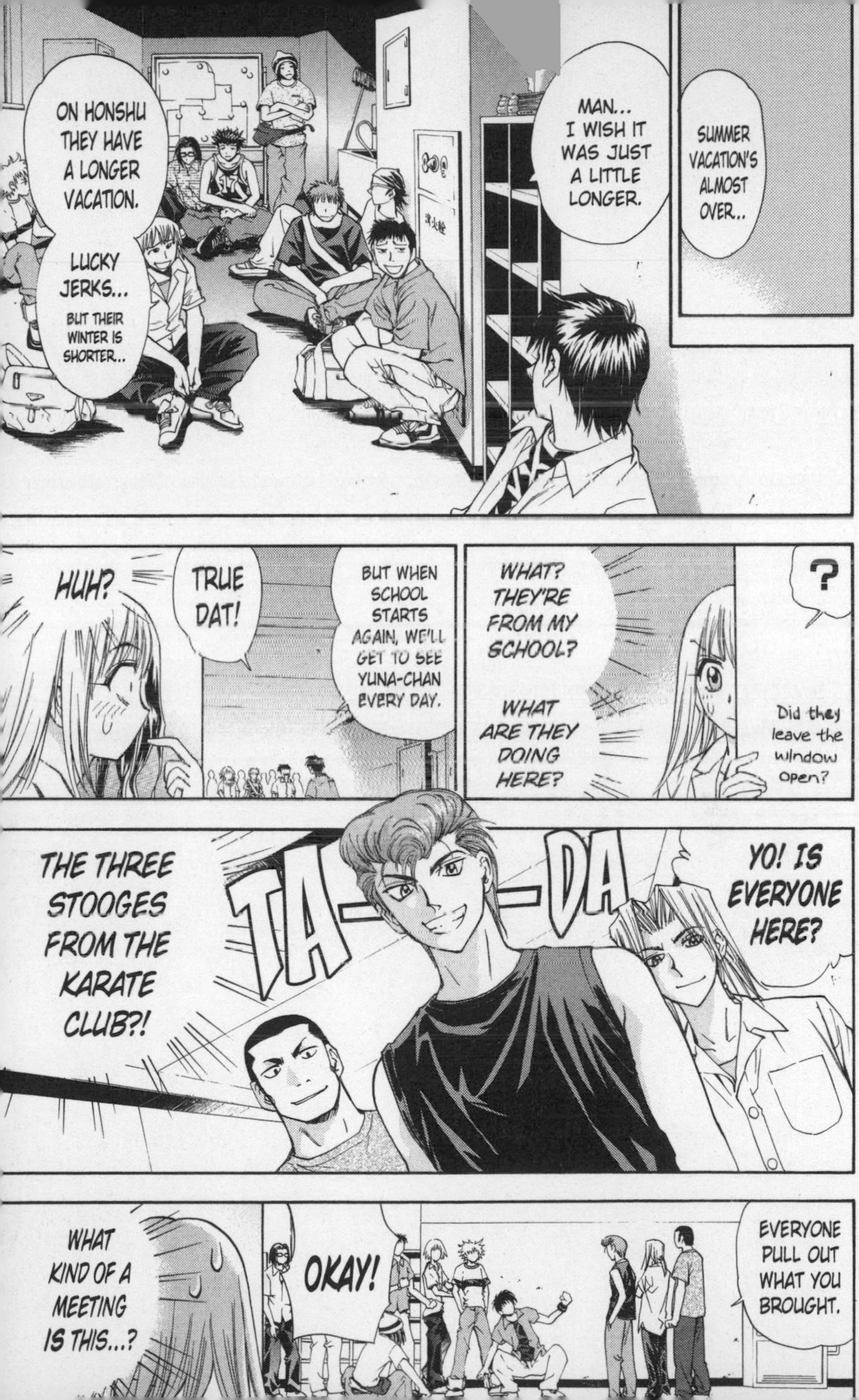
SUMMER VACATION'S ALMOST OVER...
MAN... I WISH IT WAS JUST A LITTLE LONGER.
ON HONSHU THEY HAVE A LONGER VACATION.
LUCKY JERKS...
BUT THEIR WINTER IS SHORTER...
?
Did they leave the window open?
WHAT? THEY'RE FROM MY SCHOOL?
WHAT ARE THEY DOING HERE?
BUT WHEN SCHOOL STARTS AGAIN, WE'LL GET TO SEE YUNA-CHAN EVERY DAY.
TRUE DAT!
HUH?
YO! IS EVERYONE HERE?
TA--DA
THE THREE STOOGES FROM THE KARATE CLUB?!
EVERYONE PULL OUT WHAT YOU BROUGHT.
OKAY!
WHAT KIND OF A MEETING IS THIS...?

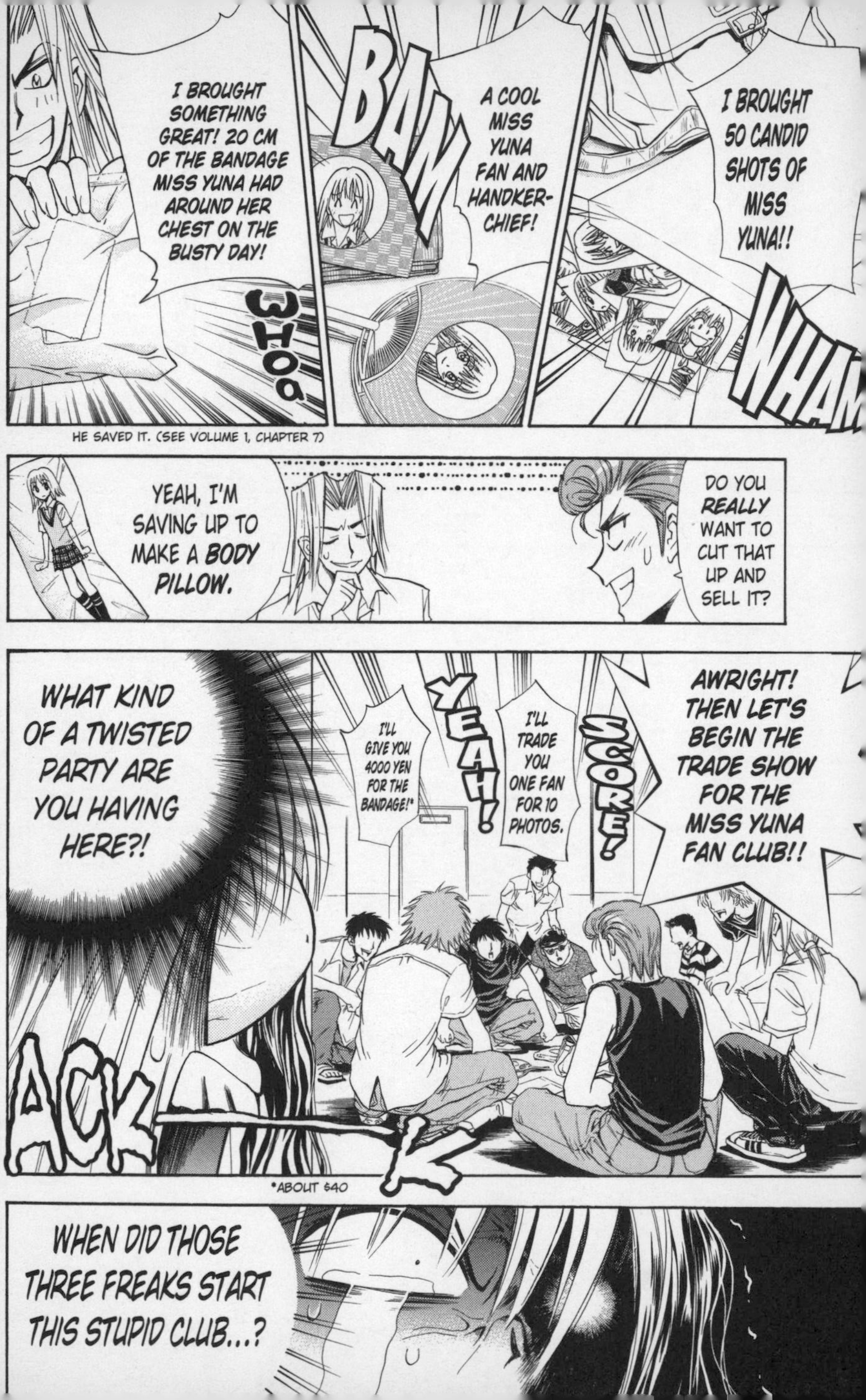
I BROUGHT 50 CANDID SHOTS OF MISS YUNA!!
WHAM
BAM
A COOL MISS YUNA FAN AND HANDKERCHIEF!
I BROUGHT SOMETHING GREAT! 20 CM OF THE BANDAGE MISS YUNA HAD AROUND HER CHEST ON THE BUSTY DAY!
WHOA
HE SAVED IT. (SEE VOLUME 1, CHAPTER 7)
DO YOU REALLY WANT TO CUT THAT UP AND SELL IT?
YEAH, I'M SAVING UP TO MAKE A BODY PILLOW.
AWRIGHT! THEN LET'S BEGIN THE TRADE SHOW FOR THE MISS YUNA FAN CLUB!!
SCORE!
I'LL TRADE YOU ONE FAN FOR 10 PHOTOS.
YEAH!
I'LL GIVE YOU 4000 YEN FOR THE BANDAGE!*
WHAT KIND OF A TWISTED PARTY ARE YOU HAVING HERE?!
ACK
*ABOUT $40
WHEN DID THOSE THREE FREAKS START THIS STUPID CLUB...?

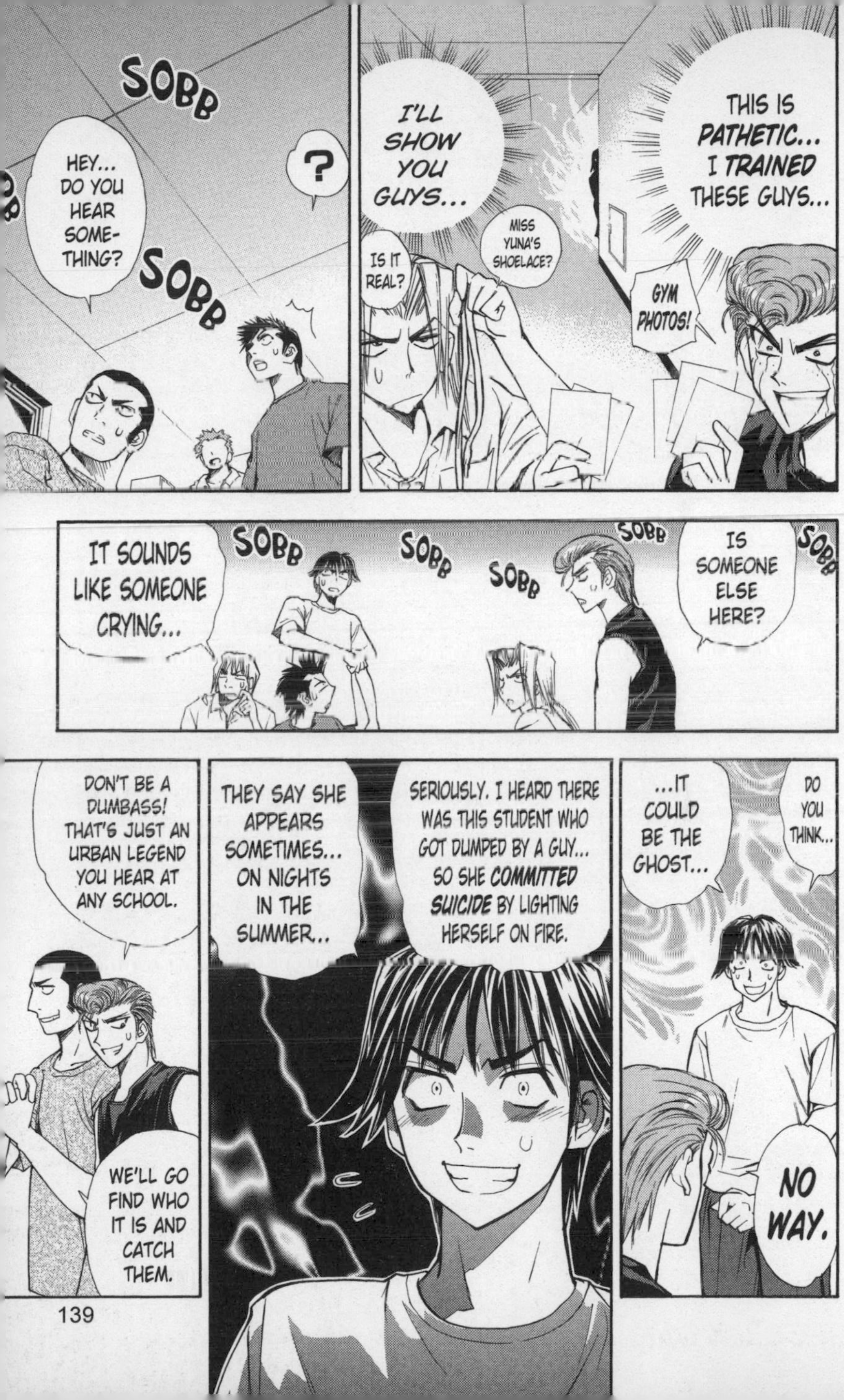
THIS IS PATHETIC... I TRAINED THESE GUYS...
GYM PHOTOS!
MISS YUNA'S SHOELACE?
IS IT REAL?
I'LL SHOW YOU GUYS...
?
SOBB
HEY... DO YOU HEAR SOME-THING?
SOBB
SOBB
IS SOMEONE ELSE HERE?
SOBB
SOBB
SOBB
SOBB
IT SOUNDS LIKE SOMEONE CRYING...
DO YOU THINK...
...IT COULD BE THE GHOST...
NO WAY.
SERIOUSLY. I HEARD THERE WAS THIS STUDENT WHO GOT DUMPED BY A GUY... SO SHE COMMITTED SUICIDE BY LIGHTING HERSELF ON FIRE.
THEY SAY SHE APPEARS SOMETIMES... ON NIGHTS IN THE SUMMER...
DON'T BE A DUMBASS! THAT'S JUST AN URBAN LEGEND YOU HEAR AT ANY SCHOOL.
WE'LL GO FIND WHO IT IS AND CATCH THEM.

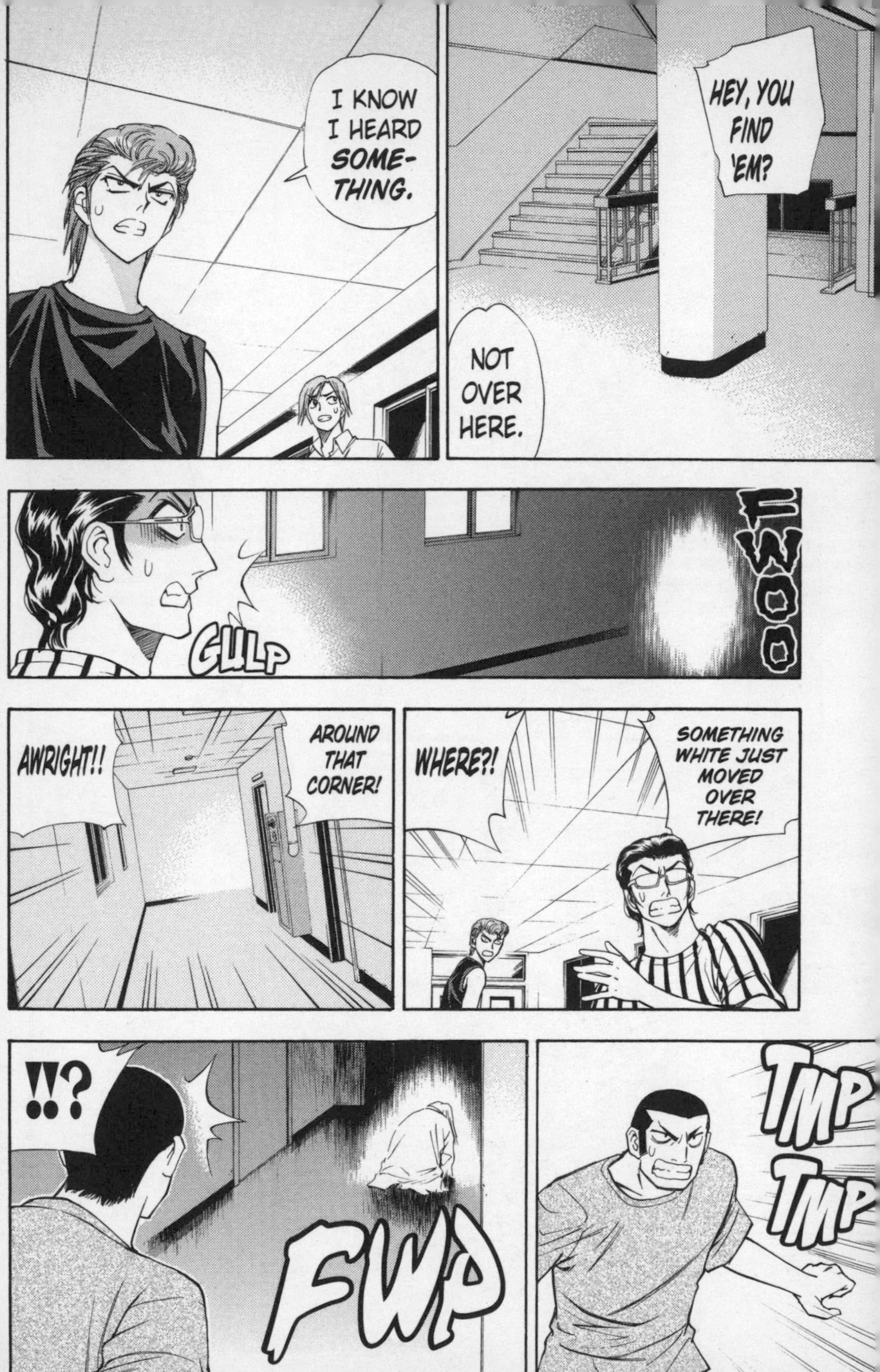
HEY, YOU FIND 'EM?
NOT OVER HERE.
I KNOW I HEARD SOMETHING.
FWOO
GULP
SOMETHING WHITE JUST MOVED OVER THERE!
WHERE?!
AROUND THAT CORNER!
AWRIGHT!!
TMP TMP
!!?
FWP

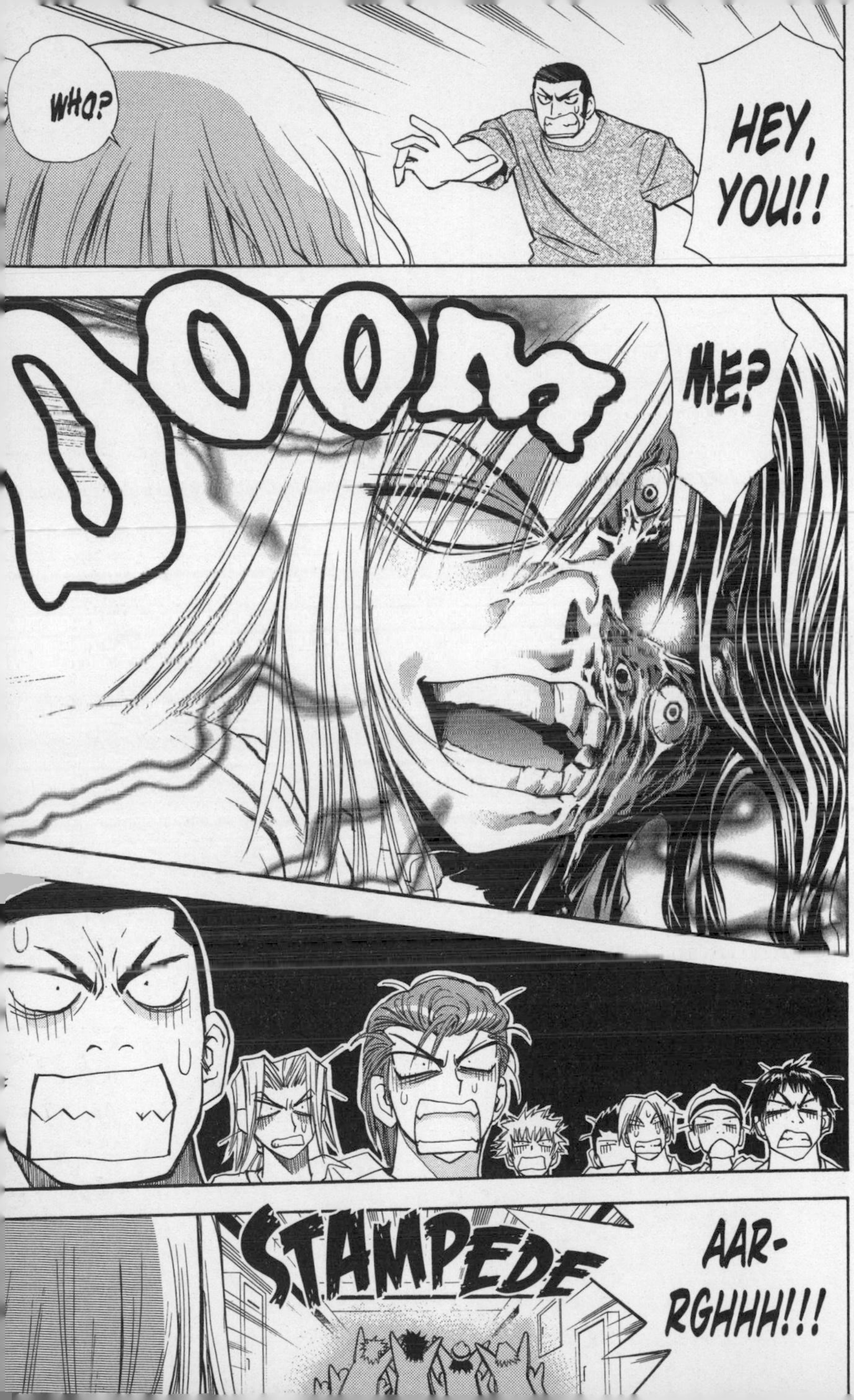
HEY, YOU!!
WHO?
ME?
DOOM
AAR-RGHHH!!!
STAMPEDE

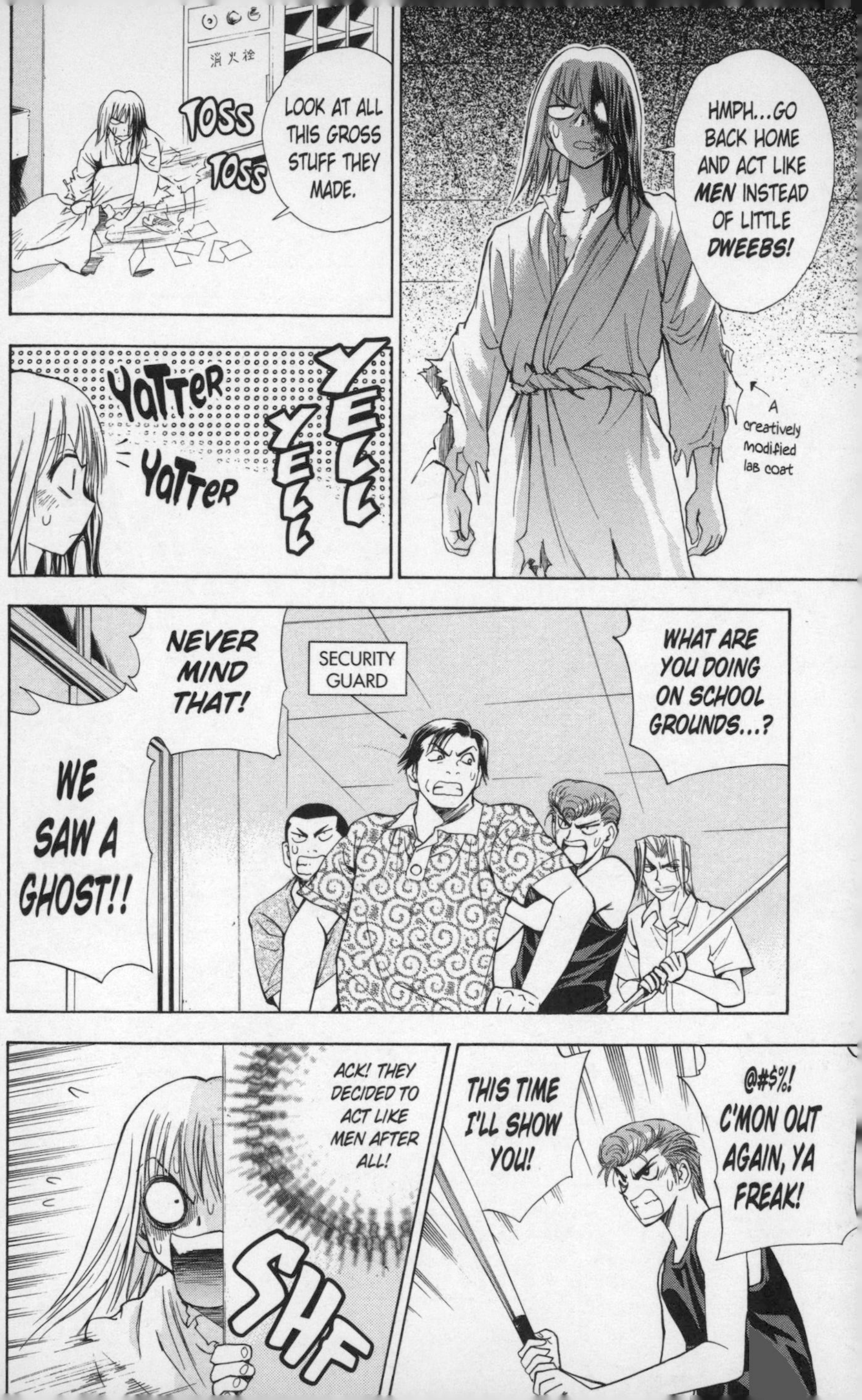

HMPH...GO BACK HOME AND ACT LIKE MEN INSTEAD OF LITTLE DWEEBS!
A creatively modified lab coat
消火栓
LOOK AT ALL THIS GROSS STUFF THEY MADE.
TOSS
TOSS
YELL
YELL
YATTER
YATTER
WHAT ARE YOU DOING ON SCHOOL GROUNDS...?
SECURITY GUARD
NEVER MIND THAT!
WE SAW A GHOST!!
@#$%! C'MON OUT AGAIN, YA FREAK!
THIS TIME I'LL SHOW YOU!
ACK! THEY DECIDED TO ACT LIKE MEN AFTER ALL!
SHF

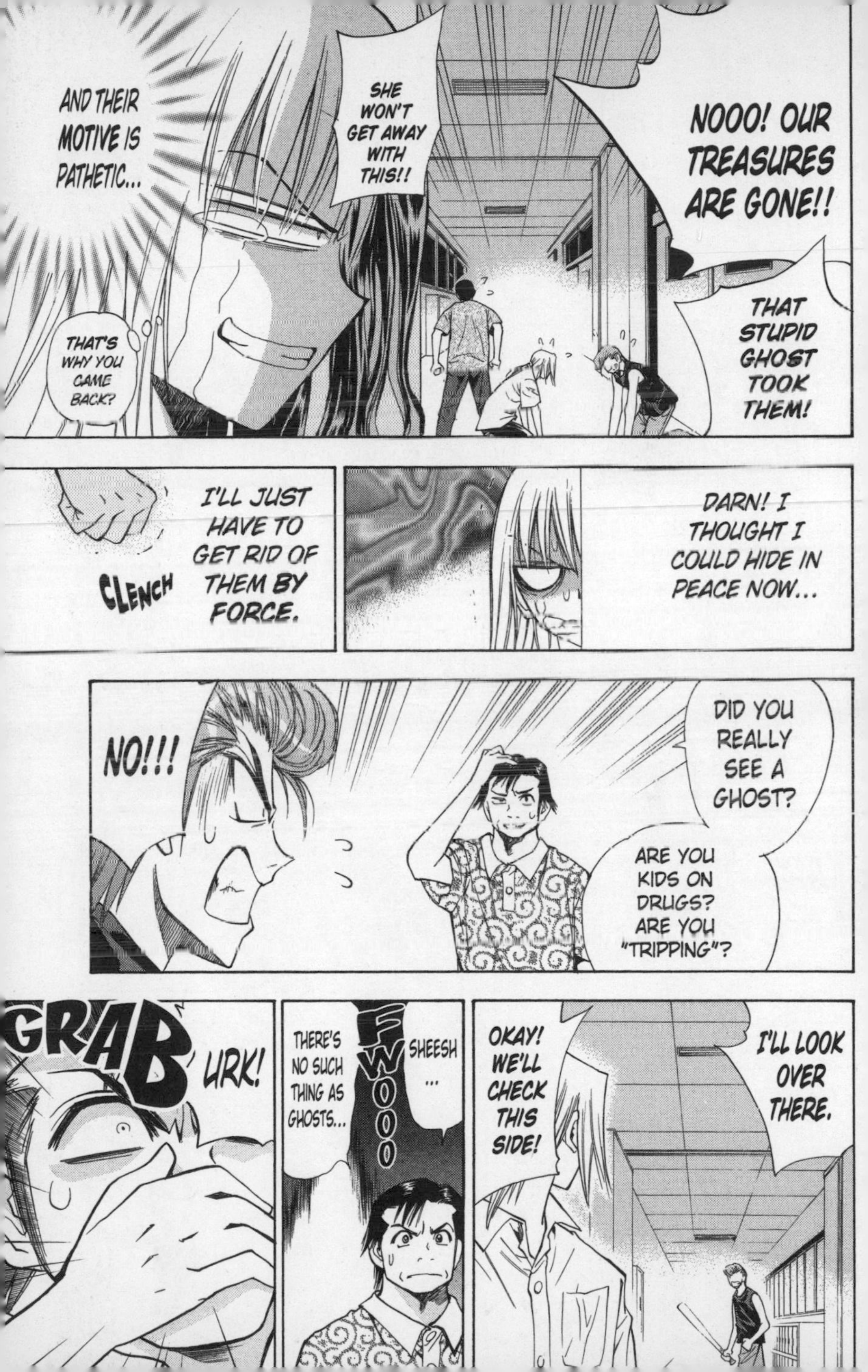
NOOO! OUR TREASURES ARE GONE!!
THAT STUPID GHOST TOOK THEM!
SHE WON'T GET AWAY WITH THIS!!
AND THEIR MOTIVE IS PATHETIC...
THAT'S WHY YOU CAME BACK?
DARN! I THOUGHT I COULD HIDE IN PEACE NOW...
I'LL JUST HAVE TO GET RID OF THEM BY FORCE.
CLENCH
DID YOU REALLY SEE A GHOST?
ARE YOU KIDS ON DRUGS? ARE YOU "TRIPPING"?
NO!!!
I'LL LOOK OVER THERE.
OKAY! WE'LL CHECK THIS SIDE!
SHEESH ...
FWOOOO
THERE'S NO SUCH THING AS GHOSTS...
URK!
GRAB

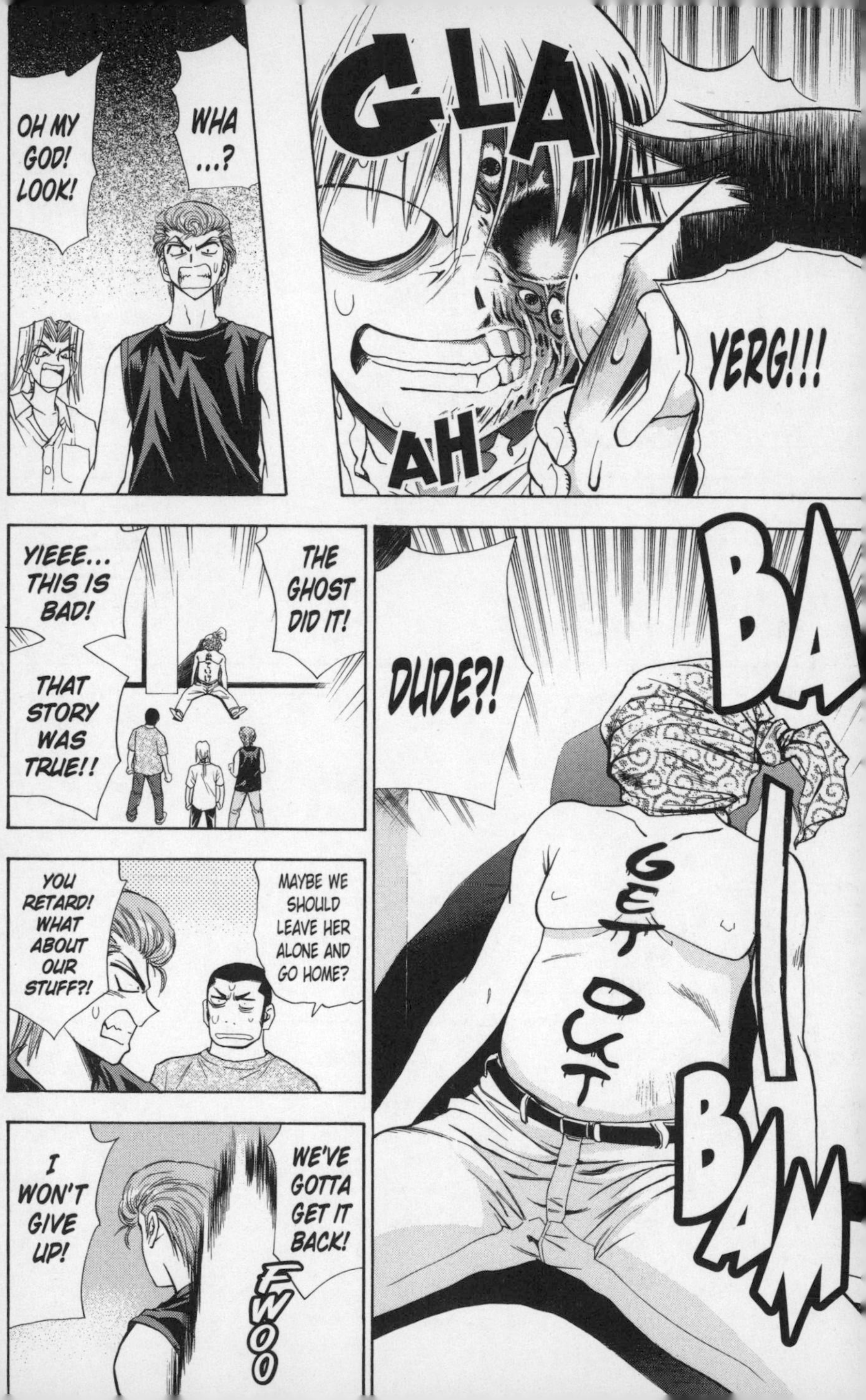
GLA
AH
YERG!!!
WHA ...?
OH MY GOD! LOOK!
BA-
BAM
DUDE?!
GET OUT
THE GHOST DID IT!
YIEEE... THIS IS BAD!
THAT STORY WAS TRUE!!
MAYBE WE SHOULD LEAVE HER ALONE AND GO HOME?
YOU RETARD! WHAT ABOUT OUR STUFF?!
WE'VE GOTTA GET IT BACK!
FWOO
I WON'T GIVE UP!

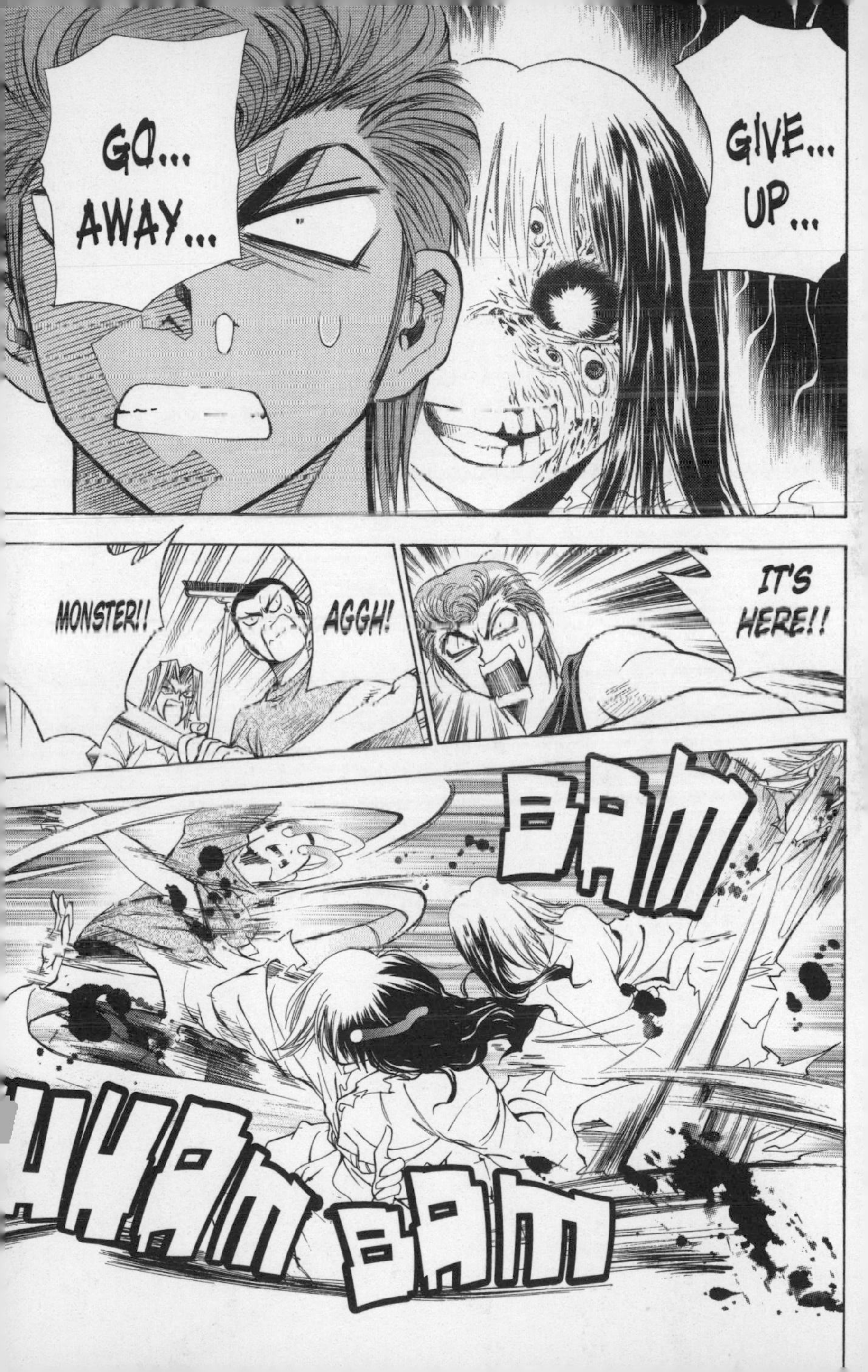
GIVE... UP...
GO... AWAY...
IT'S HERE!!
AGGH!
MONSTER!!
BAM
WHAM BAM

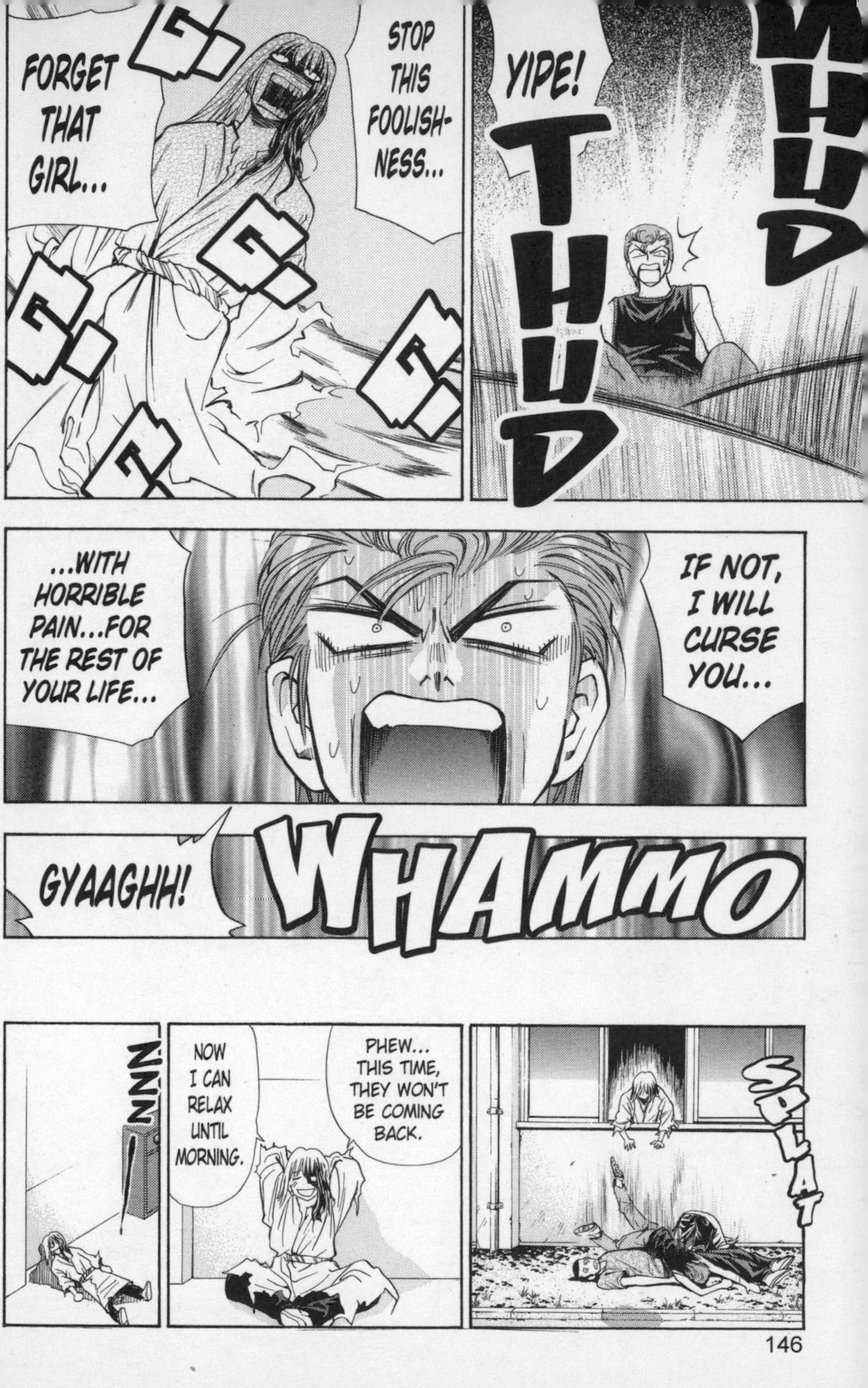
WHUD
YIPE!
THUD
STOP THIS FOOLISHNESS...
FORGET THAT GIRL...
IF NOT, I WILL CURSE YOU...
...WITH HORRIBLE PAIN...FOR THE REST OF YOUR LIFE...
WHAMMO
GYAAGHH!
SPLAT
PHEW... THIS TIME, THEY WON'T BE COMING BACK.
NOW I CAN RELAX UNTIL MORNING.
NNN

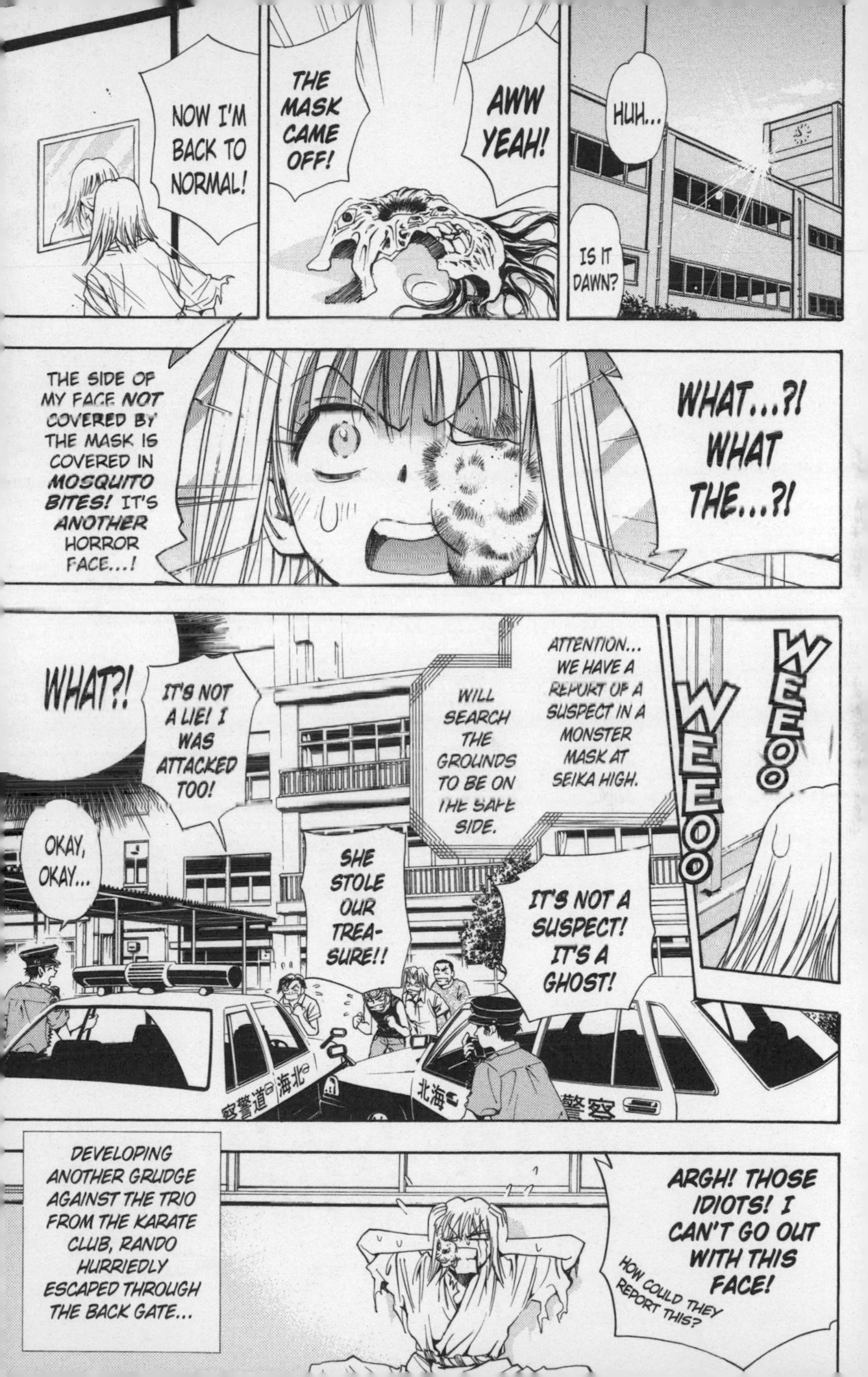
HUH...
IS IT DAWN?
AWW YEAH!
THE MASK CAME OFF!
NOW I'M BACK TO NORMAL!
WHAT...?! WHAT THE...?!
THE SIDE OF MY FACE NOT COVERED BY THE MASK IS COVERED IN MOSQUITO BITES! IT'S ANOTHER HORROR FACE...!
WEEOO WEEOO
ATTENTION... WE HAVE A REPORT OF A SUSPECT IN A MONSTER MASK AT SEIKA HIGH.
WILL SEARCH THE GROUNDS TO BE ON THE SAFE SIDE.
IT'S NOT A SUSPECT! IT'S A GHOST!
SHE STOLE OUR TREASURE!!
WHAT?!
IT'S NOT A LIE! I WAS ATTACKED TOO!
OKAY, OKAY...
ARGH! THOSE IDIOTS! I CAN'T GO OUT WITH THIS FACE!
HOW COULD THEY REPORT THIS?
DEVELOPING ANOTHER GRUDGE AGAINST THE TRIO FROM THE KARATE CLUB, RANDO HURRIEDLY ESCAPED THROUGH THE BACK GATE...

Pretty Face

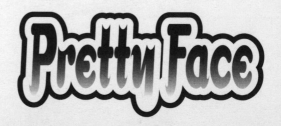

Chapter 16: The New Semester Visitor

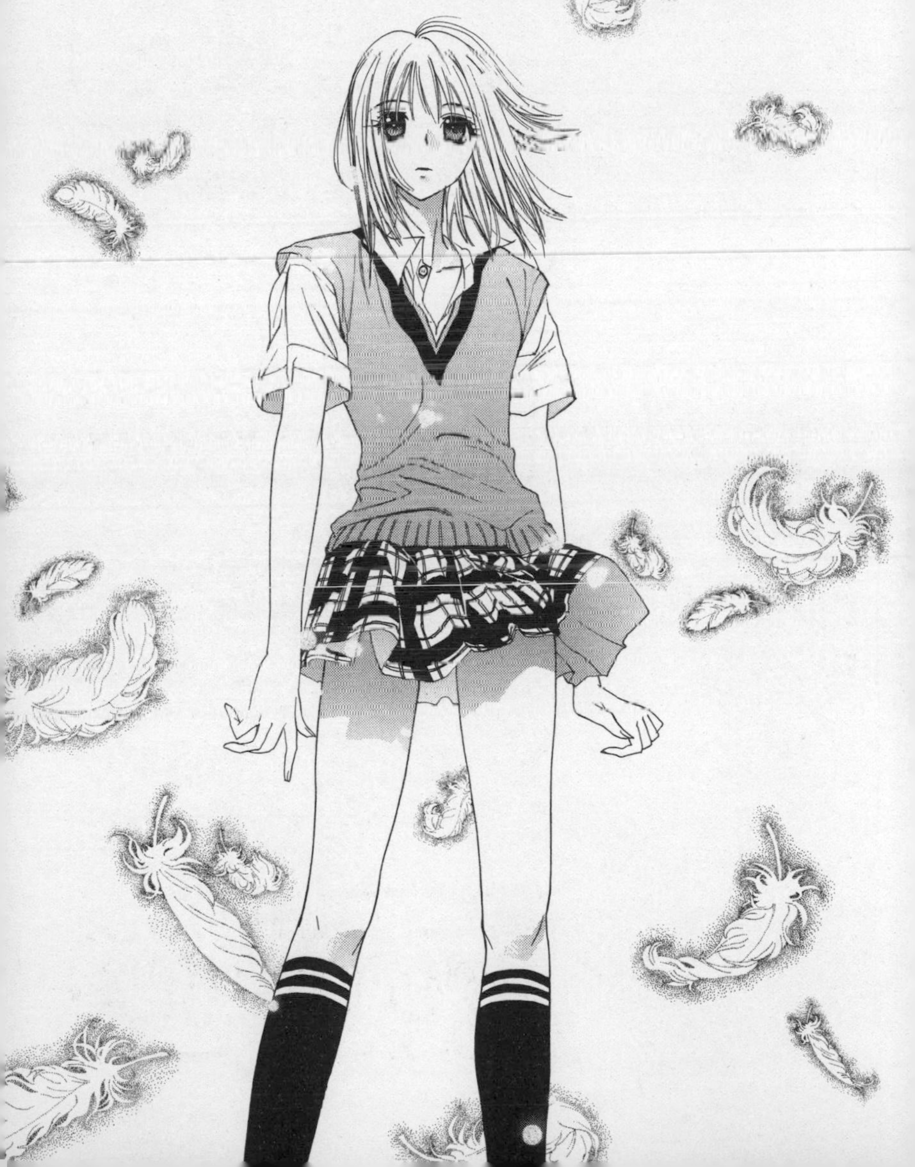

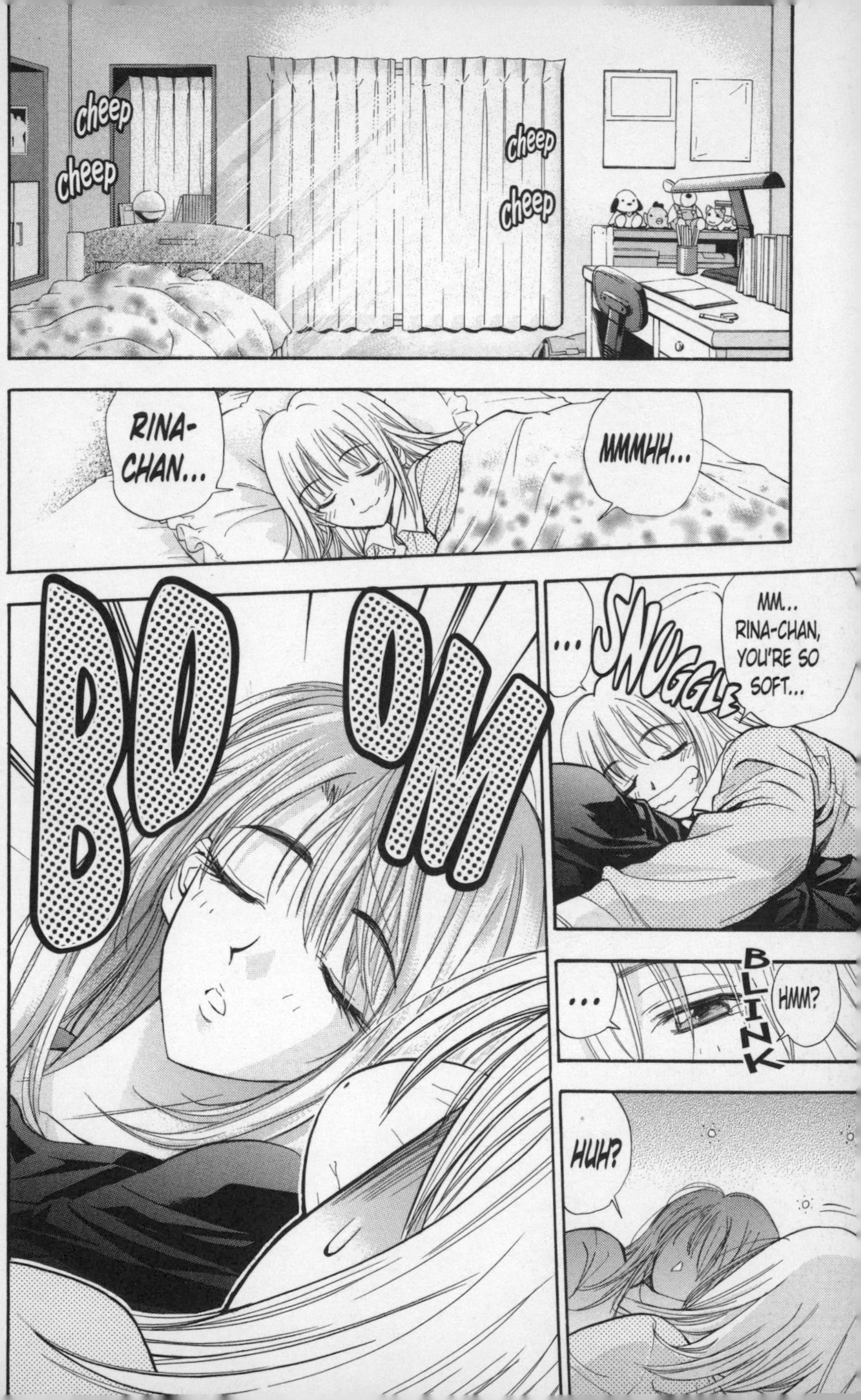
cheep
cheep
cheep
cheep
MMMHH...
RINA-CHAN...
MM... RINA-CHAN, YOU'RE SO SOFT...
SNUGGLE
...
HMM?
BLINK
...
HUH?
BOOM

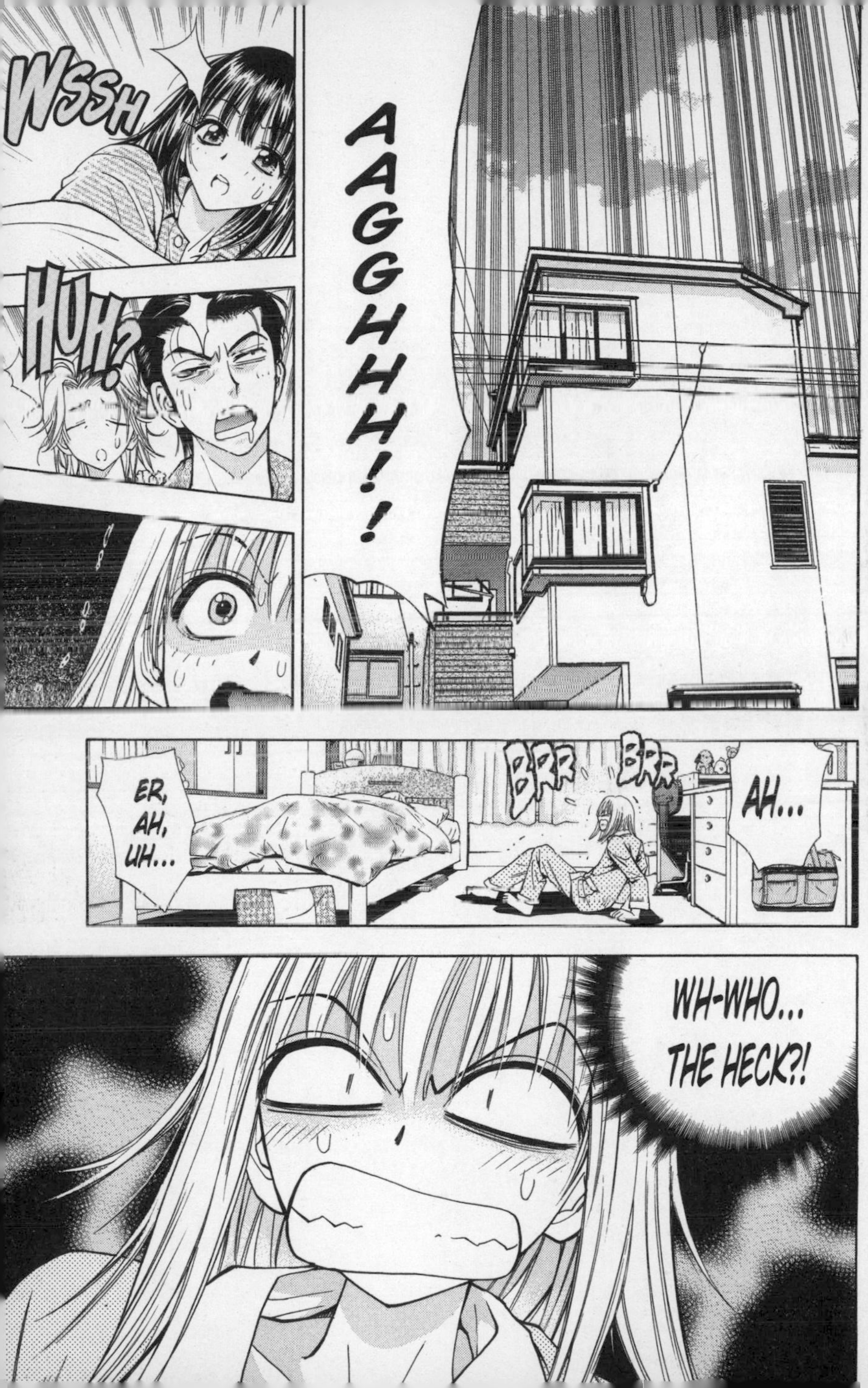
AAGGHHHH!!
WSSH
HUH?
AH...
BRR BRR
ER, AH, UH...
WH-WHO... THE HECK?!

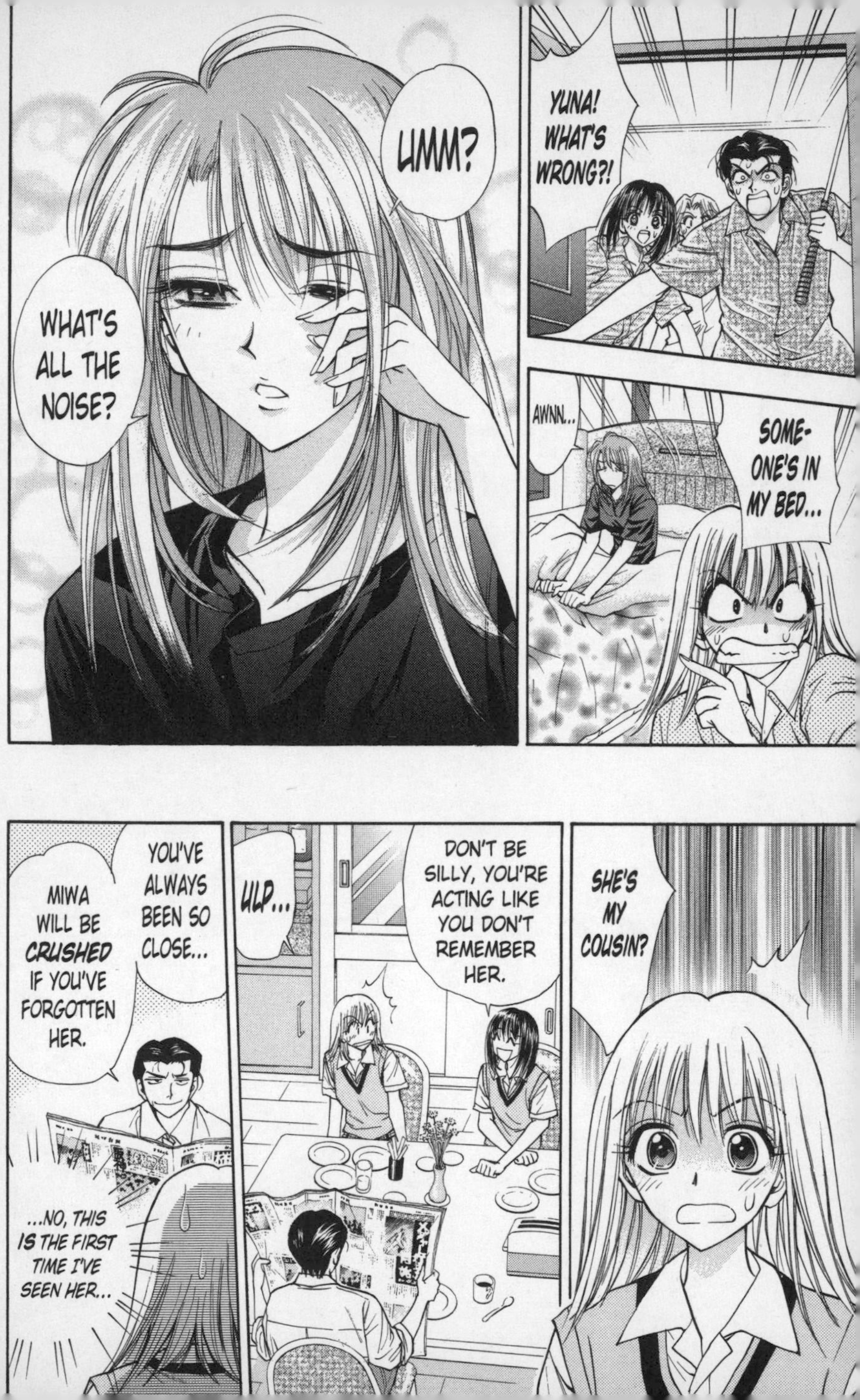
YUNA! WHAT'S WRONG?!
SOME-ONE'S IN MY BED...
AWNN...
UMM?
WHAT'S ALL THE NOISE?
SHE'S MY COUSIN?
DON'T BE SILLY, YOU'RE ACTING LIKE YOU DON'T REMEMBER HER.
ULP...
YOU'VE ALWAYS BEEN SO CLOSE...
MIWA WILL BE CRUSHED IF YOU'VE FORGOTTEN HER.
...NO, THIS IS THE FIRST TIME I'VE SEEN HER...

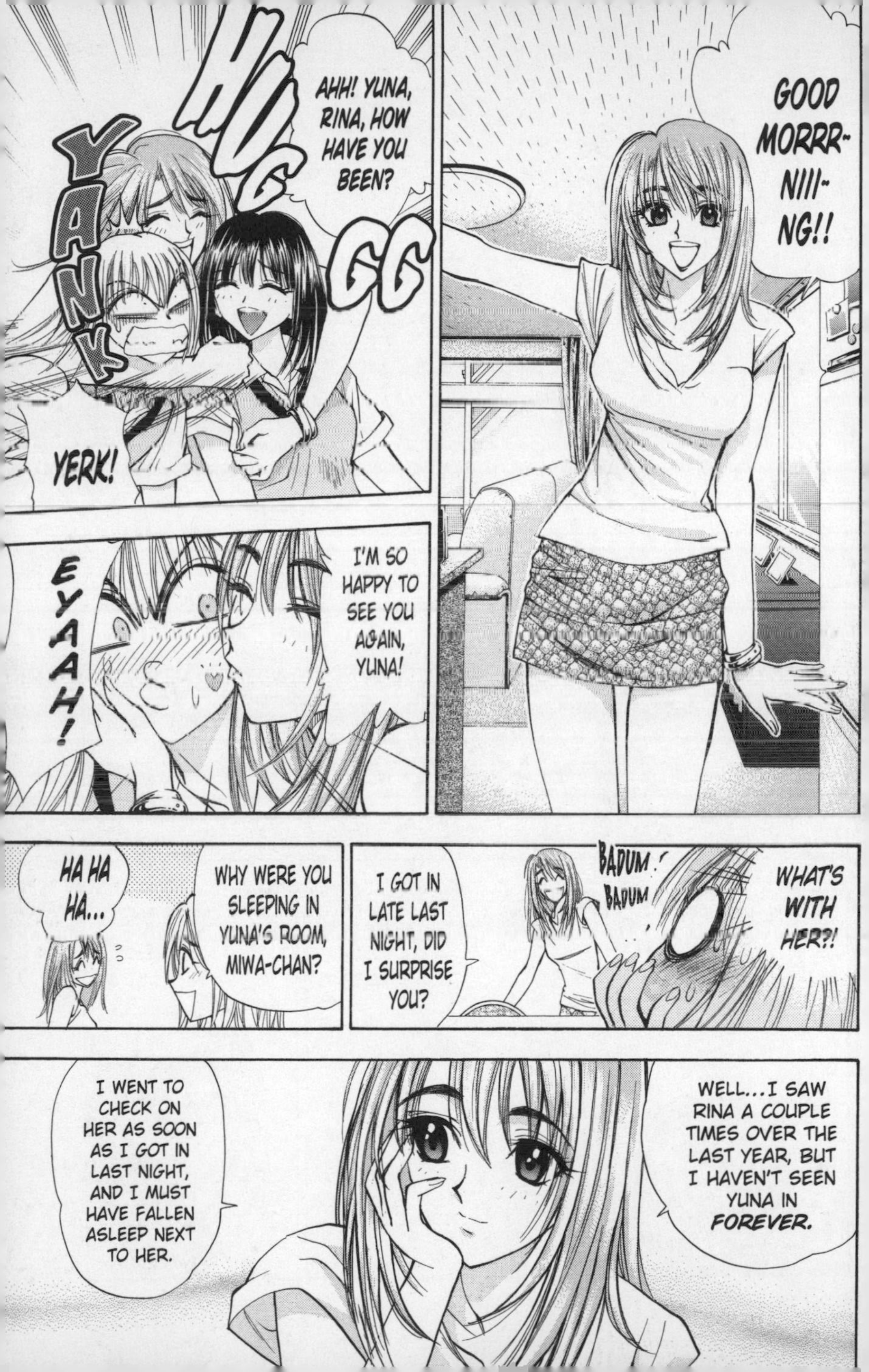
GOOD MORRR-NIII-NG!!
HUGG
AHH! YUNA, RINA, HOW HAVE YOU BEEN?
YANK
YERK!
I'M SO HAPPY TO SEE YOU AGAIN, YUNA!
EYAAAH!
WHAT'S WITH HER?!
BADUM BADUM
I GOT IN LATE LAST NIGHT, DID I SURPRISE YOU?
WHY WERE YOU SLEEPING IN YUNA'S ROOM, MIWA-CHAN?
HA HA HA...
WELL...I SAW RINA A COUPLE TIMES OVER THE LAST YEAR, BUT I HAVEN'T SEEN YUNA IN **FOREVER.**
I WENT TO CHECK ON HER AS SOON AS I GOT IN LAST NIGHT, AND I MUST HAVE FALLEN ASLEEP NEXT TO HER.

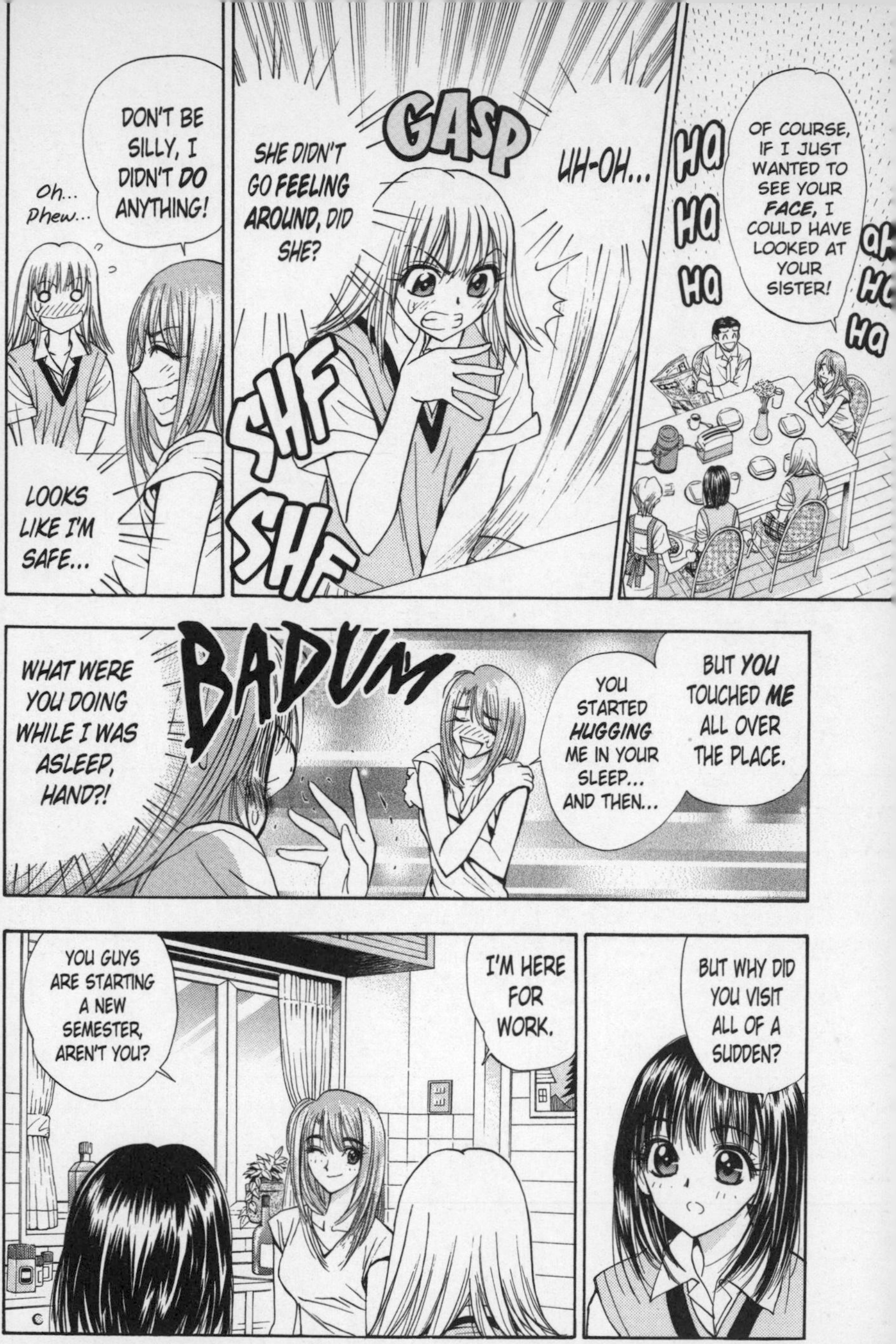

ah Ha Ha
OF COURSE, IF I JUST WANTED TO SEE YOUR FACE, I COULD HAVE LOOKED AT YOUR SISTER!
HA HA HA
UH-OH...
GASP
SHE DIDN'T GO FEELING AROUND, DID SHE?
SHF SHF
DON'T BE SILLY, I DIDN'T DO ANYTHING!
Oh... Phew...
LOOKS LIKE I'M SAFE...
BUT YOU TOUCHED ME ALL OVER THE PLACE.
YOU STARTED HUGGING ME IN YOUR SLEEP... AND THEN...
BADUM
WHAT WERE YOU DOING WHILE I WAS ASLEEP, HAND?!
BUT WHY DID YOU VISIT ALL OF A SUDDEN?
I'M HERE FOR WORK.
YOU GUYS ARE STARTING A NEW SEMESTER, AREN'T YOU?

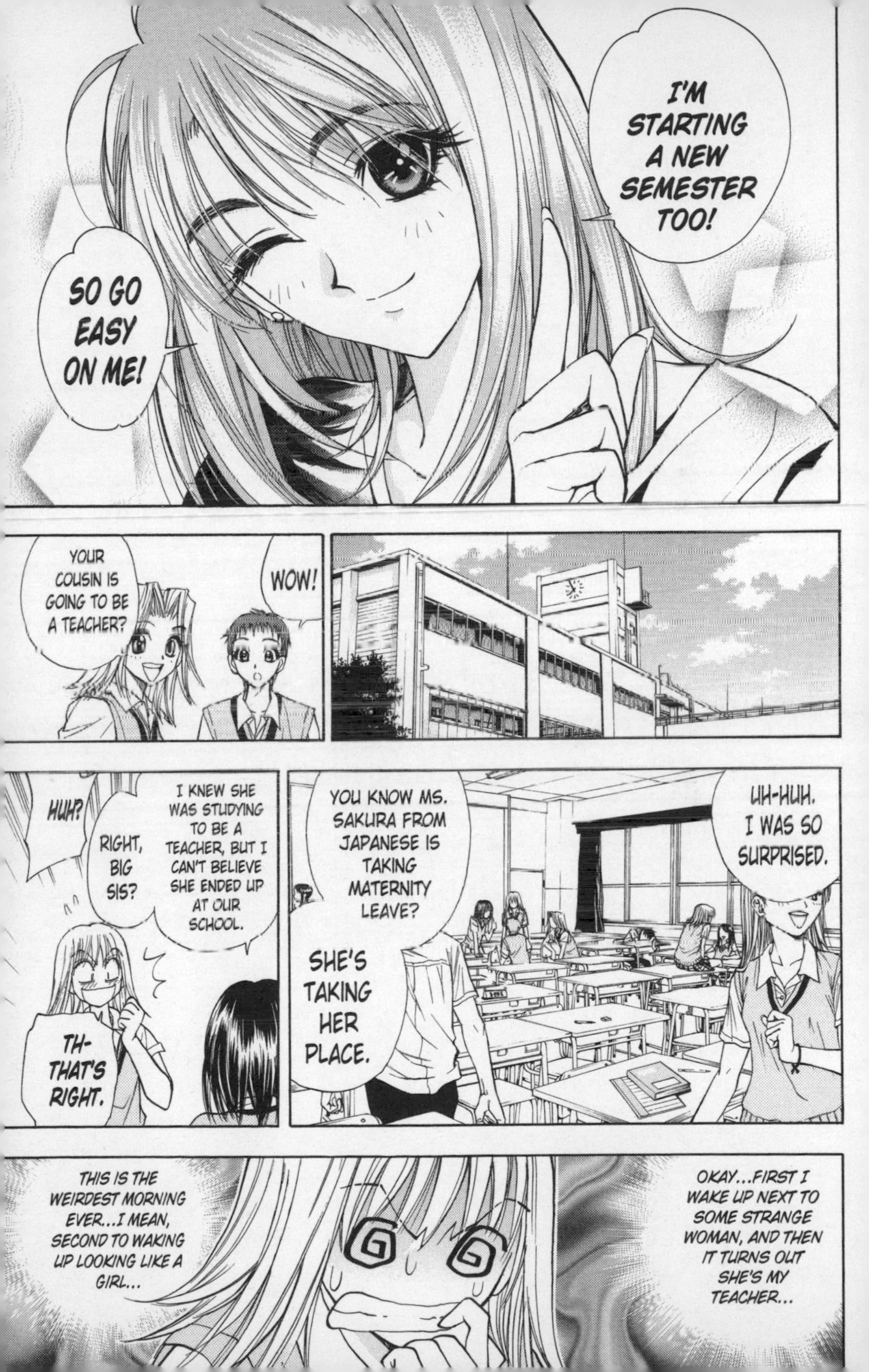
I'M STARTING A NEW SEMESTER TOO!
SO GO EASY ON ME!
WOW!
YOUR COUSIN IS GOING TO BE A TEACHER?
UH-HUH. I WAS SO SURPRISED.
YOU KNOW MS. SAKURA FROM JAPANESE IS TAKING MATERNITY LEAVE?
SHE'S TAKING HER PLACE.
I KNEW SHE WAS STUDYING TO BE A TEACHER, BUT I CAN'T BELIEVE SHE ENDED UP AT OUR SCHOOL.
RIGHT, BIG SIS?
HUH?
TH-THAT'S RIGHT.
OKAY...FIRST I WAKE UP NEXT TO SOME STRANGE WOMAN, AND THEN IT TURNS OUT SHE'S MY TEACHER...
THIS IS THE WEIRDEST MORNING EVER...I MEAN, SECOND TO WAKING UP LOOKING LIKE A GIRL...

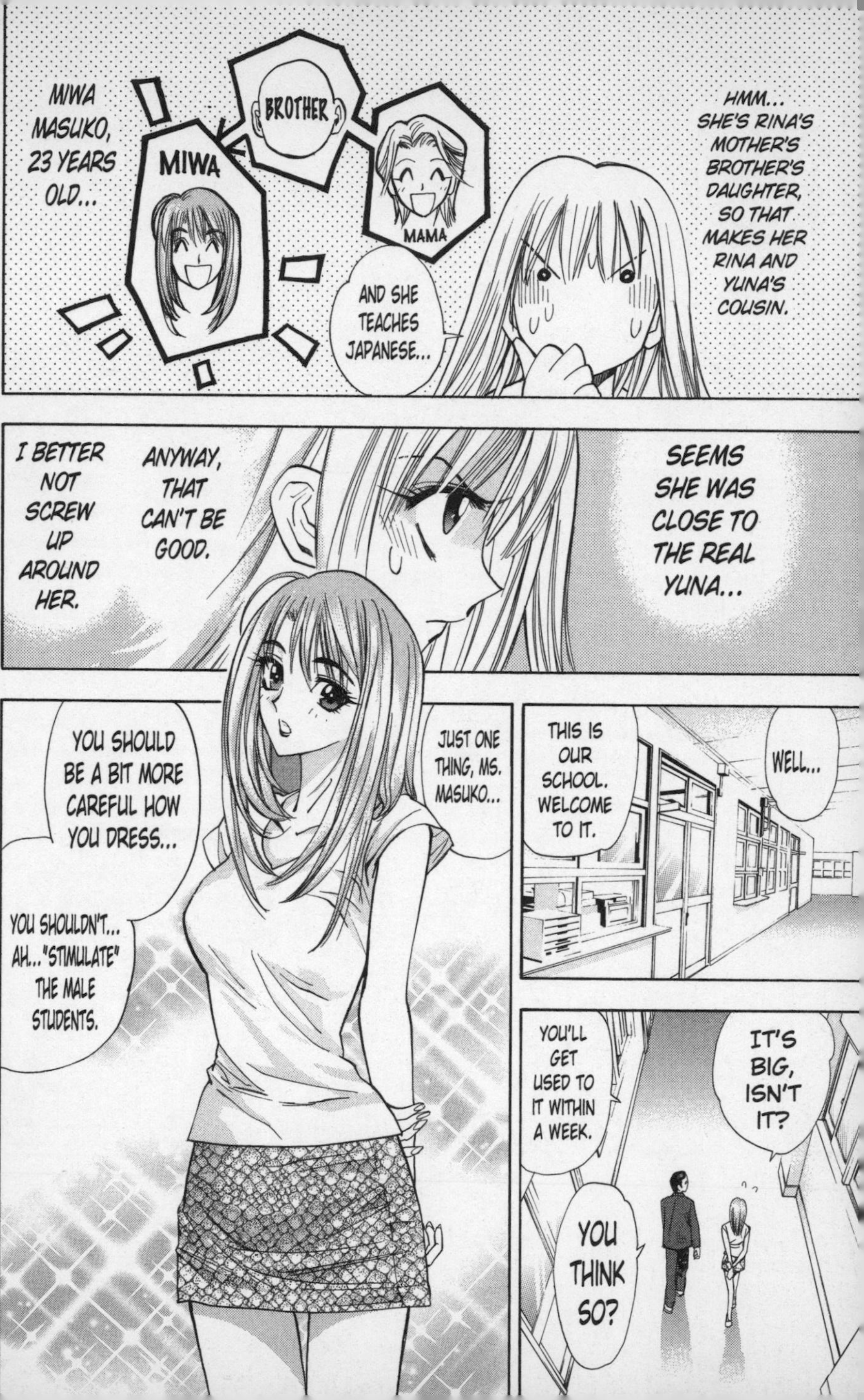
HMM... SHE'S RINA'S MOTHER'S BROTHER'S DAUGHTER, SO THAT MAKES HER RINA AND YUNA'S COUSIN.
BROTHER
MAMA
MIWA
MIWA MASUKO, 23 YEARS OLD...
AND SHE TEACHES JAPANESE...
SEEMS SHE WAS CLOSE TO THE REAL YUNA...
ANYWAY, THAT CAN'T BE GOOD.
I BETTER NOT SCREW UP AROUND HER.
WELL...
THIS IS OUR SCHOOL. WELCOME TO IT.
IT'S BIG, ISN'T IT?
YOU'LL GET USED TO IT WITHIN A WEEK.
YOU THINK SO?
JUST ONE THING, MS. MASUKO...
YOU SHOULD BE A BIT MORE CAREFUL HOW YOU DRESS...
YOU SHOULDN'T... AH..."STIMULATE" THE MALE STUDENTS.

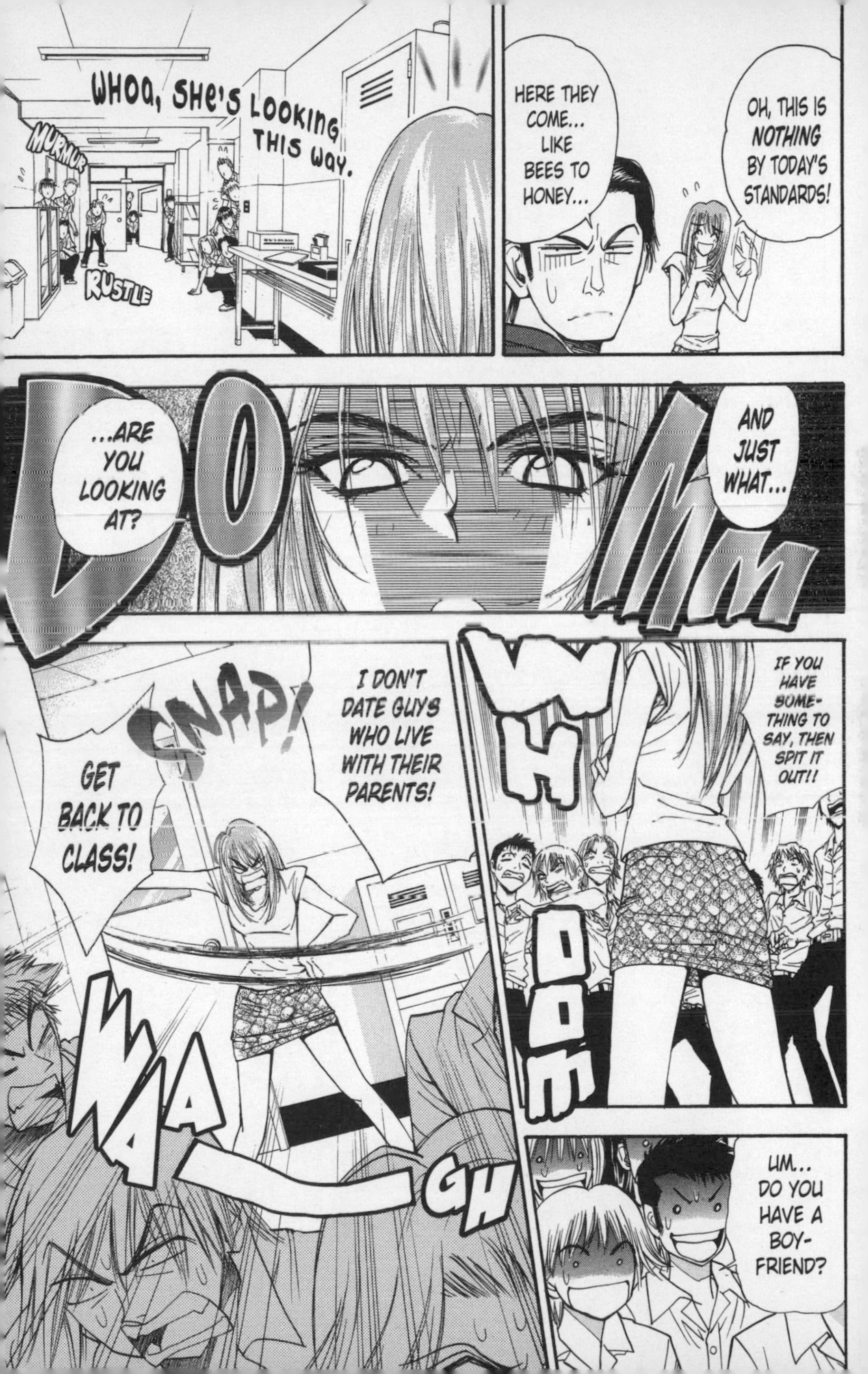
OH, THIS IS NOTHING BY TODAY'S STANDARDS!
HERE THEY COME... LIKE BEES TO HONEY...
MURMUR
WHOA, SHE'S LOOKING THIS WAY.
RUSTLE
AND JUST WHAT...
...ARE YOU LOOKING AT?
DOMM
IF YOU HAVE SOME-THING TO SAY, THEN SPIT IT OUT!!
WHOOM
UM... DO YOU HAVE A BOY-FRIEND?
I DON'T DATE GUYS WHO LIVE WITH THEIR PARENTS!
SNAP!
GET BACK TO CLASS!
WAA—GH

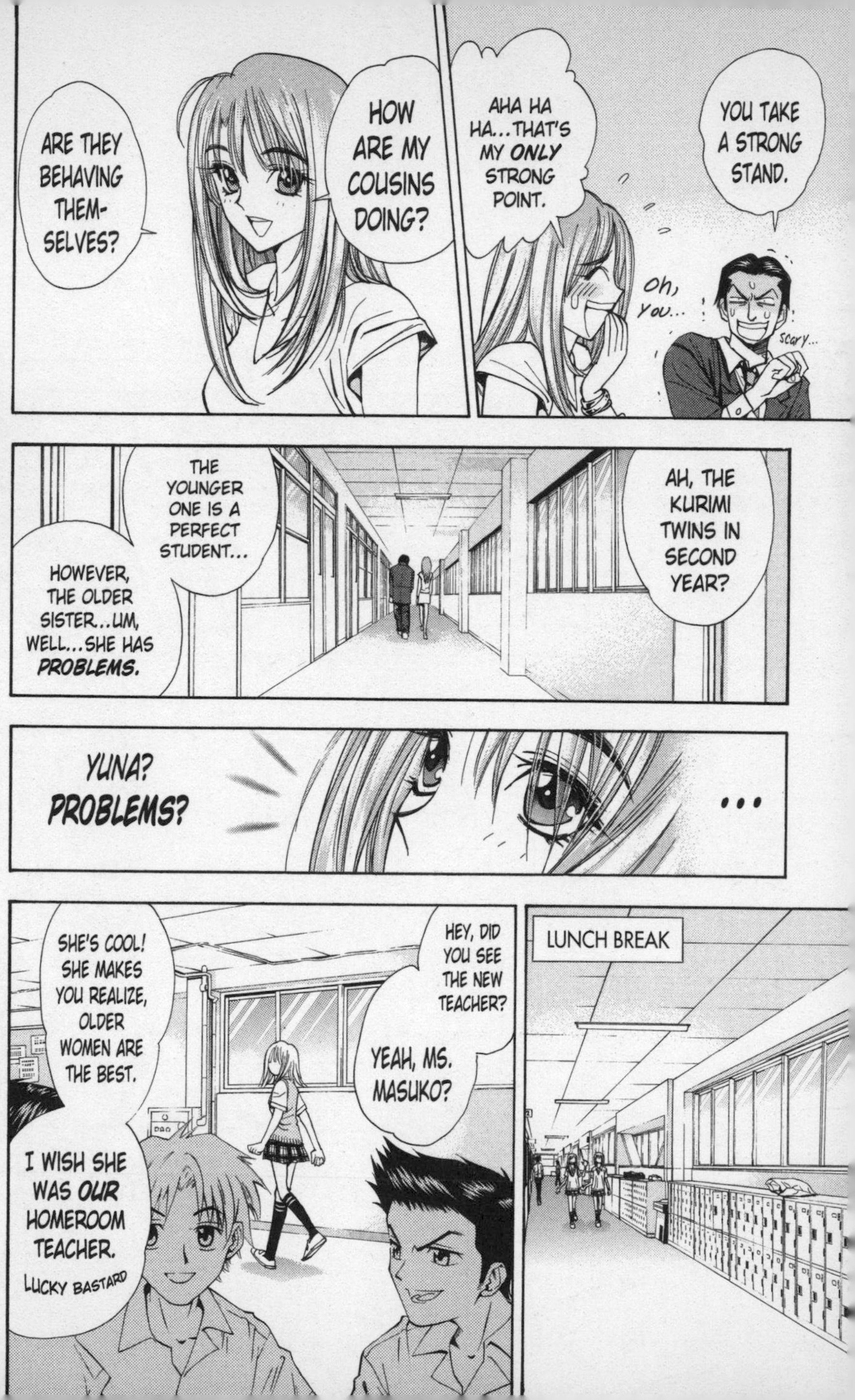
YOU TAKE A STRONG STAND.
AHA HA HA...THAT'S MY ONLY STRONG POINT.
Oh, you...
scary...
HOW ARE MY COUSINS DOING?
ARE THEY BEHAVING THEM-SELVES?
AH, THE KURIMI TWINS IN SECOND YEAR?
THE YOUNGER ONE IS A PERFECT STUDENT...
HOWEVER, THE OLDER SISTER...UM, WELL...SHE HAS PROBLEMS.
...
YUNA? PROBLEMS?
LUNCH BREAK
HEY, DID YOU SEE THE NEW TEACHER?
YEAH, MS. MASUKO?
SHE'S COOL! SHE MAKES YOU REALIZE, OLDER WOMEN ARE THE BEST.
I WISH SHE WAS OUR HOMEROOM TEACHER.
LUCKY BASTARD

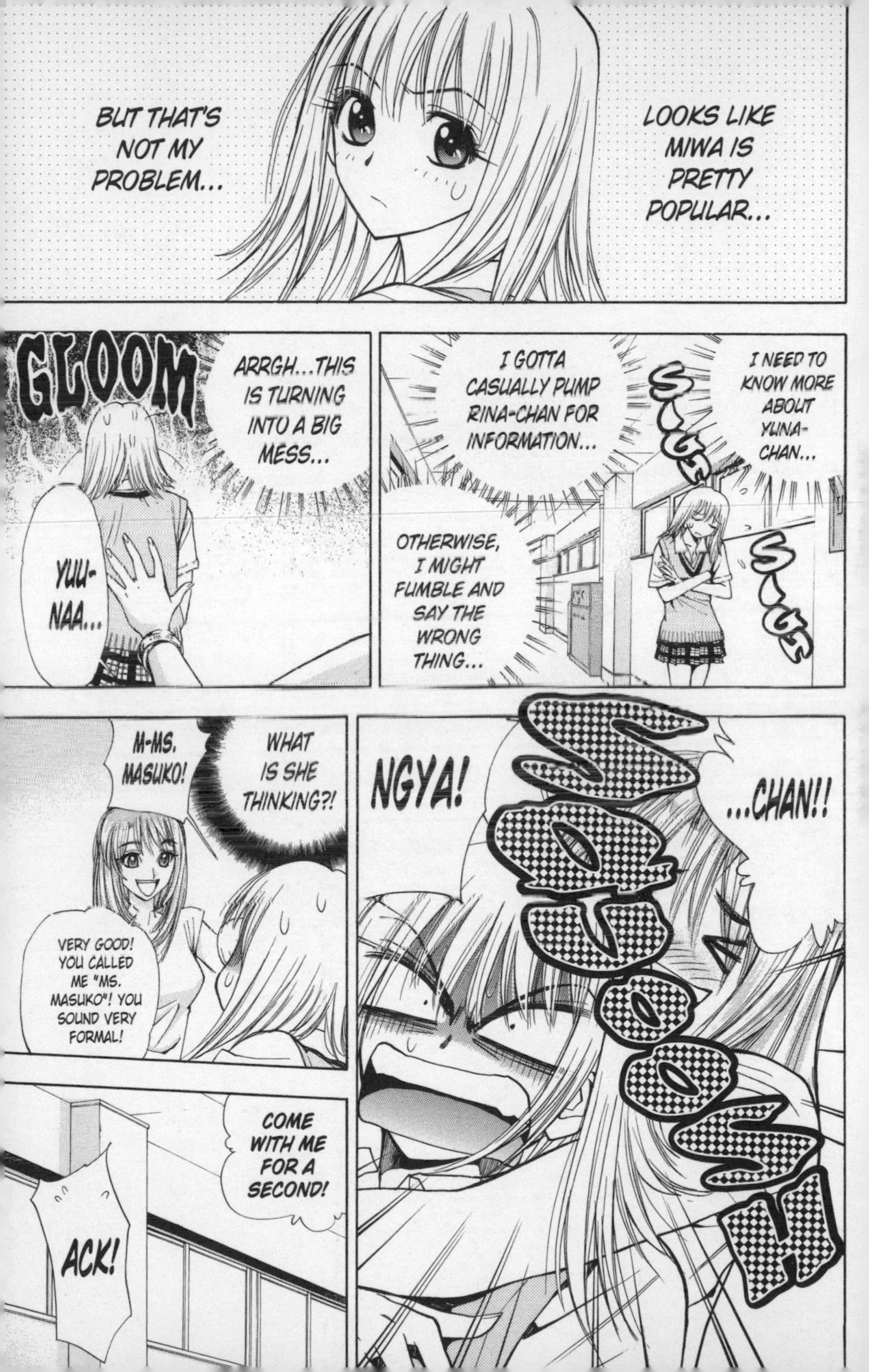
LOOKS LIKE MIWA IS PRETTY POPULAR...
BUT THAT'S NOT MY PROBLEM...
I NEED TO KNOW MORE ABOUT YUNA-CHAN...
SIGH
I GOTTA CASUALLY PUMP RINA-CHAN FOR INFORMATION...
SIGH
OTHERWISE, I MIGHT FUMBLE AND SAY THE WRONG THING...
GLOOM
ARRGH...THIS IS TURNING INTO A BIG MESS...
YUU-NAA...
...CHAN!!
SWOOSH
NGYA!
WHAT IS SHE THINKING?!
M-MS. MASUKO!
VERY GOOD! YOU CALLED ME "MS. MASUKO"! YOU SOUND VERY FORMAL!
COME WITH ME FOR A SECOND!
ACK!

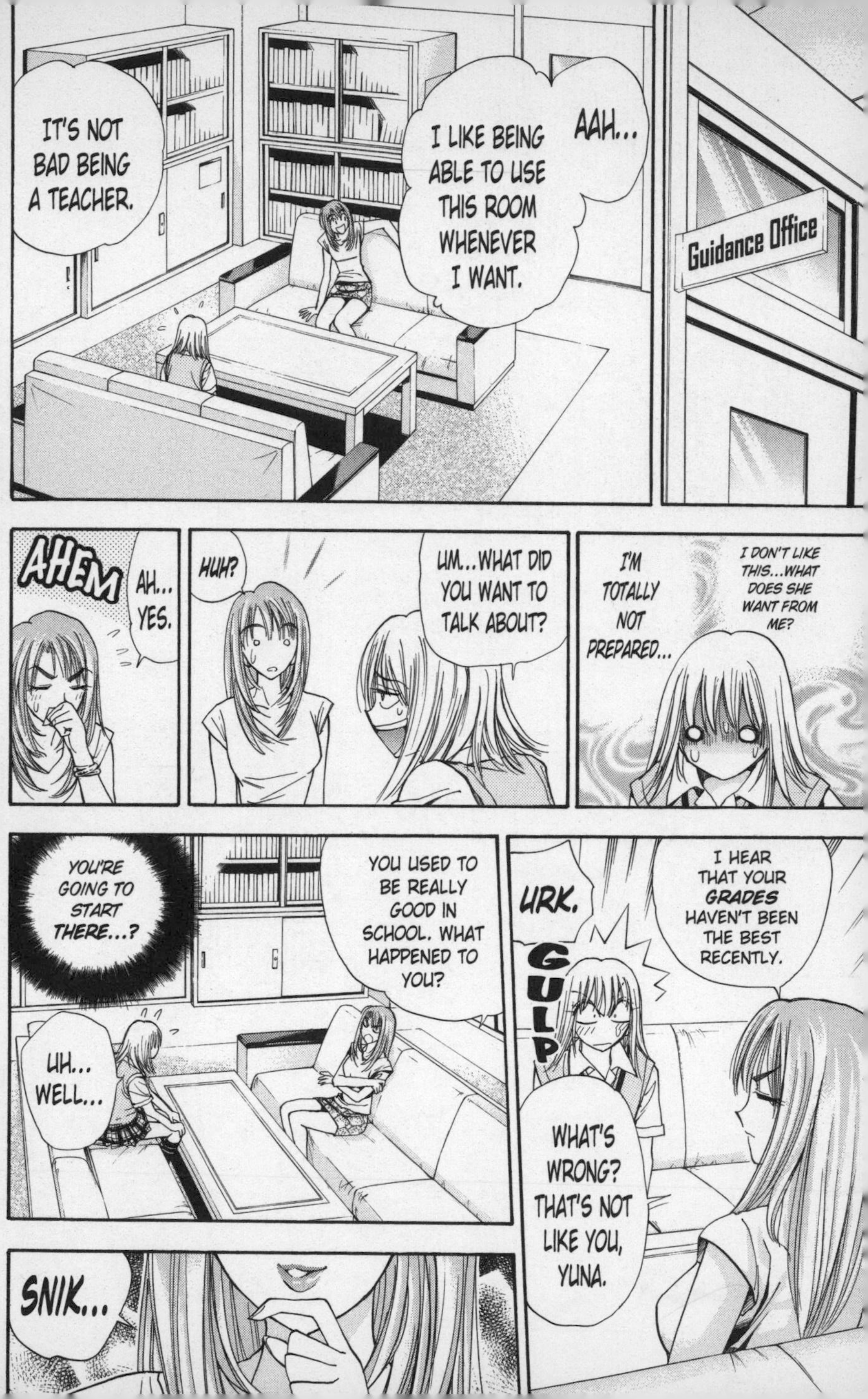
Guidance Office
AAH...
I LIKE BEING ABLE TO USE THIS ROOM WHENEVER I WANT.
IT'S NOT BAD BEING A TEACHER.
I DON'T LIKE THIS...WHAT DOES SHE WANT FROM ME?
I'M TOTALLY NOT PREPARED...
UM...WHAT DID YOU WANT TO TALK ABOUT?
HUH?
AH... YES.
AHEM
I HEAR THAT YOUR GRADES HAVEN'T BEEN THE BEST RECENTLY.
URK.
GULP
WHAT'S WRONG? THAT'S NOT LIKE YOU, YUNA.
YOU USED TO BE REALLY GOOD IN SCHOOL. WHAT HAPPENED TO YOU?
YOU'RE GOING TO START THERE...?
UH... WELL...
SNIK...

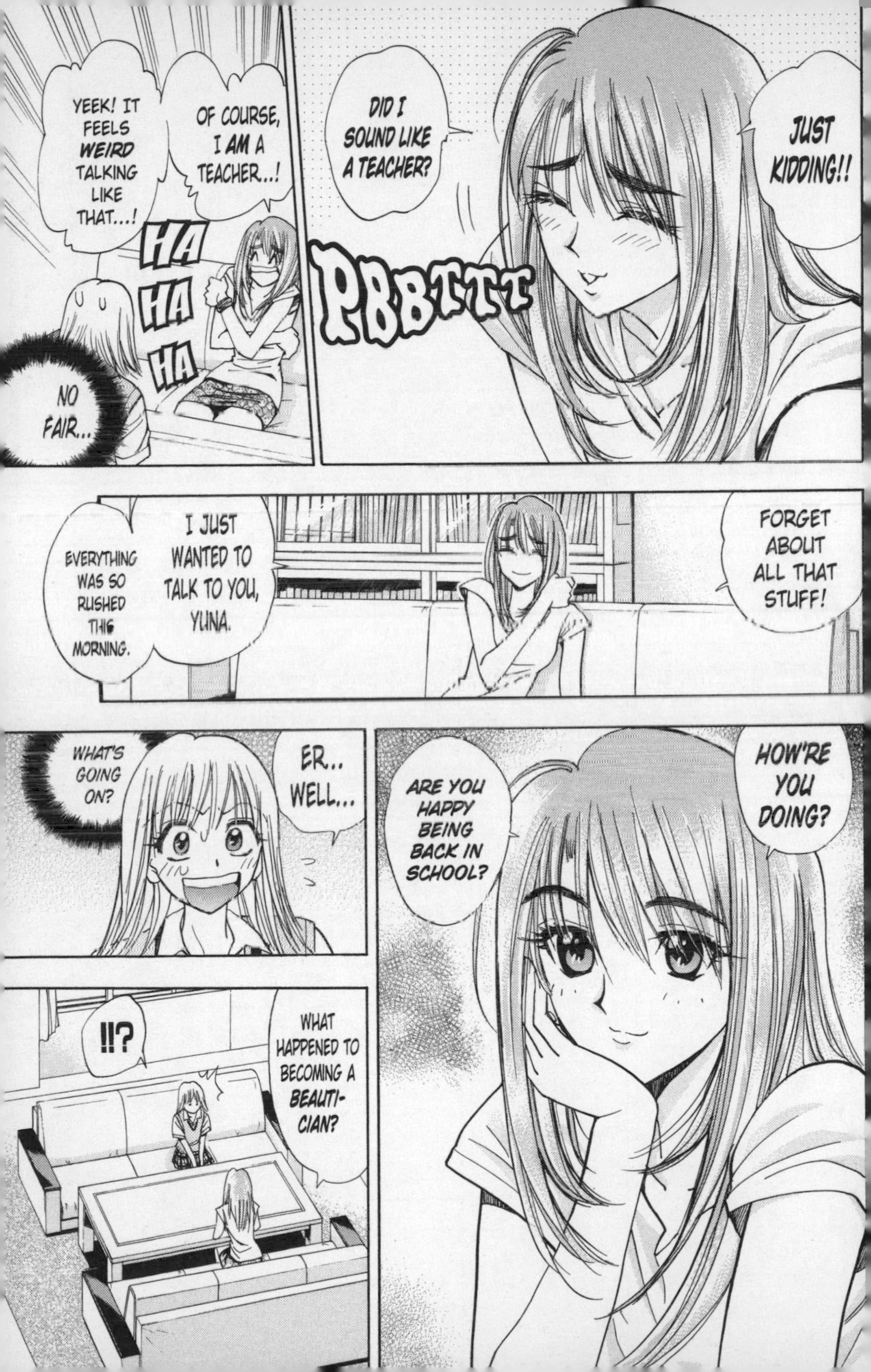
JUST KIDDING!!
DID I SOUND LIKE A TEACHER?
PBBTTT
OF COURSE, I AM A TEACHER...!
YEEK! IT FEELS WEIRD TALKING LIKE THAT...!
HA HA HA
NO FAIR...
FORGET ABOUT ALL THAT STUFF!
I JUST WANTED TO TALK TO YOU, YUNA.
EVERYTHING WAS SO RUSHED THIS MORNING.
HOW'RE YOU DOING?
ARE YOU HAPPY BEING BACK IN SCHOOL?
ER... WELL...
WHAT'S GOING ON?
WHAT HAPPENED TO BECOMING A BEAUTICIAN?
!!?

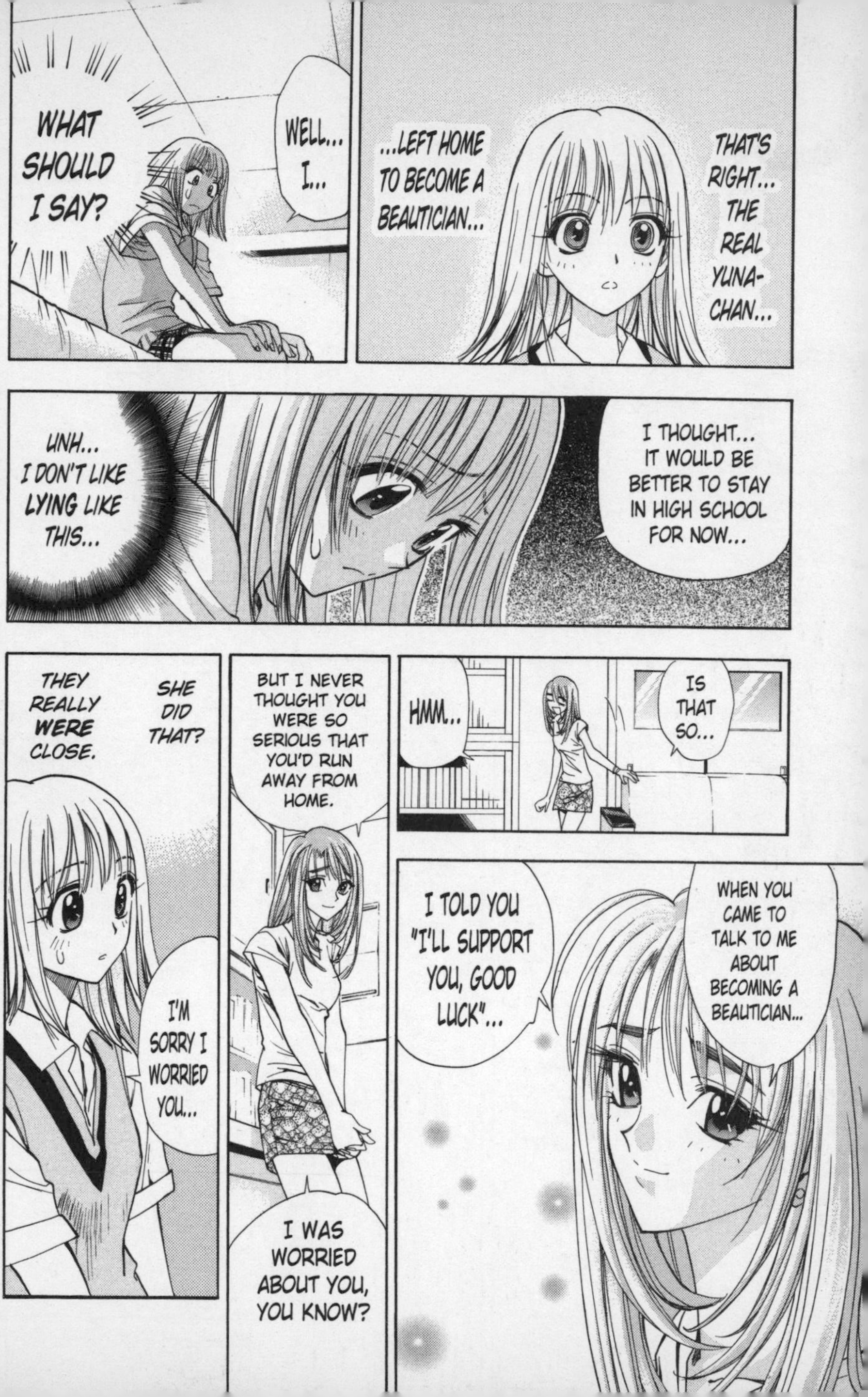
THAT'S RIGHT... THE REAL YUNA-CHAN...
...LEFT HOME TO BECOME A BEAUTICIAN...
WELL... I...
WHAT SHOULD I SAY?
I THOUGHT... IT WOULD BE BETTER TO STAY IN HIGH SCHOOL FOR NOW...
UNH... I DON'T LIKE LYING LIKE THIS...
IS THAT SO...
HMM...
WHEN YOU CAME TO TALK TO ME ABOUT BECOMING A BEAUTICIAN...
I TOLD YOU "I'LL SUPPORT YOU, GOOD LUCK"...
BUT I NEVER THOUGHT YOU WERE SO SERIOUS THAT YOU'D RUN AWAY FROM HOME.
I WAS WORRIED ABOUT YOU, YOU KNOW?
SHE DID THAT?
THEY REALLY WERE CLOSE.
I'M SORRY I WORRIED YOU...

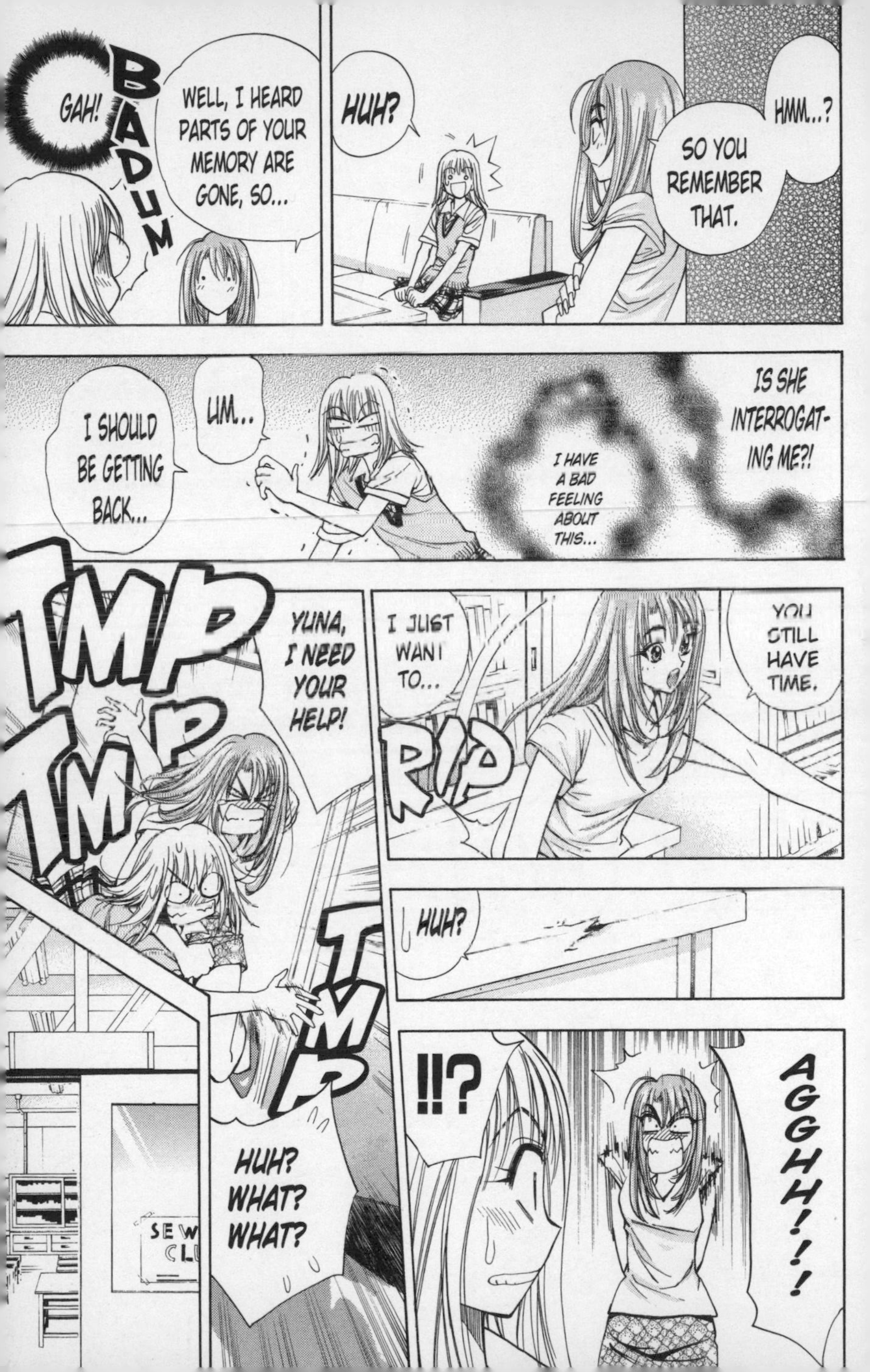
HMM..?
SO YOU REMEMBER THAT.
HUH?
WELL, I HEARD PARTS OF YOUR MEMORY ARE GONE, SO...
BADUM
GAH!
IS SHE INTERROGATING ME?!
I HAVE A BAD FEELING ABOUT THIS...
UM...
I SHOULD BE GETTING BACK...
YOU STILL HAVE TIME.
I JUST WANT TO...
RIP
HUH?
AGGH!!!
!!?
YUNA, I NEED YOUR HELP!
TMP
HUH? WHAT? WHAT?
SEW CLU

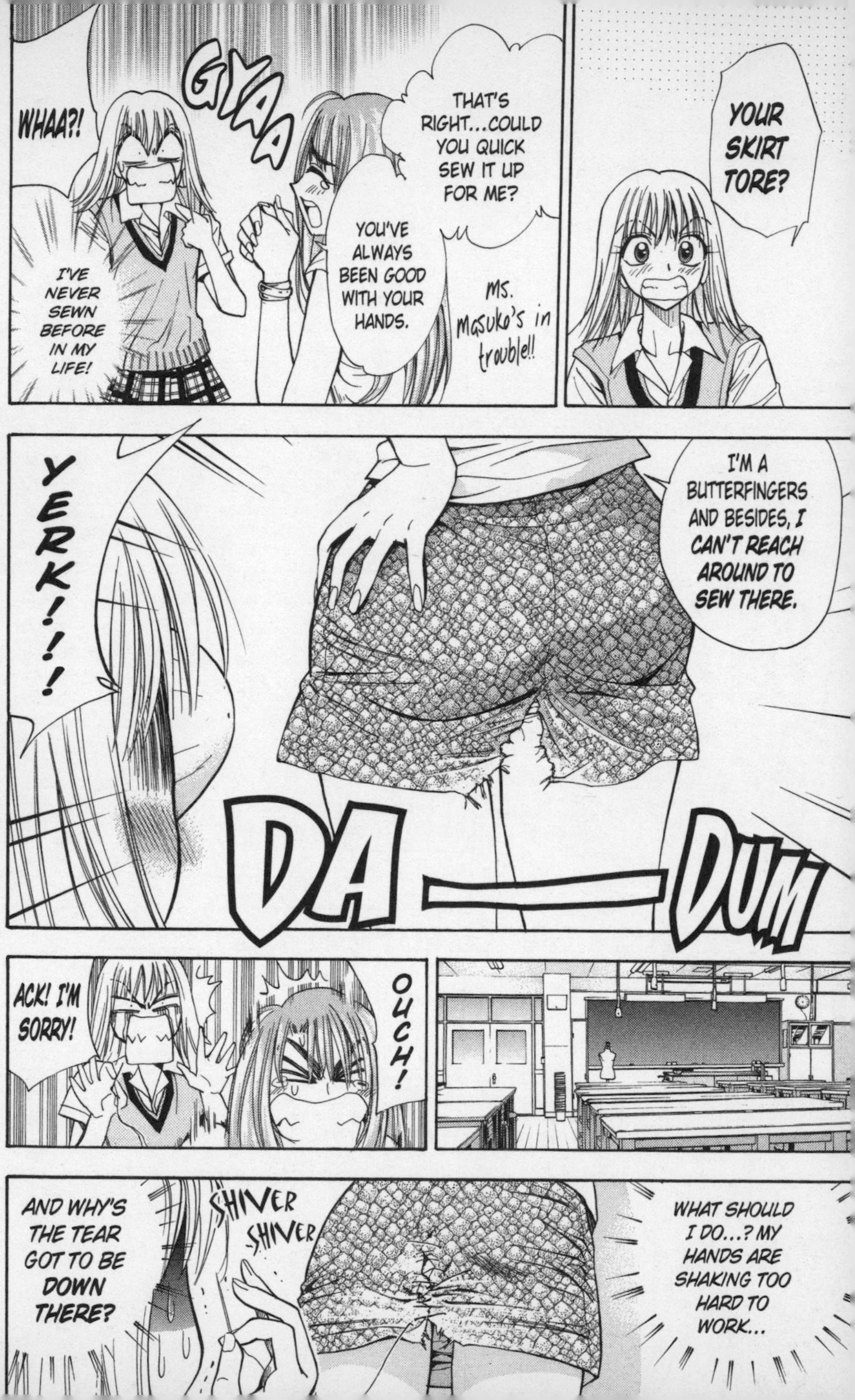
YOUR SKIRT TORE?
THAT'S RIGHT...COULD YOU QUICK SEW IT UP FOR ME?
Ms. Masuko's in trouble!!
YOU'VE ALWAYS BEEN GOOD WITH YOUR HANDS.
GYAA
WHAA?!
I'VE NEVER SEWN BEFORE IN MY LIFE!
I'M A BUTTERFINGERS AND BESIDES, I CAN'T REACH AROUND TO SEW THERE.
DA—DUM
YERK!!!
OUCH!
ACK! I'M SORRY!
WHAT SHOULD I DO...? MY HANDS ARE SHAKING TOO HARD TO WORK...
SHIVER SHIVER
AND WHY'S THE TEAR GOT TO BE DOWN THERE?

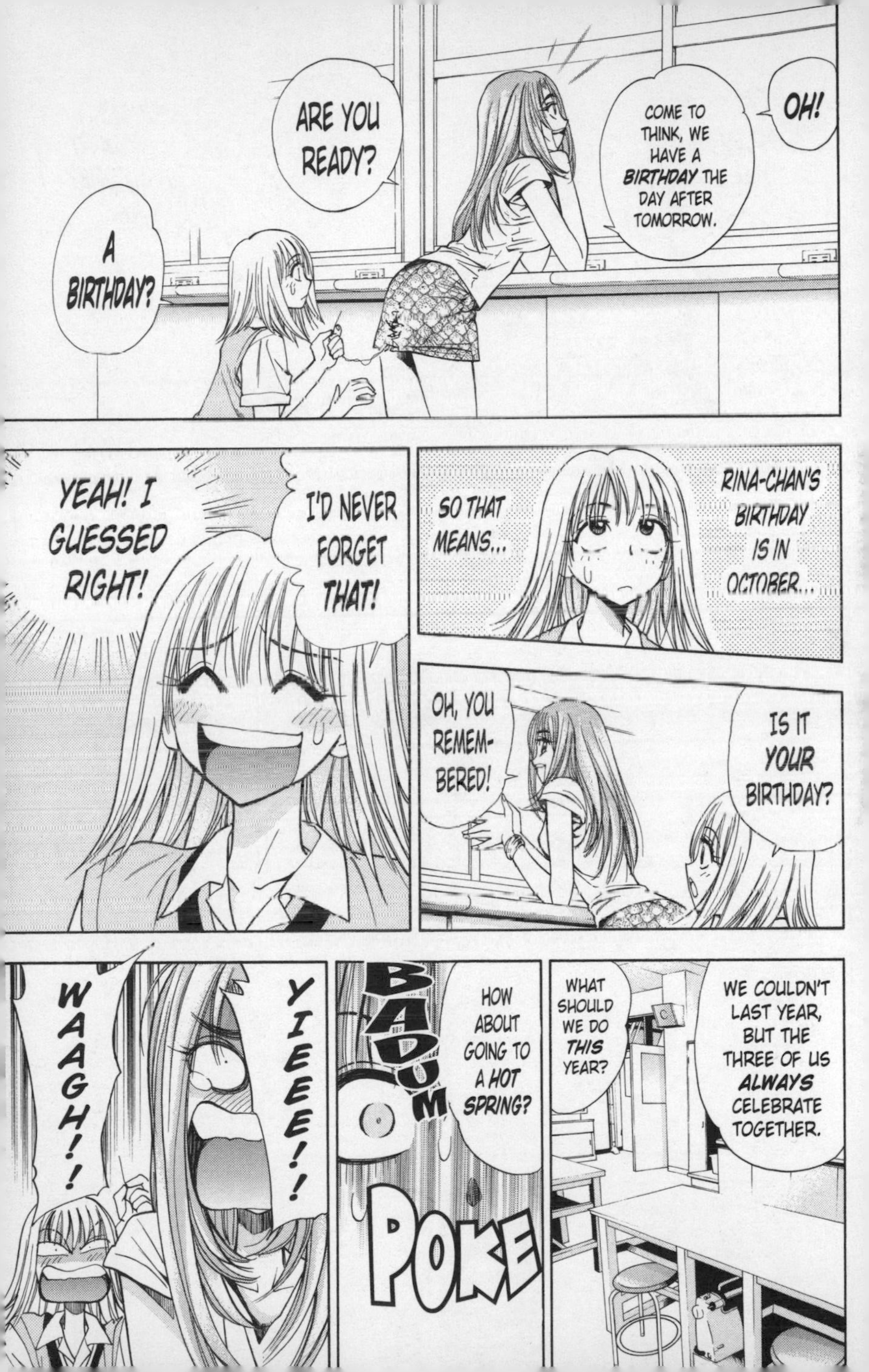
OH!
COME TO THINK, WE HAVE A BIRTHDAY THE DAY AFTER TOMORROW.
ARE YOU READY?
A BIRTHDAY?
RINA-CHAN'S BIRTHDAY IS IN OCTOBER...
SO THAT MEANS...
IS IT YOUR BIRTHDAY?
OH, YOU REMEM-BERED!
I'D NEVER FORGET THAT!
YEAH! I GUESSED RIGHT!
WE COULDN'T LAST YEAR, BUT THE THREE OF US ALWAYS CELEBRATE TOGETHER.
WHAT SHOULD WE DO THIS YEAR?
HOW ABOUT GOING TO A HOT SPRING?
BADUM
POKE
YIEEEE!!
WAAGH!!

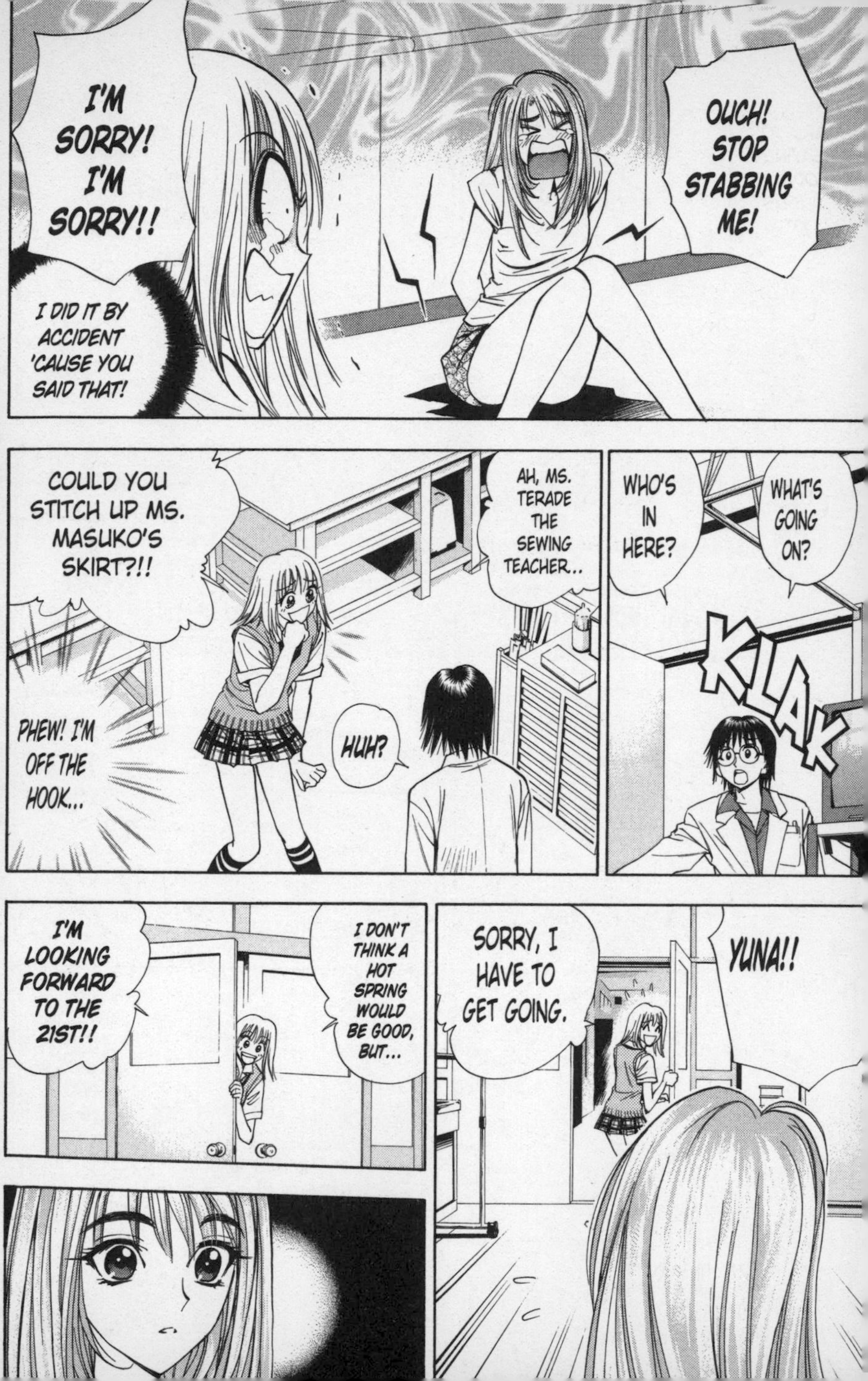
OUCH! STOP STABBING ME!
I'M SORRY! I'M SORRY!!
I DID IT BY ACCIDENT 'CAUSE YOU SAID THAT!
WHAT'S GOING ON?
WHO'S IN HERE?
KLAK
AH, MS. TERADE THE SEWING TEACHER..
COULD YOU STITCH UP MS. MASUKO'S SKIRT?!!
HUH?
PHEW! I'M OFF THE HOOK...
YUNA!!
SORRY, I HAVE TO GET GOING.
I DON'T THINK A HOT SPRING WOULD BE GOOD, BUT...
I'M LOOKING FORWARD TO THE 21ST!!

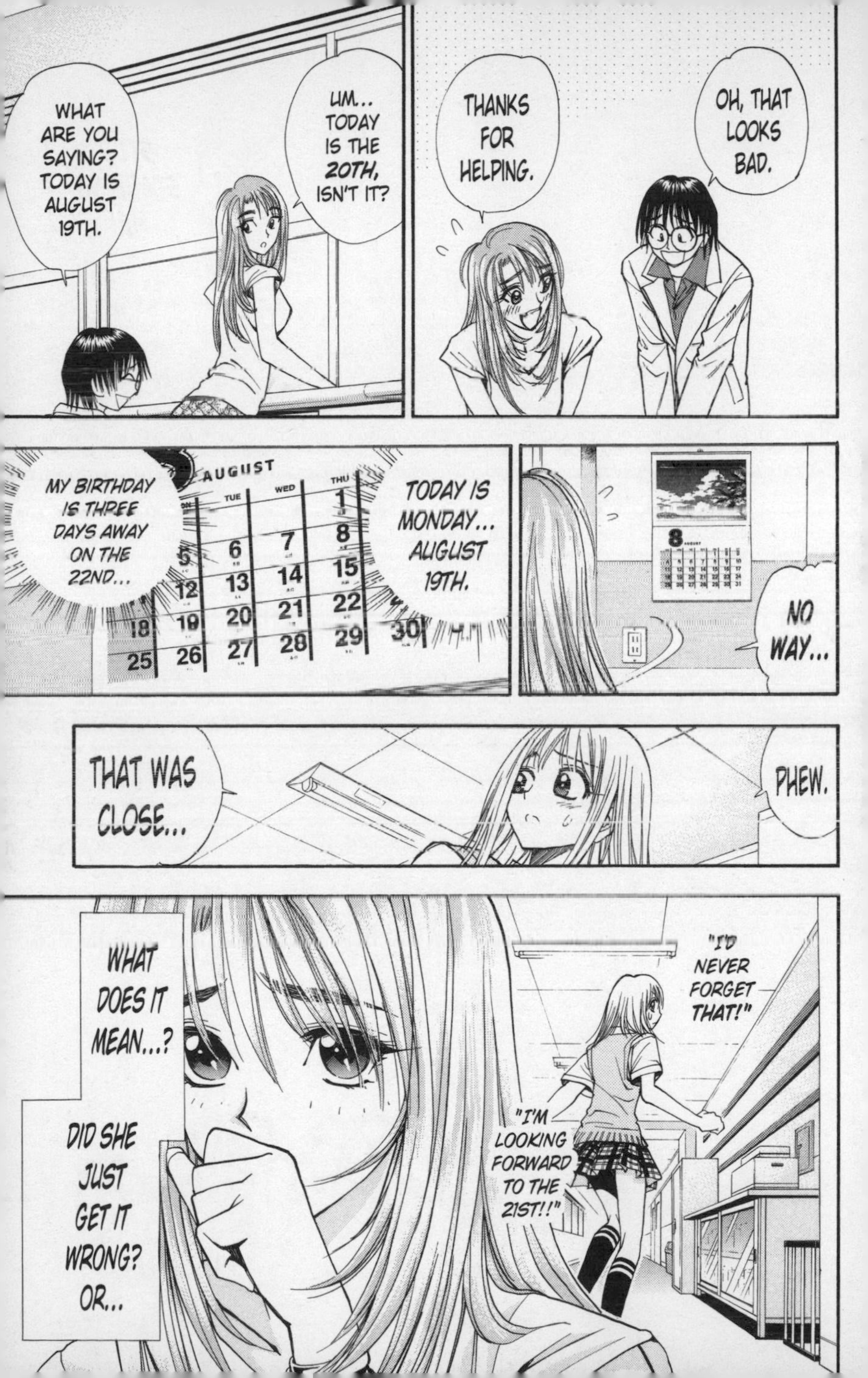
OH, THAT LOOKS BAD.
THANKS FOR HELPING.
UM... TODAY IS THE 20TH, ISN'T IT?
WHAT ARE YOU SAYING? TODAY IS AUGUST 19TH.
NO WAY...
TODAY IS MONDAY... AUGUST 19TH.
AUGUST
TUE WED THU
1
5 6 7 8
12 13 14 15
18 19 20 21 22
25 26 27 28 29 30
MY BIRTHDAY IS THREE DAYS AWAY ON THE 22ND...
PHEW.
THAT WAS CLOSE...
"I'D NEVER FORGET THAT!"
"I'M LOOKING FORWARD TO THE 21ST!!"
WHAT DOES IT MEAN...?
DID SHE JUST GET IT WRONG? OR...

Pretty Face

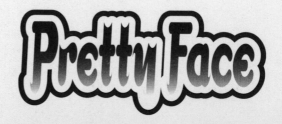

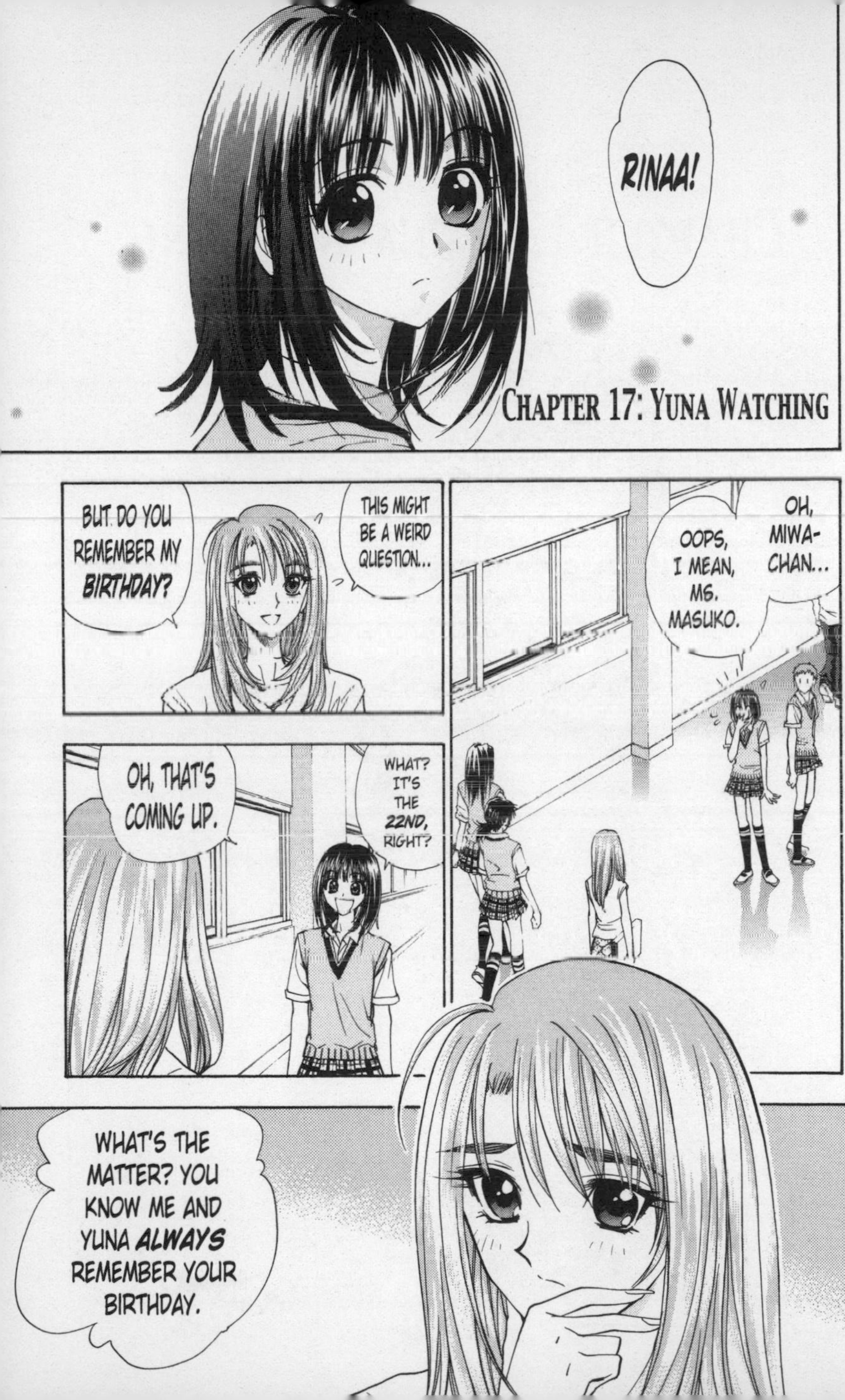
RINAA!
Chapter 17: Yuna Watching
OH, MIWA-CHAN...
OOPS, I MEAN, MS. MASUKO.
THIS MIGHT BE A WEIRD QUESTION...
BUT DO YOU REMEMBER MY BIRTHDAY?
WHAT? IT'S THE 22ND, RIGHT?
OH, THAT'S COMING UP.
WHAT'S THE MATTER? YOU KNOW ME AND YUNA ALWAYS REMEMBER YOUR BIRTHDAY.

Chapter 17: Yuna Watching

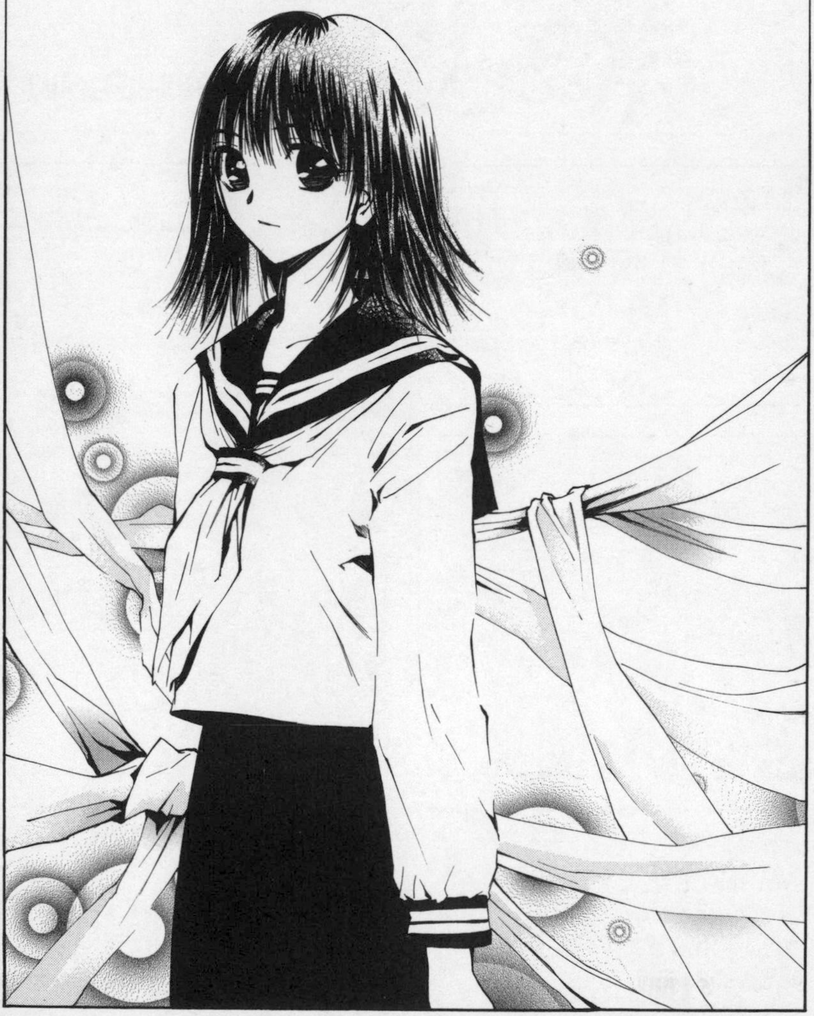

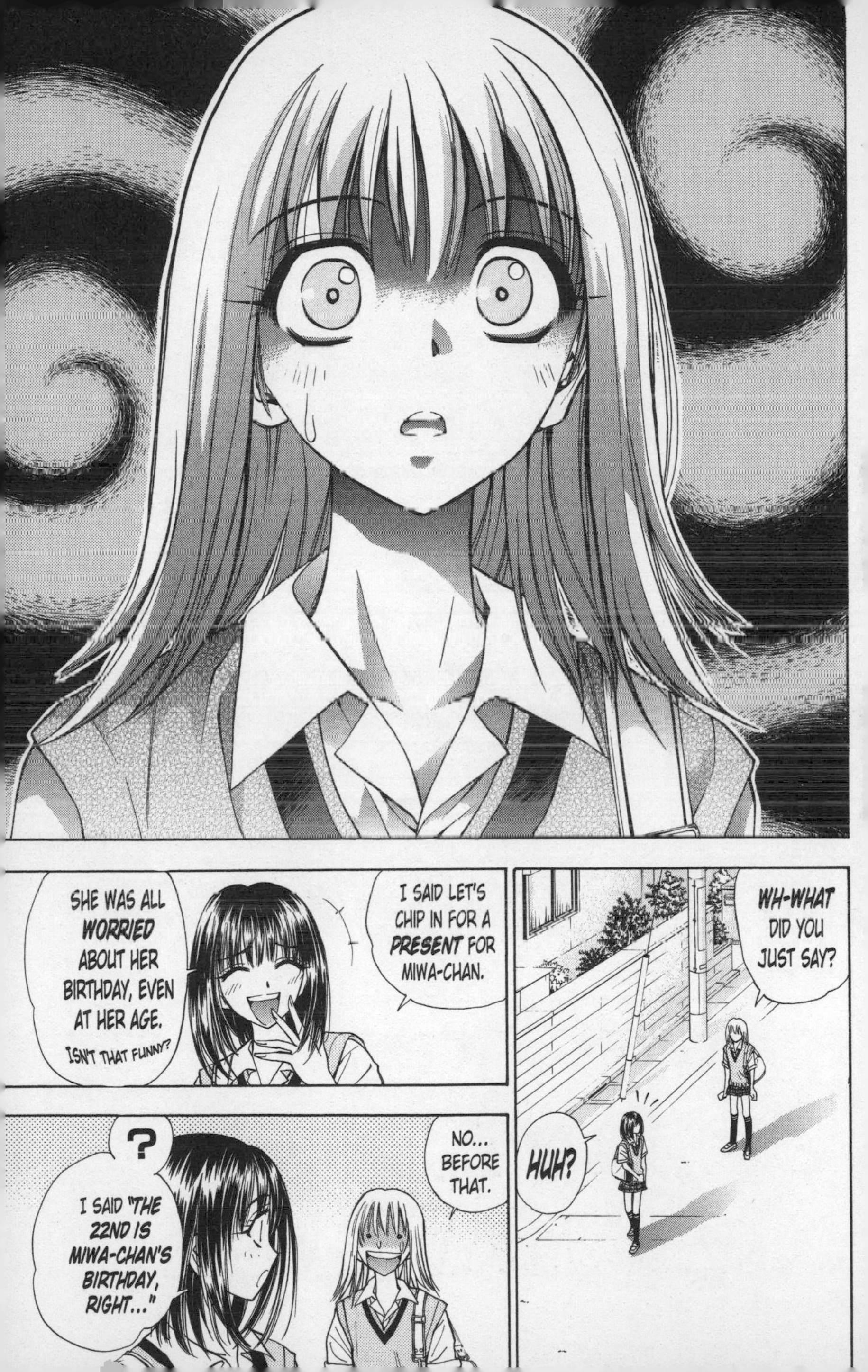
WH-WHAT DID YOU JUST SAY?
HUH?
I SAID LET'S CHIP IN FOR A PRESENT FOR MIWA-CHAN.
SHE WAS ALL WORRIED ABOUT HER BIRTHDAY, EVEN AT HER AGE. ISN'T THAT FUNNY?
NO... BEFORE THAT.
?
I SAID "THE 22ND IS MIWA-CHAN'S BIRTHDAY, RIGHT..."

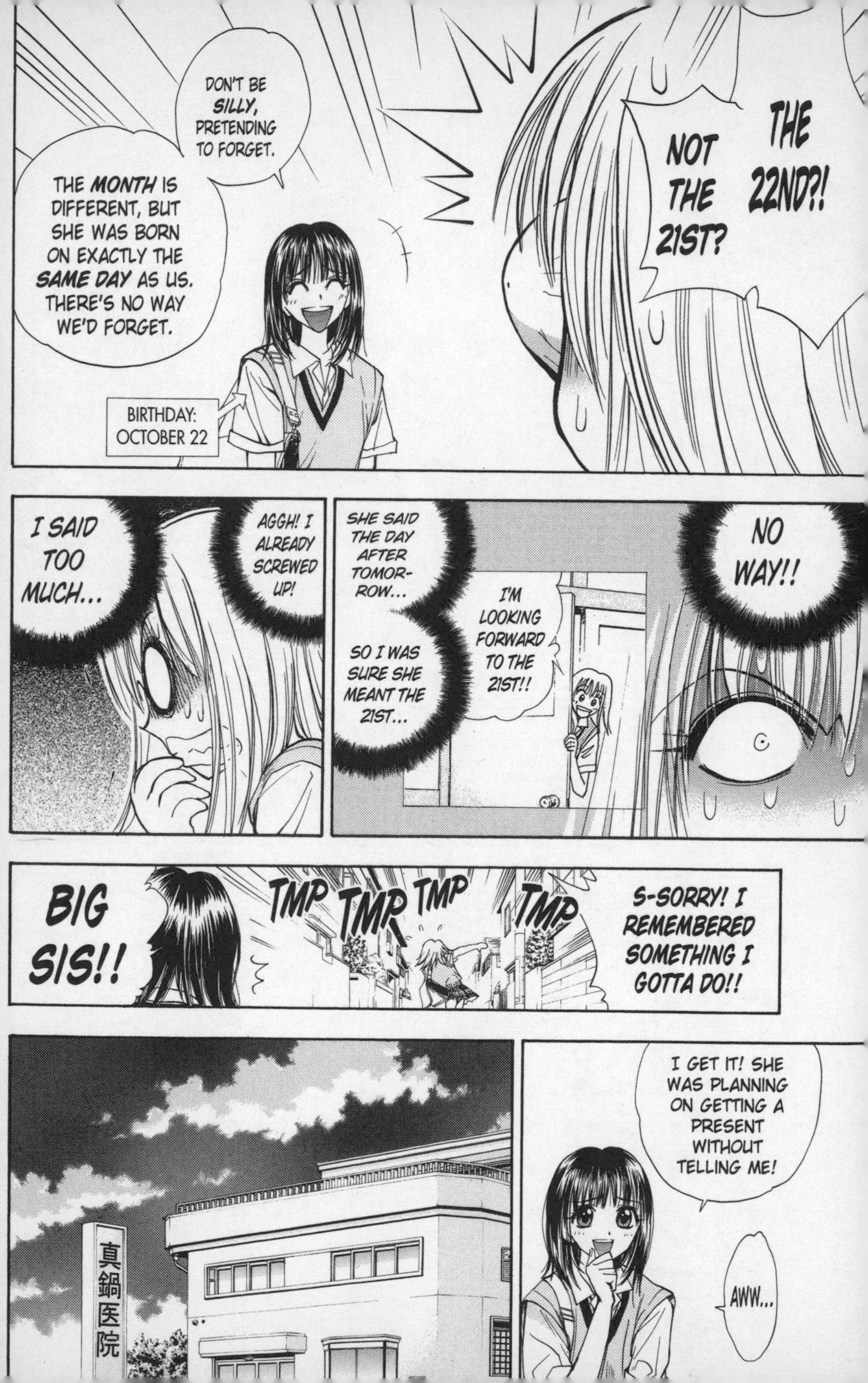
NOT THE 21ST? THE 22ND?!
DON'T BE SILLY, PRETENDING TO FORGET.
THE MONTH IS DIFFERENT, BUT SHE WAS BORN ON EXACTLY THE SAME DAY AS US. THERE'S NO WAY WE'D FORGET.
BIRTHDAY: OCTOBER 22
NO WAY!!
SHE SAID THE DAY AFTER TOMORROW...
I'M LOOKING FORWARD TO THE 21ST!!
SO I WAS SURE SHE MEANT THE 21ST...
AGGH! I ALREADY SCREWED UP!
I SAID TOO MUCH...
S-SORRY! I REMEMBERED SOMETHING I GOTTA DO!!
TMP
TMP
TMP
TMP
BIG SIS!!
I GET IT! SHE WAS PLANNING ON GETTING A PRESENT WITHOUT TELLING ME!
AWW...
真鍋医院

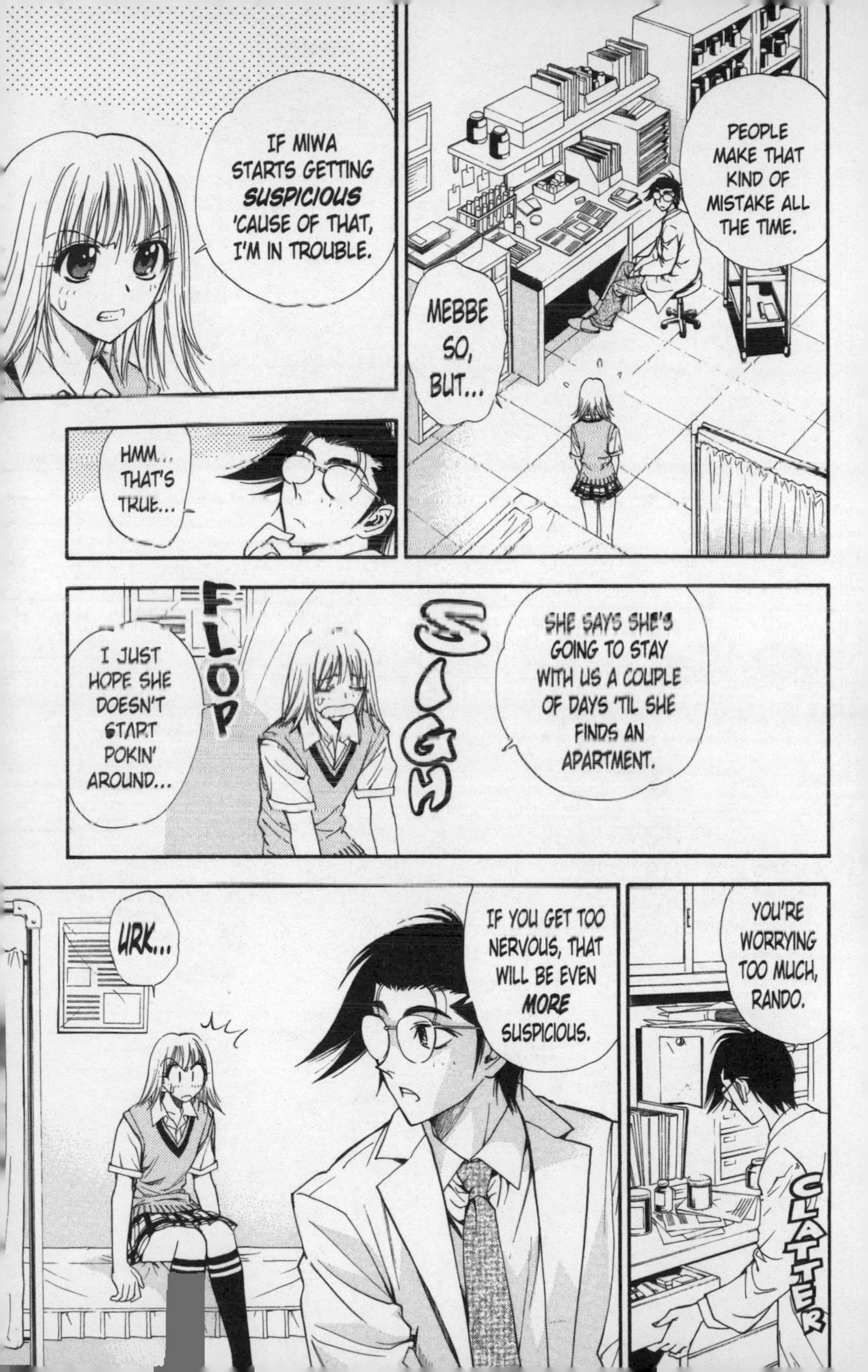
PEOPLE MAKE THAT KIND OF MISTAKE ALL THE TIME.
MEBBE SO, BUT...
IF MIWA STARTS GETTING *SUSPICIOUS* 'CAUSE OF THAT, I'M IN TROUBLE.
HMM... THAT'S TRUE...
SHE SAYS SHE'S GOING TO STAY WITH US A COUPLE OF DAYS 'TIL SHE FINDS AN APARTMENT.
SIGH
FLOP
I JUST HOPE SHE DOESN'T START POKIN' AROUND...
YOU'RE WORRYING TOO MUCH, RANDO.
CLATTER
IF YOU GET TOO NERVOUS, THAT WILL BE EVEN *MORE* SUSPICIOUS.
URK...

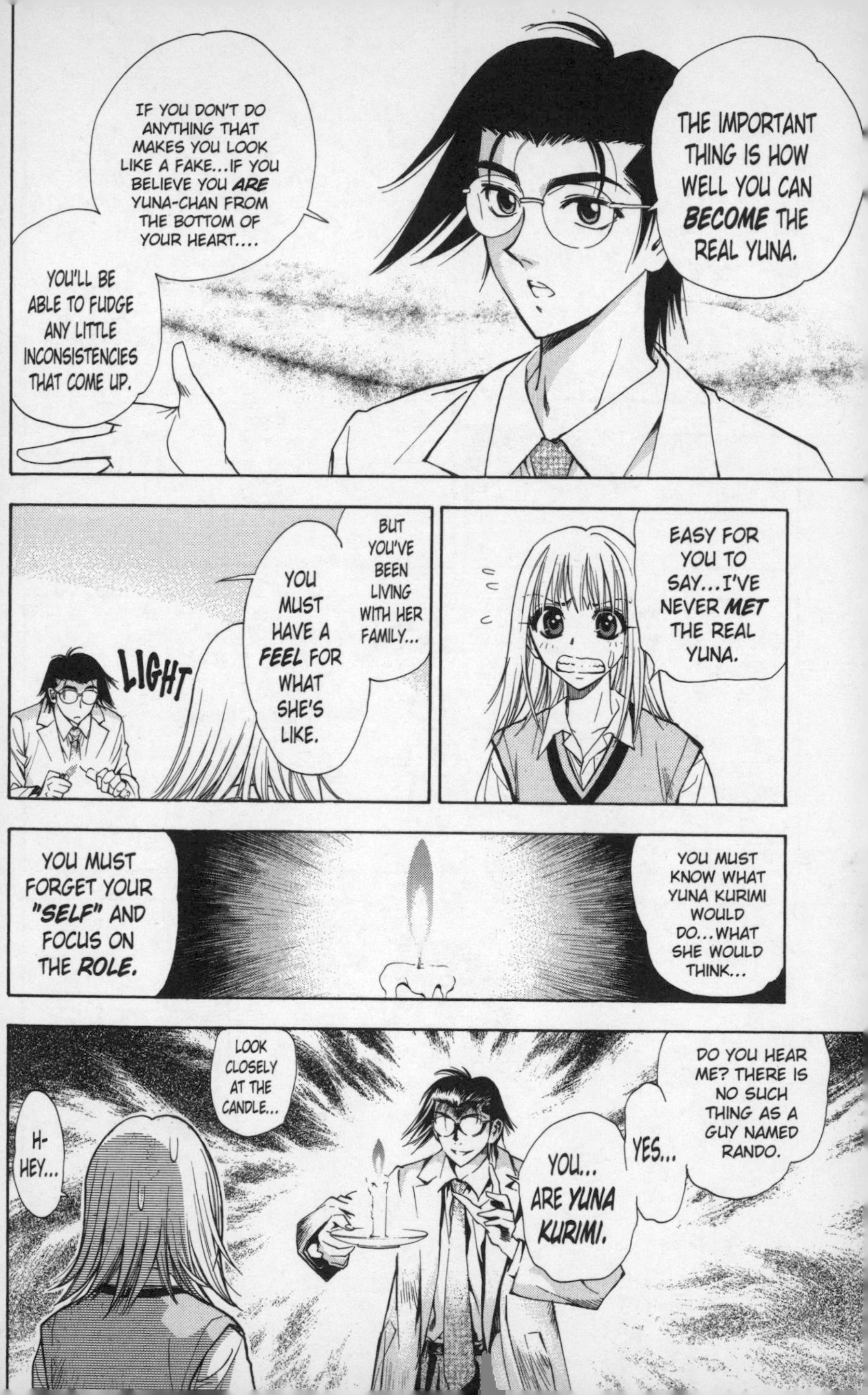
THE IMPORTANT THING IS HOW WELL YOU CAN **BECOME** THE REAL YUNA.
IF YOU DON'T DO ANYTHING THAT MAKES YOU LOOK LIKE A FAKE...IF YOU BELIEVE YOU **ARE** YUNA-CHAN FROM THE BOTTOM OF YOUR HEART....
YOU'LL BE ABLE TO FUDGE ANY LITTLE INCONSISTENCIES THAT COME UP.
EASY FOR YOU TO SAY...I'VE NEVER **MET** THE REAL YUNA.
BUT YOU'VE BEEN LIVING WITH HER FAMILY...
YOU MUST HAVE A **FEEL** FOR WHAT SHE'S LIKE.
LIGHT
YOU MUST KNOW WHAT YUNA KURIMI WOULD DO...WHAT SHE WOULD THINK...
YOU MUST FORGET YOUR **"SELF"** AND FOCUS ON THE **ROLE.**
DO YOU HEAR ME? THERE IS NO SUCH THING AS A GUY NAMED RANDO.
YES...
LOOK CLOSELY AT THE CANDLE...
YOU... ARE **YUNA KURIMI.**
H-HEY...

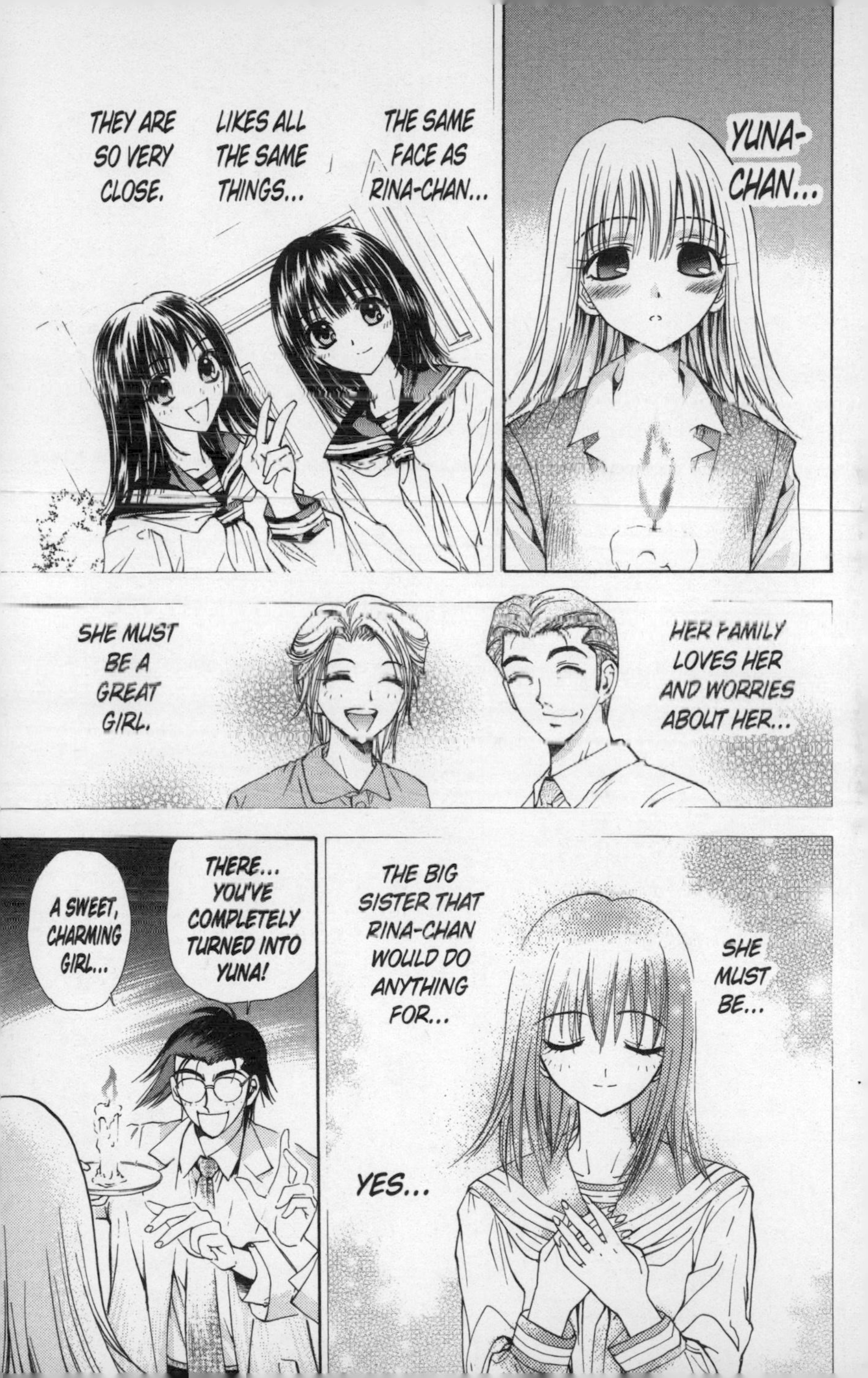
YUNA-CHAN...
THE SAME FACE AS RINA-CHAN...
LIKES ALL THE SAME THINGS...
THEY ARE SO VERY CLOSE.
HER FAMILY LOVES HER AND WORRIES ABOUT HER...
SHE MUST BE A GREAT GIRL.
SHE MUST BE...
THE BIG SISTER THAT RINA-CHAN WOULD DO ANYTHING FOR...
YES...
THERE... YOU'VE COMPLETELY TURNED INTO YUNA!
A SWEET, CHARMING GIRL...

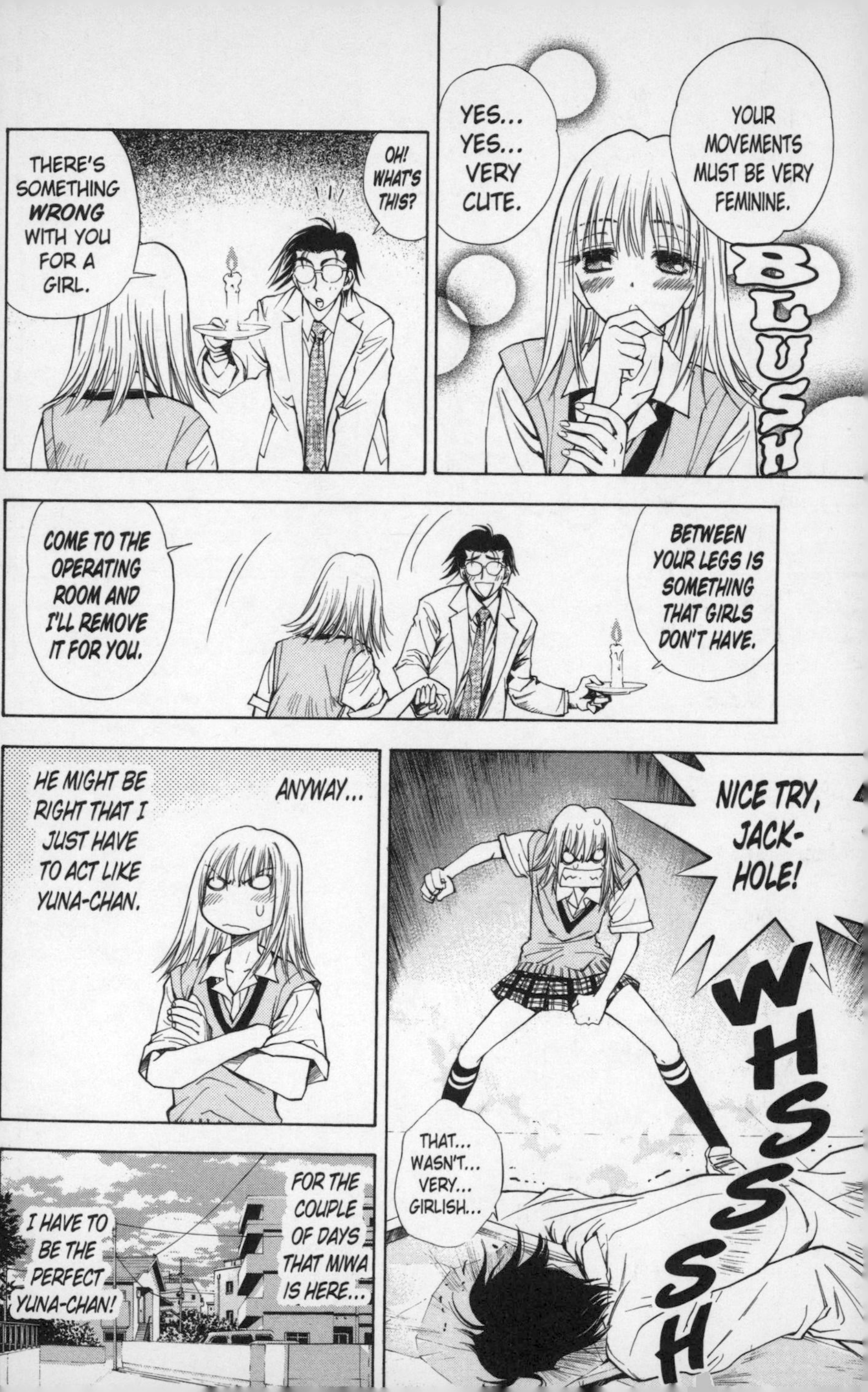
YOUR MOVEMENTS MUST BE VERY FEMININE.
YES... YES... VERY CUTE.
BLUSH
OH! WHAT'S THIS?
THERE'S SOMETHING WRONG WITH YOU FOR A GIRL.
BETWEEN YOUR LEGS IS SOMETHING THAT GIRLS DON'T HAVE.
COME TO THE OPERATING ROOM AND I'LL REMOVE IT FOR YOU.
NICE TRY, JACK-HOLE!
WHSSSSH
THAT... WASN'T... VERY... GIRLISH...
ANYWAY...
HE MIGHT BE RIGHT THAT I JUST HAVE TO ACT LIKE YUNA-CHAN.
FOR THE COUPLE OF DAYS THAT MIWA IS HERE...
I HAVE TO BE THE PERFECT YUNA-CHAN!

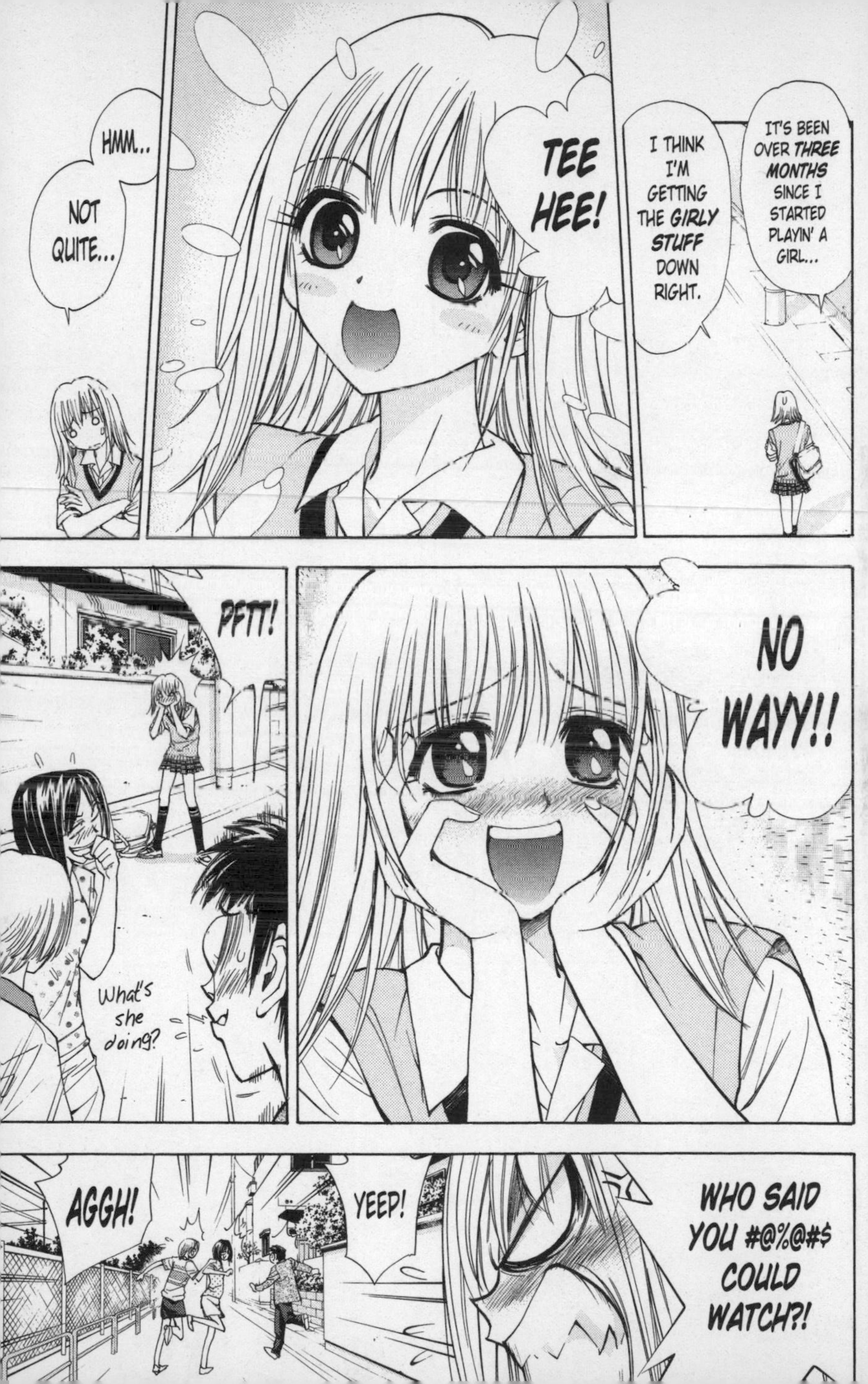
IT'S BEEN OVER THREE MONTHS SINCE I STARTED PLAYIN' A GIRL...
I THINK I'M GETTING THE GIRLY STUFF DOWN RIGHT.
TEE HEE!
HMM...
NOT QUITE...
NO WAYY!!
PFTT!
What's she doing?
WHO SAID YOU #@%@#$ COULD WATCH?!
YEEP!
AGGH!

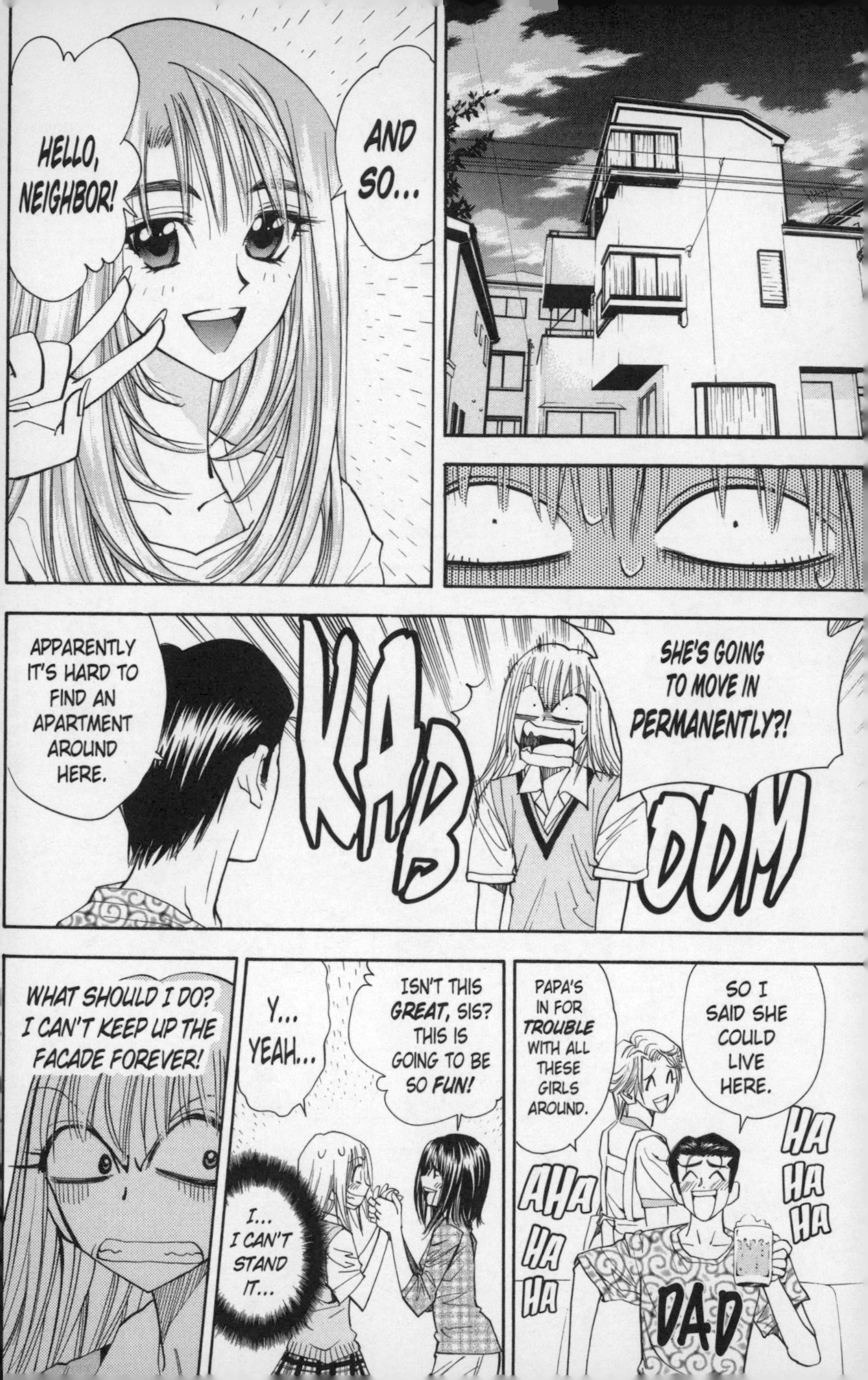
AND SO...
HELLO, NEIGHBOR!
SHE'S GOING TO MOVE IN PERMANENTLY?!
KABOOM
APPARENTLY IT'S HARD TO FIND AN APARTMENT AROUND HERE.
SO I SAID SHE COULD LIVE HERE.
HA HA HA
PAPA'S IN FOR TROUBLE WITH ALL THESE GIRLS AROUND.
AHA HA HA
DAD
ISN'T THIS GREAT, SIS? THIS IS GOING TO BE SO FUN!
Y... YEAH...
I... I CAN'T STAND IT...
WHAT SHOULD I DO? I CAN'T KEEP UP THE FACADE FOREVER!

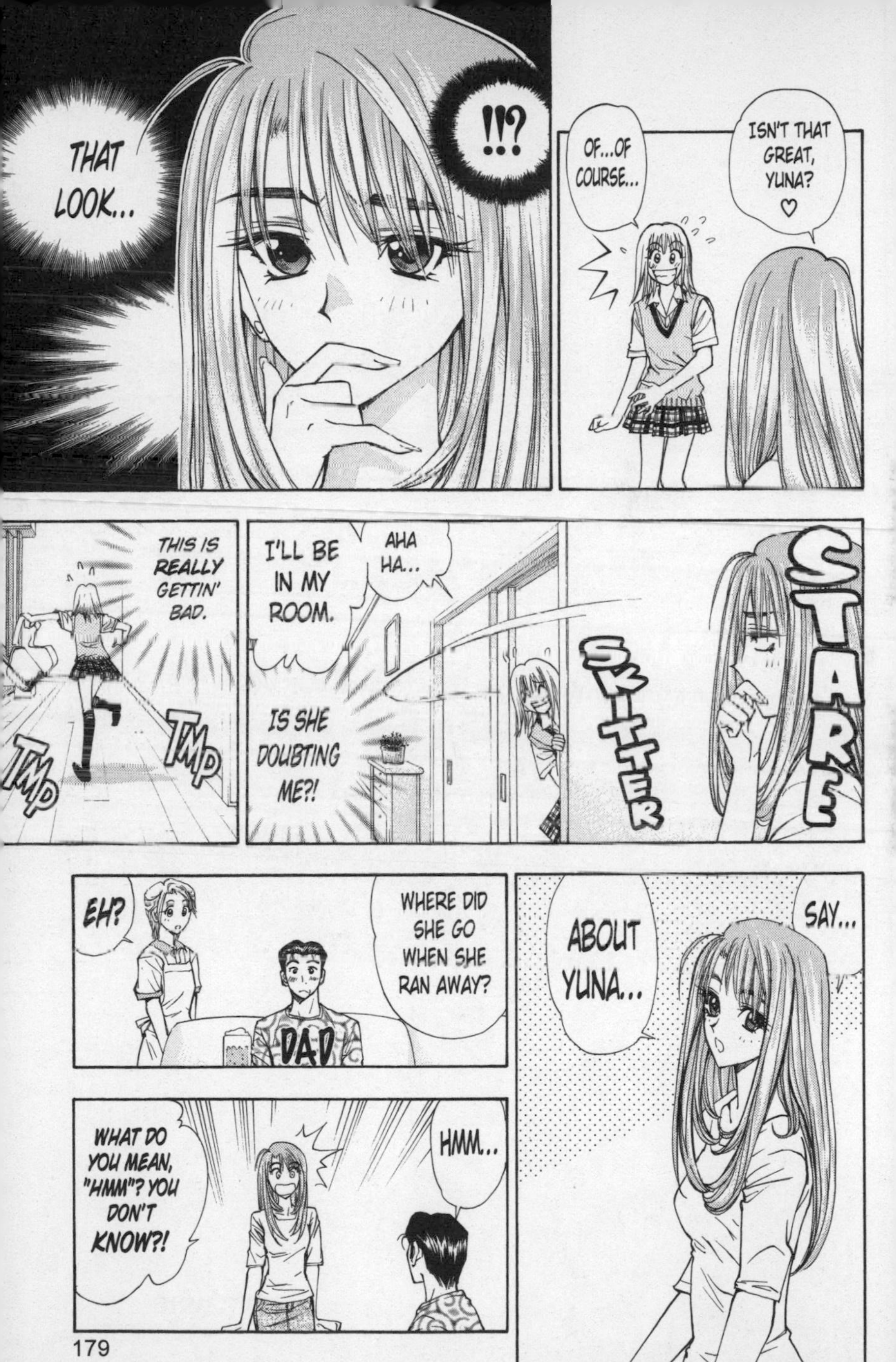
ISN'T THAT GREAT, YUNA? ♡
OF...OF COURSE...
!!?
THAT LOOK...
STARE
SKITTER
AHA HA...
I'LL BE IN MY ROOM.
IS SHE DOUBTING ME?!
THIS IS REALLY GETTIN' BAD.
TMP
TMP
SAY...
ABOUT YUNA...
WHERE DID SHE GO WHEN SHE RAN AWAY?
EH?
DAD
HMM...
WHAT DO YOU MEAN, "HMM"? YOU DON'T KNOW?!

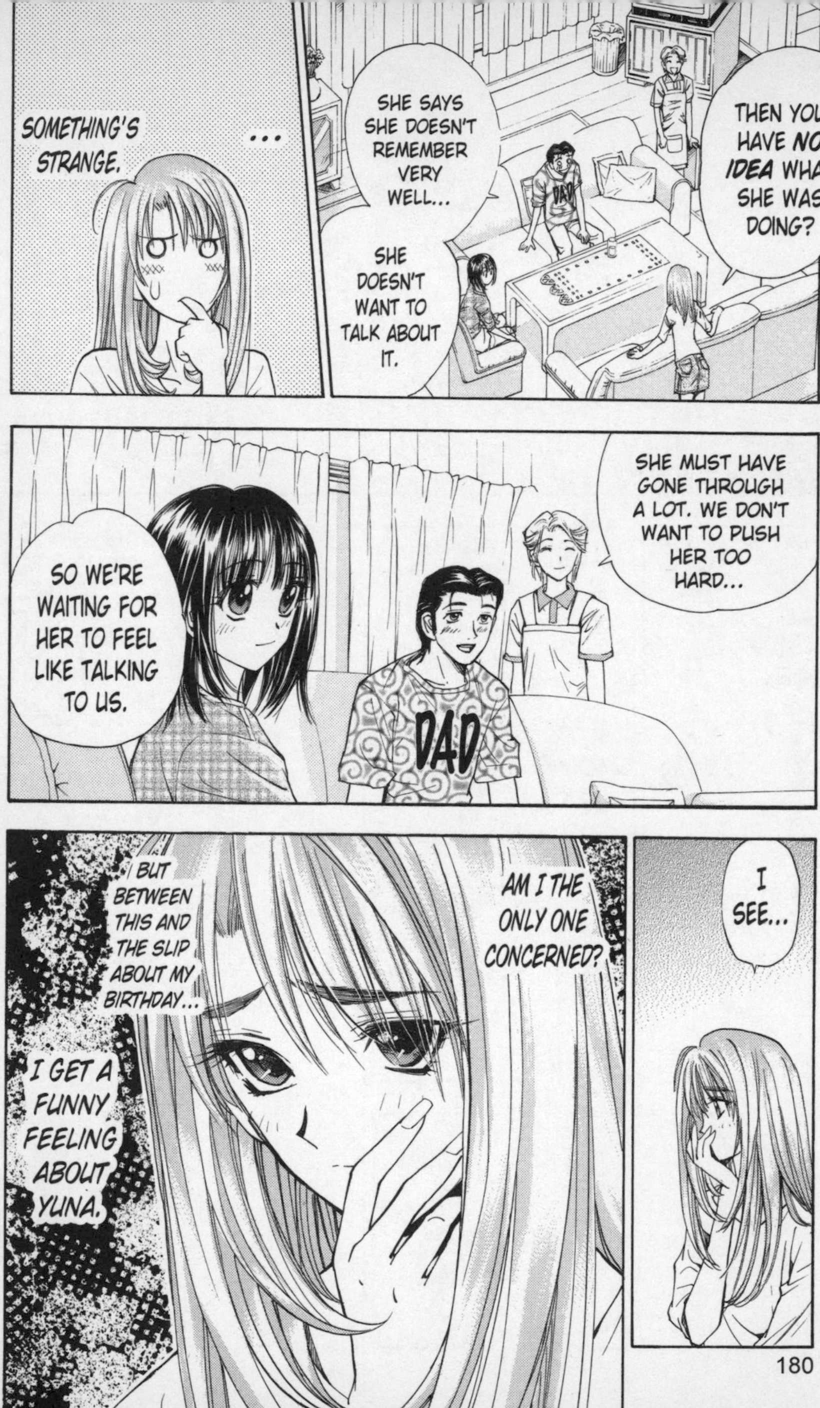
THEN YOU HAVE NO IDEA WHAT SHE WAS DOING?
SHE SAYS SHE DOESN'T REMEMBER VERY WELL...
SHE DOESN'T WANT TO TALK ABOUT IT.
...
SOMETHING'S STRANGE.
SHE MUST HAVE GONE THROUGH A LOT. WE DON'T WANT TO PUSH HER TOO HARD...
DAD
SO WE'RE WAITING FOR HER TO FEEL LIKE TALKING TO US.
I SEE...
AM I THE ONLY ONE CONCERNED?
BUT BETWEEN THIS AND THE SLIP ABOUT MY BIRTHDAY...
I GET A FUNNY FEELING ABOUT YUNA.

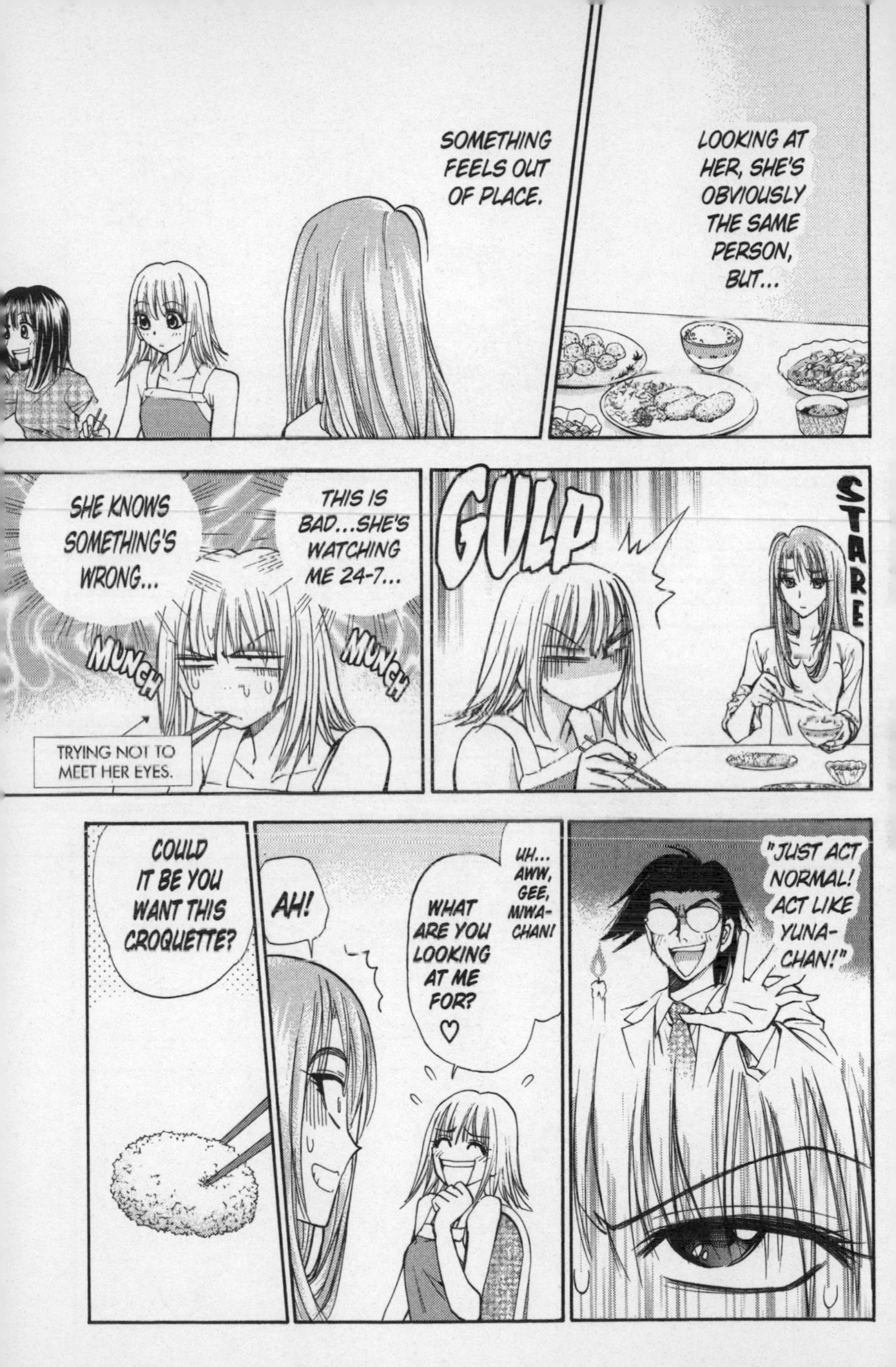
LOOKING AT HER, SHE'S OBVIOUSLY THE SAME PERSON, BUT...
SOMETHING FEELS OUT OF PLACE.
STARE
GULP
THIS IS BAD...SHE'S WATCHING ME 24-7...
SHE KNOWS SOMETHING'S WRONG...
MUNCH
MUNCH
TRYING NOT TO MEET HER EYES.
"JUST ACT NORMAL! ACT LIKE YUNA-CHAN!"
UH... AWW, GEE, MIWA-CHAN!
WHAT ARE YOU LOOKING AT ME FOR? ♡
AH!
COULD IT BE YOU WANT THIS CROQUETTE?

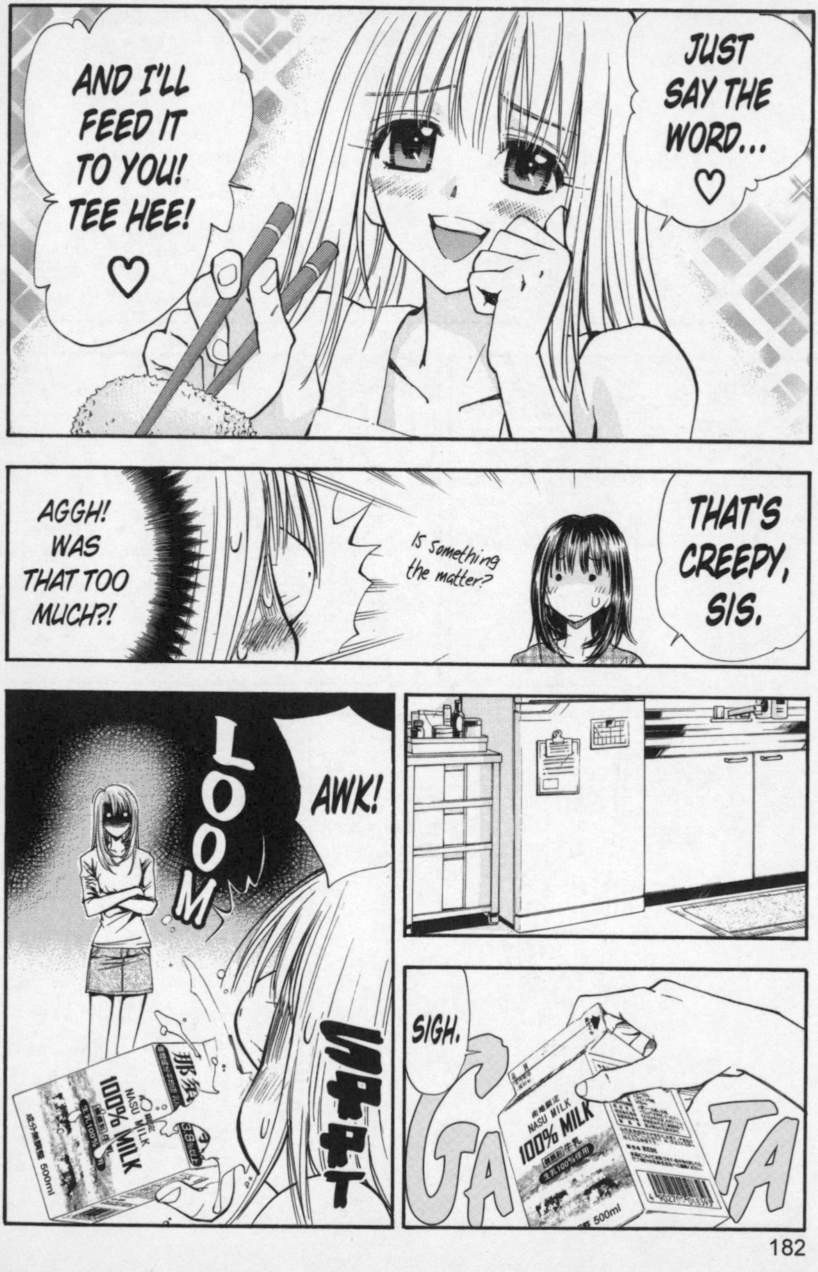
JUST SAY THE WORD... ♡
AND I'LL FEED IT TO YOU! TEE HEE! ♡
THAT'S CREEPY, SIS.
Is something the matter?
AGGH! WAS THAT TOO MUCH?!
SIGH.
GA TA
NASU MILK
100% MILK
500ml
AWK!
LOOM
SPPT

READ THIS WAY

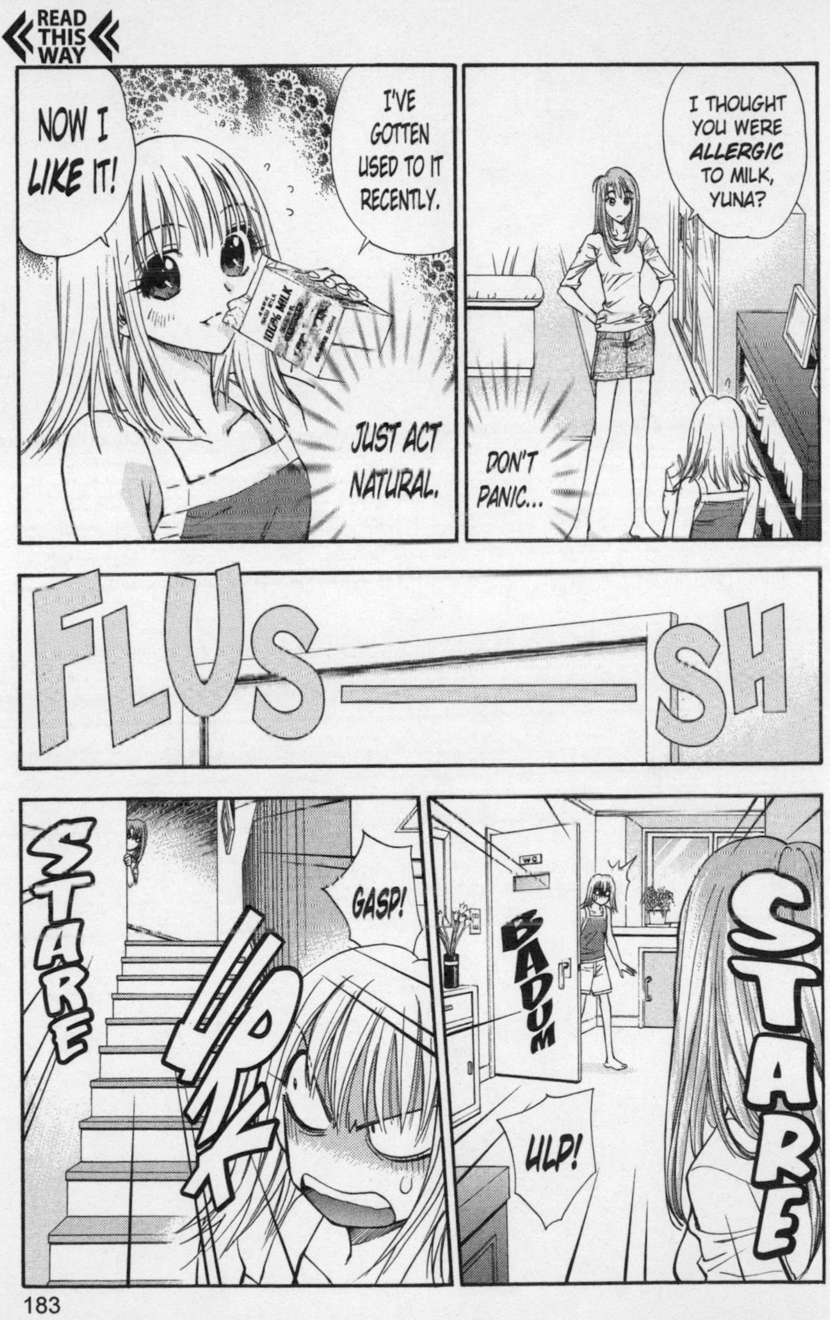

I THOUGHT YOU WERE ALLERGIC TO MILK, YUNA?
DON'T PANIC...
I'VE GOTTEN USED TO IT RECENTLY.
NOW I LIKE IT!
JUST ACT NATURAL.
FLUS—SH
STARE
BADUM
ULP!
GASP!
URK
STARE

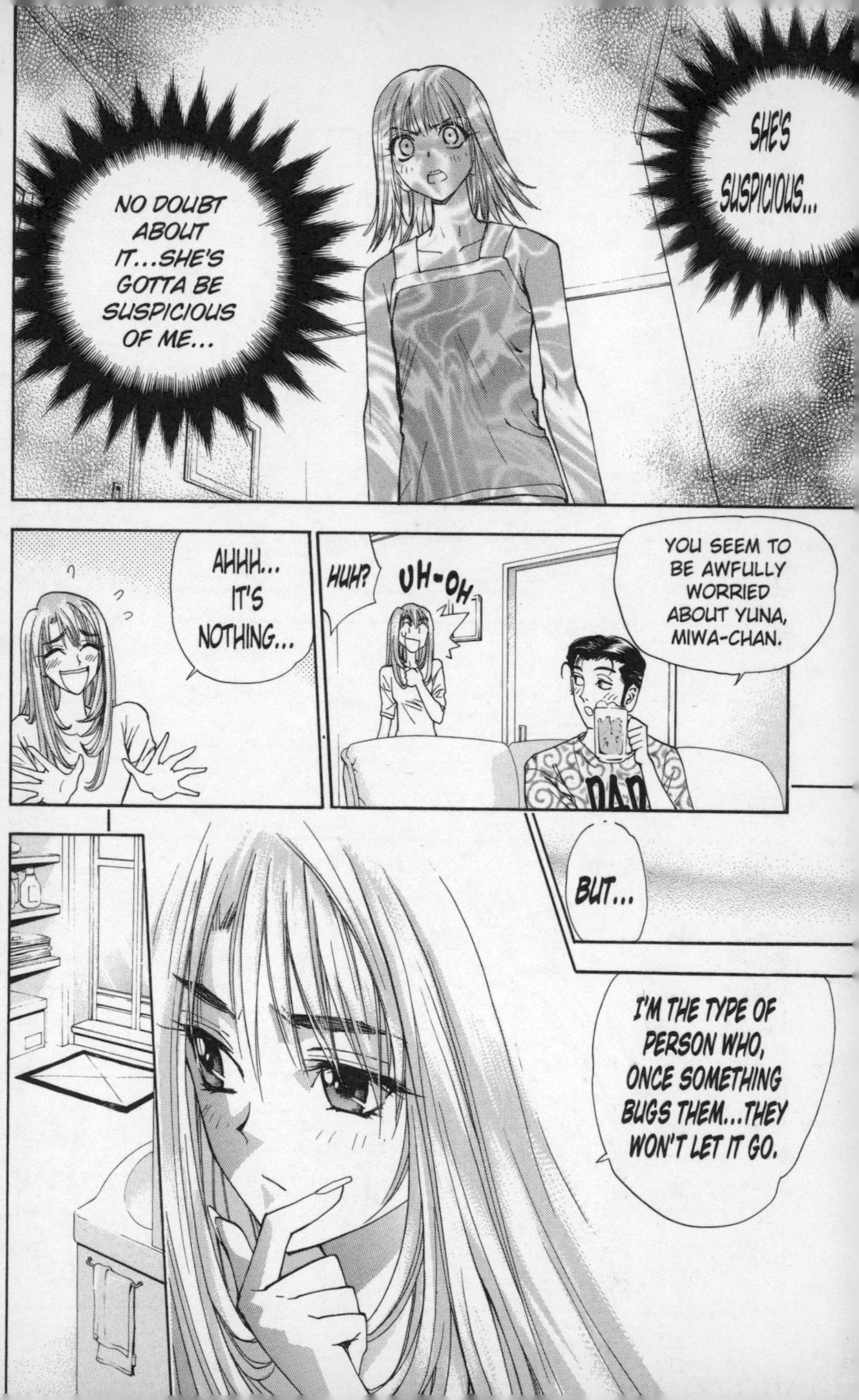
SHE'S SUSPICIOUS...
NO DOUBT ABOUT IT...SHE'S GOTTA BE SUSPICIOUS OF ME...
YOU SEEM TO BE AWFULLY WORRIED ABOUT YUNA, MIWA-CHAN.
UH-OH
HUH?
AHHH... IT'S NOTHING...
BUT...
I'M THE TYPE OF PERSON WHO, ONCE SOMETHING BUGS THEM...THEY WON'T LET IT GO.

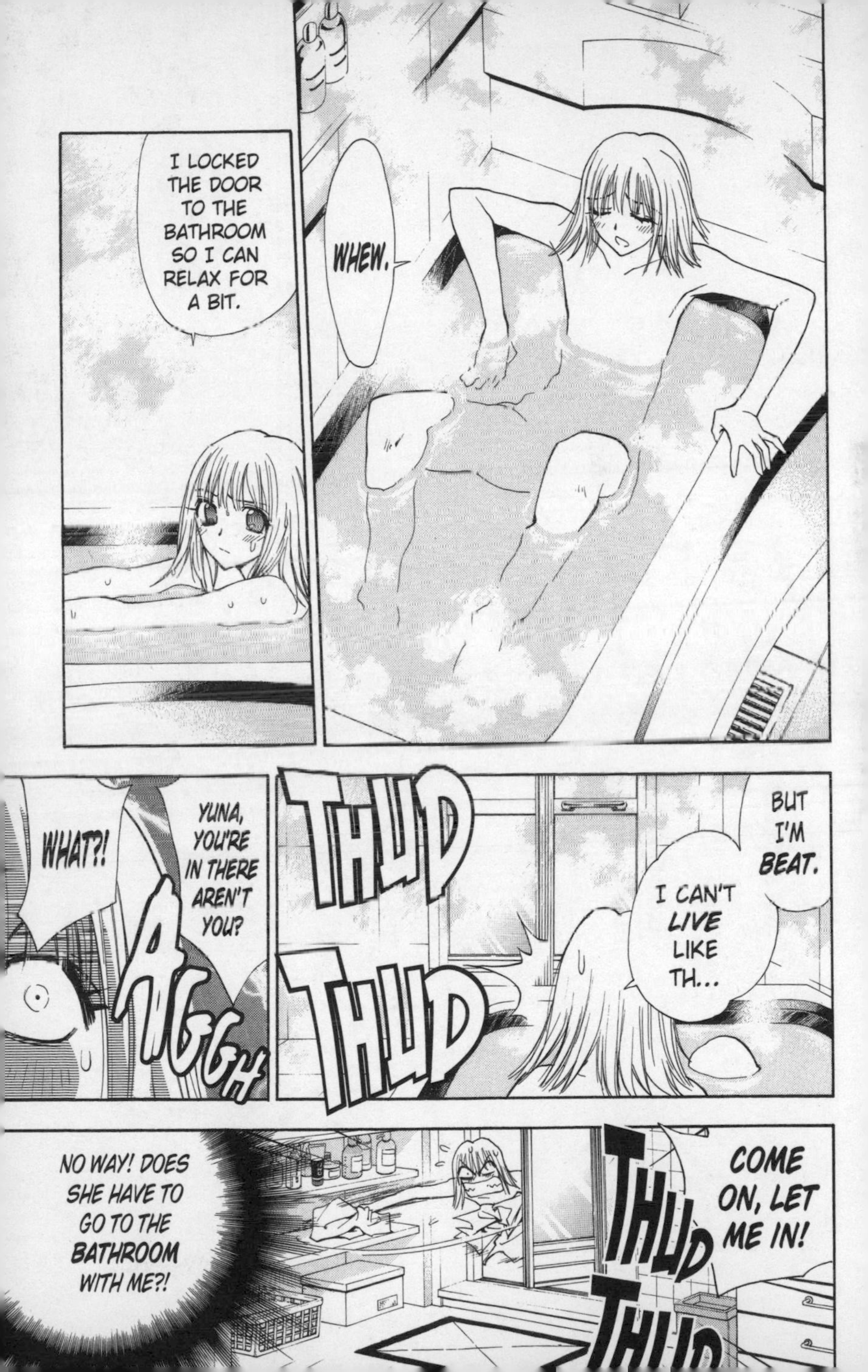
WHEW.
I LOCKED THE DOOR TO THE BATHROOM SO I CAN RELAX FOR A BIT.
BUT I'M BEAT.
I CAN'T LIVE LIKE TH...
THUD
THUD
YUNA, YOU'RE IN THERE AREN'T YOU?
WHAT?!
AGGH
COME ON, LET ME IN!
THUD
NO WAY! DOES SHE HAVE TO GO TO THE BATHROOM WITH ME?!

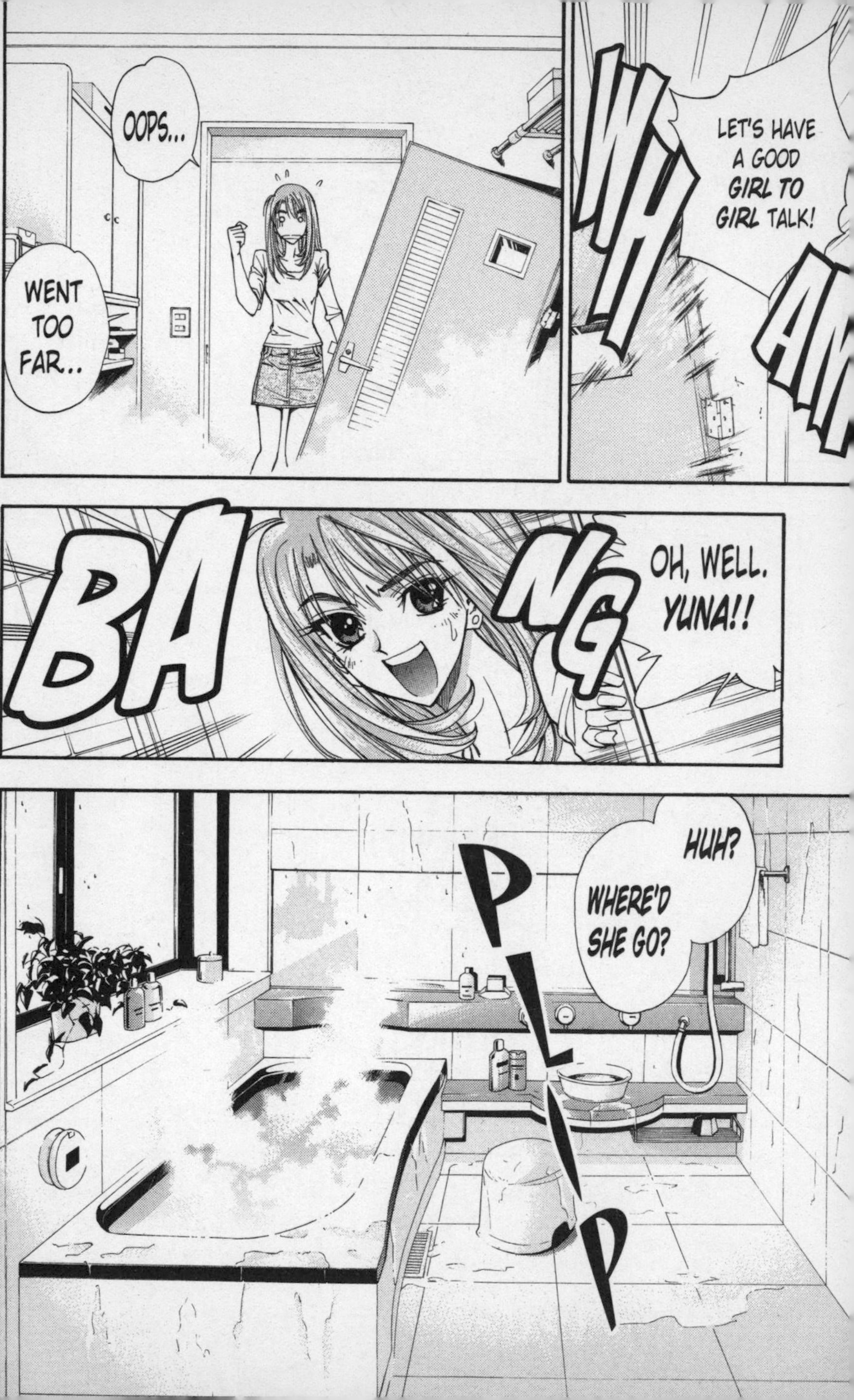
LET'S HAVE A GOOD GIRL TO GIRL TALK!
WH
AM
OOPS...
WENT TOO FAR...
OH, WELL. YUNA!!
BANG
HUH?
WHERE'D SHE GO?
PLIP

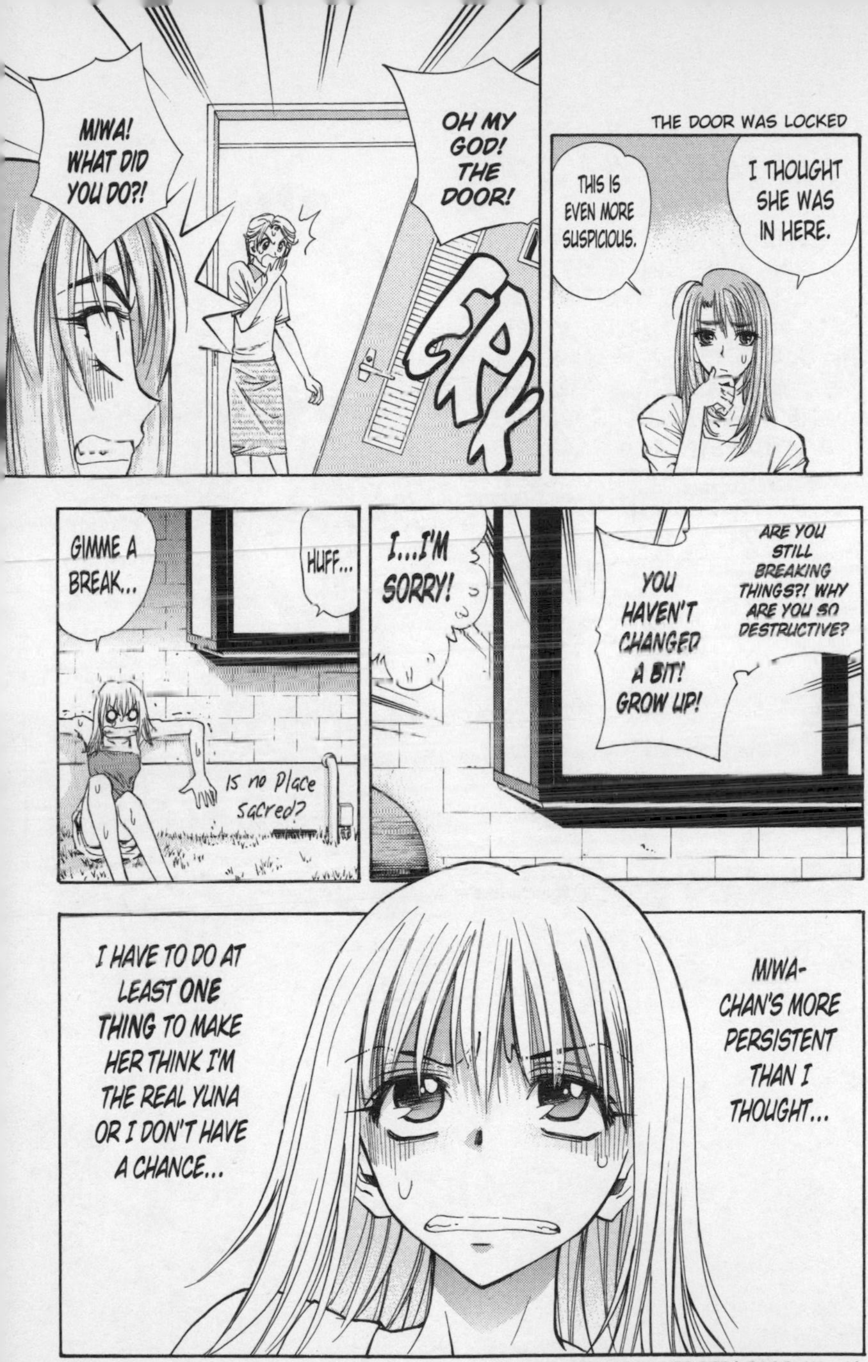
THE DOOR WAS LOCKED
I THOUGHT SHE WAS IN HERE.
THIS IS EVEN MORE SUSPICIOUS.
OH MY GOD! THE DOOR!
CRK
MIWA! WHAT DID YOU DO?!
ARE YOU STILL BREAKING THINGS?! WHY ARE YOU SO DESTRUCTIVE?
YOU HAVEN'T CHANGED A BIT! GROW UP!
I...I'M SORRY!
HUFF...
GIMME A BREAK...
Is no place sacred?
MIWA-CHAN'S MORE PERSISTENT THAN I THOUGHT...
I HAVE TO DO AT LEAST ONE THING TO MAKE HER THINK I'M THE REAL YUNA OR I DON'T HAVE A CHANCE...

TO BE CONTINUED IN *PRETTY FACE* VOL. 3!

YUKIE SANO (16 YEARS OLD)

SHE IS THE ONLY GIRL IN RINA AND YUNA'S GROUP OF FRIENDS WHO HAS A BOYFRIEND. WHAT'S MORE, HE GOES TO A DIFFERENT HIGH SCHOOL. MOST OF THE TIME, SHE'S QUITE RESERVED AND A LITTLE BIT OF A SCAREDY-CAT. SHE'S PRETTY GOOD AT HER STUDIES, BUT NOT GOOD AT SPORTS, AND HATES ANY BALL-BASED SPORTS. SHE WAS BORN IN JANUARY AND IS A CAPRICORN.

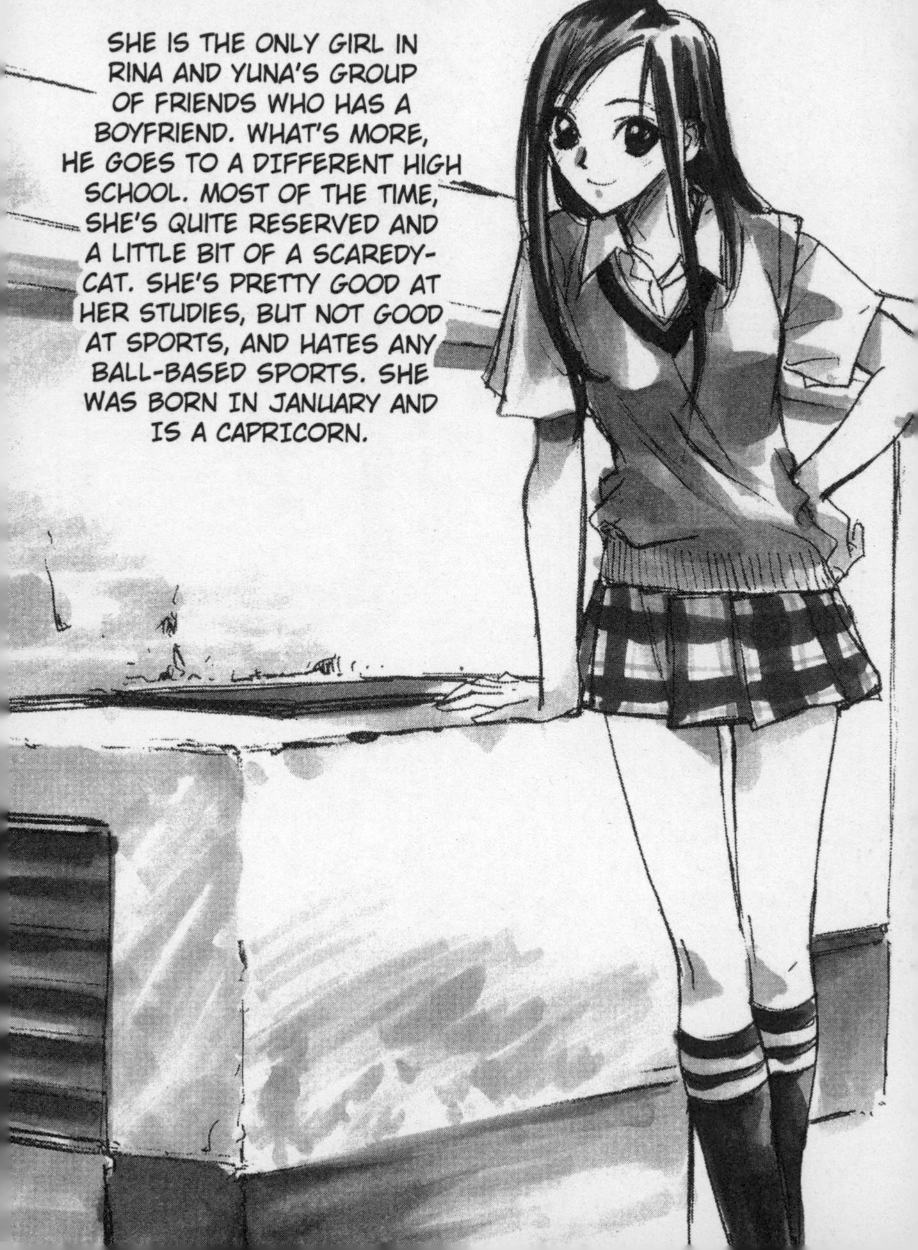

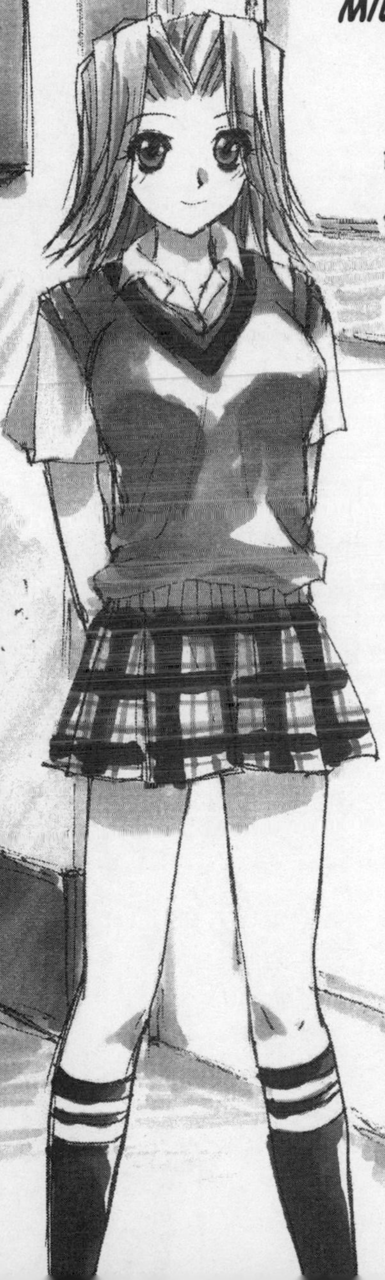

MIDORI AKAI (17 YEARS OLD)

BECAUSE HER FIRST NAME IS "MIDORI" (GREEN), HER LAST NAME IS "AKAI" (RED). PRETTY BASIC, HUH? FROM THE TIME SHE SHOWED HER PANTIES IN THE SECOND CHAPTER, SHE'S BECOME THE STRIPPER CHARACTER. HER CURRENT GOAL IS TO GET A BOYFRIEND BEFORE SHE GRADUATES FROM HIGH SCHOOL. BUT HER IDEALS ARE SO HIGH, IT'LL BE A SURPRISE IF SHE CAN CHANGE HER HISTORY OF 17 YEARS WITHOUT A BOYFRIEND. SHE WAS BORN IN AUGUST AND IS A LEO.

KEIKO TSUKAMOTO (17 YEARS OLD)

SHE'S A SPORTS FANATIC WHO IS IN THE VOLLEYBALL CLUB. SHE'S THE AUTHOR'S THIRD FAVORITE CHARACTER AFTER RINA AND YUNA. SHE LOVES ANIMALS AND OWNS A HAMSTER AND A DOG. HER DREAM IS TO ONE DAY OWN A WHITE TIGER. SHE HAS NO INTEREST IN MALES OF THE HUMAN SPECIES. SHE WAS BORN IN MAY AND IS A TAURUS.

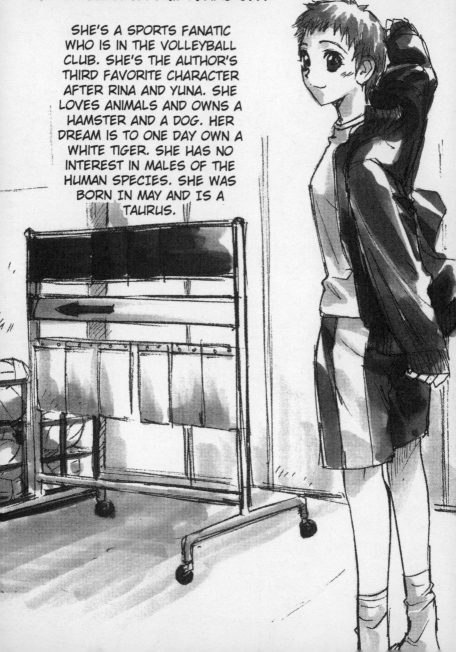

MIWA MASUKO (23 YEARS OLD)

RINA'S COUSIN ON HER MOTHER'S SIDE. SHE'S LIKE A SISTER TO YUNA AND RINA, AND THE REAL YUNA GETS A LOT OF HER PERSONALITY FROM HER. SHE'S FAIRLY POPULAR, BUT HAS NO INTEREST IN HAVING A BOYFRIEND AT THIS TIME. I'D LIKE TO WRITE A STORY ABOUT WHEN SHE WAS A HIGH SCHOOL STUDENT, BUT I DON'T THINK RANDO WOULD BE INVOLVED, SO THAT MAY NOT BE POSSIBLE.

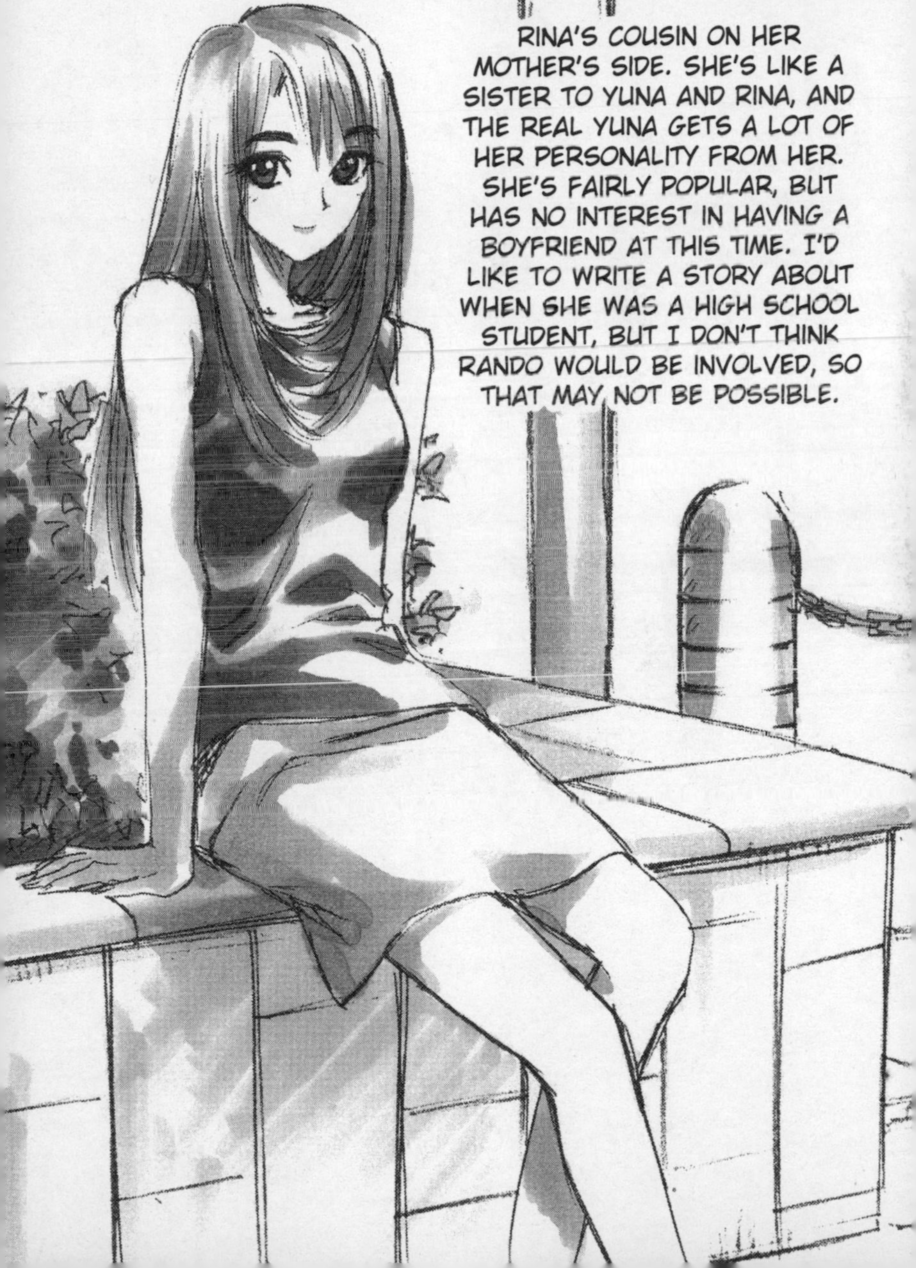

IN THE NEXT VOLUME...

Rando is tempted by some girl-on-girl action when he
meets Nozomi, a girl who just loves beautiful women who
kick men's butts. Too bad Rando *has* a man's butt that he
has to hide when he's forced to spend the day at the pool!
Can he get help from Dr. Manabe, whose solution to every
problem is to ask Rando to trade up to a "G-cup" set of
fake breasts? Then, the need for extra cash leads Rando
to accept a dubious job offer involving a full-coverage
bodysuit...and does Rando have a *male* admirer too?

COMING DECEMBER 2007!

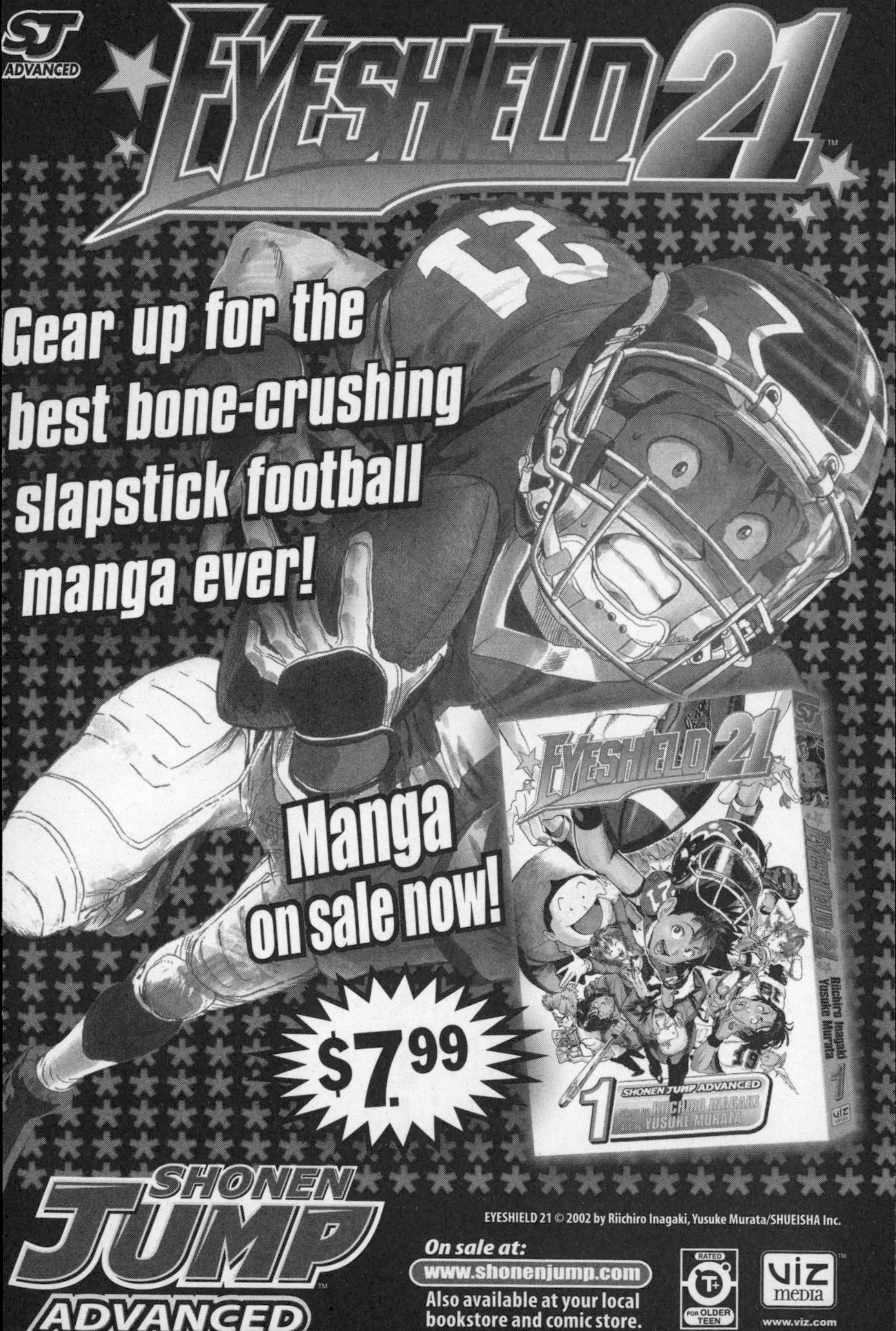
SJ ADVANCED
EYESHIELD 21™
Gear up for the best bone-crushing slapstick football manga ever!
Manga on sale now!
$7.99
EYESHIELD 21
SHONEN JUMP ADVANCED
Riichiro Inagaki Yusuke Murata
1
SHONEN JUMP ADVANCED
EYESHIELD 21 © 2002 by Riichiro Inagaki, Yusuke Murata/SHUEISHA Inc.
On sale at:
www.shonenjump.com
Also available at your local bookstore and comic store.
RATED T+ FOR OLDER TEEN
VIZ media
www.viz.com

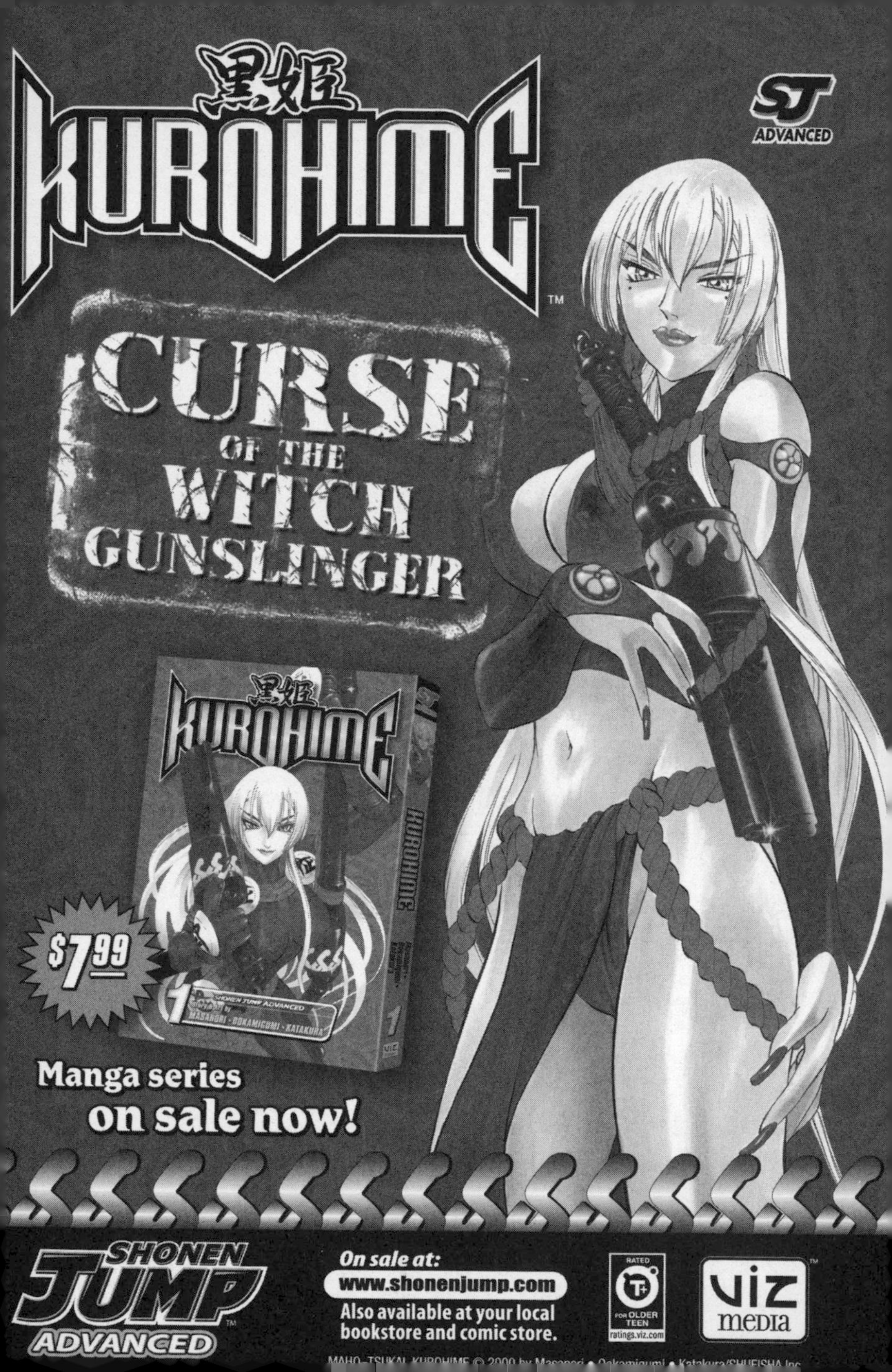

Crossing the globe to
avenge the Joestars
of generations past!

JoJo's Bizarre Adventure
by HIROHIKO ARAKI

ONLY
$7.99

**Manga series
on sale now**

Tell us what you think about SHONEN JUMP manga!

Our survey is now available online.
Go to: www.SHONENJUMP.com/mangasurvey

Help us make our product offering better!

THE REAL ACTION STARTS IN...

THE WORLD'S MOST POPULAR MANGA
www.shonenjump.com

ADVANCED

Save **50% OFF** the cover price!

SHONEN JUMP™

THE WORLD'S MOST POPULAR MANGA

Over **300 pages** per issue!

Each issue of SHONEN JUMP contains the coolest manga available in the U.S., anime news, and info on video & card games, toys AND more!

☑ **YES!** Please enter my one-year subscription (12 HUGE issues) to **SHONEN JUMP** at the LOW SUBSCRIPTION RATE of **$29.95!**

NAME

ADDRESS

CITY   STATE   ZIP

E-MAIL ADDRESS   P7GNC1

☐ **MY CHECK IS ENCLOSED** (PAYABLE TO SHONEN JUMP)   ☐ **BILL ME LATER**

CREDIT CARD: ☐ **VISA**   ☐ **MASTERCARD**

ACCOUNT #   EXP. DATE

SIGNATURE

CLIP AND MAIL TO ➤

SHONEN JUMP
Subscriptions Service Dept.
P.O. Box 515
Mount Morris, IL 61054-0515

Make checks payable to: **SHONEN JUMP**. Canada price for 12 issues: $41.95 USD, including GST, HST and QST. US/CAN orders only. Allow 6-8 weeks for delivery.

BLEACH © 2001 by Tite Kubo/SHUEISHA Inc. NARUTO © 1999 by Masashi Kishimoto/SHUEISHA Inc.
ONE PIECE © 1997 by Eiichiro Oda/SHUEISHA Inc.

RATED **T** FOR TEEN

ratings.viz.com